Introduction to Software Testing and Analysis

Introduction to Software Testing and Analysis

Volume I

V.K. Jain

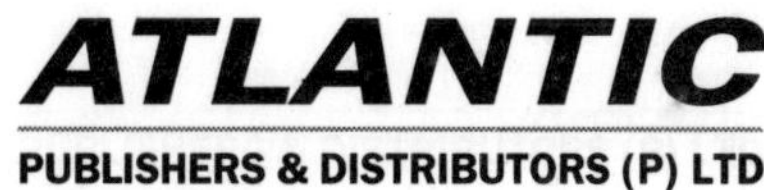

Published by
ATLANTIC
PUBLISHERS & DISTRIBUTORS (P) LTD
7/22, Ansari Road, Darya Ganj,
New Delhi-110002
Phones : +91-11-40775252, 23273880, 23275880, 23280451
Fax : +91-11-23285873
Web : www.atlanticbooks.com
E-mail : orders@atlanticbooks.com

Branch Office
5, Nallathambi Street, Wallajah Road,
Chennai-600002
Phones : +91-44-64611085, 32413319
E-mail : chennai@atlanticbooks.com

ISBN 978-81-269-1426-5 (Vol. I)
ISBN 978-81-269-1428-9 (Set)

Printed in India at Nice Printing Press, A-33/3A, Site-IV,
Industrial Area, Sahibabad, Ghaziabad, U.P.

PREFACE

Software testing is a fast growing discipline. Software industry increases Information Technology (IT) hiring each year, and recent years have seen a marked increase in emphasis on quality of software engineering in general, and testing in particular. Bill Gates recently said of Microsoft, "We have as many testers as we have developers. And developers spend half their time testing. Software testing is not only science but art as well for which contents of the books have to be very exhaustive".

The currently available books on the subject are having outdated contents and do not deal the subject with respect to fifth generation software testing techniques. This book covers well-established techniques (equivalence classes, boundary value analysis, decision tables, state transition, etc.), less known techniques (domain analysis, control path and data flow testing), and also newer techniques (use case testing, pairwise testing and exploratory testing). With this coverage, the book will become the tester's handbook.

Following Beizer's lead in his landmark book *Software Testing Techniques*, I have presented testing as a mental discipline that helps all IT professionals develop higher quality software. It includes information on the types of environments required at different stages in the life cycle.

Computer science has the greatest drawback in non-standardization of the stuff, not only of its software but in courseware also. A vast amount of curriculum exists at different levels. Department of Electronics (now Department of Information Technology) and Computer Society of India together have done a great service to the nation by way of accrediting the courses and thus prescribing the syllabi for different levels.

This book is composed generally as per syllabi prescribed for degree level (also MCA) courses prescribed by various universities and institutions including IITs and NIITs and as per DOEACC. I have adopted most recent version so as to keep contents of book most modern and up to date.

The various facades of computer science are changing its attributes at such a fast speed that it is very difficult to keep track of latest development and it is an onerous task to be aware of the latest happenings in the field. Therefore, in presenting the state-of-the-art testware, immense help has been sought by me from various sources. I express my gratitude to the authors of the works from where information has been derived.

I wish to put on record my thanks to Heera Jain, Amitabh Bajaj, Naveena Bajaj, Anurag Jain, Director NICT (Vikas Marg, New Delhi branch) and Jyotsna Agarwal for the great help provided in preparation of this book.

V.K. Jain

CONTENTS

Volume II

THE SOFTWARE DEVELOPMENT PROCESS

1

1.1 Software

1.1.1 Definition of Software

Over the past two decades, computer systems and the software that runs them have made their way into all aspects of life. Software is present in our cars, ovens, cell phones, games, and workplaces. It drives billing systems, communications systems, and Internet connections. The proliferation of software systems has reached the point that corporate and national economies are increasingly dependent on the successful development and delivery of software.

IEEE Standard Glossary defines software as computer programming language instructions, data, information, and documentation that comprise or constitute a software product (e.g., shrink wrapped word processor with disks, programs, and user guides).

Software is the task and result of modeling and implementation of the philosophy, methodology and knowledge of accomplishing a task into computer codes in humanly understandable manner.

Software is the assembly of instruction codes and data necessary to accomplish some task on a computer. We also include all representations of those instructions and data. In particular, representations include not only program source code and data files, but models created during analysis and design activities. Software can and should be tested in all its representations. Just as architects and builders can examine blueprints for a new building to spot problems even before ground is broken, so we can examine analysis and design models for software before the first line of program source code is written.

1.1.2 Open Source versus Closed Source

Open source vs. Free software: Open source software and free software are different terms for software which comes with certain rights, or freedoms, for the user. They describe two approaches and philosophies towards free software. Open source and Free software (or libre software) both describe software which is free from onerous licensing restrictions. It may be used, copied, studied, modified and redistributed without restriction. Free software is not the same as freeware, software available at zero price.

The distinction between Open Source and Free Software is a matter of philosophy and approach.

The term "Open Source" was originally intended to be trademarkable, however, the term was deemed too descriptive, so no trademark exists. OSI would prefer that people treat Open Source as if it were a trademark, and use it only to describe software licensed under an OSI approved license. Not everyone agrees with this idea.

OSI Certified is a trademark licensed only to people who are distributing software licensed under a license listed on the Open Source Initiative web page. There is also a graphic form of the trademark.

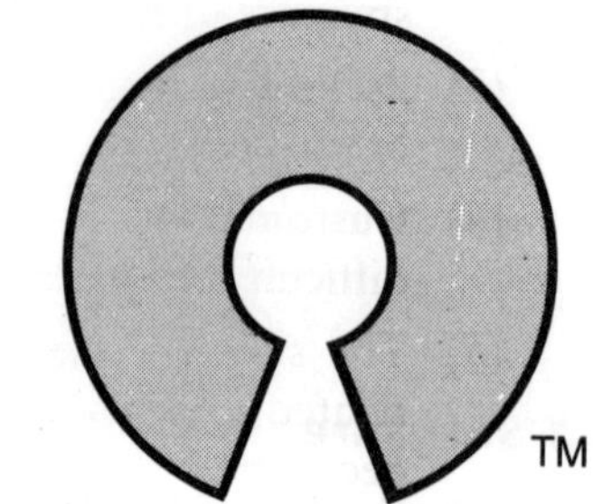

Fig. 1.1: Logo of open source initiative

Open source software and Free software share an almost identical set of licenses. According to the Free Software Foundation (FSF), the open source movement is philosophically distinct from the free software movement. The FSF's free software definition is more restrictive than the Open Source Definition (OSD). In practice, nearly all open source licenses are also classed as free software licences by FSF—which means they meet the free software definition. The difference is more a matter of philosophical emphasis. One exception is an early version of the Apple Public Source License, which was accepted by OSI but rejected by FSF because it did not allow private modified versions; this restriction was removed in later version of the license. There are now new versions that are approved by both OSI and the Free Software Foundation.

Free software licences are not only written by the Free Software Foundation. Both FSF and OSI list licences which meet their definition of free software.

The Open Source Initiative believes that more people will be convinced by the experience of freedom. The Free Software Foundation believes that more people will be convinced by the concept of freedom. The Free Software Foundation believes that knowledge of the concept is an essential requirement, insists on the use of the term free[2], and seperates itself from the Open Source movement. The Open Source Initiative believes that free has three meanings: free as in beer, free as in freedom, and free as in unsellable. Open Source says nothing about the freedom to modify and redistribute, so it is being misused by people who think that source access without freedom is sufficient. This is the case with most of the licences that make up Microsoft's "shared source" initiative, and to a lesser extent with the "license-free" software of Daniel J. Bernstein.

One of the most intensely debated topics in the computer field continues to be the relative merits of **open source and closed source** software. The former is software for which the source code is freely available (i.e., at no cost and easily accessible) for anyone to use for any purpose, including studying, modifying, extending, giving away or even selling. Although there are some philosophical differences behind the movements, in most cases open source software is basically the same as free software.

The latter provide their source code either with the compiled software or by allowing it to be downloaded from the Internet. The GNU General Public License (GPL), the most widely used free software license, actually makes it a legal requirement that the source code for all software released under it be made freely available to all users.

Closed source software is software for which the source code is kept secret. Most proprietary (i.e., commercial) software is closed source. There are several reasons that developers of proprietary software take great pains to keep their source code secret, including the concerns that:

(1) Other developers might copy some of their code and use it in other programs.

(2) Hackers will find vulnerabilities in the code that will enable them to develop viruses, spyware or other malware (i.e., malicious software) for it.

(3) Public disclosure of the source code could expose its developers to charges that some of the code was plagiarized from other programs.

(4) Customers will try to modify the source code, resulting in new problems that could be difficult for either the customers or developer to correct.

(5) The source code could be used as evidence in legal proceedings, particularly those related to whether the developer has been complying with certain legislation or court decisions.

(6) The source code could contain unfavorable comments inserted by programmers about their employer, customers or competitors. Comments are words, phrases, sentences or paragraphs that are interspersed in source code but which do not affect the operation of the code. Their official purpose is to document the code and explain it to other programmers (who may have to repair or revise the code at some future date), although they are frequently used for other purposes as well. It can be difficult to find and remove potentially offensive comments because of the great length of the code for large programs and the subtlety with which some comments are written.

1.1.3 Reasons to not Keep Source Code Secret

There are also reasons for not keeping source code secret and for allowing, or even encouraging others to view and study it. Advocates of open source point out that this approach makes it possible for a much larger and more diverse set of qualified people to examine the source code, thus resulting in the discovery of more bugs and providing more and better suggestions for improvements and extensions.

That this approach has been extremely successful is evidenced by the rapid improvements in performance of numerous open source programs, many of which are equal to or superior to their closed source counterparts. One of the most outstanding examples is the Apache web server, which currently hosts more than 70 per cent of all websites on the Internet.

Undoubtedly, the most famous example is Linux, the use of which is continuing to grow rapidly for a wide range of applications, including supercomputers, enterprise computing systems, personal computers and embedded systems. Another example is the GNU Compiler Collection (GCC), which contains very highly rated and widely used compilers for C, C++, Fortran, Java and other programming languages. In fact, the concept of open source is so appealing that there are currently thousands of open source projects in various stages of development.

Some advocates of open source contend that source code be considered a legally protected form of free speech, i.e. it should not be illegal to publish source code obtained by reverse engineering or other legal means. An example of where this is particularly controversial is the source code for the encryption algorithms for DVDs and electronic books. Several cases have reached the courts, but as yet no definitive precedents have been set.

1.1.4 Shared Source

There is an alternative to closed source and open source. It is a compromise that attempts to attain the advantages of both approaches. Microsoft is using this alternative for some of its software and has dubbed it as shared source.

Under the company's Shared Source Initiative, a few outsiders, chiefly security researchers, universities and government agencies, are allowed to view selected portions of the code under tightly restricted conditions and after signing strict non-disclosure agreements.

Shared source is seen by some as being a strategic move to address concerns by corporations and governments (both domestic and foreign) that there are security holes and backdoors in the software. A backdoor is intentionally inserted secret code that allows its developer or a government agency to search or modify software on a remote computer without the knowledge or permission of the owner of that computer. The unavailability of the source code for Microsoft software has been a major source of concern to foreign (i.e., non-U.S.) governments, which have feared that it could compromise their security. The availability of the source code for Linux, FreeBSD, Apache and other free software is thus viewed as another major advantage of such software.

Occasionally, portions of the source code for some proprietary software are leaked to the Internet. This could be evidenced of the frequently made assertion by proponents of open source that it is difficult to keep source code secret, and thus the use of code secrecy as a means of providing security is unreliable.

However, it is possible that some such leaks have, in fact, been made intentionally by the developers themselves. One motive for this is that it would allow them to receive comments about bugs and other problems with selected sections of the code from a far larger and more diverse group of people than would be possible in-house while still preventing others from legally copying or reusing the code.

1.1.5 Proprietary Software Definition

Proprietary software is software that is owned by an individual or a company (usually the one that developed it). There are almost always major restrictions on its use, and its source code is almost always kept secret.

Source code is the form in which a program is originally written by a human using a programming language and prior to being converted to machine code which is directly readable by a computer's CPU (central processing unit). It is necessary to have the source code in order to be able to modify or improve a program.

Software that is not proprietary includes free software and public domain software. Free software which is generally the same as open source software, is available at no cost to everyone, and it can be used by anyone for any purpose and with only very minimal restrictions.

These restrictions vary somewhat according to the license, but a typical requirement is that they include a copy of the original license. The most commonly used license, the GNU Public License (GPL), additionally requires that if a modified version of the software is distributed, the source code for such modified version must be made freely available. The best known example of software licensed under the GPL is Linux.

Public domain software is software that has been donated to the public domain by its copyright holder. Thus, it is no longer under copyright. Consequently, such software is completely free and can be used by anybody for any purpose without restriction.

Freeware, not to be confused with free software, is a type of proprietary software that is offered for free use of monetary charges. However, as is the case with other types of proprietary software, there are generally severe restrictions on its use and the source code is kept secret. Examples of freeware include Adobe's Acrobat Reader and Microsoft's Internet Explorer web browser.

The restrictions on the use of **proprietary software** are usually enumerated in the end user license agreements (EULAs) that users must consent to. For software provided by large companies, EULAs are generally long and complex contracts. Among the most common of the prohibitions for such programs are making unauthorized copies, using it on more than a certain number of computers and reverse engineering it.

Some Unix-like operating systems are also proprietary. Among the most popular are AIX (developed by IBM), HP-UX (developed by Hewlett-Packard), QNX (developed by QNX Software Systems) and Solaris (developed by Sun Microsystems). Others are free software, including Linux and the BSD systems (the most widely used of which is FreeBSD).

Virtually all Microsoft software is proprietary, including the Windows family of operating systems and Microsoft Office. This includes software that is given away at no charge, such as Internet Explorer. Other major producers of proprietary software include Adobe, Borland, IBM, Macromedia, Sun Microsystems and Oracle.

In the early days of computing, software was generally free, and it was something that was shared among researchers and developers, who were usually eager to improve it. However, that situation changed as computers became more common, and the production of proprietary software became an excellent business model for many companies. However, in recent years some companies have begun to realise that free software can also be highly profitable. The most outstanding example of this is IBM, which continues to reap high returns from its approximately one billion dollar investment in Linux.

Some industry observers think that the role of proprietary software will decrease in the future because of the growing competition from free software. This view holds that free software will eventually come to dominate operating systems and major application programs. Proprietary software will remain strong in some niche markets, mainly for business and technical applications for which the demand is relatively small or specialized and for which users will be willing to pay relatively high prices.

1.2 Software Development and Engineering: A Definition

Software Engineering: An early definition of software engineering was proposed by Fritz Bauer at the first major conference [NAU 69] dedicated to the subject:

- The establishment and use of sound engineering principles in order to obtain economically software that is reliable and works efficiently on real machines.

- Software engineering is an outgrowth of hardware and system engineering. It encompasses a set of three key elements—methods, tools, and procedures—that enable the manager to control the process of software development and provide the practitioner with a foundation for building high quality software in productive manner. In the paragraphs that follow, we briefly examine each of these elements.
- Software engineering is the practical application of scientific knowledge to the design and construction of computer programs and the associated documentation required to develop, operate and maintain them.
- Software engineering is the systematic application of an appropriate set of techniques to the whole process of software development.

This definition conoselystes the three most important principles of software engineering:

- A set of techniques is used to increase quality and productivity.
- The techniques are applied in a disciplined, not a haphazard way.
- The techniques are applied to the whole process of software development.

One of the important themes of software engineering is the emphasis on a clear structure for software development. This is usually contrasted with the traditional, ad hoc, approach to software development.

Software engineering tools provide automated or semi-automated support for methods. Today, tools exist to support each of the methods noted above. When tools are intergrated so that information created by one tool can be used by another, a system for the support of software development, called computer-aided software engineering (CASE) is established. CASE combines software, hardware, and a software engineering database (a data structure containing important information about analysis, design, code, and testing) to create a software engineering environment that is analogous to computer-aided design/computer-aided engineering (CAD/CAE) for hardware.

Software Development: The IEEE Standard Glossary (1990) defines software development as the transformation of user needs into a software product involving requirements analysis, software design, computer programming, and testing (e.g., the combination of multiple computer programming language statements into a product that performs a useful function).

Software Management: The IEEE Standard Glossary (1990) defines software management as the process of planning, estimating resources, scheduling, conducting, coordinating, and controlling software development.

Software Process Improvement (SPI): Harrington (1991) defines process improvement as a systematic methodology that significantly helps businesses simplify and streamline operational processes. Harrington states that the objective of process improvement is to ensure that business processes eliminate errors, minimise delays, promote understanding, are easy to use, are customer friendly, adaptable, enhance competitiveness and reduce excess capacity.

1.2.1 Basic Definitions of Process

Shari Pfleeger (2001) defines a process as "a series of steps involving activities, constraints, and resources that produce an intended output of some kind."

The following is adapted from Pfleeger's list of the attributes of a process:

- The process prescribes all of the major process activities.
- The process uses resources, subject to a set of constraints (such as a schedule), and provides intermediate and final products.
- The process may be composed of subprocesses that are linked in some way. The process may be defined as a hierarchy of processes, organized so that each subprocess has its own process model.
- Each process activity has entry and exit criteria, so that we know when the activity begins and ends.

The activities are organised in a sequence or in parallel to other independent sub-processes, so that it is clear when one activity is performed relative to the other activities.

Every process has a set of guiding principles that explains the goals of each activity.

Constraints or controls may apply to an activity, resource, or product. For example, the budget or schedule may constrain the length of time an activity may take or a tool may limit the way in which a resource may be used.

Strategy: McKechnie (1983) defines strategy as the science of planning and directing large scale operations, specifically by maneuvering resources into the most advantageous position prior to actual deployment, implementation, and engagement in order to ensure that goals and objectives have a high probability of being successfully achieved.

Software Process Improvement (SPI) Strategy: Combining Harrington's (1991) and McKechnie's (1983) definitions of process improvement and strategy, a SPI strategy is one of many optional methodologies, plans, and tactical maneuvers that will increase the likelihood of successfully achieving one or more business objectives. That is, a SPI strategy is prefabricated management or technical approach that will likely result in successful software development.

1.3 Planning Software Project

1.3.1 Project Size Categories

Project size is a major factor that determines the level of management control and the types of tools and techniques required on a software project. The following categories give some indication of software project size. These categories have been adapted from material originally presented by Yourdon.

(1) Trivial Projects

A trivial software project involves one programmer working, perhaps part-time, for a few days or a few weeks and results in a program of less than 500 statements, packaged in 10 to 20 sub-routines. Such programs are often personal software; they are developed for the exclusive use of the programmer and are usually discarded after a new months.

There is little need for formal analysis, elaborate design documentation, extensive test planning, or supporting documents for trivial programs; however, even trivial programs can be improved by some analysis, systematic design, structured coding, and methodical testing. One of the dangers of personal software development (of whatever size) is that a program intended for personal use becomes a software product, but without benefit of the planning and support required for a product.

(2) Small Projects

A small project employs one programmer for 1 to 6 months and results in a product containing 1000 to 2000 lines of source code packaged in perhaps 25 to 50 routines. Small programs usually have no interactions with other programs. Examples of such programs include scientific applications written by engineers to solve numerical problems; small commercial applications written by data processing personnel to perform straightforward data manipulation and report generation; and student projects written in compiler and operating system courses.

A small project requires little interaction among programmers or between programmers and customers. Standardized techniques and notations, standardized documents and systematic project reviews should be used even on small projects, but the degree of formality will be much less than is required on larger projects.

(3) Medium-size Projects

A project of medium size requires two to five programmers working for 1 to 2 years and results in 10,000 to 50,000 lines of source code packaged in 250 to 1000 routines.

Products of medium size have few, if any, interactions with other programs. Medium-size programs include assemblers, compilers, small management information systems, inventory systems, and process control applications.

Development of medium-size programs requires interaction among programmers and communication with customers. Thus, a certain degree of formality is required in planning, documents and project reviews. It is undoubtedly true that the vast majority of software projects and the resulting programs, are of small or medium size. Most applications programs and many systems programs are developed in 2 years or less by five or fewer programmers.

Use of systematic software engineering principles on medium-size projects can result in vastly improved product quality, increased programmer productivity, and better satisfaction of customer needs.

(4) Large Projects

A new computer game software requires from six months to a couple of years to develop and release. Before release of a new game, the developer must make it sure that it is of a very high quality because otherwise customers won't think to look for an upgrade. Because of the short lifespan of most computer games and their dependence on transient technology, opportunities to improve a released product based on customer feedback are minimal.

In the real world, the process is easily complicated by the fact that the real programs that people use aren't tiny things at all. You can roughly have idea from following:

- 300 lines, a typical lab assignment solution.
- 7,500 lines Logisim, an educational circuit-building program.
- 2,000,000 lines Solaris, the operating system running on our Sun computers.
- 29,000,000 lines Windows 2000 operating system.

Logisim represents a single-person effort, spanning a few weeks of development time. Even it's in a different class than our lab programs. But it bears no resemblance to a heavy-duty operating system like Solaris or Windows 2000, which involves huge teams of programmers working full-time for years on a system.

A large project may require 5 to 20 programmers for a period of 2 to 3 years and results in a system of 50,000 to 1000,000 source statements, packaged in several subsystems. A large program often has significant interactions with other programs and software systems.

Examples of large programs include large compilers, small time sharing systems, data-base packages, graphics programs for data acquisition and display, and real-time control systems.

Communication problems among programmers, managers, and customers often become severe on large projects. A large project generally requires more than one programming team (e.g. three teams of five persons each) and often involves more than one level of management. In addition, there is a great likelihood that there will be some turnover of project personnel during the development cycle. This will require training and indoctrination of new personnel or distribution of the responsibilities of a departed team member among the remaining members.

The size and complexity of a large project make it difficult, if not impossible, to foresee all eventualities during planning and analysis. Changes to the product requirements may be initiated by both customers and developers as the product requirements may be initiated by both customers and developers as the project evolves. Systematic processes, standardized documents, and formal reviews are essential throughout a large project.

(5) Very Large Projects

A very large project requires 100 to 1000 programmers for a period of 4 to 5 years and results in a software system of 1 million source instructions. A very large system generally consists of several major subsystems, each of which forms a large system. The subsystems typically have complex interactions with one another and with other separately developed systems.

Very large systems often involve real-time processing, telecommunications, and multitasking. Examples of such systems include large operating systems, large data-base systems and military command and control systems.

IBM operating system OS/360 was developed by 5000 programmers over a period of 5 years and contained more than 1 million source instructions (Brooks, BRO 75). A recent study forecasts the size of typical operating systems for data processing applications growing to 4 million lines of code by 1990.

(6) Extremely Large Projects

An extremely large project employs 2000 to 5000 programmers for periods of up to 10 years and results in 1 million lines of source code. Extremely large systems consist of several very large subsystems and often involve real-time processing, telecommunications, multitasking, and distributed processing. Such systems often have extremely high reliability requirements and involve life-and-death processes.

Examples of extremely large systems include air traffic control, ballistic missile defense, and military command and control systems. Very few extremely large systems have been built.

A U.S. Department of Defense project involving an antiballistic missile system was abandoned a few years ago after computer experts testified before a congressional committee that the necessary software for the system was beyond the capabilities of current technology. It is fair to assume, however, that increasing pressures of modern society and new advances in software technology will result in increasing numbers of extremely large projects in the future.

1.4 Some Important Software Projects

1.4.1 Semi Automatic Ground Equipment (SAGE)

It has been estimated that SAGE took 1800 man-years to write the original programs. Dividing 600,000 instructions by 1800 man-years and 250 working days per year yield 1.33 instructions per day.

For its time SAFEGUARD was the largest and most complex real-time system ever undertaken. The purpose of the system was to provide a defense against an attack by intercontinental ballistic missiles. The system consisted of four major components: the long-range radar to detect incoming attack missiles, a short-range radar to aim the defensive missiles so as to intercept the attacking missiles, the defensive missiles, and a very large multiprocessor computer for data processing and control. The system entailed the development of approximately 2 million instructions and required 5000 man-years of effort.

For the overall project, 2,261,000 instructions were written and 5407 man-years of effort were required. Based upon 250 working days per year, this represents an overall productivity of 1.7 instructions per man-day. The variation in productivity varied from a low of 0.98 to a high of 6.40, depending on the type of program being written.

1.4.2 Sabre

For developing the Air Reservation system, total effort has been estimated as 400 man-years, and about 1 million lines of code were written. Assuming 250 working days per year, this yields a productivity figure of 5 instuctions per man-day, quite a bit higher than SAGE or SAFEGUARD.

However, SAGE was a real-time system, while SABRE was an operational data-base system.

1.4.3 UNIX Operating System

The size of the present operating system is about 90,000 bytes or 45,000 two-bytes words. No formal accounting of the resources expended in the development of UNIX is available in the literature. However, the authors estimate that the first version of the main system software took less than 2 man-years. Dividing 45,000 machine language words by 500 man-days yields the truly prodigious productivity rate of 90 words per day. Even though operating system software is perhaps an easier job than some of the embedded real-time computer system projects we have just discussed—Thompson and Ritchie are super programmers—it was still a significant feat.

Some of the most important features of the UNIX system are centered about the major programs listed in Table 6.39. The C-programming language, developed by Ritchie, is a high-level, semi-PL/1-like language suitable for applications programming. It contains certain features such as register manipulation which also make it a useful systems programming language. In fact, the UNIX system was rewritten predominantly in the C language in 1973. This development resulted in essentially a self-maintaining system, a clearer expression and documentation of the design, and a more portable design. The rewriting increased memory size and run time by about one-third; however, the C-language version also included many enhancements and improvements of the original design.

Clearly, the designer felt that any disadvantages in abandoning assembly language were far outweighed by the advantages which were realised. As an illustration of how useful the C-language is in systems programming we cite its use in the so-called kernel of the operating system, which represents 5 to 10 per cent of the total code. This kernel contained 10,000 lines of C-language and 1000 lines of assembler code. About 200 of the lines of assembly code were written for efficiency reasons, and 800 were written to provide functions which were available in assembler but not in the C-language.

1.5 Software Testing Life Cycle

The test development life cycle contains the following components:

- Requirements
- Use Case Document
- Test Plan
- Test Case
- Test Case Execution
- Report Analysis
- Bug Analysis
- Bug Reporting

A use case describes the use of a system from start to finish. Use cases focus attention on aspects of a system useful to people outside of the system itself. Users of a program are called users or clients. Users of an enterprise are called customers, suppliers, etc.

Use Case is a collection of possible scenarios between the system under discussion and external actors, characterized by the goal the primary actor has toward the system's declared responsibilities, showing how the primary actor's goal might be delivered or might fail.

Use cases are goals (use cases and goals are used interchangeably) that are made up of scenarios. Scenarios consist of a sequence of steps to achieve the goal, each step in a scenario is a sub (or mini) goal of the use case. As such each sub-goal represents either another use case (subordinate use case) or an autonomous action that is at the lowest level desired by our use case decomposition.

This hierarchical relationship is needed to properly model the requirements of a system being developed. A complete use case analysis requires several levels. In addition the level at which the use case is operating at, it is important to understand the scope it is addressing. The level and scope are important to assure that the language and granularity of scenario steps remain consistent within the use case.

There are two scopes that use cases are written from:

- Strategic, and
- System.

There are also three levels: Summary, User and Sub-function.

Strategic Scope

The goal (Use Case) is a strategic goal with respect to the system. These goals are goals of value to the organization. The use case shows how the system is used to benefit the organization. These strategic use cases will eventually use some of the same lower level (subordinate) use cases.

System Scope

Use cases at system scope are bounded by the system under development. The goals represent specific functionality required of the system. The majority of the use cases are at system scope. These use cases are often steps in strategic level use cases.

Levels: Summary Goal , User Goal and Sub-function.

(1) **Sub-function Level Use Case:** A sub-goal or step is below the main level of interest to the user. Examples are "logging in" and "locate a device in a DB". Always at System Scope.

(2) **User Level Use Case:** This is the level of greatest interest. It represents a user task or elementary business process. A user level goal addresses the question "Does your job performance depend on how many of these you do in a day". For example "Create Site View" or "Create New Device" would be user level goals but "Log In to System" would not. Always at System Scope.

(3) **Summary Level Use Case:** Written for either strategic or system scope. They represent collections of User Level Goals. For example summary goal "Configure Data Base" might include as a step, user level goal "Add Device to database". Either at System or Strategic Scope.

1.6 Analysis of Programmer's Efforts

Bairdain of Bell Labs conducted a time and motion study of 70 programmers to determine how they spent their time (Bell Labs Study [1964, 70 Programmers], BA164). The results of that study are presented in Table 1.1. At first glance, the fact that a typical programmer spends only 13 per cent of the time writing programs appears to be unreasonable, but some analysis indicates that these figures are, in fact, quite reasonable. For example, consider the personal time of 13 per cent in Table 1.1. Assuming 260 potential work days per year (5 × 52 = 260), and assuming 11 paid holidays, 15 paid vacation days, 5 days of sick leave, and 3 days for jury duty, extra vacation, etc. gives a total of 34 days personal time, which is approximately 13 per cent of 260.

Similarly, 1 hour per day for coffee breaks, personal phone calls, and visits to the restroom plus 13 days travel time results in 39 days, or 15 per cent, miscellaneous time. Although this experiment was conducted in 1964, there is no reason to expect the results to have changed.

Table 1.1: Analysis of Time Consumed by Typical Programmer

Writing Programs	13%
Reading programs and manuals	16%
Job communication	32%
Personal	13%
Miscellaneous	15%
Other	39%
Training	6%
Mail	5%

Major reasons for underestimating the cost of a software project are failure to account for the 39 per cent overhead time for programmers (13 + 15 + 5 + 6 = 39) and failure to account for the 48 per cent of time spent in job communication and reading of programs and manuals (32 + 16 = 48). To this we would add forgetting to add the 40 to 50 per cent of development time required for testing.

Software quality and programmer productivity can be improved by improving the processes used to develop and maintain software products. Some factors that influence quality and productivity are listed in Table 1.2 and discussed below. Techniques that address these factors are discussed in subsequent chapters of the text.

Table 1.2: Factors that Influence Quality and Productivity

• Individual ability	• Problem understanding
• Team communication	• Stability of requirements
• Product complexity	• Required skills
• Appropriate notations	• Facilities and resources
• Systematic approaches	• Adequacy of Training
• Change control	• Management skills
• Level of technology	• Appropriate goals
• Required reliability	• Rising expectations
• Available time	

1.6.1 Individual Ability

Production and maintenance of software products are labour-intensive activities. Productivity and quality are, thus, direct functions of individual ability and effort. There are two aspects to ability:

- The general competence of the individual, and
- Familiarity of the individual with the particular application area.

Competent data processing programmers are not usually competent in scientific application areas, nor are scientific programmers ordinarily competent system programmers. Lack of familiarity with the application area can result in low productivity and poor quality.

1.6.2 Team Communication

Programming has traditionally been regarded as an individual and private activity. Many programmers have low social needs and prefer to work alone. Programs are seldom perceived as public documents, and programmers seldom discuss the exact details of their work in a systematic manner. As a result, it is possible for programmers to misunderstand the role of their modules in an evolving system, and to make mistakes that may not be detected until some time later. Many of the recent innovations in software engineering, such as design reviews, structured walkthroughs, and code-reading exercises, have the goals of making software more visible and improving communication among programmers.

1.6.3 Product Complexity

There are the generally acknowledged levels of product complexity: applications programs, utility programs, and system-level programs. Applications programs include scientific and data processing routines written in a high-level language such as FORTRAN, Pascal, or C, C++, C#, Java, Basic or Visual Basic. Utility programs include **compilers, assemblers, linkage editors**, and **loaders**. They may be written in a high-level language such as Pascal or Ada or in assembly language. Systems programs include data communications packages, real-time process control systems, and operating systems routines, which are usually written in assembly language or a high-level systems language such as PL/1 or Ada.

Applications programs have the highest productivity and systems programs the lowest productivity, as measured in lines of code programmer-day. Utility programs can be produced at a rate 5 to 10 lines, and applications programs at a rate 25 to 100 times that of systems programs. Some typical figures for lines of code per programmer day as a function of project complexity are: less than one line per day for systems programs, 5 to 10 lines per day for utility programs, and 25 to 100 lines per programmer-day for applications programs. These figures are only rule-of-thumb approximations and should not be regarded as definitive. They are strongly influenced by other factors.

The effort required to develop and maintain a software product is a nonlinear function of product size and complexity. A product that is twice as large or twice as complex as a known product by whatever measure other than effort, may require 10 times or even 100 times the amount of effort required for the known product. Failure to allow for the non-linear scaling of size and complexity is a primary reason for cost and schedule overruns on many software projects.

1.6.4 Level of Technology

Modern programming practices include use of systematic analysis and design techniques, appropriate notations, structured coding, systematic techniques for examining design documents and source code, and systematic testing. Software tools span the spectrum from elementary tools such as assemblers and primitive debugging aids to fully integrated development environments that incorporate tools for managing and controlling the software development process.

1.6.5 Level of Reliability

Every software product must possess a basic level of reliability; however, extreme reliability is gained only with great care in analysis, design, implementation, system testing, and maintenance of software product. Both human and machine resources are required to obtain increased reliability. This results in decreased productivity when productivity is measured in lines of code produced per programmer-month. Boehm estimates that the productivity ratio between very low and extremely high required reliability is in the order of 2:1.

1.6.6 Problem Understanding

Failure to understand the true nature of the problem to be solved is a common and difficult issue. There are several factors that contribute to this lack of understanding. Often, the customer does not truly understand the nature of the problem and/or does not understand the capabilities and limitations of computers. Most customers (most people in general) are not trained to think in logical, algorithmic terms, and often do not understand the true nature of their needs. Often, the software engineer does not understand the application area and has trouble communicating with the customer because of differences in educational backgrounds, viewpoints, and technical jargon. Sometimes the customer is not the end user of the system and the software engineer has no opportunity to investigate the user's problem. Sometimes the true nature of the problem does not become apparent until the software product, or some major portion of it, is constructed and operated. Sometimes the automated solution changes the nature of the problem (for better or worse) and the change may not be apparent until the system is installed.

Careful planning, customer interviews, task observation, prototyping, a preliminary version of the user's manual and precise product specifications can increase both customer and developer understanding of the problem to be solved.

1.6.7 Available Time

While it might appear that a software project requiring six programmer-months of effort can be completed by one programmer in 6 months or by six programmers in one month, software projects are sensitive not only to total effort but also to elapsed time and the number of people involved. Utilizing six programmers for 1 month will probably be less effective than using one programmer for 6 months because the learning curve for six programmers on a 1-month schedule will occupy a large percentage of the elapsed time, and because the effort required for coordination and communication among six programmers will drastically increase project overhead. On the other hand, using two programmers for 3 months may be more effective than using one programmer for 6 months due to the reinforcement that each programmer gains from the other.

Programmer productivity is also sensitive to the calendar time available for project completion. A well-known rule of thumb states that it takes 2 years to develop a compiler for a new language, regardless of the number of people involved. There is quantitative evidence to suggest that development time cannot be compressed below about 75 per cent of the nominal development time regardless of the personnel and resources expended. It is not clear that extending development time beyond some reasonable limit (say 2 years for a compiler) makes the project any easier.

1.6.8 Facilities and Resources

Studies of factors that motivate programmers have shown that work-related factors, such as good machine access and a quiet place to work, are more important to the typical programmer than status-related factors, such as reserved parking places and keys to the executive restroom. Most programmers feel that the positive aspects of their jobs are the creative challenges, the variety of tasks, and the opportunities of professional advancement, while the negative aspects of their jobs involve management ineptness, company policies, and organizational bureaucracy. Most programmers receive their motivational rewards from the nature of the work itself and are thus quite sensitive to, and easily frustrated by, poor facilities

Table 1.3: A Table of Contents for a Typical Requirements Document

Chapter		Contents
1.	Introduction	Organization principles; abstracts for other sections, notation guide.
2.	Computer characteristics	If the computer is predetermined, a general description with particular attention to its idiosyncrasies; otherwise a summary of its required characteristics.
3.	Hardware interface	Concise description of information received or transmitted by the computer.
4.	Software functions	What the software must do to meet its requirements, in various situations and in response to various events?
5.	Timing constraints	How often and how fast each function must be performed? This section is separate from section 3 since "what" and "when" can change independently.
6.	Accuracy constraints	How close output values must be to ideal values to be acceptable?
7.	Response to undesired events	What the software must do if sensors go down, the pilot keys in invalid data, etc.?
8.	Subsets	What the program should do if it cannot do everything ?
9.	Fundamental assumptions	The characteristics of the program that will stay the same, no matter what changes are made.
10.	Changes	The types of changes that have been made or are expected.
11.	Glossary	Most documentation is fraught with acronyms and technical terms. At first we prepared this guide for ourselves; as we learned the language, we retained it for newcomers.
12.	Source	Annotated list of documentation and personnel, indicating the types of questions each can answer.

and inadequate resources. Software project managers must be effective in dealing with the factors that motivate and frustrate programmers if they are to maintain high project quality, high programmer productivity, and high job satisfaction.

1.7 The Software Development Life Cycle

Software Development Life Cycle Models

A running joke in the computer industry is that three things should never be seen in the process of being created: laws, sausage, and software. Software creation process is so messy and disgusting that it's best to just wait and see the final result. That may or may not be totally true, but with most old sayings, there is a trace of truth behind the words. Some software is developed with the rigor and discipline of a fine craftsman, some software with tightly controlled chaos, and other software is stuck together with duct tape and chewing gum. Usually, in the end, it's apparent to the customer what process was used. The process used to create a software product from its initial conception to its public release is known as the software development life cycle model.

Software Development as a Part of System Design

The decision to implement system functionality using software is one that is typically made during system design. Software requirements are typically derived from the overall system requirements and design for those aspects in the system that are to be implemented using software. There are user needs and intended uses for a finished device, but users typically do not specify whether those requirements are to be met by hardware, software, or some combination of both. Therefore, software validation must be considered within the context of the overall design validation for the system.

Software Life Cycle

When a process relates to the building of a product, it is often called a life cycle. The development of a software product is, therefore, called a software life cycle. A software life cycle can be described in a variety of ways, but often a model is used that represents key features of the process with some combination of text and illustrations.

There are many different methods that can be used for developing software, and no model is necessarily the best for a particular project. There are four frequently used models, with most others just variations of these:

- Big-Bang
- Code-and-Fix
- Waterfall
- Spiral

Each model has its advantages and disadvantages. As a tester, you will likely encounter them all and will need to tailor your test approach to fit the model being used for your current project. Refer to these model descriptions as you read the rest of this book and think about how you would apply the various testing techniques you learn under each of them.

1.7.1 Big-Bang Model

One theory of the creation of the universe is the big-bang theory. It states that billions of years ago, the universe was created in a single huge explosion of nearly infinite energy. Everything that exists is the result of energy and matter lining up to produce software, Lee and Bill Gates. If the atoms didn't line up just right, these things might all be just quivering masses of goop.

The big-bang model for software development shown in Figure 1.2 follows much the same principle. A huge amount of matter (people and money) is put together, a lot of energy is expended often violently and out comes the perfect software product or it doesn't.

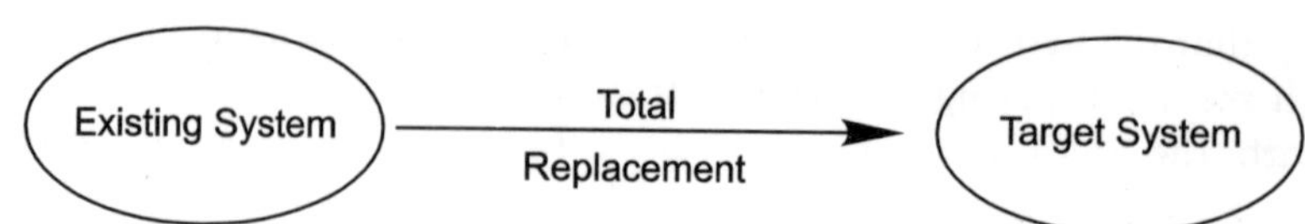

Fig. 1.2: The big-bang model is by far the simplest method of software development.

1.7.2 Code-and-Fix Model

Code and fix development is not so much a deliberate strategy as an artifact of schedule pressure on software developers. Without much in the way of a design, programmers immediately begin producing code. At some point, testing begins (often late in the development cycle), and the inevitable bugs must then be fixed before the product can be shipped.

The code-and-fix model shown in Figure 1.3 is usually the one that project teams fall into by default if they don't consciously attempt to use something else. It's a step up, procedurally, from the big-bang model, in that it at least requires some idea of what the product requirements are.

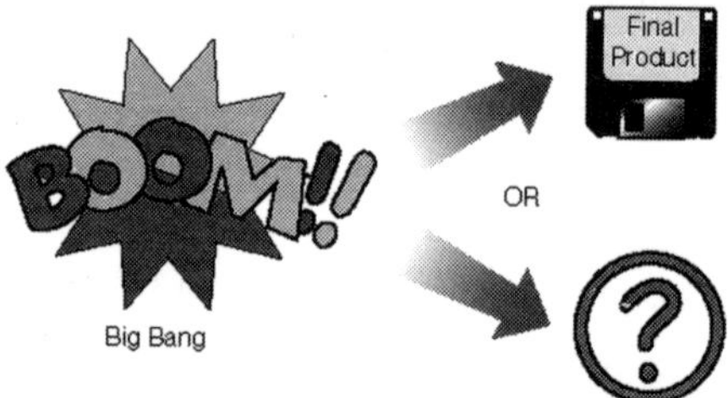

Fig. 1.3: The code-and-fix model repeats until someone gives up.

A wise man once said, "There's never time to do it right, but there's always time to do it over." That pretty much sums up this model. A team using this approach usually starts with a rough idea of what they want, does some simple design, and then proceeds into a long repeating cycle of coding, testing, and fixing bugs. At some point they decide that enough is enough and release the product.

As there's very little overhead for planning and documenting, a project team can show results immediately. For this reason, the code-and-fix model works very well for small projects intended to be created quickly and then thrown out shortly after they're done, such as prototypes and demos. Even so, code-and-fix model has been used on many large and well-known software products. If your word processor or spreadsheet software has lots of little bugs or it just doesn't seem quite finished, it was likely created with the code-and-fix model.

Like the big-bang model, testing isn't specifically called out in the code-and-fix model but does play a significant role between the coding and the fixing.

As a tester on a code-and-fix project, you need to be aware that you, along with the programmers, will be in a constant state of cycling. As often as every day you'll be given new or updated releases of the software and will set off to test it. You'll run your tests, report the bugs, and then get a new software release. You may not have finished testing the previous release when the new one arrives, and the new one may have new or changed features. Eventually, you'll get a chance to test most of the features, find fewer and fewer bugs, and then someone (or the schedule) will decide that it's time to release the product.

You will most likely encounter the code-and-fix model during your work as a software tester. It's a good introduction to software development and will help you appreciate the more formal methods.

1.7.3 Waterfall Model

In General Systems Theory, Life Cycle methodology is sometimes called the Waterfall method. In this classic view of system development the cycle is seen as a journey down a river with the end of each phase being a waterfall. The project moves forward in a linear fashion just as you would paddle down the stream. A preceding phase must be completed before the next starts. And, once you go over a waterfall (i.e., complete a phase) you can't go back.

The waterfall method is usually the first one taught in programming school. It's been around forever. It's simple, elegant, and makes sense. And, it can work well on the right project. Figure 1.4 shows the steps involved in this model.

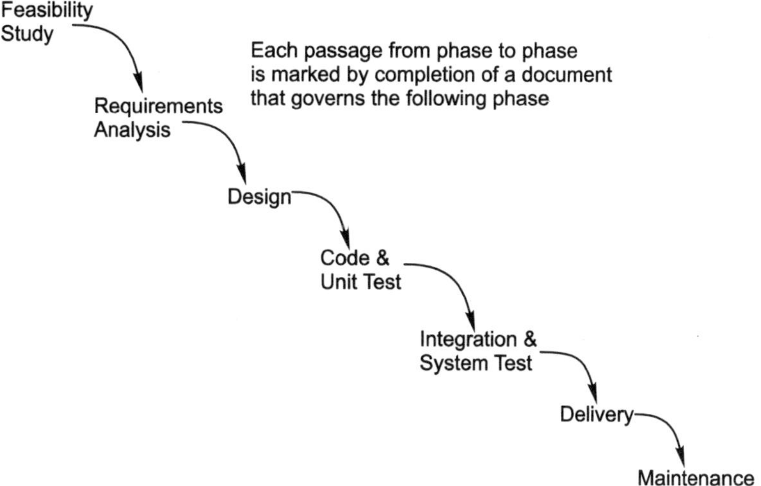

Fig. 1.4: The software development process flows from one step to the next in the waterfall model.

Early in the history of computing (around 1970), people started noticing how big programs were getting—and more crucially, how buggy they were. They invented the field of software engineering within computer science to study the process of developing reliable, large software.

One of the first problems was trying to get some handle on how people should develop large-scale software, and one of their first efforts was called the waterfall model, a picture that looks like the following. (The details of the waterfall model vary, but two things remain constant. There are boxes going from left downward to the right; and there are arrows connecting each to its successor [preferably blue, to connote the idea of water falling]. But people aren't unanimous as to how many boxes there are, or what goes into the boxes. This is my own variation.)

A project using the waterfall model moves down a series of steps starting from an initial idea to a final product. At the end of each step, the project team holds a review to determine if they're ready to move to the next step. If the project isn't ready to progress, it stays at that level until it's ready.

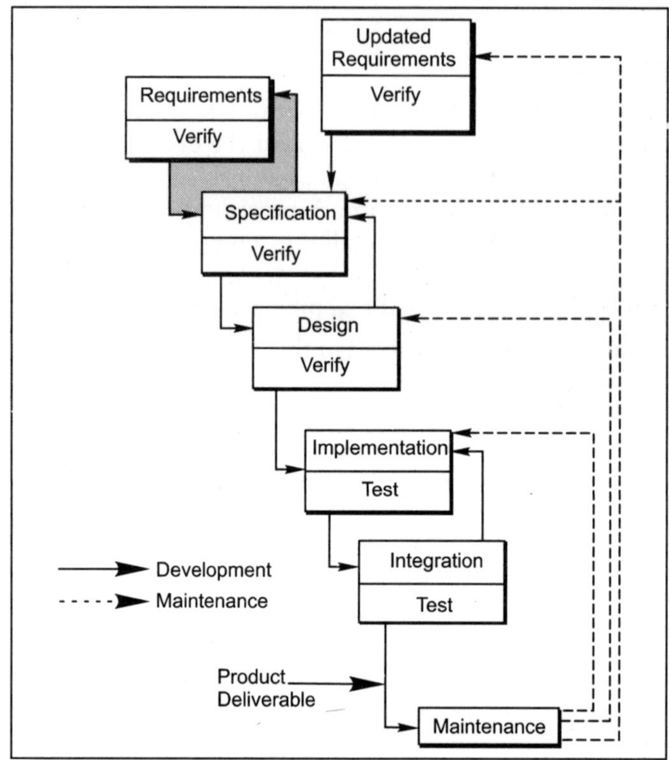

Fig. 1.5: Waterfall model as applied to software Development

One of the first software life cycle models used was the waterfall, shown in Figure 1.5. A main characteristic of the waterfall model is that each phase or component of the model is completed before the next stage begins. The process begins with a definition of the requirements for the system, and in the waterfall model the requirements are elicited, analysed, and written into one or more requirements documents before any design work begins. The system design, program design, coding, and testing activities are all self-contained and thoroughly documented phases of the process. It should be noted that different names are commonly used for some of the phases; for example, the system design phase is often called "preliminary design", and the program design phase is often called "detailed design".

The waterfall model has a number of critics. One criticism questions the possibility of capturing all the requirements at the front-end of a project. Suppose you are asked to state all the requirements for a new car before it is designed and built. It would be impossible as a customer to conceive of all the detailed requirements that would be needed to design and build a car from scratch. Yet, this is the kind of demand that the waterfall model places upon customers and analysts at the front-end of a waterfall process.

Notice three important things about the waterfall method:

- There's a large emphasis on specifying what the product will be. Note that the development or coding phase is only a single block.
- The steps are discrete; there's no overlap.
- There's no way to back up. As soon as you're on a step, you need to complete the tasks for that step and then move on—you can't go back. Variations of the waterfall model loosen the rules a bit, allowing some overlap of the steps and the ability to back up one step if necessary.

This may sound very limiting, and it is, but it works well for projects with a well-understood product definition and a disciplined development staff. The goal is to work out all the unknowns and nail down all the details before the first line of code is written. The drawback is that in today's fast moving culture, with products being developed on Internet time, by the time a software product is so carefully thought out and defined, the original reason for its being may have changed.

From a testing perspective, the waterfall model offers one huge advantage over the other models presented so far. Everything is carefully and thoroughly specified. By the time, the software is delivered to the test group, every detail has been decided on, written down, and turned into software. From that, the test group can create an accurate plan and schedule. They know exactly what they're testing, and there's no question about whether something is a feature or a bug.

But, with this advantage, comes a large disadvantage. Because testing occurs only at the end, a fundamental problem could creep in early on and not be detected until days before the scheduled product release. Remember from Chapter 1, "Software Testing Background", how the cost of bugs increases over time? What's needed is a model that folds the testing tasks in earlier to find problems before they become too costly.

Kendall and Kendall do not use the waterfall analogy in describing SDLC. Further, their description of SDLC allows for some degree of overlapping or concurrence in SDLC activities rather than being rigidly linear.

Kendall and Kendall say, "Although each phase is presented discretely it is never accomplished as a separate step. Instead, several activities can occur simultaneously, and activities may be repeated. It is more useful to think of the SDLC as accomplished in phases (with activities in full swing overlapping with others and then tapering off) and not in separate steps."

Curtis, Krasner, Shen, and Iscoe (1987, cited in Pfleeger, 2000) state that the major shortcoming of the waterfall model is that it fails to treat software as a problem-solving process. The waterfall was adapted from the world of hardware development, and represents a manufacturing or assembly-line view of software development in which a component is developed and then replicated many times over. But software is a creation process rather than a manufacturing process. Software evolves iteratively as the understanding of a problem grows. There are a lot of back and forth activities that involve trying various things to determine what works best. It is not possible, in other words, to accurately model the software development process as a set of self-contained phases as the waterfall attempts to do. Other models such as the spiral, staged delivery and evolutionary prototype models are better suited to the iterative nature of software development.

If you have worked as a test engineer in a waterfall environment, you may have direct experience with another problem that is all too common with the waterfall. Unless certain precautions are taken, all the errors made in defining the requirements, designing the system, and writing the code flow downhill to the test organization. If the waterfall is used, the test team may find a lot of bugs near the end of development bugs that have to be sent back upstream to be fixed in the requirements, design, or coding of the product. Going back upstream in a waterfall process is difficult, expensive, and time-consuming because all the work products that came from the supposedly "completed" phases now must be revised.

In spite of its problems, the waterfall model is worth understanding because it contains the basic components that are necessary for software development. Regardless of the model used, software development should begin with an understanding of what needs to be built; in other words, an elicitation and analysis of the requirements. The development process should include design, coding and testing activities, whether they are done in a linear sequence as in the waterfall, or in an iterative sequence as in the evolutionary prototyping or staged delivery models. We use the waterfall as a context for discussing process improvement, but the basic principles of rapid testing should be applicable to whatever life cycle model is used.

According to the waterfall model of software development model, software companies,

- determine the needs and requirements for the software.
- translate the requirements into specifications.
- code implementations for the specifications.
- test the code: find mistakes.
- debug: eliminate the mistakes.
- deploy: insert the software into the context where it is supposed to work, which implies installing hardware and software, testing in context, training users, assisting users (help desk), etc.
- maintain the code: port to new hardware, to new operating systems, fix errors, add functionality, and more.

In its pure form, the process is linear. One stage concludes, the other one starts, though coders may move into the debugging stage and requirements engineer may be involved in the deployment process. People have tried to develop according to this model, but they now understand that this model doesn't work. Can you imagine why?

To this day, large companies stick to some variant of this process. In detail, however, the process is much more feedback oriented and is close to the scientific process of discovering the proper (in the sense of predictive) scientific model of the world.

1.7.4 The Iterative Refinement Model

This iterative process works roughly like that:

- write up the story of the software

- find the use cases end-to-end interactions between the desired system and users and other contexts
- pick a central/important use case and implement it to the point where it is useful deploy and observe consumers/clients' reactions
- go back to the first or second step; check whether the preliminary product affects your customer's story; or find the next use cases to extend the product.

For a company, the customer is the paying entity or a representative example of some segment of the mass market consumer. For you, the customer is your boss and in reality the person to whom your boss delivers the software in a working context.

Where do all the requirement engineering, specification writing, etc. go?

It is still there, but it is a part of a cycle. Specifically:

- "writing up the story of software" means writing up what the customer tells you so that the customer understands what you wrote and you can use your story to guide your efforts—this is informal communication about requirements and specifications;
- "extracting/writing use cases" from the stories means to break up your story into small doable tasks, which are specifications of what you want, not how you want them solved with a program;
- "implementing" means that not just writing some code and hoping for the best; it means
  - to lay out the concepts of the story and the use case
  - to formulate the kind of data this involves
  - to illustrate the desired use case with behavioral examples
  - to turn the examples into tests (code)
  - to design and write code that passes all these tests.

One big difference between "waterfall" and "iterative refinement" is that you get to code much sooner and that you have a much closer interaction with your customer.

One recent evolution of iterative refinement is extreme programming, a sellable buzzword-compliant version of the idea. While "iterative refinement" has evolved in the prototype-oriented academic community-think Scheme and Prolog and similar languages—the extreme programming community evolved in the academic fringe of industry, again fostered in an interactive language community (Smalltalk, now known as Squeak).

1.7.5 Spiral Model

The spiral model (see Fig. 1.6) solves many of the problems inherent with the other models while adding a few of its own nice touches.

The spiral model was introduced by Barry Boehm in 1986 in his Association for Computing Machinery (ACM) paper, "A Spiral Model of Software Development and Enhancement." It's used fairly often and has proven to be an effective approach to developing software.

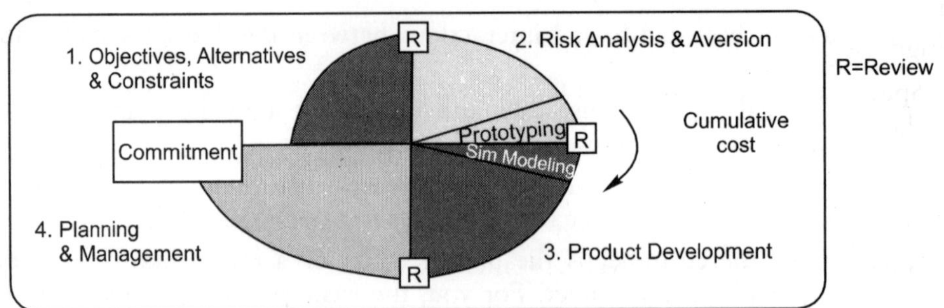

Fig. 1.6: The spiral model starts small and gradually expands as the project becomes better defined and gains stability.

The general idea behind the spiral model is that you don't define everything in detail at the very beginning. You start small, define your important features, try them out, get feedback from your customers, and then move on to the next level. You repeat this until you have your final product.

Each time around the spiral involves six steps:

1. Determine objectives, alternatives, and constraints.
2. Identify and resolve risks.
3. Evaluate alternatives.
4. Develop and test the current level.
5. Plan the next level.
6. Decide on the approach for the next level.

Built into the spiral model is a bit of waterfall (the steps of analysis, design, develop, test), a bit of code-and-fix (each time around the spiral), and a bit of big-bang (look at it from the outside). Couple this with the lower costs of finding problems early, and you have a pretty good development model.

A sincere tester, will always like this model. The tester gets a chance to influence the product early by being involved in the preliminary design phases. You'll see where the project has come from and where it's going. And, at the very end of the project, you won't feel as rushed to perform all your testing at the last minute. You've been testing all along, so the last push should only be a validation that everything is okay.

1.7.6 Deployment: The Waterfall Model of Software Development

The basic concept of the waterfall model is that software development is a sequence of stages, and software developers should clearly delineate the stages: First we design; and after we finish designing, we begin coding; and after we finish coding, we begin testing; and after we finish testing, we deploy.

The arrows on the bottom are for handling errors in executing the process. As we're coding, we may discover that there's something wrong with our design, and so we would halt coding and go back to the previous stage to modify our design to correct for the error. Or, during testing, we may discover a minor coding bug—but we may also discover a larger design bug.

Design

Design itself breaks down into smaller stages.

- **Specification:** You meet with the person paying for the work to determine what exactly the software's purpose is, and what particular things it ought to do.
- **User interface design:** You decide on how exactly the software should appear to the user, and how the user will be able to accomplish things. Frequently, this is a matter of simply designing menus and dialog boxes. But there are radically different user interfaces too (a voice interface via telephone, perhaps).
- **Module design:** You decide on how to break up the overall task into smaller, more manageable pieces. In an object-oriented system, this is basically a matter of deciding what the classes will be.

Coding

This is the most emphasized stage.

Verification and Testing

Software engineers distinguish strongly between verification and testing. Verification refers to formal mathematical proofs of program correctness, while Testing refers to experimental trials to test for potential errors. Verification is quite rare—it's more of a subject for researchers and nuclear weapons control systems programming. For most software, the only step toward determining correctness is the experimental trials.

Properly done, large-scale testing has three stages.

- **Module tests:** As each person codes a module, they test it themselves before releasing it to be part of the overall package. Often, this will involve writing some specialized test code (maybe even more code as there is in the module itself) to exercise the various parts of the module thoroughly.
- Basically, a programmer won't release the module until confident that it has no problems within it internally. It may not interact with other modules well, but independently of the rest it should work.
- **System tests (Alpha testing):** With enough modules complete, they begin to put modules together into a program, running their own tests. In a large system, you may want to gradually work yourself up, testing coherent groups of modules separately, before testing all the groups put together.
- Basically, you want to avoid big-bang testing as much as possible—the system where each person writes a draft of their code and ensures it compiles. The first test is on a draft of the complete program. What you will find is simply that nothing even remotely resembles a working product. Also, big-bang testing tends to be highly sequential—you can't distribute the work among many people, and one bug frequently prohibits you from testing any other pieces of the system.
- **Beta testing:** After the system appears to be working, they release it to beta testers—people who know the product well, but aren't necessarily programmers. They exercise the system in a more lifelike situation. A good beta tester will find aspects that the

developers may not have considered—like some rare situation that doesn't occur often, but is worth considering.

In its large systems, Microsoft works with a testing system that works as follows:

Programmers check out and work on a set of modules. When they complete a module, they check it in. The system will automatically run it through a sequence of tests to verify that the module checks internally. Overnight, each night, the system will compile all the checked modules, and it will run a sequence of tests automatically on the complete system to ensure it still passes all the tests. (There are many tests that it does automatically, so it can only be done overnight.) If it does not with the new module incorporated, it will reject the module and produce a report of the error for the person who produced the latest update to verify.

Microsoft employs a large division of people dedicated to beta testing. Their job is simply to run software, looking for problems. When they find a problem, they have to nail it down as much as possible, and then they produce a report for the software developers to tackle.

Implementation

Documentation: The group develops final documentation of how to use the system, and possibly how the system works. People like to skimp on this stage, but for large-scale systems, poor documentation means that people can't really use the system at all.

Distribution: The software is distributed to its users. In software companies, this means marketing and selling the software. For internally written software in a company, it means installing it on the proper computers so that people can access the new software.

Maintenance: As people use it, bugs will pop up. Also, as hardware and software develops, new compatibility issues will arise. Finally, people may need new, relatively small features to be added to the system. A relatively small group of programmers will have the job of updating the system to meet this challenges.

Conclusion

How big are all these pieces? Fred Brooks, author of *The Mythical Man-Month* (an extremely readable short book about software engineering, which I highly recommend), estimated the following for a large-scale project he supervised (OS/360, an IBM operating system that at the time was among the largest systems ever developed):

- 1/3 design
- 1/6 coding
- 1/4 module tests
- 1/4 system tests

So you see, the coding stage (which this course has emphasized almost exclusively) is only a small piece of the overall process.

1.8 Creating Software

The process of Creating software involves:

- Requirements analysis
- Specification from the user

- Designing Software architecture/Layout
- Coding the complete program to achieve first three
- Compilation of program
- Software testing
- Documentation for the software
- Integration into the system
- Maintenance

1.8.1 Requirements Analysis

A requirement can be any need or expectation for a system or for its software. Requirements reflect the stated or implied needs of the customer, and may be market-based, contractual, or statutory, as well as an organization's internal requirements. There can be many different kinds of requirements (e.g. design, functional, implementation, interface, performance, or physical requirements).

Software requirements are typically derived from the system requirements for those aspects of system functionality that have been allocated to software. Software requirements are typically stated in functional terms and are defined, refined, and updated as a development project progresses. Success in accurately and completely documenting software requirements is a crucial factor in successful validation of the resulting software.

1.8.2 Specification from the User

A specification is a set of requirements. Normally, a specification is the specific set of (high level) requirements agreed to by the sponsor/user and the manufacturer/producer of a system. The specification may also contain both the systems requirements and the test requirements by which it is determined that the systems requirements have been met, known as the acceptance test requirement(s), and a mapping between them.

A specification is defined as "a document that states requirements". It may refer to or include drawings, patterns, or other relevant documents and usually indicates the means and the criteria whereby conformity with the requirement can be checked. There are many different kinds of written specifications, e.g. system requirements specification, software requirements specification, software design specification, software test specification, software integration specification, etc. All of these documents establish "specified requirements" and are design outputs for which various forms of verification are necessary.

While the Quality System regulation states that design input requirements must be documented, and that specified requirements must be verified, the regulation does not further clarify the distinction between the terms "requirement" and "specification".

A program specification is the definition of what a computer program is expected to do. It can be informal, in which case it can be considered as a blueprint or user manual from a developer point of view, or formal, in which case it has a definite meaning defined in mathematical or programmatic terms.

A formal specification is a technical and mathematical description of software or hardware that may be used to develop an implementation. It describes what the system should do, not (necessarily) how the system should do it. Given such a specification, it is possible to use formal verification techniques to demonstrate that a candidate system design is correct with respect to the specification. This has the advantage that incorrect candidate system designs can be revised before a major investment has been made in actually implementing the design. An alternative approach is to use provably correct refinement steps to transform a specification into a design and ultimately into an actual implementation, that is correct by construction.

It is important to note that a design (or implementation) cannot ever be declared correct in isolation, but only correct with respect to a given specification. Whether the formal specification correctly describes the problem to be solved is a separate issue. It is also a difficult issue to address, since it ultimately concerns the problem constructing abstracted formal representations of an informal concrete problem domain, and such an abstraction step is not amenable to formal proof. However, it is possible to validate a specification by proving challenge theorems concerning properties that the specification is expected to exhibit. If correct, these theorems reinforce the specifiers understanding of the specification and its relationship with the underlying problem domain. If not, the specification probably needs to be changed to better reflect the domain understanding of those involved with producing (and implementing) the specification.

The Z notation is an example of a leading formal specification language. Others include the VDM Specification Language (VDM-SL) of the Vienna Development Method and the Abstract Machine Notation (AMN) of the B-Method.

1.8.3 Software Architecture

Software architecture or software systems architecture can best be thought of as a representation of an engineered (or To Be Engineered) software system, and the process and discipline for effectively implementing the design(s) for such a system. Such a software system is generally part of a larger system encompassing information and general and/or special purpose computer hardware.

It is a representation because it is used to convey the information content of the related elements comprising a system, the relationships among those elements, and the rules governing those relationships. It is a process because a sequence of steps is prescribed to produce or change the architecture, and/or a design from that architecture, of a system within a set of constraints. It is a discipline because a body of knowledge or a general set of principles of (software) architecture is used to inform practitioners as to the most effective way to design the system within a set of constraints.

A Software architecture is primarily concerned with the external interfaces among the system's software entities, and between the system and its external environment.

(1) Background

Prior to the advent of digital computers, the electronics and other engineering disciplines used the term system as it is still commonly used today. However, with the arrival of digital computers on the scene and the development of software engineering as a separate discipline, it was often necessary to distinguish between engineered hardware artifacts, software artifacts, and the combined artifacts. A programmable hardware artifact, or machine, that lacks its software program is impotent; even as a software artifact, or program, is equally impotent unless it can be used to alter the sequential states of a suitable (hardware) machine. However, a hardware machine and its software program can be designed to perform an almost illimitable number of abstract and physical tasks. Within the computer and software engineering disciplines (and, often, other engineering disciplines, such as communications) then, the term system came to be defined as containing all of the elements necessary (which generally includes both hardware and software) to perform a useful function.

The hardware engineer or architect deals (more or less) exclusively with the hardware device; the software engineer or architect deals (more or less) exclusively with the software program; and the systems engineer is responsible for seeing that the software program is capable of properly running within the hardware device, and that the system composed of the two entities is capable of properly interacting with its external environment and performing its intended function.

A software architecture, then, is an abstract representation of the software part of a system, capable of running on a special or general purpose computer. A good architecture may be viewed as a partitioning scheme, or algorithm, which partitions all of the system's present and foreseeable software requirements into a workable set of cleanly bounded subsystems with nothing left over. That is, it is a partitioning scheme which is exclusive, inclusive, and exhaustive. A major purpose of the partitioning is to arrange the elements in the software subsystems so that there is a minimum of communications needed among them. In both software and hardware, a good subsystem tends to be seen to be a meaningful "object". Moreover, a good architecture provides for an easy mapping to the user's requirements and the user's validation/acceptance tests of the user's (software) requirements. If everyone keeps to the religion, a mapping also exists from every least element to every requirement and test.

A robust software architecture is said to be one that exhibits an optimal degree of fault-tolerance, backward compatibility, forward compatibility, extensibility, reliability, maintainability, availability, serviceability, usability, and such other ilities as necessary and/or desirable.

To bring a software architecture user's perspective into the software architecture, it can be said that software architecture gives the direction to take steps and do the tasks involved in each such user's speciality area and interest e.g. the stake holders of software systems, the software developer, the software system operational support group, the software maintenance specialists, the deployer, the tester and also the business end user. In this sense software architecture is really the amalgamation of the multiple perspectives a system always embodies. The fact that those several different perspectives can be put together into a software architecture stands as the vindication of the need and justification of creation of software architecture before the software development in a project attains maturity.

Software architecture as a concept was touched upon already in the 1960s by (for example) Edsger Dijkstra, but has increased in popularity since the early 1990s due to the greatly increased activity with very large software systems, e.g. the Boeing 777 aircraft uses in excess of 10 million lines of code just for the basic aircraft. That could represent anywhere from about 5,000 person-years to 50,000 person-years of effort, depending on how thoroughly the coding was controlled and tested.

- Architecture Description Languages (ADL)

ADL are used to describe Software Architecture. Now, there are several ADLs, such as Wright (developed by Carnegie Mellon), Acme (developed by Carnegie Mellon), xADL (developed by UCI), Darwin (developed by Imperial College London), DAOP-ADL (developed by University of Málaga). Common elements of an ADL are component, connector and configuration.

(2) Views

Software architecture is commonly organized in views, which are analogous to the different types of blueprints made in common architecture. Some possible views are:

- Functional/logic view
- Code view
- Development/structural view
- Concurrency/process/thread view
- Physical/deployment view
- User action/feedback view

Several languages for describing software architectures have been devised, but no consensus has yet been reached on which symbol-set and view-system should be adopted. Some believe that UML will establish a standard for software architecture views. Others believe that effective development of software relies on understanding unique constraints of each problem, and so universal notations are doomed because each provides a notational bias that necessarily makes the notation useless or dangerous for some set of tasks. They point to the proliferation of programming languages and a succession of failed attempts to impose a single 'universal language' on programmers, as proof that software thrives on diversity and not on standards.

(3) Architecture Examples

There are many common ways of designing computer software modules and their communications, among them:

- Client-server
- Distributed computing
- Peer-to-peer
- Blackboard
- Implicit invocation
- Pipes and filters
- Plugin
- Monolithic system
- Three-tier model
- Structured (module-based but usually monolithic within modules)

- Software componentry (strictly module-based, usually object-oriented programming within modules, slightly less monolithic)
- Service-oriented architecture

1.9 Design Review

Design reviews are documented, comprehensive, and systematic examinations of a design to evaluate the adequacy of the design requirements, to evaluate the capability of the design to meet these requirements, and to identify problems. While there may be many informal technical reviews that occur within the development team during a software project, a formal design review is more structured and includes participation from others outside the development team. Formal design reviews may reference or include results from other formal and informal reviews. Design reviews may be conducted separately for the software, after the software is integrated with the hardware into the system, or both.

Design reviews should include:

- Examination of development plans;
- Requirements specifications;
- Design specifications;
- Testing plans and procedures;
- All other documents and activities associated with the project;
- Verification results from each stage of the defined life cycle; and
- Validation results for the overall device.

Design review is a primary tool for managing and evaluating development projects. For example, formal design reviews allow management to confirm that all goals defined in the software validation plan have been achieved. The Quality System regulation requires that at least one formal design review be conducted during the device design process. However, it is recommended that multiple design reviews be conducted (e.g. at the end of each software life cycle activity, in preparation for proceeding to the next activity). Formal design review is especially important at or near the end of the requirements activity, before major resources have been committed to specific design solutions. Problems found at this point can be resolved more easily, save time and money, and reduce the likelihood of missing a critical issue.

Answers to some key questions should be documented during formal design reviews. These include:

- Have the appropriate tasks and expected results, outputs or products been established for each software life-cycle activity?
- Do the tasks and expected results, outputs or products of each software life cycle activity:
  - Comply with the requirements of other software life cycle activities in terms of correctness, completeness, consistency and accuracy?
  - Satisfy the standards, practices and conventions of that activity?
  - Establish a proper basis for initiating tasks for the next software life cycle activity?

Following are the basic popular models used by many software development firms.

(a) System Development Life Cycle (SDLC) Model
(b) Prototyping Model
(c) Rapid Application Development Model
(d) Component Assembly Model

1.9.1 System Development Life Cycle Model (SDLC Model)

This is also known as Classic Life Cycle Model (or) Linear Sequential Model (or) Waterfall Method. This has the following activities.

1. System/Information Engineering and Modeling
2. Software Requirements Analysis
3. Systems Analysis and Design
4. Code Generation
5. Testing
6. Maintenance.

1.9.2 System/Information Engineering and Modeling

As software is always of a large system (or business), work begins by establishing requirements for all system elements and then allocating some subset of these requirements to software. This system view is essential when software must interface with other elements such as hardware, people and other resources. System is the basic and very critical requirement for the existence of software in any entity. So if the system is not in place, the system should be engineered and put in place. In some cases, to extract the maximum output, the system should be re-engineered and spruced up. Once the ideal system is engineered or tuned, the development team studies the software requirement for the system.

1.9.3 Software Requirement Analysis

This is also known as feasibility study. In this phase, the development team visits the customer and studies their system. They investigate the need for possible software automation in the given system. By the end of the feasibility study, the team furnishes a document that holds the different specific recommendations for the candidate system. It also includes the personnel assignments, costs, project schedule, and target dates. The requirements gathering process is intensified and focussed specially on software. To understand the nature of the program(s) to be built, the system engineer ("analyst") must understand the information domain for the software, as well as required function, behavior, performance and interfacing. The essential purpose of this phase is to find the need and to define the problem that needs to be solved.

1.9.4 System Analysis and Design

In this phase; the software development process, the software's overall structure and its nuances are defined. In terms of the client/server technology, the number of tiers needed for the package architecture, the database design, the data structure design, etc. are all defined in this phase. A software development model is created. Analysis and Design, are very crucial in the whole development cycle. Any glitch in the design phase could be very expensive to solve in the later stage of the software development. Much care is taken during this phase. The logical system of the product is developed in this phase.

1.9.5 Code Generation

The design must be translated into a machine-readable form. The code generation step performs this task. If the design is performed in a detailed manner, code generation can be accomplished without much complication. Programming tools like Compilers, Interpreters, Debuggers are used to generate the code. Different high level programming languages like C, C++, Pascal, Java are used for coding. With respect to the type of application, the right programming language is chosen.

1.9.6 Testing

Once the code is generated, the software program testing begins. Different testing methodologies are available to unravel the bugs that were committed during the previous phases. Different testing tools and methodologies are already available. Some companies build their own testing tools that are tailor-made for their own development operations.

1.9.7 Maintenance

Software will definitely undergo change once it is delivered to the customer. There are many reasons for the change. Change could happen because of some unexpected input values into the system. In addition, the changes in the system could directly affect the software operations. The software should be developed to accommodate changes that could happen during the post-implementation period.

1.10 Prototyping Model

This is a cyclic version of the linear model. In this model, once the requirement analysis is done and the design for a prototype is made, the development process gets started. Once the prototype is created, it is given to the customer for evaluation. The customer tests the package and gives his/her feedback to the developer who refines the product according to the customer's exact expectation. After a finite number of iterations, the final software package is given to the customer. In this methodology, the software is evolved as a result of periodic shuttling of information between the customer and developer. This is the most popular development model in the contemporary IT industry. Most of the successful software products have been developed using this model—as it is very difficult (even for a whizkid!) to comprehend all the requirements of a customer in one shot. There are many variations of this model skewed with respect to the project management styles of the companies. New versions of a software product evolve as a result of prototyping.

1.11 Rapid Application Development (RAD) Model

The RAD is a linear sequential software development process that emphasises an extremely short development cycle. The RAD software model is a "high speed" adaptation of the linear sequential model in which rapid development is achieved by using a component-based construction approach. Used primarily for information systems applications, the RAD approach encompasses the following phases:

1.11.1 Business Modeling

The information flow among business functions is modeled in a way that answers the following questions:

- What information drives the business process?
- What information is generated?
- Who generates it?
- Where does the information go?
- Who processes it?

1.11.2 Data Modeling

The information flow defined as part of the business modeling phase is refined into a set of data objects that are needed to support the business. The characteristic (called attributes) of each object is identified and the relationships between these objects are defined.

1.11.3 Process Modeling

The data objects defined in the data-modeling phase are transformed to achieve the information flow necessary to implement a business function. Processing the descriptions are created for adding, modifying, deleting, or retrieving a data object.

1.11.4 Application Generation

RAD assumes the use of the RAD tools like VB, VC++, Delphi, etc. rather than creating software using conventional third generation programming languages. The RAD works to reuse existing program components (when possible) or create reusable components (when necessary). In all cases, automated tools are used to facilitate construction of the software.

1.11.5 Testing and Turnover

Since the RAD process emphasises reuse, many of the program components have already been tested. This minimises the testing and development time.

1.11.6 Component Assembly Model

Object technologies provide the technical framework for a component-based process model for software engineering. The object oriented paradigm emphasises the creation of classes that encapsulate both data and the algorithm that are used to manipulate the data. If properly designed and implemented, object oriented classes are reusable across different applications and computer-based system architectures. Component Assembly Model leads to software reusability. The integration/assembly of the already existing software components accelerate the development process. Nowadays, many component libraries are available on the Internet. If the right components are chosen, the integration aspect is made much simpler.

1.12 Using Hybrid of Different Model

All these different software development models have their own advantages and disadvantages. Nevertheless, in the contemporary commercial software development world, the fusion of all these methodologies is incorporated. Timing is very crucial in software development. If a delay happens in the development phase, the market could be taken over by the competitor. Also if a 'bug' filled product is launched in a short period of time (quicker than the competitors), it may affect the reputation of the company. So, there should be a tradeoff between the development time and the quality of the product. Customers don't expect a bug free product but they expect a user-friendly product. That results in Customer Ecstasy.

1.13 Software Life Cycle Activities

The use of any specific life cycle model for a particular software cannot be recomended. Software developers should establish a software life cycle model that is appropriate for their product and organisation. The software life cycle model that is selected should cover the software from its birth to its retirement. Activities in a typical software life cycle model include the following:

- Quality Planning
- System Requirements Definition
- Detailed Software Requirements Specification
- Software Design Specification
- Construction or Coding
- Testing
- Installation
- Operation and Support
- Maintenance Retirement

Verification, testing, and other tasks that support software validation occur during each of these activities. A life cycle model organises these software development activities in various ways and provides a framework for monitoring and controlling the software development project.

1.14 Typical Tasks Supporting Validation

For each of the software life cycle activities, there are certain "typical" tasks that support a conclusion that the software is validated. However, the specific tasks to be performed, their order of performance, and the iteration and timing of their performance will be dictated by the specific software life cycle model that is selected and the safety risk associated with the software application. For very low risk applications, certain tasks may not be needed at all. However, the software developer should at least consider each of these tasks and should define and document which tasks are or are not appropriate for their specific application. The following discussion is generic and is not intended to prescribe any particular software life cycle model or any particular order in which tasks are to be performed.

1.14.1 Quality Planning

Design and development planning should culminate in a plan that identifies necessary tasks, procedures for anomaly reporting and resolution, necessary resources, and management review requirements, including formal design reviews. A software life cycle model and associated activities should be identified, as well as those tasks necessary for each software life cycle activity. The plan should include:

- The specific tasks for each life cycle activity;
- Enumeration of important quality factors (e.g., reliability, maintainability, and usability);
- Methods and procedures for each task;
- Task acceptance criteria;
- Criteria for defining and documenting outputs in terms that will allow evaluation of their conformance to input requirements;
- Inputs for each task;
- Outputs from each task;
- Roles, resources, and responsibilities for each task;
- Risks and assumptions; and
- Documentation of user needs.

Management must identify and provide the appropriate software development environment and resources. Typically, each task requires personnel as well as physical resources. The plan should identify the personnel, the facility and equipment resources for each task, and the role that risk (hazard) management will play. A configuration management plan should be developed that will guide and control multiple parallel development activities and ensure proper communications and documentation. Controls are necessary to ensure positive and correct correspondence among all approved versions of the specifications documents, source code, object code, and test suites that comprise a software system. The controls also should ensure accurate identification of, and access to the currently approved versions.

Procedures should be created for reporting and resolving software anomalies found through validation or other activities. Management should identify the reports and specify the contents, format, and responsible organizational elements for each report. Procedures also are necessary for the review and approval of software development results, including the responsible organizational elements for such reviews and approvals.

Typical Tasks : Quality Planning

- Risk (Hazard) Management Plan
- Configuration Management Plan
- Software Quality Assurance Plan: Software Verification and Validation Plan
- Verification and Validation Tasks, and Acceptance Criteria
- Schedule and Resource Allocation (for software verification and validation activities)
- Reporting Requirements
  - Formal Design Review Requirements
  - Other Technical Review Requirements
- Problem Reporting and Resolution Procedures
- Other Support Activities

1.14.2 Requirements

Requirements development includes the identification, analysis, and documentation of information about the device and its intended use. Areas of special importance include allocation of system functions to hardware/software, operating conditions, user characteristics, potential hazards, and anticipated tasks. In addition, the requirements should state clearly the intended use of the software.

The software requirements specification document should contain a written definition of the software functions. It is not possible to validate software without predetermined and documented software requirements. Typical software requirements specify the following:

- All software system inputs;
- All software system outputs;
- All functions that the software system will perform;
- All performance requirements that the software will meet (e.g. data throughput, reliability, and timing);
- The definition of all external and user interfaces, as well as any internal software-to-system interfaces;
- How users will interact with the system;
- What constitutes an error and how errors should be handled;
- Required response times;
- The intended operating environment for the software, if this is a design constraint (e.g. hardware platform, operating system);
- All ranges, limits, defaults, and specific values that the software will accept; and
- All safety related requirements, specifications, features, or functions that will be implemented in software.

Software safety requirements are derived from a technical risk management process that is closely integrated with the system requirements development process. Software requirement specifications should identify clearly the potential hazards that can result from a software failure in the system as well as any safety requirements to be implemented in software. The consequences of software failure should be evaluated, along with means of mitigating such failures (e.g. hardware mitigation, defensive programming, etc.). From this analysis, it should be possible to identify the most appropriate measures necessary to prevent harm.

The Quality System regulation requires a mechanism for addressing incomplete, ambiguous or conflicting requirements. Each requirement (e.g. hardware, software, user, operator interface, and safety) identified in the software requirements specification should be evaluated for accuracy, completeness, consistency, testability, correctness, and clarity. For example, software requirements should be evaluated to verify that:

- There are no internal inconsistencies among requirements;
- All of the performance requirements for the system have been spelled out;
- Fault tolerance, safety, and security requirements are complete and correct;

- Allocation of software functions is accurate and complete;
- Software requirements are appropriate for the system hazards; and
- All requirements are expressed in terms that are measurable or objectively verifiable.

A software requirements traceability analysis should be conducted to trace software requirements to (and from) system requirements and to risk analysis results. In addition to any other analyses and documentation used to verify software requirements, a formal design review is recommended to confirm that requirements are fully specified and appropriate before extensive software design efforts begin. Requirements can be approved and released incrementally, but care should be taken that interactions and interfaces among software (and hardware) requirements are properly reviewed, analyzed, and controlled.

1.14.3 Design

In the design process, the software requirements specification is translated into a logical and physical representation of the software to be implemented. The software design specification is a description of what the software should do and how it should do it. Due to complexity of the project or to enable persons with varying levels of technical responsibilities to clearly understand design information, the design specification may contain both a high level summary of the design and detailed design information. The completed software design specification constrains the programmer/coder to stay within the intent of the agreed upon requirements and design. A complete software design specification will relieve the programmer from the need to make ad hoc design decisions.

The software design needs to address human factors. Use error caused by designs that are either overly complex or contrary to users' intuitive expectations for operation is one of the most persistent and critical problems encountered by FDA. Frequently, the design of the software is a factor in such use errors. Human factors engineering should be woven into the entire design and development process, including the device design requirements, analyses, and tests. Device safety and usability issues should be considered when developing flowcharts, state diagrams, prototyping tools, and test plans. Also, task and function analyses, risk analyses, prototype tests and reviews, and full usability tests should be performed. Participants from the user population should be included when applying these methodologies.

The software design specification should include:

- Software requirements specification, including predetermined criteria for acceptance of the software;
- Software risk analysis;
- Development procedures and coding guidelines (or other programming procedures);
- Systems documentation (e.g. a narrative or a context diagram) that describes the systems context in which the program is intended to function, including the relationship of hardware, software, and the physical environment;
- Hardware to be used;
- Parameters to be measured or recorded;
- Logical structure (including control logic) and logical processing steps (e.g. algorithms);

- Data structures and data flow diagrams;
- Definitions of variables (control and data) and description of where they are used;
- Error, alarm, and warning messages;
- Supporting software (e.g. operating systems, drivers, other application software);
- Communication links (links among internal modules of the software, links with the supporting software, links with the hardware, and links with the user);
- Security measures (both physical and logical security); and
- Any additional constraints not identified in the above elements.

The first four of the elements noted above usually are separate pre-existing documents that are included by reference in the software design specification. Software requirements specification was discussed in the preceding section, as was software risk analysis. Written development procedures serve as a guide to the organization, and written programming procedures serve as a guide to individual programmers. As software cannot be validated without knowledge of the context in which it is intended to function, systems documentation is referenced. If some of the above elements are not included in the software, it may be helpful to future reviewers and maintainers of the software if that is clearly stated (e.g. There are no error messages in this program).

The activities that occur during software design have several purposes. Software design evaluations are conducted to determine if the design is complete, correct, consistent, unambiguous, feasible, and maintainable. Appropriate consideration of software architecture (e.g. modular structure) during design can reduce the magnitude of future validation efforts when software changes are needed. Software design evaluations may include analyses of control flow, data flow, complexity, timing, sizing, memory allocation, criticality analysis, and many other aspects of the design. A traceability analysis should be conducted to verify that the software design implements all of the software requirements. As a technique for identifying where requirements are not sufficient, the traceability analysis should also verify that all aspects of the design are traceable to software requirements. An analysis of communication links should be conducted to evaluate the proposed design with respect to hardware, user, and related software requirements. The software risk analysis should be re-examined to determine whether any additional hazards have been identified and whether any new hazards have been introduced by the design.

At the end of the software design activity, a Formal Design Review should be conducted to verify that the design is correct, consistent, complete, accurate, and testable, before moving to implement the design. Portions of the design can be approved and released incrementally for implementation; but care should be taken that interactions and communication links among various elements are properly reviewed, analyzed, and controlled.

Most software development models will be iterative. This is likely to result in several versions of both the software requirement specification and the software design specification. All approved versions should be archived and controlled in accordance with established configuration management procedures.

Typical Tasks: Design

- Updated Software Risk Analysis
- Traceability Analysis—Design Specification to Software Requirements (and vice versa)
- Software Design Evaluation
- Design Communication Link Analysis
- Module Test Plan Generation
- Integration Test Plan Generation
- Test Design Generation (module, integration, system and acceptance)

1.14.4 Construction or Coding

Software may be constructed either by coding (i.e., programming) or by assembling together previously coded software components (e.g. from code libraries, off-the-shelf software, etc.) for use in a new application. Coding is the software activity where the detailed design specification is implemented as source code. Coding is the lowest level of abstraction for the software development process. It is the last stage in decomposition of the software requirements where module specifications are translated into a programming language.

Coding usually involves the use of a high-level programming language, but may also entail the use of assembly language (or microcode) for time-critical operations. The source code may be either compiled or interpreted for use on a target hardware platform.

Decisions on the selection of programming languages and software build tools (assemblers, linkers and compilers) should include consideration of the impact on subsequent quality evaluation tasks (e.g. availability of debugging and testing tools for the chosen language). Some compilers offer optional levels and commands for error checking to assist in debugging the code. Different levels of error checking may be used throughout the coding process, and warnings or other messages from the compiler may or may not be recorded. However, at the end of the coding and debugging process, the most rigorous level of error checking is normally used to document what compilation errors still remain in the software. If the most rigorous level of error checking is not used for final translation of the source code, then justification for use of the less rigorous translation error checking should be documented. Also, for the final compilation, there should be documentation of the compilation process and its outcome, including any warnings or other messages from the compiler and their resolution, or justification for the decision to leave issues unresolved.

Firms frequently adopt specific coding guidelines that establish quality policies and procedures related to the software coding process. Source code should be evaluated to verify its compliance with specified coding guidelines. Such guidelines should include coding conventions regarding clarity, style, complexity management, and commenting. Code comments should provide useful and descriptive information for a module, including expected inputs and outputs, variables referenced, expected data types, and operations to be performed. Source code should also be evaluated to verify its compliance with the corresponding detailed design specification. Modules ready for integration and test should have documentation of compliance with coding guidelines and any other applicable quality policies and procedures.

Source code evaluations are often implemented as code inspections and code walkthroughs. Such static analyses provide a very effective means to detect errors before execution of the code. They allow for examination of each error in isolation and can also help in focusing later dynamic testing of the software. Firms may use manual (desk) checking with appropriate controls to ensure consistency and independence. Source code evaluations should be extended to verification of internal linkages between modules and layers (horizontal and vertical interfaces), and compliance with their design specifications. Documentation of the procedures used and the results of source code evaluations should be maintained as part of design verification.

A source code traceability analysis is an important tool to verify that all code is linked to established specifications and established test procedures. A source code traceability analysis should be conducted and documented to verify that:

- Each element of the software design specification has been implemented in code;
- Modules and functions implemented in code can be traced back to an element in the software design specification and to the risk analysis;
- Tests for modules and functions can be traced back to an element in the software design specification and to the risk analysis; and
- Tests for modules and functions can be traced back to source code for the same modules and functions.

Typical Tasks

- Construction or Coding Traceability Analyses
- Source Code to Design Specification (and vice versa)
- Test Cases to Source Code and to Design Specification
- Source Code and Source Code Documentation Evaluation
- Source Code Interface Analysis
- Test Procedure and Test Case Generation (module, integration, system and acceptance)

1.14.5 Test Documentation

Test documentation is a required tool for managing and maintaining the testing process. Documents produced by testers should answer the following questions:

- What to test? Test Plan
- How to test? Test Specification
- What are the results? Test Results Analysis Report
- What are 5 common solutions to software development problems?
  - **Solid requirements** - clear, complete, detailed, cohesive, attainable, testable requirements that are agreed to by all players. Use prototypes to help nail down requirements. In 'agile' type environments, continuous close coordination with customers/end-users is necessary.

- **realistic schedules** - allow adequate time for planning, design, testing, bug fixing, re-testing, changes, and documentation; personnel should be able to complete the project without burning out.
- **adequate testing** - start testing early on, re-test after fixes or changes, plan for adequate time for testing and bug-fixing. 'Early' testing ideally includes unit testing by developers and built-in testing and diagnostic capabilities.
- **stick to initial requirements as much as possible** - be prepared to defend against excessive changes and additions once development has begun, and be prepared to explain consequences. If changes are necessary, they should be adequately reflected in related schedule changes. If possible, work closely with customers/end-users to manage expectations. This will provide them a higher comfort level with their requirements decisions and minimise excessive changes later on.
- **communication** - require walkthroughs and inspections when appropriate; make extensive use of group communication tools—groupware, wiki's, bug-tracking tools and change management tools, intranet capabilities, etc. ensure that information/documentation is available and up-to-date—preferably electronic, not paper; promote teamwork and cooperation; use protoypes and/or continuous communication with end-users if possible to clarify expectations.

1.15 Life Cycle Cost

The life cycle cost of a product includes not simply the cost of materials and labor to manufacture it, but in fact all costs associated with the product from inception to retirement. The idea of a life cycle approach to cost is not specific to embedded systems, but rather is more generally applied to very expensive capital purchases such as buildings, factory machinery, and military systems (ships, planes, tanks, etc.). However, since embedded system designers are often embedding computers in such expensive systems, it behoves them to understand the financial model for life cycle costing so that they can take this into account in their work.

Kirk & Dell'Isola's book [Kirk 95] provides a comprehensive look at life cycle costing from the perspective of operating a commercial building, such as an office building (the following discussion is based on material from that book with some augmentation). However, the concepts they discuss apply to many embedded systems in general (As an aside, an office building is in fact an embedded system. There are computers controlling the climate, operating the elevator system, and in many cases controlling the lighting. In some buildings these three systems are beginning to be coordinated for efficient operation as well as lower cost maintenance.). In general, the factors included in the life cycle are those discussed in the previous section with respect to design and retirement of the product. In general, the idea is to minimize total cost for owning and operating an embedded system over the complete life of that system. This means that in addition to technical design factors, specific economic factors must be considered.

The life of a product is the shortest of three different aspects of system life:

- *Useful Life (utility)*: This is the obvious notion of equipment lifetime, in which eventually equipment wears out to the point it is beyond reasonable repair.

- *Technological Life (obsolescence)*: A system may become expensive or impractical to maintain even though it still is theoretically repairable or operable in general. For example, it may be impossible to find technicians trained in repairing vacuum-tube operated computers, or it may be impossible to find replacement parts for 16 Kb DRAM chips. Or the system may simply not incorporate the latest technology that in and of itself is seen desirable by users (for example, a rotary dial telephone system).
- *Economic Life (cost of operation)*: A system may still be functional, but become too expensive to be worth continuing to use. One example is because of a high cost of repair using obsolete components (this is a typical problem in long-lived embedded systems).
- Another reason may be that newer versions can be purchased and have lower operating costs so that the "payback" period of making that purchase is brief. This has, for example, happened recently with fuel-efficient furnaces and air conditioners.

Although it may not be possible to completely predict the lifetime of a system in advance, it is estimated taking these three factors into account. Then, the direct costs of ownership are considered, including:

- *Initial purchase cost*: Clearly, purchase cost is part of total cost. The usual issue is optimizing whether one should pay a higher up-front purchase cost in hopes of reaping lower operating costs. In some cases there is a limit on the amount of money that can be spent, such as a credit line limit, which may cap the allowable purchase cost.
- *Energy costs*: Operating equipment usually requires energy, and can be a significant portion of total costs. In many cases embedded computers are used to increase energy consumption efficiency, and thus reducing energy cost is a primary goal. As an example, high-end home furnaces perform energy management to maximize heat delivered to the house and minimize heat that escapes into a basement from hot water "stranded" in the basement heating elements when the thermostat reaches its set point.
- *Maintenance/Repair/Custodial costs*: A low initial purchase cost may be indicative of a system which will need frequent maintenance, repairs, or upkeep. Presumably a higher purchase cost indicates a system that contains more durable components. For an embedded system, it is more likely that components other than computers will break. However, installing sensors, data logging, and diagnostic capabilities for the system can substantially reduce these costs. As an example, elevators may come with minimal diagnostic sensors, but a contract maintenance company may well add sensors in an up-front investment to reduce the cost of later service calls.
- *Alteration/replacement costs*: In a long-lived system that will be upgraded, it is important to take into account eventually removing or upgrading the equipment. As an example, a component or housing may be glued into place to save on installation costs, but be very difficult to remove, whereas a bolted-in system is more expensive to install, but cheaper to replace. A more specifically electronic

example is the use of flash memory to permit field software upgrades without replacing read-only-memory chips.

Additionally, there are many indirect costs that must be taken into account in a complete financial model. These indirect costs of ownership include:

- *Interest (debt service)*: In some cases the most important indirect cost is the cost of borrowing money to pay the initial purchase cost in order to reduce later operating costs (or, alternately, the opportunity cost of not investing the purchase cost in some other way). Thus, any life cycle savings must be higher than extra initial cost savings to take into account the fact that extra money may need to be borrowed early in the system life cycle, but the savings are reaped later in the life cycle.
- *Administrative costs*. These can vary considerably, but might include such factors as periodic safety inspections, the cost of arranging for and administering service agreements, the cost of tracking capital equipment via property tags, and the like.
- *Staffing of equipment to operate it*: In some embedded systems computers are used to automate tasks previously performed by people. Perhaps the best everyday example of this is in elevators, which used to be operated by a trained person, but now are completely automatic. Clearly, saving operator wages is worth a significant increase in initial purchase cost in industrialized countries (but not necessarily in countries with low standards of living).
- *Opportunity cost of down time*: A system that is frequently unavailable for service may not be as cost-effective as a more dependable system because of reduced productivity, the cost of stockpiling against potential service outages, or the cost of paying operators while their equipment is broken. Minimizing down time is extremely important most embedded system industries, including manufacturing and transportation. Embedded computers often contribute significantly to dependability by permitting operating in degraded modes while awaiting repair, by alerting maintenance personnel to impending failures, or by helping diagnose problems for quick repair.
- *Other non-quantitative factors*: Some factors are important, but hard to set a fixed price on. These include potential productivity increases from comfortable employees and comfort taken from dealing with a company with a track record for standing behind their products.

The above life cycle costing approach works well for many large-scale embedded systems, where consumers are very sophisticated and equipped to invest for the long-term. However, with consumer products it may be much more difficult to create a design that is optimized both to achieve profitable sales as well as maximum utility for the purchaser.

Antonides discusses a combination of economics and psychology for durable goods purchases. While they come to the conclusion that frequency of use is generally related to reliability, and the cost of the good is generally related to its lifetime (when comparing different similar goods of different prices). While this is probably no surprise, the finding that makes life difficult for embedded system designers is that the decision of when to scrap a product is made on a potentially distorted view of life cycle economics. It should be noted that this is a European study and thus not necessarily representative of North American consumers. However, the specific points mentioned seem to ring true in general (the following is an interpretation and amplification, not a quotation):

The opinion of consumers with respect to how their equipment works does not agree with objective technical measurements. In particular, there is a bias to replacing rather than repairing, even when repair would be more economical in a life cycle cost sense.

Consumers, and especially low-income consumers, tend to underestimate the benefit of paying a higher purchase cost and reaping lower operating costs. This is presumably because they have little cash, and they have little credit or only have access to expensive credit such as credit cards rather than home equity loans. (Thus, many such systems are extremely cost-sensitive, squeezing the budget for embedded system components.)

The age of the consumer may affect the degree of patience and tendency to perform long-term planning (thus, younger or very old people may not value features such as diagnostics or upgradability; additionally they may not be inclined to wait and save for buying a high-end model).

When taken as a whole, the point of life cycle costing is to take into account all the direct and indirect costs of a product, and optimize for the lowest total cost given the constraints of customer preferences/behaviors.

Questions without Answer

1. Describe the code-and-fix model of software development. List some problems associated with this model, and suggest a phase of software development that can be introduced to eliminate some of these problems.
2. Describe three problems associated with viewing the software development process as a black box. In this view, the only visible flows are the product's inputs and outputs, and not the internal structure or operation.
3. List and briefly describe the seven main activities of software production, and identify the documents that result from each activity.
4. Identify six characteristics of a requirements specification document.
5. Define vertical and horizontal modularity, and describe the salient differences between the two.
6. A typical way to use horizontal modularity is to view functional requirements in terms of three separate models. List and describe these three views.
7. Describe the following four aspects of a requirements specification document, and indicate how each guides the engineer during production of the software:
   (i) The domain;
   (ii) Functional requirements;
   (iii) Non-functional requirements;
   (iv) Requirements on the development and maintenance process.
8. Define and explain the purpose of "alpha testing", "beta testing", and the deployment stage of a software product.

9. Describe the "waterfall model", including brief descriptions of each individual stage.
10. Describe the documents that result from each individual stage of the waterfall model.
11. The underlying philosophy of the waterfall model is based upon three principles. List and describe these three principles.
12. Describe a primary weakness associated with the waterfall model.
13. Describe the evolutionary (incremental) approach to the software life cycle.
14. Describe the meaning of "incremental delivery" (to the customer), as it relates to the evolutionary life cycle approach.
15. Three specific points or stages can be used to describe the evolutionary process model. What are these stages, and what is the usefulness of each stage?
16. Describe the "incremental development-and-delivery model".
17. Describe how the evolutionary model of software development solves some of the problems associated with the waterfall model of software development.

REFERENCES

Boris Beizer, *Black Box Testing, Techniques for Functional Testing of Software and Systems,* John Wiley & Sons, 1995.

Boris Beizer, *Software System Testing and Quality Assurance*, International Thomson Computer Press, 1996.

Edward Kit, *Software Testing in the Real World,* Addison-Wesley Longman, 1995.

Elfriede Dustin, Jeff Rashka, and John Paul, *Automated Software Testing – Introduction, Management and Performance,* Addison Wesley Longman, Inc., 1999.

"Guidance for Industry, FDA Reviewers and Compliance on Off-the-Shelf Software Use in Medical Devices, Office of Device Evaluation, Center for Devices and Radiological Health, Food and Drug Administration, September 1999.

"Guideline on General Principles of Process Validation" Center for Drugs and Biologics, & Center for Devices and Radiological Health, Food and Drug Administration, May 1987.

M. S. Deutsch, *Software Verification and Validation Realistic Project Approaches,* Prentice Hall, 1982.

Martha A. Branstad, John C. Cherniavsky, and W. Richards Adrion, NBS Special Publication 500-56, *Validation, Verification, and Testing for the Individual Programmer,* Center for Programming Science and Technology, Institute for Computer Sciences and Technology, National Bureau of Standards, U.S. Department of Commerce, February 1980.

Richard E. Fairley, *Software Engineering Concepts*, McGraw-Hill Publishing Company, 1985.

Technical Report No. 18, "Validation of Computer-Related Systems". PDA Committee on Validation of Computer-Related Systems. *PDA Journal of Pharmaceutical Science and Technology,* Volume 49, Number 1, January-February 1995 Supplement.

W. Richards Adrion, Martha A. Branstad, and John C. Cherniavsky. NBS Special Publication 500-75, *Validation, Verification, and Testing of Computer Software,* Center for Programming Science and Technology, Institute for Computer Sciences and Technology, National Bureau of Standards, U.S. Department of Commerce, February 1981.

International and National Consensus Standards

1. ANSI / ANS-10.4.1987, Guidelines for the Verification and Validation of Scientific and Engineering Computer Programs for the Nuclear Industry, American National Standards Institute, 1987.
2. ANSI/ASQC Standard D1160-1995, Formal Design Reviews, American Society for Quality Control, 1995.

3. ANSI/UL 1998:1998, Standard for Safety for Software in Programmable Components, Underwriters Laboratories, Inc., 1998.
4. IEEE Std. 1012-1986, Software Verification and Validation Plans, Institute for Electrical and Electronics Engineers, 1986.
5. IEEE Standards Collection, Software Engineering, Institute of Electrical and Electronics Engineers, Inc., 1994.
6. ISO 9000-3:1997, Quality Management and Quality Assurance Standards—Part 3: Guidelines for the application of ISO 9001:1994 to the development, supply, installation and maintenance of computer software. International Organization for Standardization, 1997.
7. ISO 9001:1994, Quality Systems—Model for Quality Assurance in Design, Development, Production, Installation, and Servicing. International Organization for Standardization, 1994.
8. ISO/IEC 12207:1995, Information Technology – Software Life Cycle Processes, Joint Technical Committee. ISO/IEC JTC 1, Subcommittee SC 7, International Organization for Standardization and International Electrotechnical Commission, 1995.

SOFTWARE FAULTS, FAILURE AND DEBUGGING

2

2.1 Program Definition

A program is a sequence of instructions understandable by a computer's Central Processing Unit (CPU) that indicates which operations the computer should perform on a set of data.

Programs are stored in executable files that reside in storage, but are copied into memory when they are launched so that their machine code will be immediately available to the CPU, which is the main logic unit of a computer. Storage refers to devices or media that can retain data for relatively long periods of time (e.g., years or even decades), such as hard disk drives (HDDs), floppy disks, optical disks (e.g., CDs and DVDs) and magnetic tape. This contrasts with memory, whose contents are retained only temporarily (i.e., while in use or only as long as the power supply remains on) but which can be accessed (i.e., read and written to) at extremely high speeds.

An executable file is a file that has been converted from source code into machine code, which is directly understandable by the CPU, by a specialized program called a compiler. Source code is the version of software as it is originally written (i.e. typed into a computer) by a human in plain text (i.e., human readable alphanumeric characters). Source code can be written in any of the hundreds of programming languages that have been developed, some of the most popular of these are C, C++, Cobol, Fortran, Java, Perl, PHP, Python and Tcl/Tk.

Software is usually used as a generic term for programs. However, in its broadest sense it can refer to all information (i.e. both programs and data) in electronic form and can provide a distinction from hardware, which refers to computers or other electronic systems on which software can exist and be used.

Programs are often divided into two broad categories:

- Systems programs, and
- Application programs.

The former refers to operating systems and utility programs that manage computer resources at a low level, i.e. that enable a computer to function. Examples of such utilities include compilers, device drivers and the X Window System (which provides basic graphic capabilities on Unix-like operating systems). Major categories of application programs include word processors, databases and games. Many computer users are only familiar with application programs, and many may not even realize that systems programs exist.

A program is a passive entity until it is launched; then it spawns (i.e., gives birth to) one or more processes. A process can be thought of as an instance of a program in action. On multitasking operating systems (i.e., systems that allow multiple processes to run seemingly simultaneously), multiple instances of a program can run concurrently, each a different process (or set of processes).

Programs are commonly launched directly by a user by clicking on an icon (i.e., a small image representing the program) in a GUI (graphical user interface) or by typing in a command at the command line (i.e., all-text user interface) and then pressing the ENTER key. Some programs are launched automatically by the system as it boots up (i.e., starts up) or in response to certain events.

A command is an instruction telling a computer to do something, such as launch a program. It consists of the name of one or more programs and any options and arguments for each command. An option is a (usually) single letter code that modifies the behavior of a command line program in some specific way. An argument is a file name or other input data for such a program. The ability of command line programs (i.e., programs which operate in the all-text mode) to use options and arguments adds greatly to their flexibility.

Executable programs are usually stored in one of several standard directories on Unix-like operating systems, including /bin,/sbin, /usr/bin, /usr/sbin and /usr/local/bin. Although it is not necessary for them to be in these locations in order to be operable, it is often more convenient.

Programs can range all the way in size and complexity from just a few lines of code that merely displays a simple phrase such as Hello World on the monitor screen to a massive operating system which contains hundreds of megabytes of code.

Many of the most widely used computer programs are proprietary software, i.e. commercial programs that usually are not available free of charge and for which there are restrictions on its use. However, the past several years have seen a rapid growth in the development and use of free software, i.e. programs that can be obtained at no cost and can be used for any desired purpose (including modifying them and making copies to give away or sell).

In contrast to many products, the quality and value of programs should definitely not be judged on the basis of their price. This is because many free programs are as good as or superior to their non-free counterparts, plus they have some additional advantages of not having any onerous EULAs (end user licensing agreements) and allowing users to modify them in any way desired. In fact, some of the most popular programs are free (e.g., the Apache Web Server which hosts more than 60 per cent of all Internet web sites).

An important tenet of the efficient programs like Unix philosophy is to write small programs that do only one thing but do it well, rather than to write massive programs that attempt to do numerous things. One reason is that a huge program is too complex for even the brightest human mind to comprehend in its entirety, and thus it is extremely difficult to remove all bugs (i.e., errors) and make it as efficient and secure as possible.

Moreover, small, specialized programs in Unix-like operating systems can be designed to work well with each other when they are connected via pipes to form pipelines of commands, which can perform highly specific tasks that would be very tedious or impractical by any other means.

2.2 Developing Codes

Programming is the creation of programs. It is performed by programmers, also frequently referred to as developers, who write the source code for a program using one or more programming languages and a text editor and often with a variety of more sophisticated tools as well, such as iLINFO

2.2.1 Source Code Definition

Source code (also referred to as source or code) is the version of a software or part of it as it is originally written (i.e., typed into a computer) by a human in plain text (i.e., human readable alphanumeric characters).

The term software refers to all operating systems, application programs and data that is used by products containing microprocessors (also called processors or central processing units). Such products include not only personal computers but also a vast array of other products, such as aircraft electronic systems, railway signaling systems, industrial robots, electronic medical equipment, space vehicle guidance systems, electronic cameras and even simple electronic toys.

Source code can be written in any of the hundreds of programming languages that have been developed. Some of the most popular of these are C, C++, Cobol, Fortran, Java, Perl, PHP, Python and Tcl/Tk.

There are many programs that can be used for writing source code in the desired programming language, ranging from simple, general purpose text editors (such as vi or gedit on Linux or Notepad on Microsoft Windows) to integrated development environments (such as Visual C++ on Microsoft Windows or the cross-platform Eclipse Platform for constructing and running integrated software-development tools). After writing, the source code is saved in a single file or, more commonly, in multiple files, with the number of files depending on such factors as the programming language and the size of the project.

Very often it is the case that source code intended for use on one platform can be written on another platform. A platform is any combination of processor and/or operating system. However, there are some notable exceptions. For example, the popular Microsoft text editors Notepad and Wordpad cannot be used to write code for deployment on Unix-like operating systems because they do not treat new lines of text correctly.

To be usable by a computer or other microprocessor-based product, source code must be compiled (i.e., translated by a computer) into machine language by a special program called a compiler. Also referred to as object code or binaries, machine language consists of a sequence of instructions (in the form of zeros and ones) that the processor can understand—but which is very difficult for humans to read or modify.

A program's source code is not necessarily all written in the same programming language. For example, it is common for programs that are written primarily in C to contain portions that are in an assembly language for optimization of processor efficiency. This is the case with the Linux kernel (i.e., the core of the Linux operating system).

An assembly language is a human-readable notation for machine language for a specific processor. It is far easier for programmers to remember and write assembly language commands than it is the zeros and ones that constitute machine language because they are short, mnemonic series of alphanumeric characters. In contrast to high-level programming languages such as C, Java and Perl, there is a close correspondence between assembly languages and machine languages.

Even moderately complex software can require the compilation of dozens, or hundreds of separate source code files. However, this complexity can be reduced considerably by the inclusion of a makefile, which is a file that describes the relationships among the source code files and contains information about how they are to be compiled.

2.2.2 Uses for Source Code

Software is distributed (i.e., sold or given away) primarily in compiled form (i.e., binaries) rather than in source code form. There are good reasons for this, including the fact that it is usually much easier to install (particularly for ordinary users), it keeps the source code secret and the file sizes are much smaller (thereby speeding downloads from the Internet and conserving disk space).

As an example of the huge size differences in file size that can exist between the source and binary versions of a program, AbiWord (a popular, stand alone and free word processing program that is available for the Linux, Microsoft Windows and QNX operating systems) has a source code size of 25.3MB but a binary (RPM format) size of only 3.54MB (both for version 2.0.6 for Linux).

The contrast is even greater for the Linux kernel. For example, the source code for version 2.4 is approximately 100MB and contains nearly 3.38 million lines of code, whereas its compiled binary is only about 1.1MB on a typical system. (The size of the Linux kernel source code has been increasing nearly exponentially ever since its inception, soaring from 0.2MB and 10,239 lines of code for version 0.01 in 1991 to 212MB and 5.93 million lines of code for version 2.6.0 in 2003.)

Although its primary purpose is usually to generate ready-to-install binaries, source code has several other important uses as well, and thus there is often a demand for it along with, or even in place of, the precompiled versions of the software. The reasons for this relate to the fact that the source code is generally the most versatile, informative and permanent form of any software:

(1) System administrators and other experienced users frequently prefer to compile software themselves prior to installation because of the increased number of options and consequent greater control that it can provide in tailoring the software to particular requirements.

(2) It is relatively easy to fix bugs (i.e., errors), find viruses or other malicious content as well as to enhance or otherwise modify software using the source code, whereas it would be extremely difficult using the binaries.

(3) Having the source code version of software makes it practical to port the software to other platforms (i.e., develop versions for other processors and/or operating systems). Without the source for a particular piece of software, such porting is usually extremely difficult.

(4) Source code can be a valuable tool for learning, particularly for beginning programmers, who often find it helpful to study existing code to gain insight into programming techniques and methodology.

(5) Source code also serves as a communication tool between experienced programmers. This is because of its (at least ideally) concise and unambiguous nature. The sharing of source code between developers is frequently cited as a contributing factor to the refinement of their programming skills.

(6) Programmers often want source code because of their tendency to recycle parts of it into new projects, a practice referred to as software reusability.

When the source code for a software package has been lost or is otherwise unobtainable, it is possible to reverse engineer it in order to obtain the code. However, reverse engineering is not easy, and there are frequently legal and contractual restrictions. In particular, it constitutes a violation of copyright law if done for the sole purpose of copying or duplicating programs. Reverse engineering for any purpose is often prohibited by EULAs (end user license agreements).

2.3 Software Faults (Errors, Bugs and Defects)

2.3.1 Difference between Error, Bug, Defect and Fault

Error is an undesirable deviation from requirements. Bug is an error found before the application goes into production but *defect* is an error found after the application goes into production. Broadly they are one and the same. The issue is whether to call them bugs or defects.

Bug is an unwanted and unintended property of a program or piece of hardware, esp. one that causes it to malfunction. Antonym of feature. Examples: "There's a bug in the editor: it writes things out backwards." "The system crashed because of a hardware bug." "Fred is a winner, but he has a few bugs" (i.e., Fred is a good guy, but he has a few personality problems).

The name "bug" gives off a subliminal impression that somehow the defect crawled into the code quite independently of the software engineer.

Historical note: Admiral Grace Hopper (an early computing pioneer better known for inventing COBOL) liked to tell a story in which a technician solved a glitch in the Harvard Mark II machine by pulling an actual insect out from between the contacts of one of its relays, and she subsequently promulgated bug in its hackish sense as a joke about the incident (though, as she was careful to admit, she was not there when it happened). For many years the logbook associated with the incident and the actual bug in question (a moth) sat in a display case at the Naval Surface Warfare Center (NSWC).

The text of the log entry (from September 9, 1947), reads "1545 Relay #70 Panel F (moth) in relay. First actual case of bug being found". This wording establishes that the term was already in use at the time in its current specific sense —and Hopper herself reports that the term 'bug' was regularly applied to problems in radar electronics during WWII.

The name "defect" presents the cold harsh reality that the engineer, analyst or designer actually got something wrong.

That which is subject to a defect is missing a requisite element and, therefore, is not legally binding. Defective service of process, for example, is service that does not comply with a procedural or jurisdictional requirement. A defective will is one that has not been properly drawn up, has been obtained by unlawful means, or does not comply with a particular law. In some cases, however, defects can be cured; for example, defective service of process can be cured by the service of an amended complaint.

In product liability, a defective product is one that cannot be used for the purposes intended or is made dangerous as a result of a flaw or imperfection. Such a defect might exist in the entire design of a product or in the production of a particular individual product. A latent defect is one that is not readily observable by the buyer of an item, whereas a patent defect is obvious or immediately apparent upon observation.

A fatal defect is one that, due to its serious nature, serves to nullify a contract.

2.3.2 Faults

The word Fault is used to denote an error or failure. A software fault, also known as a "crash" or "abend," is when the program directs the computer to go outside of its restricted memory boundary. A hardware fault is a failure in one of the circuits.

- In document ISO/CD 10303-226, a fault is defined as an abnormal condition or defect at the component, equipment, or sub-system level which may lead to a failure.
- According to Federal Standard 1037C, the term fault has the following meanings:
  - An accidental condition that causes a functional unit to fail to perform its required function.
  - A defect that causes a reproducible or catastrophic malfunction. A malfunction is considered reproducible if it occurs consistently under the same circumstances.

2.3.3 Software Failures

The terms failure and fault are key to any understanding of system reliability.

The Failure is the inability of a system or system component to perform a required function within specified limits. A failure may be produced when a fault is encountered. A system is said to have a failure if the service it delivers to the user deviates from compliance with the system specification for a specified period of time.

Failure in general refers to the state or condition of not meeting a desirable or intended objective. It may be viewed as the opposite of success.

2.3.4 Classification of Software Faults

Software faults may be:

- Permanent
- Transient

Some studies have suggested that since software is not a physical entity and hence not subject to transient physical phenomena (as opposed to hardware), software faults are permanent in nature. Some other studies classify software faults as both permanent and transient.

Gray classifies software faults into:

- Bohrbugs, and
- Heisenbugs.

Bohrbugs are essentially permanent design faults and hence almost deterministic in nature. They can be identified easily and weeded out during the testing and debugging phase (or early deployment phase) of the software life cycle. Heisenbugs, on the other hand, belong to the class of temporary internal faults and are intermittent. They are essentially permanent faults whose conditions of activation occur rarely or are not easily reproducible. Hence these faults result in transient failures, i.e. failures which may not recur if the software is restarted. Some typical situations in which Heisenbugs might surface are boundaries between various software components, improper or insufficient exception handling and interdependent timing of various events. It is for this reason that Heisenbugs are extremely difficult to identify through testing. Hence a mature piece of software in the operational phase, released after its development and testing stage, is more likely to experience failures caused by Heisenbugs than due to Bohrbugs. Most recent studies on failure data have reported that a large proportion of software failures are transient in nature, caused by phenomena such as overloads or timing and exception errors. The study of failure data from Tandem's fault tolerant computer system indicated that 70 per cent of the failures were transient failures, caused by faults like race conditions and timing problems.

2.4 Bugs and Their Sources

A bug, also referred to as a software bug, is an error or flaw in a computer program or software that may prevent it from working correctly or produce an incorrect or unintended result.

Bugs arise from mistakes made by humans in designing programs and writing their source code. Source code, also referred to as code, is the version of software (usually an application program or an operating system) as it is originally written (i.e., typed into a computer) by programmers using any of numerous programming languages, some of the most popular of which are C, C++, Java, Perl, PHP, Python and Tcl/Tk.

It is likely that there are bugs in virtually all useful computer programs. This is because of:

(1) the huge number of lines of code required for such programs,

(2) the complexity of programming and the consequent ease of making errors, and

(3) the difficulty of detecting some types of errors.

For example, a modern operating system typically contains several million lines of code (e.g., roughly 40 million for Microsoft Windows XP).

As programs continue to grow longer and more complex, bugs are becoming even more common and more difficult to find. Thus programmers now often devote more time and effort to finding and fixing bugs than to writing new code.

The frequency of bugs (e.g., the average number of bugs per million lines of code) can vary greatly according to the program. Well-written programs typically have few if any bugs that prevent them from functioning as intended nearly all of the time.

A program that contains a large number of bugs and/or bugs that seriously interfere with its functionality is said to be buggy. Reports about bugs in a program are referred to as bug reports or change requests.

Bugs can have a wide variety of effects, with varying levels of inconvenience to the users of a program. Some bugs affect a program's functionality only under very unusual circumstances and/or have only a subtle effect on a program's functionality, and they can thus lie undetected for a long time. More serious bugs can cause the program to crash or freeze in relatively common situations.

In some operating systems, such as the Microsoft Windows systems, a single crashing or freezing application program can make the entire computer unusable until it is rebooted (i.e., restarted). This can be not only inconvenient but also very costly for a large organization. Linux and other Unix-like operating systems are designed from the ground up so that bugs in application programs will usually not affect other programs or require the system to be rebooted.

Some bugs can result in security problems. One of the most common types is a buffer overflow, which can permit a malicious user or intruder to enter a system and execute programs that ordinary users are not normally allowed to run. A buffer overflow occurs any time a program writes more information into the buffer than there is memory space allocated for it. A buffer is a portion of memory that is set aside as a temporary holding place to store data, often before it is sent to or received from an external device.

Some bugs arise from unintended interactions between different parts of a program. This happens because programs are typically very complicated and thus programmers cannot visualize every possible way in which different parts could interact. Race condition bugs often fall into this category. A race condition occurs when the final state of a system depends on the order in which independently scheduled sequences of instructions are executed.

The results of bugs can be extremely serious. For example, in 1996, the European Space Agency's Ariane 5 rocket, which was valued at approximately US $500 million, exploded 40 seconds after launching due to a bug in its on-board guidance software 1.

The software industry has devoted much effort to finding methods for reducing the number of bugs. Among the approaches that are being used are improved design of programming languages (e.g., the elimination of pointers, which are a major cause of programming errors), better compilers (which can detect more types of errors) and improved testing techniques.

The use of the term bug to describe inexplicable defects has been a part of engineering jargon for well in excess of a century. For example, Thomas Edison used it in a letter to an associate in 1878. The term may have first been used in a computer context around 1947 by Grace Hopper, an early computer pioneer, who traced an error made by a computer to an actual insect stuck between the contacts of an electrical relay in the system.

The following are the Sources of bugs (Errors or Faults due to errors):

- Programming Errors—programmers, like anyone else, can make mistakes.
- Changing requirements (whether documented or undocumented)—the end-user may not understand the effects of changes, or may understand and request them anyway—redesign, rescheduling of engineers, effects on other projects, work already completed that may have to be redone or thrown out, hardware requirements that may be affected, etc. If there are many minor changes or any major changes, known and unknown dependencies among parts of the project are likely to interact and cause problems, and the complexity of coordinating changes may result in errors. Enthusiasm of engineering staff may be affected. In some fast-changing business environments, continuously modified requirements may be a fact of life. In this case, management must understand the resulting risks, and QA and test engineers must adapt and plan for continuous extensive testing to keep the inevitable bugs from running out of control.
- Miscommunication or no communication—as to specifics of what an application should or shouldn't do (the application's requirements).
- Software Complexity—the complexity of current software applications can be difficult to comprehend for anyone without experience in modern-day software development. Multi-tiered applications, client-server and distributed applications, data communications, enormous relational databases, and sheer size of applications have all contributed to the exponential growth in software/system complexity.
- Time pressures—scheduling of software projects is difficult at best, often requiring a lot of guesswork. When deadlines loom and the crunch comes, mistakes will be made. For example, people prefer to say things like:
  - 'no problem'
  - 'piece of cake'
  - 'I can whip that out in a few hours'
  - 'it should be easy to update that old code'

  instead of:
  - 'that adds a lot of complexity and we could end up making a lot of mistakes'
  - 'we have no idea if we can do that; we'll wing it'
  - 'I can't estimate how long it will take, until I take a close look at it'
  - 'we can't figure out what that old spaghetti code did in the first place'

  If there are too many unrealistic 'no problems', the result is bugs.
  - Poorly documented code—it's tough to maintain and modify code that is badly written or poorly documented; the result is bugs. In many organizations management provides no incentive for programmers to document their code or write clear, understandable, maintainable code. In fact, it's usually the opposite: they get points mostly for quickly turning out code, and there's job security if nobody else can understand it ('if it was hard to write, it should be hard to read').

- Software development tools—visual tools, class libraries, compilers, scripting tools, etc. often introduce their own bugs or are poorly documented, resulting in added bugs.

2.5 Programming Errors

Even the most experienced programmers make mistakes, and knowing how to debug an application and find those mistakes is an important part of programming. Before you learn about the debugging process, however, it helps to know the types of bugs that you will need to find and fix.

Programming errors fall into three categories:

- Compilation errors,
- Run-time errors, and
- Logic errors.

The techniques for debugging each of these are covered in the next three lessons.

2.5.1 Compilation Errors

Compilation errors, also known as compiler errors, are errors that prevent your program from running. When you press F5 to run a program, Visual Basic compiles your code into a binary language that the computer understands. If the Visual Basic compiler comes across code that it does not understand, it issues a compiler error.

If there is a syntax error in the code, the compiler will detect the error and the program won't even compile. At this point, the programmer is unable to form an executable that a user can run until the error is fixed. Forgetting a semi-colon at the end of a statement, for example, is a compile-time error. It's something the compiler can detect as an error.

Most compiler errors are caused by mistakes that you make when typing code. For example, you might misspell a keyword, leave out some necessary punctuation, or try to use an End If statement without first using an If statement.

Fortunately the Visual Basic Code Editor was designed to identify these mistakes before you try to run the program. You will learn how to find and fix compilation errors in the next lesson, Oops, a Typo: Finding and Getting Rid of Compiler Errors.

2.5.2 Run-Time Errors

Run-time errors are errors that occur while your program runs. These typically occur when your program attempts an operation that is impossible to carry out.

An example of this is division by zero. Suppose you had the following statement:

Speed = Miles/Hours

If the variable **Hours** has a value of 0, the division operation fails and causes a run-time error. The program must run in order for this error to be detected, and if Hours contains a valid value, it will not occur at all.

When a run-time error does occur, you can use the debugging tools in Visual Basic to determine the cause.

Compilers aren't perfect and so can't catch all errors at compile time. This is especially true for logic errors such as infinite loops. For example, the actual syntax of the code looks okay. But when you follow the code's logic, the same piece of code keeps executing over and over again infinitely so that it loops. In such a case, compilers aren't really smart enough to catch all of these types of errors at compile-time. Therefore, the program compiles file into an executable file. However, and unfortunately, when the end-user runs the program, the program (or even their whole computer) freezes up due to an infinite loop. Other types of run-time errors are when an incorrect value is computed, the wrong thing happens, etc. Basically, a run-time error is anything that goes wrong in a program. It's any error or problem with the program that slipped by the compiler's error checker.

2.5.3 Logic Errors

Logic errors are errors that prevent your program from doing what you intended it to do. Your code may compile and run without error, but the result of an operation may produce a result that you did not expect.

For example, you might have a variable named **`FirstName`** that is initially set to a blank string. Later in your program, you might concatenate **`FirstName`** with another variable named **`LastName`** to display a full name. If you forgot to assign a value to **`FirstName,`** only the last name would be displayed, not the full name as you intended.

Logic errors are the hardest to find and fix, but Visual Basic has debugging tools that make this job easier, also.

2.6 Need for Debugging

Why people must test programs is often debated. If people were ethical, we would not have to test for security risks, but the world is not entirely full of ethical people who ensure that correct data is computed into a system—that is why safe practices need to be developed. The only way for this to take place is through bug testing. There are two categories that effect the client and the programmer, as each have different needs and wants.

From the client's perspective, having a stable program that is guaranteed to perform its desired task is not only a reflection of the program, but also of the company itself. Poor products shine the light dimly on the company, so a solid and well-tested product needs to be ensured through bug testing, before manufacturing takes place.

Management doesn't always know about product flaws; company directors assume that every function works smoothly without any defects. However, experience shows that no product/system can be deemed completely secure without controversy. There will always be bugs in a program; whether they are found or not is another question. Open Source makes it much easier to spot bugs and code flaws, and active security checks by the public help create a much more stable and operable program. This is one of the reasons why Microsoft products fail consistently when it comes to testing; their products are not Open Source, and therefore it is much harder to create a secure and flexible program without the aid of the programming community to help optimize code.

The importance to the client, purchaser of the software, is without doubt a key aspect in performing their daily tasks successfully. If the program is vulnerable to overflows, lack of input checks, or even lack of encryption, it will quickly become known for its instability, and product sales will drop dramatically. Customers will purchase alternative products that perform the same task and that have been carefully checked by multiple tests, as will be seen in the testing section of this document.

There is a high level of ethics involved when a programmer is contracted to develop a program. The programmer is the top of the chain for importance in testing and coding a proficient software application. He/she is responsible for ensuring that all functions of the program work, and work efficiently; code optimization should be at its peak, with security functions in check. Better programs are known to have been thoroughly tested, with all sorts of data sets being properly dealt with. Operating systems like Linux are tested every day by programmers and crackers alike. Yes, security problems do exist in this environment, but most are patched or fixed, pushing towards one of the most stable systems currently around.

Sloppy programmers will not care about ethics, and will simply code the program to minimally function with all its client side requirements implemented. Some programmers deem financial security more important than ethical security—be careful whom you contract to fulfill your programming requirements.

2.7 Debugging vs Testing

The term bug is often used to refer to a problem or fault in a computer. There are software bugs and hardware bugs.

Common Problems	Solutions
Poor requirements: If requirements are unclear, incomplete, too general, or not testable, there will be problems	**Solid requirements**—clear, complete, detailed, cohesive, attainable, testable requirements that are agreed to by all players, use prototypes to help nail down requirements
Unrealistic schedule: If too much work is crammed in too little time, problems are inevitable	**Realistic schedules**—allow adequate time for planning, design, testing, bug fixing, re-testing, changes, and documentation; personnel should be able to complete the project without burning out.
Inadequate testing: No one will know whether or not the program is any good until the customer complains or systems crash	**Adequate testing**—start testing early on, re-test after fixes or changes, plan for adequate time for testing and bug-fixing.
Requirements change: Requests to pile on new features after development is underway are common	**Stick to initial requirements as much as possible**—be prepared to defend against excessive changes and additions once development has begun, and be prepared to explain consequences. If changes are necessary, they should be adequately reflected in related schedule changes. If possible, use rapid prototype during the design phase so that customer can see what to expect. This will provide them a higher comfort level with their requirements decisions and minimize changes later on.
Miscommunication: If developers don't know what is needed or customers have erroneous expectations, problems are guaranteed	Check list should be prepared at requirement formation level itself.
Poorly documented code: Sufficient comments not built into the source code, requirement changes not updated in the impacted documents	The programmer should have the practice of providing code at each level.

Software testing should not be confused with debugging. Debugging is the process of analyzing and locating bugs when software does not behave as expected. Although the identification of some bugs will be obvious from playing with the software, a methodical approach to software testing is a much more thorough means of identifying bugs. Debugging is therefore an activity, which supports testing, but cannot replace testing. However, no amount of testing can be guaranteed to discover all bugs.

2.8 Software Fault Metrics

Metrics in the area of software fault tolerance, (or software faults) are generally pretty poor. The data sets that have been analyzed in the past are surely not indicative of today's large and complex software systems. The analysis by of various POSIX systems has the largest applicable data set found in the literature. Some of the advantages of the research are the fact that the systems are commercially developed, the systems adhere to the same specification, and the systems are large enough that testing them shows an array of problems. Still, the research is not without its problems; operating systems may be a more unique case than application software; operating systems may share more heritage from projects like Berkeley's Unix or the Open Software Foundation's research projects. The issue with gathering good metrics data is the cost involved in developing multiple versions of complex robust software. Operating systems offer the advantage of many organizations building their own versions of this complex software.

The results of the research show that software errors may be correlated in N-version software systems. The results of these studies imply that the failure mode for programmers is not unique, destroying a major tenant of the N-version software fault tolerance technique. It is important to remember however, the research, like most other publications in this area, are case studies, and may not be an in-depth study across enough variety of software systems to be a conclusive result.

2.8.1 Tools

Software fault tolerance has an extreme lack of tools in order to aide the programmer in making reliable system. This lack of adequate tools is not very different from the general lack of functional tools in software development that go beyond an editor and a compiler. The ability to semi-automate the adding of fault tolerance into software would be a significant enhancement to the market today. One of the biggest issues facing the development of software fault tolerant systems is the cost currently required to develop these systems. Enhanced and functional tools, that can easily accomplish their task, would surely be welcomed in the market place.

2.8.2 Techniques Recovery Blocks

The recovery block method is a simple method developed by Randell from what was observed as somewhat current practice at the time. The recovery block operates with an adjudicator which confirms the results of various implementations of the same algorithm. In a system with recovery blocks, the system view is broken down into fault recoverable blocks. The entire system is constructed of these fault tolerant blocks. Each block contains at least a primary, secondary, and exceptional case code along with an adjudicator (It is important to note that this definition can be recursive, and that any component may be composed of another fault tolerant block composed of primary, secondary, exceptional case, and adjudicator components.). The adjudicator is the component which determines the correctness of the various blocks to try. The adjudicator should be kept somewhat simple in order to maintain execution speed and aide in correctness. Upon first entering a unit, the adjudicator first executes the primary alternate (There may be N alternates in a unit which the adjudicator may try.). If the adjudicator determines that the primary block failed, it then tries to roll back the state of the system and tries the secondary alternate. If the adjudicator does not accept the results of any of the alternates, it then invokes the exception handler, which then indicates the fact that the software could not perform the requested operation.

Recovery block operation still has the same dependency which most software fault tolerance systems have—design diversity. The recovery block method increases the pressure on the specification to be specific enough to create different multiple alternatives that are functionally the same. This issue is further discussed in the context of the N-version method.

The recovery block system is also complicated by the fact that it requires the ability to roll back the state of the system from trying an alternate. This may be accomplished in a variety of ways, including hardware support for these operations. This try and rollback ability has the effect of making the software to appear extremely transactional, in which only after a transaction is accepted is it committed to the system. There are advantages to a system built with a transactional nature, the largest of which is the difficult nature of getting such a system into an incorrect or unstable state. This property, in combination with checkpointing and recovery may aide in constructing a distributed hardware fault tolerant system.

2.9 Cost of Fixing Errors (Debugging)

The National Institute of Standards & Technology (NIST) found, in a 2002 study, that software errors cost the U.S. economy an aggregate of $59.5 billion annually. Furthermore, these defects cost more than their correction efforts—tarnishing reputations, crippling performance and impacting revenue. Testing is crucial for reducing these impacts, yet the soaring cost, time and effort required for adequate testing limits corporate flexibility and responsiveness to changing business conditions.

Always a burden for IT organizations, the mounting demands of testing strain development resources and budgets, and overrun tight schedules. Software developers typically are not testing experts and avoid it whenever possible. Testing today's highly complex and integrated software is a distinct competency that requires trained specialists, automated tools, and a readiness to respond to the cyclical resource demands of release-driven development efforts. Yet, the high costs of testing coupled with budget cutbacks have limited the testing capacity of many IT organizations. Compounding the issue is that developers traditionally have taken a tactical approach to testing—focused on defect detection at the end of the development process. However, as Figure 2.1 shows, inadequate testing in the early stages of development leaves defects that are increasingly expensive to fix later in the lifecycle.

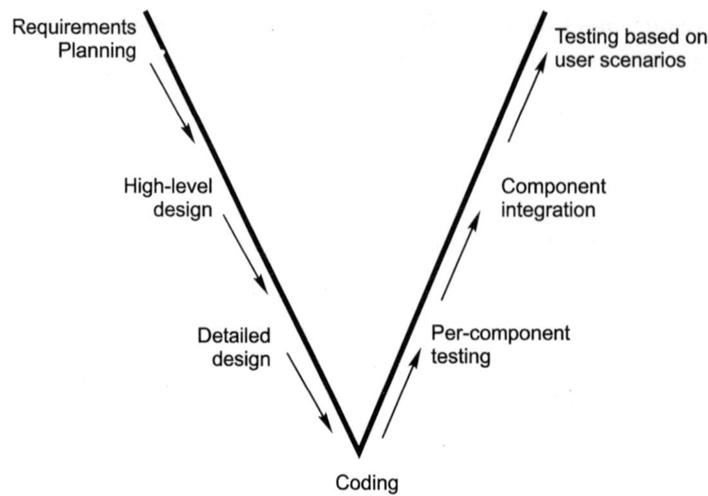

Fig. 2.1: Relative cost of defect correction

According to the NIST, the cost of remediation in post-release is up to 30 times higher than in requirements and analysis.

2.9.1 Measurements of Expenditures

To determine how much more economical automated GUI-testing really is compared to manual testing, certain firms have measured and compared the expenditures for both methods during our PIE.

The table in Figure 2.2 shows the result:

	Preparation V		Execution **D**		**N**	Expenditure **E** for **n** aut.			tests:
Test	manual	auto	manual	auto		1	5	10	20
Test 1	16	56	24	1	1,74	143%	45%	26%	15%
Test 2	10	14	2	0,1	2,11	118%	73%	50%	32%
Test 3	10	16	4,5	0,2	1,40	112%	52%	33%	20%
Test 4	20	28	1,5	0,2	6,15	131%	105%	86%	64%
Test 5	10	15	1	0,1	5,56	137%	103%	80%	57%
Test 6	10	15	1,5	0,1	3,57	131%	89%	64%	43%
Test 7	10	11,5	0,75	0,1	2,31	108%	87%	71%	54%
Test 8	10	11,5	0,5	0,1	3,75	110%	96%	83%	68%
Test 9	10	14	3	0,1	1,38	108%	58%	38%	23%
Test 10	10	10,6	0,5	0,1	1,50	102%	89%	77%	63%
Total	**116**	**191,6**	**39,25**	**2,1**	**2,03**	**125%**	**65%**	**42%**	**26%**

Fig. 2.2

The baseline project chosen for measuring this data was the development of an integrated PC software tool for radio base stations (for GSM radio communication). This application provides a graphical interface for commissioning, parameterization, hardware diagnostics, firmware downloading, equipment data base creation, and in-field and off-line diagnostics of multiple types of base stations, including a full-graphics editor for equipment definition. The application was developed using Microsoft Visual C++/Visual Studio and is approximately 100000 lines of C++ Code in size.

Vm: = Expenditure for test specification. Va: = Expenditure for test specification + implementation.

Dm: = Expenditure for single, manual test execution.

Da: = Expenditure for test interpretation after automated testing. Time for test process not counted since executed without supervision via CR-Tool. V and D are given in hours of work.

*En: = Aa /Am = (Va + n*Da)/ (Vm + n*Dm).*

This equivalence shows "Break-even" of GUI Test Automation

The question of main interest is: How often does a specific test have to be repeated before automated testing becomes cheaper than manual testing? In the above table this "break-even" point is represented by the N-factor, in accordance with the equation EN = Aa /Am = 100%. The measurements undertaken within our experiments show that a break-even can already be attained by the 2nd regression test cycle (Ntotal =2, 03). This break-even, however, does have two prerequisites: the tests must run completely without human interaction (e.g. overnight test runs), and no further test script modifications are necessary to rerun the tests in later releases of the product. As already mentioned in this lecture, this is not easy to achieve.

If all you do is buy a CR-Tool and begin capturing, then your testing costs will increase to between 125% and 150% of manual testing costs (see E1 in Fig. 2.2). And there will be additional costs associated with each test run because of traps such as test script maintenance. On the other hand, if you establish a complete framework for GUI test automation (where the CR-Tool is a cornerstone and not the complete solution), then a decrease of costings down to about 40 per cent for a typical product test cycle (E10) is realistic.

2.9.2 Early Problem Detection

A broad range of testing occurs during the software development process. Each review, inspection, walk-through, group code test, and desk check is in reality a form of test.

The earlier an error can be detected and corrected, the lower the additional development cost associated with fixing the error. Many sources have stated that the cost of early detection and fixing of problems is on the order of 1 per cent of the cost incurred when problems are detected at final test or worse, by the customer.

Late problem detection is also a major cause of schedule slips and late completion of final software.

Many have claimed that as many as 80 per cent of software errors that occur before a software product reaches final quality assurance testing can be caught by using certain techniques such as specification reviews, audits, inspections, group code reviews, and walkthroughs. Without these "pre-filters", error rates would be much higher. Cost of Random (Smart Monkey) testing the bugs is discussed in section 6.13.5 of this book.

2.10 The Life of a Fault or Bug

The life of a software bug may be described as follows: A bug is born when a person makes an error in some activity that relates to software development, such as defining a requirement, designing a program, or writing code. This error gets embedded in that person's work product (requirement document, design document, or code) as a fault.

As long as this fault (also known as a bug or defect) remains in the work product, it can give rise to other bugs. For example, if a fault in a requirements document goes undetected, it is likely to lead to related bugs in the system design, program design, code, and even in the user documentation.

A bug can go undetected until a failure occurs, which is when a user or tester perceives that the system is not delivering the expected service. In the system test phase, the goal of the test engineer is to induce failures through testing and thereby uncover and document the associated bugs so they can be removed from the system. Ideally the life of a bug ends when it is uncovered in static or dynamic testing and fixed.

In addition to the threat of attacks, substantial time and money is spent keeping software up to date. As intimated earlier software bugs cost the United State economy $59.5 billion annually. Even bugs without security implications can be problematic for users and companies. According to a PC Magazine article, Microsoft founder Bill Gates was quoted to claim that on average 5 per cent of all Windows machines crash twice a month. In order for secure protocols to fully protect against malicious users, they must be perfectly implemented in software—a very difficult task. Most of the errors detected in secure systems are implementation errors. While some of the errors are due to improperly matching the specification, many errors are caused by complications introduced when programming—especially when using an inherently unsafe language like C. If programmers are not careful, it may be possible for an attacker to overwrite regions of memory in such a manner they are able to execute arbitrary code and gain access to private data.

```
Unsigned int x;
int array[5];
Scanf ("%d", 8x);
If(x > 4  fatal (" Intx out of bounds");
5 x++;
6 a = array[x];
```

Fig. 2.3: Example of common bug

An example of a common bug is shown in Fig. 2.3. This code segment will cause an array bounds error if the value of four is provided as an input since the array will be indexed with the value five which is outside the bounds of the array. Complete software verification for arbitrary programs with unbounded memory is undecidable.

Frequently, software verification is limited to a set of properties that must be satisfied for correct behavior. Some examples include memory access checking (pointers must point to valid data when dereferenced), array overflows, and proper use of network protocols. These properties exhibit well-known behavior that can be easily specified and are a common source of bugs.

2.11 Software Failure

According to Laprie "a system failure occurs when the delivered service no longer complies with the specifications, the latter being an agreed description of the system's expected function and/or service". This definition applies to both hardware and software system failures. Faults or bugs in a hardware or a software component cause errors. An error is defined by Laprie as that part of the system which is liable to lead to subsequent failure, and an error affecting the service is an indication that a failure occurs or has occurred. If the system comprises of multiple components, errors can lead to a component failure. As various components in the system interact, failure of one component might introduce one or more faults in another. Figure 2.4 shows this cyclic behavior

→ Failure → Fault → Error → Failure → Fault

Fig. 2.4: Fault Behavior

Software project failure is often devastating to an organization. Schedule slips, buggy releases and missing features can mean the end of the project or even financial ruin for a company. Oddly, there is disagreement over what it means for a project to fail.

2.11.1 Criteria for Failure

The criteria for failure are heavily dependent on context of use, and may be relative to a particular observer or belief system. A situation considered to be a failure by one might be considered a success by another, particularly in cases of direct competition or a zero-sum game. As well, the degree of success or failure in a situation may be differently viewed by distinct observers or participants, such that a situation that one considers to be a failure, another might consider to be a success, a qualified success or a neutral situation.

It may also be difficult or impossible to ascertain whether a situation meets criteria for failure or success due to ambiguous or ill-defined definition of those criteria. Finding useful and effective criteria, or heuristics, to judge the success or failure of a situation may itself be a significant task.

Failure is defined in ISO/CD 10303-226 as the lack of ability of a component, equipment, sub-system, or system to perform its intended function as designed. Failure may be the result of one or many faults.

2.11.2 Types of Failure

Failure can be differentially perceived from the viewpoints of the evaluators. A person who is only interested in the final outcome of an activity would consider it to be an Outcome Failure if the core issue has not been resolved or a core need is not met. A failure can also be a process failure whereby although the activity is completed successfully, a person may still feel dissatisfied if the underlying process is perceived to be below expected standard or benchmark.

The advantages of defining faults as failures of component/interacting systems are: One can consider faults without the need to establish a direct connection with a failure, so we can discuss faults that do not cause failures. The definition of a fault is the same as the definition of a failure with only the boundary of the relevant system or sub-system being different.

Solid and Soft Faults

- A soft software fault is a fault which is temporary and recoverable
- A solid software fault is a fault which is permanent or which cannot be recovered

The term error often is used in addition to the terms fault and failure. Often, errors are defined to be the result of faults, leading to failures. Informally, errors seem to be a passive concept associated with incorrect values in the system state. However, it is extremely difficult to develop unambiguous criteria for differentiating between faults and errors.

Fault tolerance is the ability of a system to respond gracefully to an unexpected hardware or software failure. There are many levels of fault tolerance, the lowest being the ability to continue operation in the event of a power failure. Many fault-tolerant computer systems mirror all operations—that is, every operation is performed on two or more duplicate systems, so if one fails the other can take over. This is called *redundancy*.

Consider a computer system running a program to control the temperature of a boiler. If a bit in memory becomes stuck at one, that is a fault. If the computer system outputs cause the boiler temperature to rise out of the normal zone, that is a computer system failure. If there is a gauge showing the temperature of the boiler, and its needle moves into the "yellow" zone, that is system fault—if the boiler explodes because of the faulty firing calculation, that is a system failure.

Software faults are most often caused by design faults. Design faults occur when a designer (in this case a programmer), either misunderstands a specification or simply makes a mistake. Software faults are common for the simple reason that the complexity in modern systems is often pushed into the software part of the system. It is estimated that 60-90 per cent of current computer errors are from software faults. Software faults may also occur from hardware; these faults are usually transitory in nature, and can be masked using a combination of current software and hardware fault tolerance techniques.

The current assumption is that software cannot be made without bugs. This assumption may be mostly true, but software does not have to be as traditional buggy as it is now. For example, the Tandem Guardian 90 operating system showed that for all of installed field systems, that for a period of less than a year, (specific time period not given) that a total of 200 errors were reported; 179 of those error were attributed to software faults. The Tandem data shows that it is not necessary for software to be inherently buggy, however, the cost and overhead for replicated processes and the time and effort spent on making software correct must be taken into account.

2.11.3 The Cost, Feature, Product Spiral

Economics determines the success of any software project and its value to a company. The amount of money spent on development determines the cost of the asset. The return generated by the product is its value. The difference between the return and the cost is the return on investment (ROI).

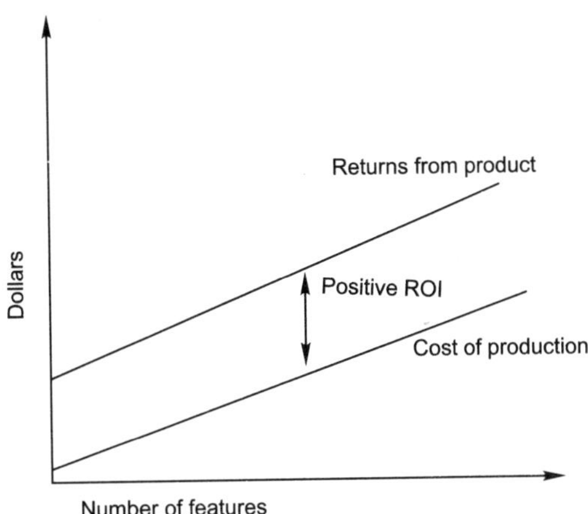

Fig. 2.5: The ROI of a product is the difference between its cost of production and its return. If the return is greater than the cost of production then it is said to possess a positive ROI.

Economics of Adding Features

Organizations must consider the cost of adding features to a product. Figure 2.5 shows a software project whose returns outpace the cost of production, thus producing a positive ROI.

Figure 2.6 shows a product that initially has a positive ROI, but whose added features cost (marginal cost) more than the amount of return generated by the features. This initially profitable product becomes a drag on the company.

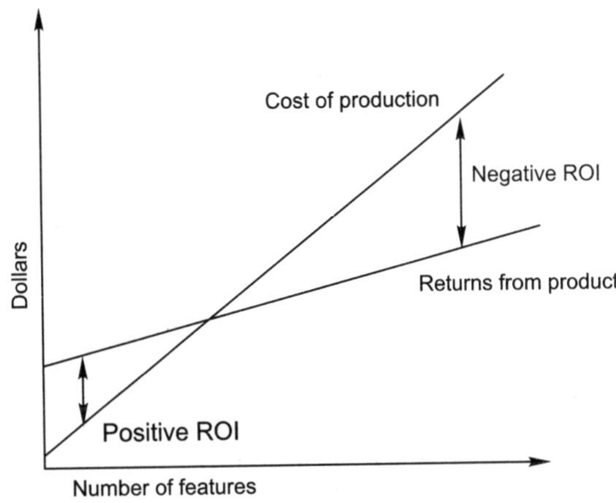

Fig. 2.6: ROI is said to be negative if it costs more to produce a product than it generates.

Figures 2.5 and 2.6 are deceptive because under most software processes, the cost of changing software is not linear, but exponential. Brooks attributes the exponential rise in costs to the cost of communication. Changes to software include new features, bug fixes and scaling.

The effects of exponential cost of production can be characterized by three properties. First, new projects are successful because the cost curve is flat. Second, once the costs start increasing, they quickly overcome any additional value added from the new features. Finally, if changes are made after the costs become exponential, the additional costs will quickly overwhelm all returns garnered from the product to date. Figure 2.7 details the effects of an exponential cost of change.

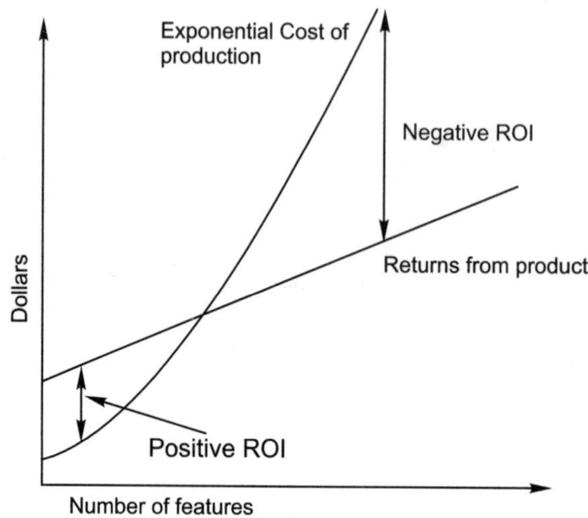

Fig. 2.7: Exponential costs of change can quickly subsume the worth of any product

Software processes are designed to manage the cost of change. An examination of cost management and processes is beyond the scope this article but will be the topic of a future article. Briefly, processes that follow waterfall and iterative models control costs by reducing need for change as costs increase. In contrast, processes based on the spiral model ensure that the cost of change is fixed. This article assumes an exponential cost of change as most projects are based on waterfall or iterative models.

Changes are often unavoidable because there are no successful medium-sized software projects. Successful projects require a significant amount of development and become a company asset.

Maximizing ROI means expanding the market and the addition of features which, in turn, increase the investment in the product. If the next version is successful, this increased investment leads to an even greater desire to maximize returns. If the cost of change becomes exponential, high cost makes adding features impractical and development must stop. Unfortunately, most companies do not realize this point exists and spend huge sums on dead products.

2.11.4 Software Failure Modes

Exponential costs of change belie a stark reality: Unless the product is shipped before the cost of change becomes exponential, it will very likely fail. Many projects become races to see if enough features can be created to make a viable product before adding the additional required features becomes too expensive.

There are four failure modes that prevent product completion:

(1) Hitting the wall before release

A small team of programmers is making good progress adding features to a product. Before the needed features can be delivered, some event makes the cost of change exponential and all progress stops. These events may include losing a key team member, adding team members to accelerate production, unforeseen difficulties with technology choices, unforeseen requirements, and major changes in target audience/market. Figure 2.8 shows how the minimum number of features will never be reached.

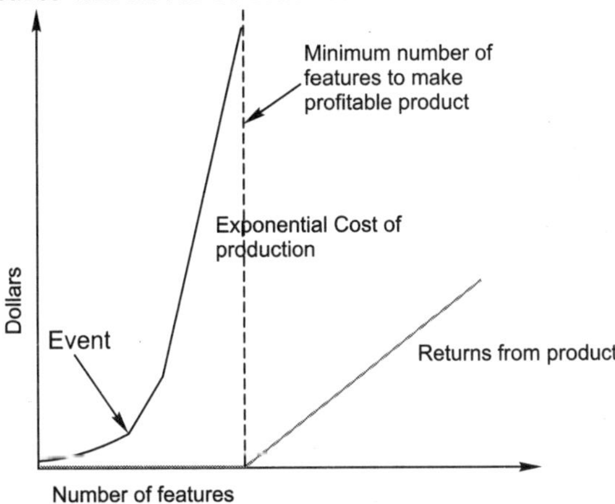

Fig.2.8: Teams hit a wall in production when some event causes the cost of change to be exponential so that all progress seems to stop.

(2) 90% done

A team of programmers is making steady progress but never finishes the required features because of a gradual rise in the cost of change.

This failure mode is often unavoidable because the riskiest features are often put off until last. These features often require so much complexity that their solutions overwhelm the development process. Proper risk mitigation is essential to avoiding this failure mode.

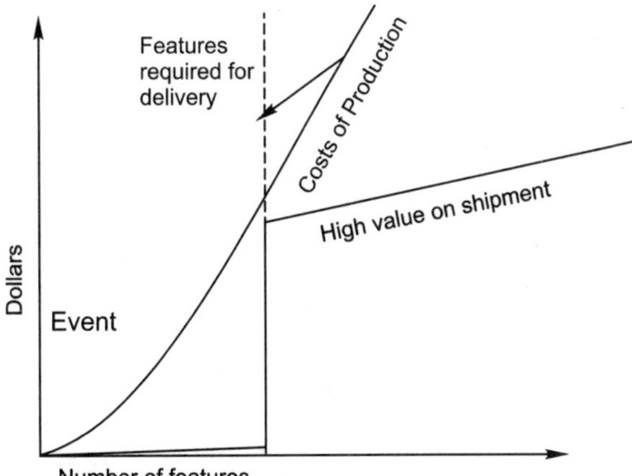

Fig. 2.9: 90% done is difficult to detect because the cost of change increases slower with no propagating event. The higher the value on delivery and the more required features, the more likely this failure mode.

(3) Endless QA

Endless QA occurs when a product ships with all features completed, but still has too many bugs to make it into production. If the cost curve has become exponential, these bugs will take longer and longer to fix. As the cost of change increases, any given change will likely cause more bugs. Figure 2.10 demonstrates how the fixing of bugs once the product is released to QA can ruin ROI. The higher the cost of change before delivery to QA, the larger the number of bugs. Indeed, the number of bugs at QA is a good indirect metric of the cost of change.

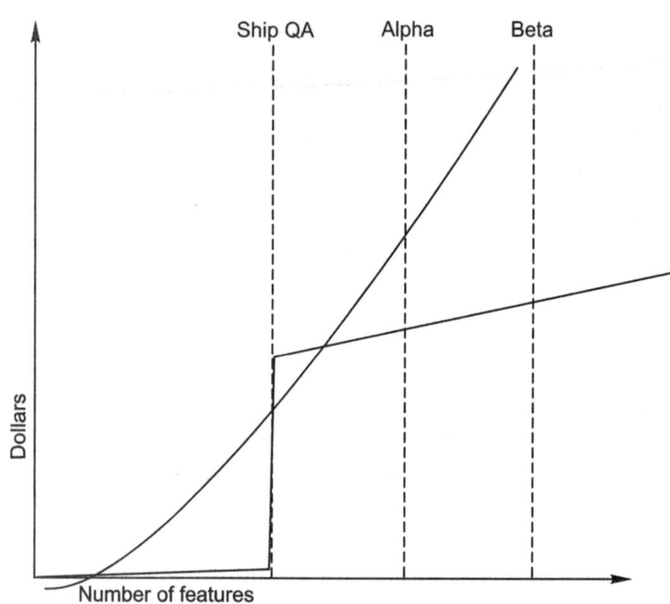

Fig. 2.10: A product shipped to QA with a fair number of bugs when the cost of change is exponential is in danger of never being shipped as each attempt to fix bugs will probably produce more, each one costing more to fix.

(4) Version 2.0

Most failures of version 2.0 of any product can be traced to exponential cost of change. During version 1.x, the cost of change has become exponential. The new features will never generate high-enough returns to make up for the costs of producing the version. Figure 2.11 diagrams this effect. What is most frustrating for many teams is that after a successful first version, the costs of change may have become so high, that it is unlikely the second version will ever ship.

2.11.5 Failure Traps

If costs do increase exponentially, development teams must ensure cost is managed until delivery of the product. If they don't, failure is all but guaranteed.

Unfortunately, there are several traps for developers that accelerate the onset of exponential costs of change. Interestingly, all of these techniques are designed to accelerate development at the beginning of the project, but the costs of using may overwhelm any savings. Here are four of the most common traps:

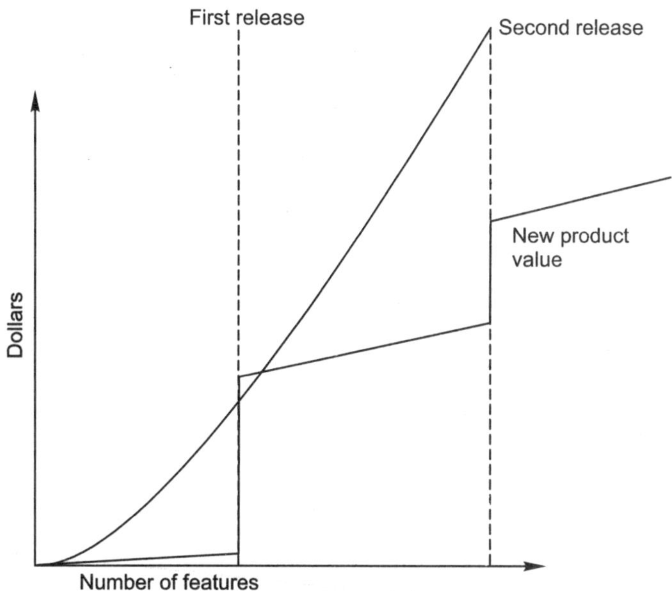

Fig. 2.11: Second releases often fail because the cost of change has become so great it easily overwhelms the value of the second release.

(1) Prototype Trap

Product prototypes are great ways to prove technologies, techniques and reduce risk. However, unless the economics of development are understood, they become liabilities. The problem is how much money is spent on the prototype. If enough resources are spent on any given prototype it becomes too valuable to throw away.

Most developers intend to throw away a prototype once it is completed and the resulting code quickly becomes expensive to change.

The prototype trap can be avoided by ensuring that no significant investment is spent on any given prototype. There are many situations where prototypes are necessary, but they must never endanger a project by reducing the amount of resources available to finish.

(2) 4GL Trap

4GLs such as Visual Basic (VB), Forte, 4GL, and Magic allow developers to rapidly develop applications by making assumptions about how data will be accessed and displayed.

The problem with 4GLs is that the code is very hard to modify after it has been created. This accelerates the cost of change. In addition, a language that makes some applications easy to create, becomes a hindrance when the problem domain exceeds the design of that language.

Often, the only way around these limitations is to use some other language such as Java or C++ to solve the unsupported problem. The interfaces between multiple languages are notoriously expensive to maintain and extend. Anyone who has tried to make a VB application perform and look like a professional, highly polished standalone application will immediately realize these limitations.

The 4GL trap is easily avoided by understanding the limitations of each language and only using it if all of the features required by the product fit within the assumed model of the language. This is the most insidious part of this trap. Most 4GLs are marketed as being designed for novice programmers with little training. Microsoft has been particularly aggressive in marketing VB to companies as the way to hire 'cheap' programmers. Unfortunately, these are precisely the people who should not be making the decision about when a particular language is adequate for solving a given problem. Choosing the wrong language will ensure that the product will never ship.

(3) Scripting Trap

Scripting languages allow the easy creation of sophisticated software by sewing together existing applications. Advanced scripting languages such as Perl are very powerful and can be used for a variety of purposes. Operating systems such as Unix are designed to be easily integrated through scripting languages and have far lower cost of ownership than those whose management tools are grafted on with pretty user interfaces.

The trap lies in the sophistication of these languages and the mechanisms that make it easy to write programs. Most scripts are not maintainable or even readable by those people who created them. This does not mean that scripts are bad things. They are the perfect solution for integrating existing tools and making small programs. However, since they are always expensive to maintain, the amount of effort put into any single script should be below the threshold of throwaway code: essentially, it is usually cheaper to rewrite the script than to try to modify it.

A stark example of the scripting trap comes from Excite. Excite built its original search and Web serving infrastructure in Perl on Unix machines. Perl allowed Excite to quickly create products that competed with more mature companies such as Yahoo and Web Crawler. However, by 1998, maintenance expenses made it impossible to add new features. Excite had to stop all production and rewrite its infrastructure in Java. This transition took many months and hindered Excite's competion in the other markets such as online shopping and video streaming.

Avoiding the trap is relatively easy. There are many applications that are small and will remain small forever. These are perfect for scripting languages. If new features are required, this small size makes it easy to rewrite in an OO language to control cost of change.

(4) Integrated Development Environment (IDE) Trap

Many companies product IDEs that allow developers to quickly deploy code that they write. Examples include Microsoft's Visual Interdev Studio and .NET framework, IBM's Visual Age and Oracle's 8i. The problem with these environments is that they make assumptions about the target deployment environment and workgroup configuration.

The problem is that companies do not design these tools to help developers, but lock developers who use their IDE's into their platforms.

In the real world of changing requirements, platform restrictions are often deadly. These restrictions include limited OS support, limited APIs that may make certain features impossible, or platform bugs. Often, the only way around these restrictions is to rewrite major amounts of code.

The IDE trap is easily avoided by choosing tools that do not lock you into a vendor's technology. In addition, development teams must deploy to production style systems early in the development process. This allows adequate time to develop the necessary scripts and procedures to ensure proper delivery.

(5) Reengineering Trap

Reengineering project is designed to address exponential cost of change of an existing system. Lessons learned in previous versions can be applied to control the cost of change.

Reengineering almost always fails because the existing code cannot be easily changed because the cost of change is exponential. If the cost of change was not exponential, there would be no reason to reengineer. This makes it extremely expensive to work with the existing code. As a result, reengineering usually takes as long or longer to complete than the original product while producing the same set of features.

If it took 10 man-years to complete the first product, it will probably take 10 man-years to complete the reengineered version with exactly the same features. Ten man-years for a zero-sum gain. This is why reengineering projects are rarely completed.

The reengineering trap is avoided by developing a migration strategy. All new features must be made separate from the original code base to avoid the exponential cost of change and the original code base is mined for completed features.

Whenever a bug is encountered in the original code base or an existing feature needs to be extended, the existing code is removed and refactored into the new code base. These migrations are expensive, but there is no way to avoid them. In this way, an organized reengineering of only those sections that are not currently adequate will be performed. The cost of changing these sections will be exponential, but will hopefully be limited.

2.12 Major Computer System Failures Caused by Software Bugs

In early 2006, problems in a state's financial monitoring software resulted in incorrect election candidate financial reports being made available to the public. The state's election finance reporting website was shut down until the software was repaired.

Trading on a major Asian stock exchange was brought to a halt in November of 2005, reportedly due to an error in a system software upgrade. The problem was rectified and trading resumed later the same day.

A May 2005 newspaper article reported that a major hybrid car manufacturer had to install a software fix on 20,000 vehicles due to problems with invalid engine warning lights and occasional stalling. In the article, an automative software specialist indicated that the automobile industry spends $2 billion to $3 billion per year fixing software problems.

Media reports in January of 2005 detailed severe problems with a $170 million high-profile U.S. government IT systems project. Software testing was one of the five major problem areas according to a report of the commission reviewing the project. In March of 2005 it was decided to scrap the entire project.

In July 2004, newspapers reported that a new government welfare management system in Canada costing several hundred million dollars was unable to handle a simple benefits rate increase after being put into live operation. Reportedly the original contract allowed for only

6 weeks of acceptance testing and the system was never tested for its ability to handle a rate increase.

Millions of bank accounts were impacted by errors due to installation of inadequately tested software code in the transaction processing system of a major North American bank, according to mid-2004 news reports. Articles about the incident stated that it took two weeks to fix all the resulting errors, that additional problems resulted when the incident drew a large number of e-mail phishing attacks against the bank's customers, and that the total cost of the incident could exceed $100 million.

A bug in site management software utilized by companies with a significant percentage of worldwide web traffic was reported in May of 2004. The bug resulted in performance problems for many of the sites simultaneously and required disabling of the software until the bug was fixed.

According to news reports in April of 2004, a software bug was determined to be a major contributor to the 2003 Northeast blackout, the worst power system failure in North American history. The failure involved loss of electrical power to 50 million customers, forced shutdown of 100 power plants, and economic losses estimated at $6 billion. The bug was reportedly in one utility company's vendor-supplied power monitoring and management system, which was unable to correctly handle and report on an unusual confluence of initially localized events. The error was found and corrected after examining millions of lines of code.

In early 2004, news reports revealed the intentional use of a software bug as a counter-espionage tool. According to the report, in the early 1980's one nation surreptitiously allowed a hostile nation's espionage service to steal a version of sophisticated industrial software that had intentionally-added flaws. This eventually resulted in major industrial disruption in the country that used the stolen flawed software.

A major U.S. retailer was reportedly hit with a large government fine in October of 2003 due to website errors that enabled customers to view one another's online orders.

News stories in the fall of 2003 stated that a manufacturing company recalled all their transportation products in order to fix a software problem causing instability in certain circumstances. The company found and reported the bug itself and initiated the recall procedure in which a software upgrade fixed the problems.

In August of 2003, a U.S. court ruled that a lawsuit against a large online brokerage company could proceed; the lawsuit reportedly involved claims that the company was not fixing system problems that sometimes resulted in failed stock trades, based on the experiences of 4 plaintiffs during an 8-month period. A previous lower court's ruling that "...six miscues out of more than 400 trades does not indicate negligence." was invalidated.

In April of 2003 it was announced that a large student loan company in the U.S. made a software error in calculating the monthly payments on 800,000 loans. Although borrowers were to be notified of an increase in their required payments, the company will still reportedly lose $8 million in interest. The error was uncovered when borrowers began reporting inconsistencies in their bills.

News reports in February of 2003 revealed that the U.S. Treasury Department mailed 50,000 Social Security checks without any beneficiary names. A spokesperson indicated that the missing names were due to an error in a software change. Replacement checks were subsequently mailed out with the problem corrected, and recipients were then able to cash their Social Security checks.

In March of 2002 it was reported that software bugs in Britain's national tax system resulted in more than 100,000 erroneous tax overcharges. The problem was partly attributed to the difficulty of testing the integration of multiple systems.

A newspaper columnist reported in July 2001 that a serious flaw was found in off-the-shelf software that had long been used in systems for tracking certain U.S. nuclear materials. The same software had been recently donated to another country to be used in tracking their own nuclear materials, and it was not until scientists in that country discovered the problem, and shared the information, that U.S. officials became aware of the problems.

According to newspaper stories in mid-2001, a major systems development contractor was fired and sued over problems with a large retirement plan management system. According to the reports, the client claimed that system deliveries were late, the software had excessive defects, and it caused other systems to crash.

In January of 2001 newspapers reported that a major European railroad was hit by the after effects of the Y2K bug. The company found that many of their newer trains would not run due to their inability to recognize the date '31/12/2000'; the trains were started by altering the control system's date settings.

News reports in September of 2000 told of a software vendor settling a lawsuit with a large mortgage lender; the vendor had reportedly delivered an online mortgage processing system that did not meet specifications, was delivered late, and didn't work.

In early 2000, major problems were reported with a new computer system in a large suburban U.S. public school district with 100,000+ students; problems included 10,000 erroneous report cards and students left stranded by failed class registration systems; the district's CIO was fired. The school district decided to reinstate it's original 25-year old system for at least a year until the bugs were worked out of the new system by the software vendors.

A review board concluded that the NASA Mars Polar Lander failed in December 1999 due to software problems that caused improper functioning of retro rockets utilized by the Lander as it entered the Martian atmosphere.

In October of 1999 the $125 million NASA Mars Climate Orbiter spacecraft was believed to be lost in space due to a simple data conversion error. It was determined that spacecraft software used certain data in English units that should have been in metric units. Among other tasks, the orbiter was to serve as a communications relay for the Mars Polar Lander mission, which failed for unknown reasons in December 1999. Several investigating panels were convened to determine the process failures that allowed the error to go undetected.

Bugs in software supporting a large commercial high-speed data network affected 70,000 business customers over a period of 8 days in August of 1999. Among those affected was the electronic trading system of the largest U.S. futures exchange, which was shut down for most of a week as a result of the outages.

In April of 1999 a software bug caused the failure of a $1.2 billion U.S. military satellite launch, the costliest unmanned accident in the history of Cape Canaveral launches. The failure was the latest in a string of launch failures, triggering a complete military and industry review of U.S. space launch programs, including software integration and testing processes. Congressional oversight hearings were requested.

A small town in Illinois in the U.S. received an unusually large monthly electric bill of $7 million in March of 1999. This was about 700 times larger than its normal bill. It turned out to be due to bugs in new software that had been purchased by the local power company to deal with Y2K software issues.

In early 1999 a major computer game company recalled all copies of a popular new product due to software problems. The company made a public apology for releasing a product before it was ready.

The computer system of a major online U.S. stock trading service failed during trading hours several times over a period of days in February of 1999 according to nationwide news reports. The problem was reportedly due to bugs in a software upgrade intended to speed online trade confirmations.

In April of 1998 a major U.S. data communications network failed for 24 hours, crippling a large part of some U.S. credit card transaction authorization systems as well as other large U.S. bank, retail, and government data systems. The cause was eventually traced to a software bug.

January 1998 news reports told of software problems at a major U.S. telecommunications company that resulted in no charges for long distance calls for a month for 400,000 customers. The problem went undetected until customers called up with questions about their bills.

In November of 1997 the stock of a major health industry company dropped 60% due to reports of failures in computer billing systems, problems with a large database conversion, and inadequate software testing. It was reported that more than $100,000,000 in receivables had to be written off and that multi-million dollar fines were levied on the company by government agencies.

A retail store chain filed suit in August of 1997 against a transaction processing system vendor (not a credit card company) due to the software's inability to handle credit cards with year 2000 expiration dates.

In August of 1997 one of the leading consumer credit reporting companies reportedly shut down their new public website after less than two days of operation due to software problems. The new site allowed website visitors instant access, for a small fee, to their personal credit reports. However, a number of initial users ended up viewing each others' reports instead of their own, resulting in irate customers and nationwide publicity. The problem was attributed to "...unexpectedly high demand from consumers and faulty software that routed the files to the wrong computers."

In November of 1996, newspapers reported that software bugs caused the 411 telephone information system of one of the U.S. RBOC's to fail for most of a day. Most of the 2000 operators had to search through phone books instead of using their 13,000,000-listing database. The bugs were introduced by new software modifications and the problem software had been installed on both the production and backup systems. A spokesman for the software vendor reportedly stated that 'It had nothing to do with the integrity of the software. It was human error.'

On June 4, 1996, the first flight of the European Space Agency's new Ariane 5 rocket failed shortly after launching, resulting in an estimated uninsured loss of a half billion dollars. It was reportedly due to the lack of exception handling of a floating-point error in a conversion from a 64-bit integer to a 16-bit signed integer.

Software bugs caused the bank accounts of 823 customers of a major U.S. bank to be credited with $924,844,208.32 each in May of 1996, according to newspaper reports. The American Bankers Association claimed it was the largest such error in banking history. A bank spokesman said the programming errors were corrected and all funds were recovered.

Software bugs in a Soviet early-warning monitoring system nearly brought on nuclear war in 1983, according to news reports in early 1999. The software was supposed to filter out false missile detections caused by Soviet satellites picking up sunlight reflections off cloud-tops, but failed to do so. Disaster was averted when a Soviet commander, based on what he said was a '...funny feeling in my gut', decided the apparent missile attack was a false alarm. The filtering software code was rewritten.

2.13 Software Fault Tolerance

Fault Tolerance

Without software fault tolerance, it is generally not possible to make a truly fault tolerant system. As previously mentioned, it is estimated that 60-90% of current failures are software failures. This means, that a larger focus on software reliability and fault tolerance is necessary in order to ensure a fault tolerant system.

Ultra Fault Tolerance

An ultra-fault tolerant system needs software fault tolerance in order to create a system that is ultra-reliable. These systems are very necessary for missions in which the system may not be accessible. For example, space missions, or very deep undersea communications systems, are not easily accessible. These missions require systems whose reliability ensures that the system will operate throughout its mission life.

Software fault tolerance is the ability for software to detect and recover from a fault that is happening or has already happened in either the software or hardware in the system in which the software is running in order to provide service in accordance with the specification. Software fault tolerance is a necessary component in order to construct the next generation of highly available and reliable computing systems from embedded systems to data warehouse systems. Software fault tolerance is not a solution unto itself however, and it is important to realize that software fault tolerance is just one piece necessary to create the next generation of systems.

Fault tolerance is defined as how to provide, by redundancy, service complying with the specification in spite of faults having occurred or occurring (Laprie, 1996). There are some important concepts buried within the text of this definition that should be examined. Primarily, Laprie argues that fault tolerance is accomplished using redundancy. This argument is good for errors which are not caused by design faults, however, replicating a design fault in multiple places will not aide in complying with a specification. It is also important to note the emphasis placed on the specification as the final arbiter of what is an error and what is not. Design diversity increases pressure on the specification creators to make multiple variants of the same specification which are equivalent in order to aide the programmer in creating variations in algorithms for the necessary redundancy. The definition itself may no longer be appropriate for the type of problems that current fault tolerance is trying to solve, both hardware and software.

In order to adequately understand software fault tolerance it is important to understand the nature of the problem that software fault tolerance is supposed to solve. Software faults are all design faults (Storey, 96). Software manufacturing, the reproduction of software, is considered to be perfect. The source of the problem being solely design faults is very different than almost any other system in which fault tolerance is a desired property. This inherent issue, that software faults are the result of human error in interpreting a specification or correctly implementing an algorithm, creates issues which must be dealt with in the fundamental approach to software fault tolerance.

Current software fault tolerance methods are based on traditional hardware fault tolerance. The deficiency with this approach is that traditional hardware fault tolerance was designed to conquer manufacturing faults primarily, and environmental and other faults secondarily. Design diversity was not a concept applied to the solutions to hardware fault tolerance, and to this end, N-Way redundant systems solved many single errors by replicating the same hardware. Software fault tolerance tries to leverage the experience of hardware fault tolerance to solve a different problem, but by doing so creates a need for design diversity in order to properly create a redundant system.

Design diversity is a solution to software fault tolerance only so far as it is possible to create diverse and equivalent specifications so that programmers can create software which has different enough designs that they don't share similar failure modes. Design diversity and independent failure modes have been shown to be a particularly difficult problem though, as evidenced in [DeVale, 99]. The issue still remains that for a complex problem, the need for humans to solve that problem error-free is not easily solvable.

Randell argues that the difference between fault tolerance versus exception handling is that exception handling deviates from the specification and fault tolerance attempts to provide services compliant with the specification after detecting a fault [Lyu, 95]. This is an important difference to realize between trying to construct robust software versus trying to construct reliable software. Reliable software will accomplish its task under adverse conditions while robust software will be able to indicate a failure correctly (hopefully without the entire system failing). (For more information on the definitions and differences between reliability, robustness, and fault masking see traditional reliability.)

2.13.1 Software Fault Tolerance, The History

Software fault tolerance is mostly based on traditional hardware fault tolerance. N-version programming closely parallels N-way redundancy in the hardware fault tolerance paradigm. Recovery blocks, are modeled after what Randell discovered was the current ad hoc method being employed in safety critical software [Lyu, 95]. The ad hoc method used the concept of retrying the same operation in hopes that the problem would be resolved when the second try occurred. Traditional hardware fault tolerance tried to solve a few common problems which plagued earlier computer hardware. One of the largest problems facing computer hardware was and may still be, manufacturing faults. Another common hardware problem, whose sources may be very diverse is transient faults. These two types of faults can generally be effectively guarded against using redundant hardware of the same type, however, redundant hardware of the same type will not mask a design fault. Recovery blocks may be a good solution to transient faults, however, it faces the same inherent problem that N-version programming does in that they do not offer (sufficient) protection against design faults. (It is possible for a limited class of design faults to be recovered from using distributed N-version programming. Memory leaks, which are a design fault, can cause a local heap to grow beyond the limits of its computer system. Using distributed N-version programming or one of its variants, it is possible that distributed heaps could run out of memory at different times and still be consistent with respect to valid data state.) [Murray, 8]

Hardware Fault Tolerance

Current software fault tolerance is based on traditional hardware fault tolerance (for better or worse). Both hardware and software fault tolerance are beginning to face the new class of problems of dealing with design faults. Hardware designers will soon face how to create a microprocessor that effectively uses one billion transistors; as part of that daunting task, making the microprocessor correct becomes more challenging. In the future, hardware and software may cooperate more in achieving fault tolerance for the system as a whole.

2.13.2 Software Methodology

Software methodology may be one of the best ways to build in software fault tolerance. Building correct software would make large strides in system dependability. Using a system that is mostly correct, with some more simple fault tolerance techniques may be the best system solution in the future.

2.13.3 Techniques for Fault Tolerance in Software

Means to cope with the existence and manifestation of faults in software are divided into three main categories:

- Fault avoidance/prevention: This includes design methodologies which attempt to make software provably fault-free.
- Fault removal: These methods aim to remove faults after the development stage is completed. This is done by exhaustive and rigorous testing of the final product.
- Fault tolerance: This method makes the assumption that the system has unavoidable and undetectable faults and aims to make provisions for the system to operate correctly even in the presence of faults.

Most Bohrbugs, which are deterministic and repeatable, can be removed through rigorous and extensive testing and debugging. But, as argued in the previous sections, no amount of testing can certify software as fault-free, i.e. fault avoidance and fault removal cannot ensure the absence of faults. Therefore, any practical piece of software can be presumed to contain faults in the operational phase and designers must deal with these faults if the software failure has serious consequences. The remaining faults in software after testing and debugging are usually Heisenbugs which eluded detection during the testing. Hence, fault tolerance, is the only remaining hope to achieve dependable software. Fault tolerance makes it possible for the software system to provide service even in the presence of faults. This means that an imminent failure needs to be prevented or recovered from. In this paper, we will only discuss methods to deal with software in the operational phase, i.e. methods to provide fault tolerance.

There are two strategies for software fault tolerance:

- error processing, and
- fault treatment.

(1) **Error Processing:** Error Processing aims to remove errors from the software state and can be implemented by substituting an error-free state in place of the erroneous state, called error recovery, or by compensating for the error by providing redundancy, called error compensation. Error recovery can be achieved by either forward or backward error recovery.

(2) **Fault Treatment:** The second strategy, fault treatment, aims to prevent activation of faults and so action is taken before the error creeps in. The two steps in this strategy are *fault diagnosis* and *fault passivation*. Figure 2.12 shows this classification. The nature of faults which typically occur in software has to be thoroughly understood in order to apply these strategies effectively. Techniques for tolerating faults in software have been divided into three classes—design diversity, data diversity and environment diversity. Table 2.1 shows the fault tolerance strategies used by these classes. All these classes are discussed briefly in the following sections.

Table 2.1: Strategies Used by Different Fault Tolerance Methods

	Design	Data	Environment	Checkpointing
	diversity	diversity	diversity	& recovery
Error compensation	X	X		
Error recovery				X
Fault treatment			X	

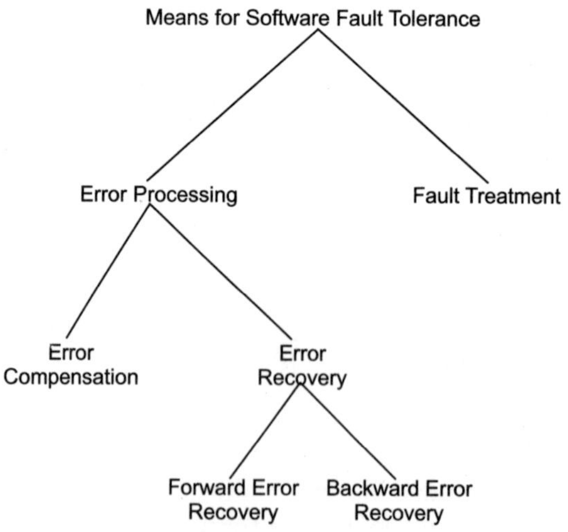

Fig. 2.12: Hierarchy of software fault tolerance

2.13.4 Design Diversity Concepts

Design diversity techniques are specifically developed to tolerate design faults in software arising out of wrong specifications and incorrect coding. Two or more variants of a software developed by different teams but to a common specification are used. These variants are then used in a time or space redundant manner to achieve fault tolerance. Popular techniques which are based on the design diversity concept for fault tolerance in software are:

- N-version programming: First introduced by Avizienis et al. in 1977, this concept is similar to the NMR (N-modular programming) approach in hardware fault tolerance. In this technique, N (N>=2) independently generated functionally equivalent programs called versions, are executed in parallel. A majority voting logic is used to compare the results produced by all the versions and report one of the results which is presumed correct. The ability to tolerate faults here depends on how "independent" the different versions of the program are. This technique has been applied to a number of real-life systems like railroad traffic control and flight control, even though the overhead involved in generating different versions and implementing the voting logic may be high.
- Recovery block: Recovery blocks were first introduced by Horning et al. This scheme is analogous to the cold standby scheme for hardware fault tolerance. Basically, in this approach, multiple variants of a software which are functionally equivalent are deployed in a time redundant fashion. An acceptance test is used to test the validity of the result produced by the primary version. If the result from the primary version passes the acceptance test, this result is reported and execution stops. If, on the other hand, the result from the primary version fails the acceptance test, another version from among the multiple versions is invoked and the result produced is checked by the acceptance test. The execution of the structure does not stop until the acceptance test is passed by one of the multiple versions or until all the versions have been exhausted. The significant differences in the recovery block approach from N-version programming are that only one version is executed at a time and the acceptability of results is decided by a test rather than by majority voting. The recovery block technique has been applied to real life systems and has been the basis for the distributed recovery block structure for integrating hardware and software fault tolerance and the extended distributed recovery block structure for command and control applications. Modeling and analysis of recovery blocks are desribed by Tomek et al.
- N-self checking programming: In N-self checking programming, multiple variants of a software are used in a hot-standby fashion as opposed to the recovery block technique in which the variants are used in the cold-standby mode. A self-checking software component is a variant with an acceptance test or a pair of variants with an associated comparison test. Fault tolerance is achieved by executing more than one self-checking component in parallel. These components can also be used to tolerate one or more hardware faults.

The design diversity approach was developed mainly to deal with Bohrbugs. It relies on the assumption of independence of between multiple variants of software. However, as some studies have shown, this assumption may not always be valid. Design diversity can also be used to treat Heisenbugs. Since there are multiple versions of software operating, it not likely that all of them will experience the same transient failure. On the disadvantages of design diversity is the high cost involved in developing multiple variants of software.

2.13.5 Data Diversity

Data diversity, a technique for fault tolerance in software, was introduced by Amman and Knight. While the design diversity approaches to provide fault tolerance rely on multiple versions of the software written to the same specifications, the data diversity approach uses only one version of the software. This approach relies on the observation that a software sometime fails for certain values in the input space and this failure could be averted if there is a minor perturbation of input data which is acceptable to the software. N-copy programming, based on data diversity, has N-copies of a program executing in parallel, but each copy running on a different input set produced by a diverse-data system. The diverse-data system produces a related set of points in the data space. Selection of the system output is done using an enhanced voting scheme which may not be a majority voting mechanism. This technique might not be acceptable to all programs since equivalent input data transformations might not be acceptable by the specification. However, in some cases like a real time control program, a minor perturbation in sensor values may be able to prevent a failure since sensor values are usually noisy and inaccurate.

Data diversity can work well with Bohrbugs and is cheaper to implement than design diversity techniques. To some extent, data diversity can also deal with Heisenbugs since different input data is presented and by definition, these bugs are non-deterministic and non-repeatable.

2.13.6 Environment Diversity

Environment diversity is the newest approach to fault tolerance in software. Although this technique has been used for long in an ad-hoc manner, only recently has it gained recognition and importance. Having its basis on the observation that most software failures are transient in nature, the environment diversity approach requires reexecuting the software in a different environment. Environment diversity deals effectively with Heisenbugs by exploiting their definition and nature.

Adams has proposed restarting the system as the best approach to masking software faults. Environment diversity is a generalization of restart. This has been proposed in as a cheap but effective technique for fault tolerance in software. There are three components which determine the behavior of a process or executing software:

- The volatile state: This consists of the program stack and static and dynamic data segments.
- The persistent state: This state refers to all the user files related to a program's execution.
- The operating system (OS) environment: This refers to all the resources the program accesses through the operating system like swap space, file systems, communication channels, keyboard and monitors.

Transient faults typically occur in computer systems due to design faults in software which result in unacceptable and erroneous states in the OS environment. Therefore environment diversity attempts to provide a new or modified operating environment for the running software. Usually, this is done at the instance of a failure in the software. When the software fails, it is restarted in a different, error-free OS environment state which is achieved by some clean up operations.

Examples of environment diversity techniques include retry operation, restart application and rebooting the node. The retry and restart operations can be done on the same node or on another spare (cold/warm/hot) node.

Tandem's fault tolerant computer system is based on the process pair approach. It was noted that these failures did not recur once the application was restarted on the second processor. This was due to the fact that the second processor provided a different environment which did not trigger the same error conditions which led to the failure of the application on the first processor. Hence, in this case, hardware redundancy was used to tolerate most of the software faults. The basic observation in all these transient failures is that the same error condition is unlikely to occur if the software is reexecuted in a different environment.

2.13.7 Checkpointing and Recovery

Checkpointing and recovery belongs to the category of error recovery for fault tolerance, as opposed to design diversity which belongs to error compensation, and data and environment diversities which belong to the fault treatment category. Error compensation, error recovery and fault treatment are complementary to one another and fault tolerance in software can be increased by deploying a combination of these techniques. The recovery block uses checkpoints in its implementation. Garg proposes and analyzes the combination of software rejuvenation (preventive fault treatment) with checkpointing and recovery to reduce the chances of activating a fault and simultaneously minimizing the loss of computation when there is a failure.

Checkpointing involves occasionally saving the state of a process in stable storage during normal execution. Upon failure, the process is restarted in the saved state (last saved checkpoint). This thus reduces the amount of lost work. Checkpointing and recovery was mainly intended to tolerate transient hardware failures, where the application is restarted upon repair of a hardware unit after failure. This technique has been implemented in both software and hardware. Checkpointing and restart was used as early as 1948 when the ENIAC was used to solve a two point boundary value problem with known conditions, although the computation was marred by a very high tube error rate. Checkpointing has also been used as a backward error recovery technique for handling intermittent software faults since then. For instance, the progressive retry technique employs checkpointing along with message logs.

2.13.8 N-version Software

The N-version software concept attempts to parallel the traditional hardware fault tolerance concept of N-way redundant hardware. In an N-version software system, each module is made with up to N different implementations. Each variant accomplishes the same task, but hopefully in a different way. Each version then submits its answer to voter or decider which determines the correct answer, (hopefully, all versions were the same and correct) and returns that as the result of the module. This system can hopefully overcome the design faults present in most software by relying upon the design diversity concept. An important distinction in N-version software is the fact that the system could include multiple types of hardware using multiple versions of software. The goal is to increase the diversity in order to avoid common mode failures. Using N-version software, it is encouraged that each different version be implemented in as diverse a manner as possible, including different tool sets, different programming languages, and possibly different environments. The various development groups must have as little interaction related to the programming between them as possible. N-version software can only be successful and successfully tolerate faults if the required design diversity is met.

The dependence on appropriate specifications in N-version software, (and recovery blocks) cannot be stressed enough. The delicate balance required by the N-version software method requires that a specification be specific enough so that the various versions are completely inter-operable, so that a software decider may choose equally between them, but cannot be so limiting that the software programmers do not have enough freedom to create diverse designs. The flexibility in the specification to encourage design diversity, yet maintain the compatibility between versions is a difficult task, however, most current software fault tolerance methods rely on this delicate balance in the specification.

The N-version method presents the possibility of various faults being generated, but successfully masked and ignored within the system. It is important, however, to detect and correct these faults before they become errors. First, the classification of faults applied to N-version software method: if only a single version in an N-version system, the error is classified as a simplex fault. If M-versions within an N-version system have faults, then the fault is declared to be an M-plex fault. M-plex faults are further classified into two classes of faults of related and independent types. Detecting, classifying, and correcting faults is an important task in any fault tolerant system for long-term correct operation.

The differences between the recovery block method and the N-version method are not too numerous, but they are important. In traditional recovery blocks, each alternative would be executed serially until an acceptable solution is found as determined by the adjudicator. The recovery block method has been extended to include concurrent execution of the various alternatives. The N-version method has always been designed to be implemented using N-way hardware concurrently. In a serial retry system, the cost in time of trying multiple alternatives may be too expensive, especially for a real-time system. Conversely, concurrent systems require the expense of N-way hardware and a communications network to connect them. Another important difference in the two methods is the difference between an adjudicator and the decider. The recovery block method requires that each module build a specific adjudicator; in the N-version method, a single decider may be used. The recovery block method, assuming that the programmer can create a sufficiently simple adjudicator, will create a system which is difficult to enter into an incorrect state. The engineering tradeoffs, especially monetary costs, involved with developing either type of system have their advantages and disadvantages, and it is important for the engineer to explore the space to decide on what the best solution for his project is.

2.13.9 Self-checking Software

Self-checking software is not a rigorously described method in the literature, but rather a more ad hoc method used in some important systems. [Lyu, 95] Self-checking software has been implemented in some extremely reliable and safety-critical systems already deployed in our society, including the Lucent ESS-5 phone switch and the Airbus A-340 airplanes.

Self-checking software are the extra checks, often including some amount checkpointing and rollback recovery methods added into fault-tolerant or safety critical systems. Other methods including separate tasks that "walk" the heap finding and correcting data defects and the options of using degraded performance algorithms. While self-checking may not be a rigorous methodology, it has shown to be surprisingly effective.

The obvious problem with self-checking software is its lack of rigor. Code coverage for a fault tolerant system is unknown. Furthermore, just how reliable a system made with self-checking software? Without the proper rigor and experiments comparing and improving self-checking software cannot effectively be done.

2.14 Fault Tracking

The bug needs to be communicated and assigned to developers that can fix it. After the problem is resolved, fixes should be re-tested, and determinations made regarding requirements for regression testing to check that fixes didn't create problems elsewhere. If a problem-tracking system is in place, it should encapsulate these processes. A variety of commercial problem-tracking/management software tools are available. The following are items to consider in the tracking process:

2.14.1 Reporting Stage

- Complete information such that developers can understand the bug, get an idea of it's severity, and reproduce it if necessary.
- Bug identifier (number, ID, etc.)
- Current bug status (e.g., 'Released for Retest', 'New', etc.)
- The application name or identifier and version
- The function, module, feature, object, screen, etc. where the bug occurred
- Environment specifics, system, platform, relevant hardware specifics
- Test case name/number/identifier
- One-line bug description
- Full bug description
- Description of steps needed to reproduce the bug if not covered by a test case or if the developer doesn't have easy access to the test case/test script/test tool
- Names and/or descriptions of file/data/messages, etc. used in test
- File excerpts/error messages/log file excerpts/screen shots/test tool logs that would be helpful in finding the cause of the problem
- Severity estimate (a 5-level range such as 1-5 or 'critical'-to-'low' is common)
- Was the bug reproducible?

- Tester name
- Test date
- Bug reporting date
- Name of developer/group/organization the problem is assigned to
- Description of problem cause

2.14.2 Fixing (Debugging)

- Description of fix
- Code section/file/module/class/method that was fixed
- Date of fix
- Application version that contains the fix
- Tester responsible for retest
- Retest date
- Retest results
- Regression testing requirements
- Tester responsible for regression tests
- Regression testing results

A reporting or tracking process should enable notification of appropriate personnel at various stages. For instance, testers need to know when retesting is needed, developers need to know when bugs are found and how to get the needed information, and reporting/summary capabilities are needed for managers.

2.15 Software Metrics

Metrics are a set of measurements that quantify results. Performance metrics quantify the units performance. Software metrics tell you whether the software is meeting its goals. Business metrics define the business' progress in measurable terms.

Metrics are a system of parameters or ways of quantitative and periodic assessment of a process that is to be measured, along with the procedures to carry out such measurement and the procedures for the interpretation of the assessment in the light of previous or comparable assessments. Metrics are usually specialized by the subject area, in which case they are valid only within certain domain and cannot be directly benchmarked or interpreted outside it.

The following elements must be known for a metric to be fully defined.

Element	Description
Metric	Name of the metric
Metric Description	Description of what is measured
Measurement Procedure	How is the metric measured
Measurement Frequency	How often is the measurement taken
Thresholds Estimation	How are the thresholds calculated
Current Thresholds	Current range of values considered normal for the metric
Target Value	Best possible value of the metric
Units	Units of measurement

Software metrics can be classified into three categories:

- Product metrics,
- Process metrics, and
- Project metrics.

Product metrics describe the characteristics of the product such as size, complexity, design features, performance, and quality level. Process metrics can be used to improve software development and maintenance. Examples include the effectiveness of defect removal during development, the pattern of testing defect arrival, and the response time of the fix process. Project metrics describe the project characteristics and execution. Examples include the number of software developers, the staffing pattern over the life-cycle of the software, cost, schedule, and productivity. Some metrics belong to multiple categories. For example, the in-process quality metrics of a project are both process metrics and project metrics.

Software quality metrics are a subset of software metrics that focus on the quality aspects of the product, process, and project. In general, software quality metrics are more closely associated with process and product metrics than with project metrics. Nonetheless, the project parameters such as the number of developers and their skill levels, the schedule, the size, and the organization structure certainly affect the quality of the product. Software quality metrics can be divided further into end-product quality metrics and in-process quality metrics. The essence of software quality engineering is to investigate the relationships among in-process metrics, project characteristics, and end-product quality, and based on the findings, to engineer improvements in both process and product quality. Moreover, we should view quality from the entire software life-cycle perspective and, in this regard, we should include metrics that measure the quality level of the maintenance process as another category of software quality metrics. In this chapter we discuss several metrics in each of three groups of software quality metrics: product quality, in-process quality, and maintenance quality. In the last sections we also describe the key metrics used by several major software developers and discuss software metrics data collection.

2.15.1 Product Quality Metrics

The de facto definition of software quality consists of two levels:

- Intrinsic product quality, and
- Customer satisfaction.

The metrics we discuss here cover both levels:

- Mean time to failure
- Defect density
- Customer problems
- Customer satisfaction.

Intrinsic product quality is usually measured by the number of "bugs" (functional defects) in the software or by how long the software can run before encountering a "crash". In operational definitions, the two metrics are defect density (rate) and mean time to failure (MTTF). The MTTF metric is most often used with safety-critical systems such as the airline traffic control systems, avionics, and weapons. For instance, the U.S. government mandates that its air traffic control system cannot be unavailable for more than three seconds per year. In civilian airliners, the probability of certain catastrophic failures must be no worse than 10-9 per hour (Littlewood and Strigini, 1992). The defect density metric, in contrast, is used in many commercial software systems.

The two metrics are correlated but are different enough to merit close attention. First, one measures the time between failures, the other measures the defects relative to the software size (lines of code, function points, etc.). Second, although it is difficult to separate defects and failures in actual measurements and data tracking, failures and defects (or faults) have different meanings. According to the IEEE/American National Standards Institute (ANSI) standard (982.2):

- An error is a human mistake that results in incorrect software.
- The resulting fault is an accidental condition that causes a unit of the system to fail to function as required.
- A defect is an anomaly in a product.
- A failure occurs when a functional unit of a software-related system can no longer perform its required function or cannot perform it within specified limits.

From these definitions, the difference between a fault and a defect is unclear. For practical purposes, there is no difference between the two terms. Indeed, in many development organizations the two terms are used synonymously. In this book we also use the two terms interchangeably.

Simply put, when an error occurs during the development process, a fault or a defect is injected in the software. In operational mode, failures are caused by faults or defects, or failures are materializations of faults. Sometimes a fault causes more than one failure situation and, on the other hand, some faults do not materialize until the software has been executed for a long time with some particular scenarios. Therefore, defect and failure do not have a one-to-one correspondence.

Third, the defects that cause higher failure rates are usually discovered and removed early. The probability of failure associated with a latent defect is called its size, or "bug size". For special-purpose software systems such as the air traffic control systems or the space shuttle control systems, the operations profile and scenarios are better defined and, therefore, the time to failure metric is appropriate. For general-purpose computer systems or commercial-use software, for which there is no typical user profile of the software, the MTTF metric is more difficult to implement and may not be representative of all customers.

Fourth, gathering data about time between failures is very expensive. It requires recording the occurrence time of each software failure. It is sometimes quite difficult to record the time for all the failures observed during testing or operation. To be useful, time between failures data also requires a high degree of accuracy. This is perhaps the reason the MTTF metric is not widely used by commercial developers.

Finally, the defect rate metric (or the volume of defects) has another appeal to commercial software development organizations. The defect rate of a product or the expected number of defects over a certain time period is important for cost and resource estimates of the maintenance phase of the software life cycle.

Regardless of their differences and similarities, MTTF and defect density are the two key metrics for intrinsic product quality. Accordingly, there are two main types of software reliability growth models—the time between failures models and the defect count (defect rate) models.

2.15.1.1 The Defect Density Metric

Although seemingly straightforward, comparing the defect rates of software products involves many issues. In this section we try to articulate the major points. To define a rate, we first have to operationalize the numerator and the denominator, and specify the time frame. The general concept of defect rate is the number of defects over the opportunities for error (OFE) during a specific time frame. We have just discussed the definitions of software defect and failure. Because failures are defects materialized, we can use the number of unique causes of observed failures to approximate the number of defects in the software. The denominator is the size of the software, usually expressed in thousand lines of code (KLOC) or in the number of function points. In terms of time frames, various operational definitions are used for the life of product (LOP), ranging from one year to many years after the software product's release to the general market. In our experience with operating systems, usually more than 95 per cent of the defects are found within four years of the software's release. For application software, most defects are normally found within two years of its release.

2.15.1.2 Lines of Code

The lines of code (LOC) metric is anything but simple. The major problem comes from the ambiguity of the operational definition, the actual counting. In the early days of Assembler programming, in which one physical line was the same as one instruction, the LOC definition was clear. With the availability of high-level languages the one-to-one correspondence broke down. Differences between physical lines and instruction statements (or logical lines of code) and differences among languages contribute to the huge variations in counting LOCs. Even within the same language, the methods and algorithms used by different counting tools can cause significant differences in the final counts. Jones (1986) describes several variations:

- Count only executable lines.
- Count executable lines plus data definitions.
- Count executable lines, data definitions, and comments.
- Count executable lines, data definitions, comments, and job control language.
- Count lines as physical lines on an input screen.
- Count lines as terminated by logical delimiters.

To illustrate the variations in LOC count practices, let us look at a few examples by authors of software metrics. In Boehm's well-known book Software Engineering Economics (1981), the LOC counting method counts lines as physical lines and includes executable lines, data definitions, and comments. In *Software Engineering Metrics and Models* by Conte et al. (1986), LOC is defined as follows:

"A line of code is any line of program text that is not a comment or blank line, regardless of the number of statements or fragments of statements on the line. This specifically includes all lines containing program headers, declarations, and executable and non-executable statements."

Thus their method is to count physical lines including prologues and data definitions (declarations) but not comments. In Programming Productivity by Jones (1986), the source instruction (or logical lines of code) method is used. The method used by IBM Rochester is also to count source instructions including executable lines and data definitions but excluding comments and program prologues.

The resultant differences in program size between counting physical lines and counting instruction statements are difficult to assess. It is not even known which method will result in a larger number. In some languages such as BASIC, PASCAL, and C, several instruction statements can be entered on one physical line. On the other hand, instruction statements and data declarations might span several physical lines, especially when the programming style aims for easy maintenance, which is not necessarily done by the original code owner. Languages that have a fixed column format such as FORTRAN may have the physical-lines-to-source-instructions ratio closest to one. According to Jones (1992), the difference between counts of physical lines and counts including instruction statements can be as large as 500%; and the average difference is about 200%, with logical statements outnumbering physical lines. In contrast, for COBOL the difference is about 200% in the opposite direction, with physical lines outnumbering instruction statements.

There are strengths and weaknesses of physical LOC and logical LOC (Jones, 2000). In general, logical statements are a somewhat more rational choice for quality data. When any data on size of program products and their quality are presented, the method for LOC counting should be described. At the minimum, in any publication of quality when LOC data is involved, the author should state whether the LOC counting method is based on physical LOC or logical LOC.

Furthermore, some companies may use the straight LOC count (whatever LOC counting method is used) as the denominator for calculating defect rate, whereas others may use the normalized count (normalized to Assembler-equivalent LOC based on some conversion ratios) for the denominator. Therefore, industrywide standards should include the conversion ratios from high-level language to Assembler. So far, very little research on this topic has been published. The conversion ratios published by Jones (1986) are the most well-known in the industry. As more and more high-level languages become available for software development, more research will be needed in this area.

When straight LOC count data is used, size and defect rate comparisons across languages are often invalid. Extreme caution should be exercised when comparing the defect rates of two products if the operational definitions (counting) of LOC, defects, and time frame are not identical. Indeed, we do not recommend such comparisons. We recommend comparison against one's own history for the sake of measuring improvement over time.

For productivity studies, the problems with using LOC are more severe. A basic problem is that the amount of LOC in a softare program is negatively correlated with design efficiency. The purpose of software is to provide certain functionality for solving some specific problems or to perform certain tasks. Efficient design provides the functionality with lower implementation effort and fewer LOCs. Therefore, using LOC data to measure software productivity is like using the weight of an airplane to measure its speed and capability. In addition to the level of languages issue, LOC data do not reflect noncoding work such as the creation of requirements, specifications, and user manuals. The LOC results are so misleading in productivity studies that Jones states "using lines of code for productivity studies involving multiple languages and full life cycle activities should be viewed as professional malpractice".

2.15.1.3 Defects Metrics

When a software product is released to the market for the first time, and when a certain LOC count method is specified, it is relatively easy to state its quality level (projected or actual). For example, statements such as the following can be made: "This product has a total of 50 KLOC; the latent defect rate for this product during the next four years is 2.0 defects per KLOC." However, when enhancements are made and subsequent versions of the product are released, the situation becomes more complicated. One needs to measure the quality of the entire product as well as the portion of the product that is new. The latter is the measurement of true development quality—the defect rate of the new and changed code. Although the defect rate for the entire product will improve from release to release due to aging, the defect rate of the new and changed code will not improve unless there is real improvement in the development process. To calculate defect rate for the new and changed code, the following must be available:

- **LOC count**: The entire software product as well as the new and changed code of the release must be available.
- **Defect tracking**: Defects must be tracked to the release origin—the portion of the code that contains the defects and at what release the portion was added, changed, or enhanced. When calculating the defect rate of the entire product, all defects are used; when calculating the defect rate for the new and changed code, only defects of the release origin of the new and changed code are included.

These tasks are enabled by the practice of change flagging. Specifically, when a new function is added or an enhancement is made to an existing function, the new and changed lines of code are flagged with a specific identification (ID) number through the use of comments. The ID is linked to the requirements number, which is usually described briefly in the module's prologue. Therefore, any changes in the program modules can be linked to a certain requirement. This linkage procedure is part of the software configuration management mechanism and is usually practiced by organizations that have an established process. If the change-flagging IDs and requirements IDs are further linked to the release number of the product, the LOC counting tools can use the linkages to count the new and changed code in new releases. The change-flagging practice is also important to the developers who deal with problem determination and maintenance. When a defect is reported and the fault zone determined, the developer can determine in which function or enhancement pertaining to what requirements at what release origin the defect was injected.

The new and changed LOC counts can also be obtained via the delta-library method. By comparing program modules in the original library with the new versions in the current release library, the LOC count tools can determine the amount of new and changed code for the new release. This method does not involve the change-flagging method. However, change flagging remains very important for maintenance. In many software development environments, tools for automatic change flagging are also available.

Example: Lines of Code Defect Rates

At IBM Rochester, lines of code data is based on instruction statements (logical LOC) and includes executable code and data definitions but excludes comments. LOC counts are obtained for the total product and for the new and changed code of the new release. Because the LOC count is based on source instructions, the two size metrics are called shipped source instructions (SSI) and new and changed source instructions (CSI), respectively. The relationship between the SSI count and the CSI count can be expressed with the following formula:

SSI (current release) = SSI (previous release)

\+ CSI (new and changed code instructions for current release)

- deleted code (usually very small)
- changed code (to avoid double count in both SSI and CSI)

Defects after the release of the product are tracked. Defects can be field defects, which are found by customers, or internal defects, which are found internally. The several post-release defect rate metrics per thousand SSI (KSSI) or per thousand CSI (KCSI) are:

(1) Total defects per KSSI (a measure of code quality of the total product)

(2) Field defects per KSSI (a measure of defect rate in the field)

(3) Release-origin defects (field and internal) per KCSI (a measure of development quality)

(4) Release-origin field defects per KCSI (a measure of development quality per defects found by customers)

Metric (1) measures the total release code quality, and metric (3) measures the quality of the new and changed code. For the initial release where the entire product is new, the two metrics are the same. Thereafter, metric (1) is affected by aging and the improvement (or deterioration) of metric (3). Metrics (1) and (3) are process measures; their field counterparts, metrics (2) and (4) represent the customer's perspective. Given an estimated defect rate (KCSI or KSSI), software developers can minimize the impact to customers by finding and fixing the defects before customers encounter them.

Customer's Perspective

The defect rate metrics measure code quality per unit. It is useful to drive quality improvement from the development team's point of view. Good practice in software quality engineering, however, also needs to consider the customer's perspective. Assume that we are to set the defect rate goal for release-to-release improvement of one product. From the customer's point of view, the defect rate is not as relevant as the total number of defects that might affect their business. Therefore, a good defect rate target should lead to a release-to-release reduction in the total number of defects, regardless of size. If a new release is larger than its predecessors, it means the defect rate goal for the new and changed code has to be significantly better than that of the previous release in order to reduce the total number of defects.

Consider the following hypothetical example:

Initial Release of Product Y

KCSI = KSSI = 50 KLOC Defects/KCSI = 2.0

Total number of defects = 2.0 × 50 = 100

Second Release

KCSI = 20

KSSI = 50 + 20 (new and changed lines of code) - 4 (assuming 20% are changed lines of code) = 66

Defect/KCSI = 1.8 (assuming 10% improvement over the first release)

Total number of additional defects = 1.8 × 20 = 36

Third Release

KCSI = 30

KSSI = 66 + 30 (new and changed lines of code) - 6 (assuming the same per cent (20%) of changed lines of code) = 90

Targeted number of additional defects (no more than previous release) = 36

Defect rate target for the new and changed lines of code: 36/30 = 1.2 defects/KCSI or lower

From the initial release to the second release the defect rate improved by 10 per cent. However, customers experienced a 64 per cent reduction [(100 - 36)/100] in the number of defects because the second release is smaller. The size factor works against the third release because it is much larger than the second release. Its defect rate has to be one-third (1.2/1.8) better than that of the second release for the number of new defects not to exceed that of the second release. Of course, sometimes the difference between the two defect rate targets is very large and the new defect rate target is deemed not achievable. In those situations, other actions should be planned to improve the quality of the base code or to reduce the volume of postrelease field defects (i.e., by finding them internally).

2.15.1.4 Function Points

Counting lines of code is but one way to measure size. Another one is the function point. Both are surrogate indicators of the opportunities for error (OFE) in the defect density metrics. In recent years the function point has been gaining acceptance in application development in terms of both productivity (e.g., function points per person-year) and quality (e.g., defects per function point). In this section we provide a concise summary of the subject.

A function can be defined as a collection of executable statements that performs a certain task, together with declarations of the formal parameters and local variables manipulated by those statements. The ultimate measure of software productivity is the number of functions a development team can produce given a certain amount of resource, regardless of the size of the software in lines of code. The defect rate metric, ideally, is indexed to the number of functions a software provides. If defects per unit of functions is low, then the software should have better quality even though the defects per KLOC value could be higher—when the functions were implemented by fewer lines of code. However, measuring functions is theoretically promising but realistically very difficult.

The function point metric, originated by Albrecht and his colleagues at IBM in the mid-1970s, however, is something of a misnomer because the technique does not measure functions explicitly (Albrecht, 1979). It does address some of the problems associated with LOC counts in size and productivity measures, especially the differences in LOC counts that result because different levels of languages are used. It is a weighted total of five major components that comprise an application:

- Number of external inputs (e.g., transaction types) = 4
- Number of external outputs (e.g., report types) = 5
- Number of logical internal files (files as the user might conceive them, not physical files) = 10
- Number of external interface files (files accessed by the application but not maintained by it) = 7
- Number of external inquiries (types of online inquiries supported) = 4

These are the average weighting factors. There are also low and high weighting factors, depending on the complexity assessment of the application in terms of the five components (Kemerer and Porter, 1992; Sprouls, 1990):

1. External input: low complexity, 3; high complexity, 6
2. External output: low complexity, 4; high complexity, 7
3. Logical internal file: low complexity, 7; high complexity, 15
4. External interface file: low complexity, 5; high complexity, 10
5. External inquiry: low complexity, 3; high complexity, 6

The complexity classification of each component is based on a set of standards that define complexity in terms of objective guidelines. For instance, for the external output component, if the number of data element types is 20 or more and the number of file types referenced is 2 or more, then complexity is high. If the number of data element types is 5 or fewer and the number of file types referenced is 2 or 3, then complexity is low.

With the weighting factors, the first step is to calculate the function counts (FCs) based on the following formula:

$$FC = \sum_{i-1}^{5} \sum_{j-1}^{5} w_{ij} \times x_{ij}$$

where w_{ij} are the weighting factors of the five components by complexity level (low, average, high) and x_{ij} are the numbers of each component in the application.

The second step involves a scale from 0 to 5 to assess the impact of 14 general system characteristics in terms of their likely effect on the application. The 14 characteristics are:

- Data communications
- Distributed functions
- Performance
- Heavily used configuration
- Transaction rate

- Online data entry
- End-user efficiency
- Online update
- Complex processing
- Reusability
- Installation ease
- Operational ease
- Multiple sites
- Facilitation of change

The scores (ranging from 0 to 5) for these characteristics are then summed, based on the following formula, to arrive at the value adjustment factor (VAF)

$$VAF = 0.65 + 0.01 \sum_{i-1}^{14} Ci$$

where is the score for general system characteristic i. Finally, the number of ci function points is obtained by multiplying function counts and the value adjustment factor:

$$FP = FC \times VAF$$

This equation is a simplified description of the calculation of function points. One should consult the fully documented methods, such as the International Function Point User's Group Standard for a complete treatment.

Over the years the function point metric has gained acceptance as a key productivity measure in the application world. In 1986 the IFPUG was established. The IFPUG counting practices committee is the de facto standards organization for function point counting methods. Classes and seminars on function points counting and applications are offered frequently by consulting firms and at software conferences. In application contract work, the function point is often used to measure the amount of work, and quality is expressed as defects per function point. In systems and real-time software, however, the function point has been slow to gain acceptance. This is perhaps due to the incorrect impression that function points work only for information systems (Jones, 2000), the inertia of the LOC-related practices, and the effort required for function points counting. Intriguingly, similar observations can be made about function point use in academic research.

There are also issues related to the function point metric. Fundamentally, the meaning of function point and the derivation algorithm and its rationale may need more research and more theoretical groundwork. There are also many variations in counting function points in the industry and several major methods other than the IFPUG standard. In 1983, Symons presented a function point variant that he termed the Mark II function point. According to Jones (2000), the Mark II function point is now widely used in the United Kingdom and to a lesser degree in Hong Kong and Canada. Some of the minor function point variants include feature points, 3D function points, and full function points. In all, based on the comprehensive software benchmark work by Jones (2000), the set of function point variants now include at least 25 functional metrics. Function point counting can be time-consuming and expensive, and accurate counting requires certified function point specialists. Nonetheless, function point metrics are apparently more robust than LOC-based data with regard to comparisons across organizations, especially studies involving multiple languages and those for productivity evaluation.

In 2000, based on a large body of empirical studies, Jones published the book Software Assessments, Benchmarks, and Best Practices. All metrics used throughout the book are based on function points. According to his study (1997), the average number of software defects in the U.S. is approximately 5 per function point during the entire software life cycle. This number represents the total number of defects found and measured from early software requirements throughout the life cycle of the software, including the defects reported by users in the field. Jones also estimates the defect removal efficiency of software organizations by level of the capability maturity model (CMM) developed by the Software Engineering Institute (SEI). By applying the defect removal efficiency to the overall defect rate per function point, the following defect rates for the delivered software were estimated. The time frames for these defect rates were not specified, but it appears that these defect rates are for the maintenance life of the software. The estimated defect rates per function point are as follows:

SEI CMM Level 1: 0.75

SEI CMM Level 2: 0.44

SEI CMM Level 3: 0.27

SEI CMM Level 4: 0.14

SEI CMM Level 5: 0.05

2.15.1.5 Customer Problems Metric

Another product quality metric used by major developers in the software industry measures the problems customers encounter when using the product. For the defect rate metric, the numerator is the number of valid defects. However, from the customers' standpoint, all problems they encounter while using the software product, not just the valid defects, are problems with the software. Problems that are not valid defects may be usability problems, unclear documentation or information, duplicates of valid defects (defects that were reported by other customers and fixes were available but the current customers did not know of them), or even user errors. These so-called non-defect-oriented problems, together with the defect problems, constitute the total problem space of the software from the customers' perspective.

The problems metric is usually expressed in terms of problems per user month (PUM): PUM = Total problems that customers reported (true defects and non-defect-oriented problems) for a time period, Total number of license-months of the software during the period where

Number of license-months = Number of install licenses of the software

Number of months in the calculation period

PUM is usually calculated for each month after the software is released to the market, and also for monthly averages by year. Note that the denominator is the number of license-months instead of thousand lines of code or function point, and the numerator is all problems customers encountered. Basically, this metric relates problems to usage. Approaches to achieve a low PUM include:

- Improve the development process and reduce the product defects.
- Reduce the non-defect-oriented problems by improving all aspects of the products (such as usability, documentation), customer education, and support.
- Increase the sale (the number of installed licenses) of the product.

The first two approaches reduce the numerator of the PUM metric, and the third increases the denominator. The result of any of these courses of action will be that the PUM metric has a lower value. All three approaches make good sense for quality improvement and business goals for any organization. The PUM metric, therefore, is a good metric. The only minor drawback is that when the business is in excellent condition and the number of software licenses is rapidly increasing, the PUM metric will look extraordinarily good (low value) and, hence, the need to continue to reduce the number of customers' problems (the numerator of the metric) may be undermined. Therefore, the total number of customer problems should also be monitored and aggressive year-to-year or release-to-release improvement goals set as the number of installed licenses increases. However, unlike valid code defects, customer problems are not totally under the control of the software development organization. Therefore, it may not be feasible to set a PUM goal that the total customer problems cannot increase from release to release, especially when the sales of the software are increasing.

The key points of the defect rate metric and the customer problems metric are briefly summarized in Table 2.2. The two metrics represent two perspectives of product quality. For each metric the numerator and denominator match each other well: Defects relate to source instructions or the number of function points, and problems relate to usage of the product. If the numerator and denominator are mixed up, poor metrics will result. Such metrics could be counterproductive to an organization's quality improvement effort because they will cause confusion and wasted resources.

Table 2.2: Defect Rate and Customer Problems Metrics

	Defect Rate	**Problems per User Month (PUM)**
Numerator	Valid and unique product defects	All customer problems (defects and non-defects, first time and repeated)
Denominator	Size of product (KLOC or function point)	Customer usage of the product (user-months)
Measurement perspective	Producer—software development organization	Customer
Scope	Intrinsic product quality	Intrinsic product quality plus other factors

The customer problems metric can be regarded as an intermediate measurement between defects measurement and customer satisfaction. To reduce customer problems, one has to reduce the functional defects in the products and, in addition, improve other factors (usability, documentation, problem rediscovery, etc.). To improve customer satisfaction, one has to reduce defects and overall problems and, in addition, manage factors of broader scope such as timing and availability of the product, company image, services, total customer solutions, and so forth. From the software quality standpoint, the relationship of the scopes of the three metrics can be represented by the Venn diagram in Figure 2.13.

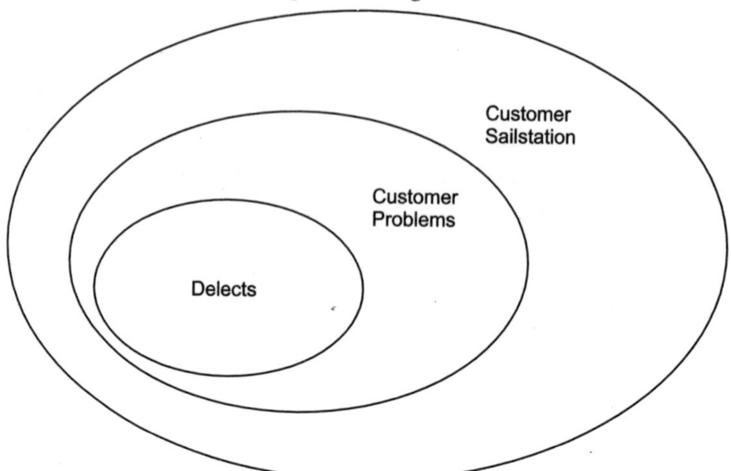

Fig. 2.13: Scopes of three quality metrics

2.15.1.6 Customer Satisfaction Metrics

Customer satisfaction is often measured by customer survey data via the five-point scale:

- Very satisfied
- Satisfied
- Neutral
- Dissatisfied
- Very dissatisfied.

Satisfaction with the overall quality of the product and its specific dimensions is usually obtained through various methods of customer surveys. For example, the specific parameters of customer satisfaction in software monitored by IBM include the CUPRIMDSO categories (capability, functionality, usability, performance, reliability, installability, maintainability, documentation/information, service, and overall); for Hewlett-Packard they are FURPS (Functionality, Usability, Reliability, Performance, and Service).

Based on the five-point-scale data, several metrics with slight variations can be constructed and used, depending on the purpose of analysis. For example:

(1) Per cent of completely satisfied customers

(2) Per cent of satisfied customers (satisfied and completely satisfied)

(3) Per cent of dissatisfied customers (dissatisfied and completely dissatisfied)

(4) Per cent of non-satisfied (neutral, dissatisfied, and completely dissatisfied)

Usually the second metric, per cent satisfaction, is used. In practices that focus on reducing the percentage of non-satisfaction, much like reducing product defects, metric is used.

In addition to forming percentages for various satisfaction or dissatisfaction categories, the weighted index approach can be used. For instance, some companies use the net satisfaction index (NSI) to facilitate comparisons across product. The NSI has the following weighting factors:

- Completely satisfied = 100%
- Satisfied = 75%
- Neutral = 50%
- Dissatisfied = 25%
- Completely dissatisfied = 0%

NSI ranges from 0 per cent (all customers are completely dissatisfied) to 100 per cent (all customers are completely satisfied). If all customers are satisfied (but not completely satisfied), NSI will have a value of 75 per cent. This weighting approach, however, may be masking the satisfaction profile of one's customer set. For example, if half of the customers are completely satisfied and half are neutral, NSI's value is also 75 per cent, which is equivalent to the scenario that all customers are satisfied. If satisfaction is a good indicator of product loyalty, then half completely satisfied and half neutral is certainly less positive than all satisfied. Furthermore, we are not sure of the rationale behind giving a 25 per cent weight to those who are dissatisfied. Therefore, this example of NSI is not a good metric; it is inferior to the simple approach of calculating percentage of specific categories. If the entire satisfaction profile is desired, one can simply show the per cent distribution of all categories via a histogram. A weighted index is for data summary when multiple indicators are too cumbersome to be shown. For example, if customers' purchase decisions can be expressed as a function of their satisfaction with specific dimensions of a product, then a purchase decision index could be useful. In contrast, if simple indicators can do the job, then the weighted index approach should be avoided.

2.15.2 In-Process Quality Metrics

Because our goal is to understand the programming process and to learn to engineer quality into the process, in-process quality metrics play an important role. In-process quality metrics are less formally defined than end-product metrics, and their practices vary greatly among software developers. On the one hand, in-process quality metrics simply means tracking defect arrival during formal machine testing for some organizations. On the other hand, some software organizations with well-established software metrics programs cover various parameters in each phase of the development cycle. In this section we briefly discuss several metrics that are basic to sound in-process quality management. In later chapters on modeling we will examine some of them in greater detail and discuss others within the context of models.

(1) Defect Density During Machine Testing

Defect rate during formal machine testing (testing after code is integrated into the system library) is usually positively correlated with the defect rate in the field. Higher defect rates found during testing is an indicator that the software has experienced higher error injection during its development process, unless the higher testing defect rate is due to an extraordinary testing effort—for example, additional testing or a new testing approach that was deemed more effective in detecting defects. The rationale for the positive correlation is simple: Software defect density never follows the uniform distribution. If a piece of code or a product has higher testing defects, it is a result of more effective testing or it is because of higher latent defects in the code. Myers (1979) discusses a counterintuitive principle that the more defects found during testing, the more defects will be found later. That principle is another expression of the positive correlation between defect rates during testing and in the field or between defect rates between phases of testing.

This simple metric of defects per KLOC or function point, therefore, is a good indicator of quality while the software is still being tested. It is especially useful to monitor subsequent releases of a product in the same development organization. Therefore, release-to-release comparisons are not contaminated by extraneous factors. The development team or the project manager can use the following scenarios to judge the release quality:

- If the defect rate during testing is the same or lower than that of the previous release (or a similar product), then ask: Does the testing for the current release deteriorate?
- If the answer is no, the quality perspective is positive.
- If the answer is yes, you need to do extra testing (e.g., add test cases to increase coverage, blitz test, customer testing, stress testing, etc.).
- If the defect rate during testing is substantially higher than that of the previous release (or a similar product), then ask: Did we plan for and actually improve testing effectiveness?
- If the answer is no, the quality perspective is negative. Ironically, the only remedial approach that can be taken at this stage of the life cycle is to do more testing, which will yield even higher defect rates.
- If the answer is yes, then the quality perspective is the same or positive.

(2) Defect Arrival Pattern During Machine Testing

Overall defect density during testing is a summary indicator. The pattern of defect arrivals (or for that matter, times between failures) gives more information. Even with the same overall defect rate during testing, different patterns of defect arrivals indicate different quality levels in the field. Figure 2.14 shows two contrasting patterns for both the defect arrival rate and the cumulative defect rate. Data were plotted from 44 weeks before code-freeze until the week prior to code-freeze. The second pattern, represented by the charts on the right side, obviously indicates that testing started late, the test suite was not sufficient, and that the testing ended prematurely.

The objective is always to look for defect arrivals that stabilize at a very low level, or times between failures that are far apart, before ending the testing effort and releasing the software to the field. Such declining patterns of defect arrival during testing are indeed the basic assumption of many software reliability models. The time unit for observing the arrival pattern is usually weeks and occasionally months. For reliability models that require execution time data, the time interval is in units of CPU time.

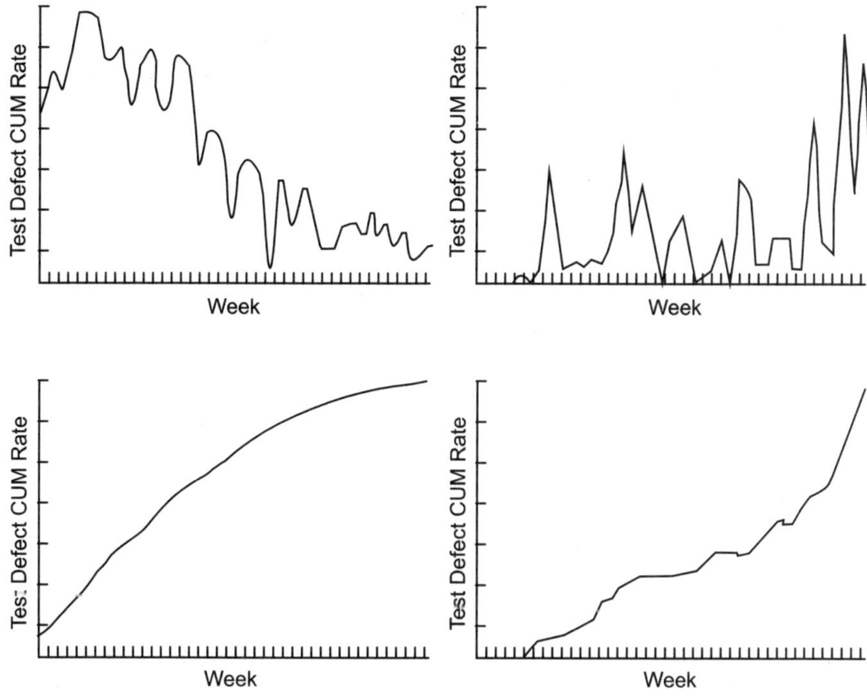

Fig. 2.14: Two contrasting defect arrival patterns during testing

When we talk about the defect arrival pattern during testing, there are actually three slightly different metrics, which should be looked at simultaneously:

The defect arrivals (defects reported) during the testing phase by time interval (e.g., week). These are the raw number of arrivals, not all of which are valid defects.

The pattern of valid defect arrivals—when problem determination is done on the reported problems. This is the true defect pattern.

The pattern of defect backlog overtime. This metric is needed because development organizations cannot investigate and fix all reported problems immediately. This metric is a workload statement as well as a quality statement. If the defect backlog is large at the end of the development cycle and a lot of fixes have yet to be integrated into the system, the stability of the system (hence its quality) will be affected. Retesting (regression test) is needed to ensure that targeted product quality levels are reached.

(3) Phase-Based Defect Removal Pattern

The phase-based defect removal pattern is an extension of the test defect density metric. In addition to testing, it requires the tracking of defects at all phases of the development cycle, including the design reviews, code inspections, and formal verifications before testing. Because a large percentage of programming defects is related to design problems, conducting formal reviews or functional verifications to enhance the defect removal capability of the process at the front end reduces error injection. The pattern of phase-based defect removal reflects the overall defect removal ability of the development process.

With regard to the metrics for the design and coding phases, in addition to defect rates, many development organizations use metrics such as inspection coverage and inspection effort for in-process quality management. Some companies even set up "model values" and "control boundaries" for various in-process quality indicators. For example, Cusumano (1992) reports the specific model values and control boundaries for metrics such as review coverage rate, review manpower rate (review work hours/number of design work hours), defect rate, and so forth, which were used by NEC's Switching Systems Division.

Figure 2.15 shows the patterns of defect removal of two development projects: project A was front-end loaded and project B was heavily testing-dependent for removing defects. In the figure, the various phases of defect removal are high-level design review, low-level design review, code inspection, unit test (UT), component test (CT), and system test (ST). As expected, the field quality of project A outperformed project B significantly.

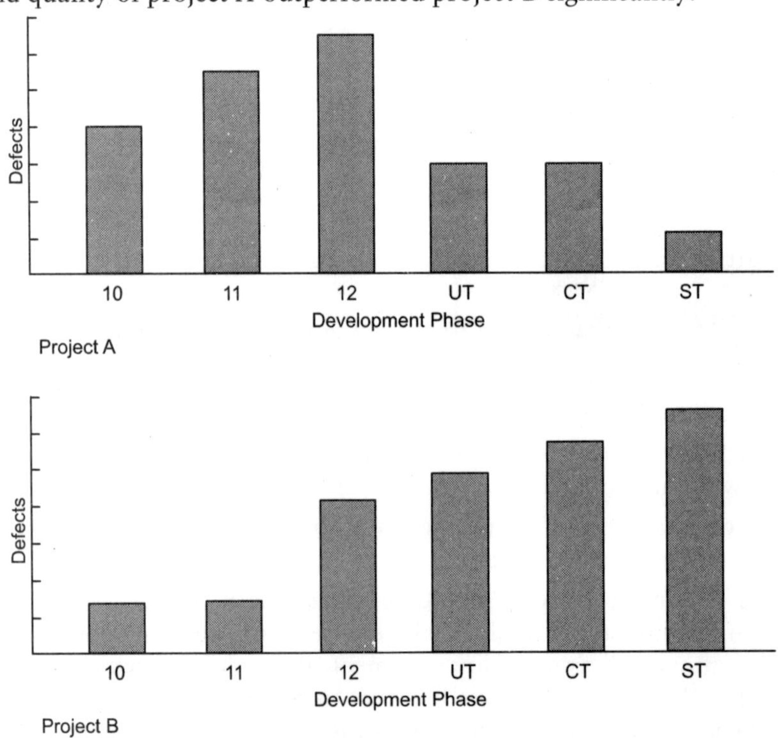

Fig. 2.15: Defect removal by phase for two products

(4) Defect Removal Effectiveness

Defect removal effectiveness (or efficiency, as used by some writers) can be defined as follows:

$$\text{DRE} = \frac{\text{Defects removed during a development phase}}{\text{Defects latent in the product}} \times 100\ \%$$

Because the total number of latent defects in the product at any given phase is not known, the denominator of the metric can only be approximated. It is usually estimated by:

Defects removed during the phase + defects found later

The metric can be calculated for the entire development process, for the front end (before code integration), and for each phase. It is called early defect removal and phase effectiveness when used for the front end and for specific phases, respectively. The higher the value of the metric, the more effective the development process and the fewer the defects escape to the next phase or to the field. This metric is a key concept of the defect removal model for software development. Figure 2.16 shows the DRE by phase for a real software project. The weakest phases were unit test (UT), code inspections and component test (CT). Based on this metric, action plans to improve the effectiveness of these phases were established and deployed.

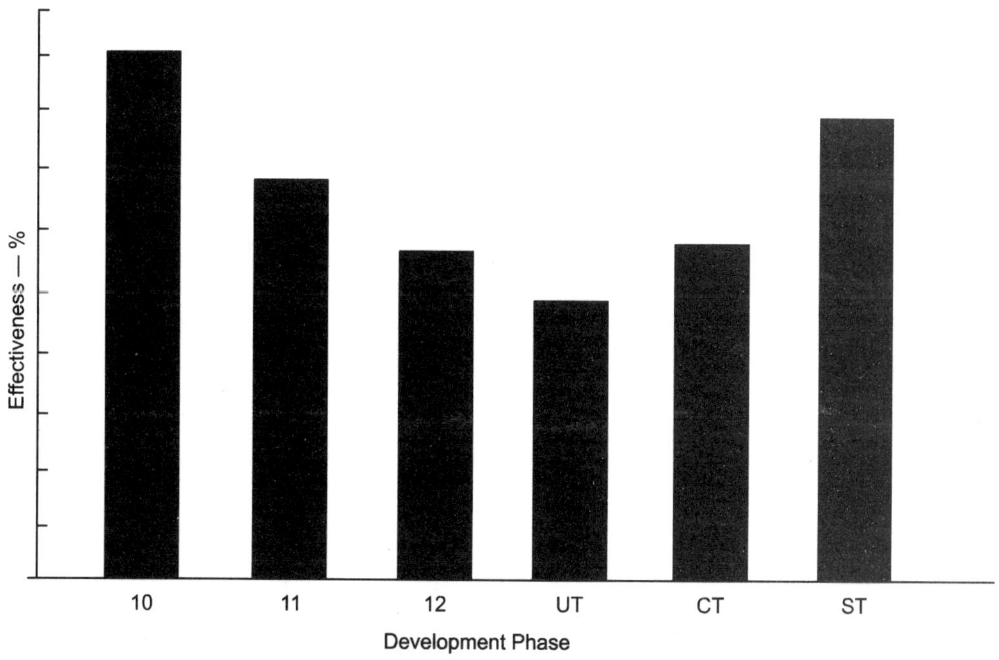

Fig. 2.16: Phase effectiveness of a software project

2.15.3 Fix Quality

Fix quality or the number of defective fixes is another important quality metric for the maintenance phase. From the customer's perspective, it is bad enough to encounter functional defects when running a business on the software. It is even worse if the fixes turn out to be defective. A fix is defective if it did not fix the reported problem, or if it fixed the original problem but injected a new defect. For mission-critical software, defective fixes are detrimental to customer satisfaction.

The metric of per cent defective fixes is simply the percentage of all fixes in a time interval (e.g., 1 month) that are defective. A defective fix can be recorded in two ways: Record it in the month it was discovered or record it in the month the fix was delivered. The first is a customer measure, the second is a process measure. The difference between the two dates is the latent period of the defective fix. It is meaningful to keep track of the latency data and other information such as the number of customers who were affected by the defective fix. Usually the longer the latency, the more customers are affected because there is more time for customers to apply that defective fix to their software system.

There is an argument against using percentage for defective fixes. If the number of defects, and therefore the fixes, is large, then the small value of the percentage metric will show an optimistic picture, although the number of defective fixes could be quite large. This metric, therefore, should be a straight count of the number of defective fixes. The quality goal for the maintenance process, of course, is zero defective fixes without delinquency.

There is no correlation between the existence of a metrics program and the size of the organization, or between the effectiveness of using metrics in software development and team size. For small teams that are starting to implement a metrics program with minimum resources, is recommended:

- Implement the defect arrival metric during the last phase of testing, augmented by a qualitative indicator of the number of critical problems (or show stoppers) and the nature of these problems. The latter is a subset of total defects. These indicators provide important information with regard to the quality of the software and its readiness to ship to customers. For example, if the defect arrival metric is trending down to a sufficiently low level and the number of show stoppers is small and becoming sparser as the test progresses, one can forecast a positive quality posture of the product in the field, and vice versa.
- After the product is shipped, a natural metric is the number of defects coming in from the field over time. As defects are reported, the organization fixes these defects for their customers, normally in the form of individual fixes, fix packages, or frequent software upgrades, depending on the organization's maintenance strategy. The inevitable question is, how many outstanding defects need to be fixed; in other words, how big is the fix backlog. If the organization intends to compare its fix efficiency to the volume of defect arrivals, the backlog management index metric can be formed easily without additional data.

When a product size metric is available, the above metrics can be normalised to form other metrics such as defect density curves over time, during testing or when the product is in the field, and overall defect rate of the product, for a specific duration or for the maintenance life of the product. These normalised metrics can serve as baselines for other projects by percentage number of source statements (LOC per function point) by language are as follows:

Maintenance quality metrics

- Fix backlog
- Backlog management index
- Fix response time and fix responsiveness
- Per cent delinquent fixes
- Defective fixes

With regard to in-process data, generally those at the back end (e.g., testing defects) are more reliable than those at the front end (e.g., design reviews and inspections). To improve data reliability, it is important to establish definitions and examples (e.g., what constitutes a defect during design reviews). Furthermore, validation must be an integral part of the data collection system and should be performed concurrently with software development and data collection.

Basic Assembly	320	Macro Assembly	213
C	128	Fortran	107
COBOL	107	Pascal	91
PL/I	80	Ada	8371
C++	53	Ada	9549
Visual Basic	32	Smalltalk	21
SQL	12		

This discussion of a few simple and useful metrics as the beginning of a good metrics practice is from the quality perspective. For overall project management, it is well known that the most basic variables to measure are product size, effort (e.g., person-year), and development cycle time.

2.15.4 National Software Quality Experiment

In 1992, the DOD Software Technology Strategy set the objective to reduce software problem rates by a factor of ten by the year 2000. The National Software Quality Experiment was conducted to benchmark the state of software product quality and to measure progress towards the national objective.

The centerpiece of the experiment was the Software Inspection Lab where data collection procedures, product checklists, and participant behaviors are packaged for operational project use. The uniform application of the experiment and the collection of consistent measurements are guaranteed through rigorous training of each participant.

Approximately three thousand participants from nearly sixty organizations have populated the experiment database with over twelve thousand defects of all types along with pertinent information needed to pinpoint their root causes. These results are highlighted below in the discussion of the common problems—Inspection Lab operations, defect type ranking, and return on investment.

(1) Common Problems Revealed

Analysis of the issues raised in the experiment to date has revealed common problems that reoccur from session to session. Typical organizations which desire to reduce their software problem rates should focus on preventing the following types of defects:

1. Software product source code components are not traced to requirements.
2. As a result, the software product is not under intellectual control, verification procedures are imprecise, and changes cannot be managed.
3. Software engineering practices for systematic design and structured programming are applied without sufficient rigor and discipline.
4. As a result, high defect rates are experienced in logic, data, interfaces and functionality.
5. Software product designs and source code are recorded in an ad hoc style. As a result, the understandability, adaptability, and maintainability of the software product are directly impacted.

6. The rules of construction for the application domain are not clearly stated, understood, and applied.
7. As a result, common patterns and templates are not exploited in preparation for later reuse.
8. The code and upload development paradigm is becoming predominant in emerging e-commerce applications.
9. As a result, the enterprise code base services only the short-term planning horizon where code rules and heroes flourish, but it mortgages the future where traceable baseline requirements, specification, and design artifacts are necessary foundations.

*(2) **Inspection Lab Operations***

The Inspection Lab is the consistent operation of software inspection sessions as part of the National Software Quality Experiment. These sessions apply the elements of software inspections including the entry, conduct, and exit processes; defined roles of participants; product checklists; and forms and reports. Through 1999, 2669 participants conducted inspection sessions. A total of 903,979 source lines of code have received strict and close examination in the Software Inspection Lab. There have been 161,139 minutes of preparation effort and 61,547 minutes of conduct time expended to detect 13,042 defects. See Table 2.3 Inspection Lab Operations.

Of these 13,042 defects, 2116 were classified as major, and 10,926 as minor. A major defect effects execution; a minor defect does not. It required 12.36 minutes of preparation effort on the average to detect a defect. To detect a major defect required 76.15 minutes of preparation effort on the average. On the average, .881 thousand source lines of code were examined each inspection conduct hour. There were 2.34 major defects detected in each thousand lines, and 12.09 minor defects. There were 4.89 defects detected in inspecting 338.70 lines per session. The preparation effort was 0.65 of conduct effort. The Software Inspection Labs produced a return on investment of 4.41.

Table 2.3: Inspection Lab Operations

Sessions	Prep Effort	Conduct Time	Major Defects	Minor Defects	Size in Lines
2317	142,306	52,196	1854	9521	788,459
Metrics:					
1.	12.51	Minutes of preparation effort per defect			
2.	76.76	Minutes of preparation effort per major defect			
3.	2.35	Major defects per KSLOC			
4.	12.08	Minor defects per KSLOC			
5.	906	Lines per conduct hour			
6.	4.91	Defects per session			
7.	4.48	Return on Investment			

(3) Defect Type Ranking

The foremost defect types that accounted for 92.97% of all defects detected include the following.

Table 2.4: Distribution of Defects Typewise

Defect Type	Distribution
Documentation	42.97% error in guidance documentation
Standards	20.68% error in compliance with product standards
Logic	7.13% error revealed through informal correctness questions function
Functionality	6.61% error in stating or meeting intended
Data	4.70% error in data definition, initial value setting, or use
Syntax	4.69% error in language defined syntax compliance
Maintainability	3.89% error in good practice impacting the supportability and evolution of the software product
Performance	2.30% error in managing or meeting constraints in computer resource allocations and capacities for CPU, memory, or I/O

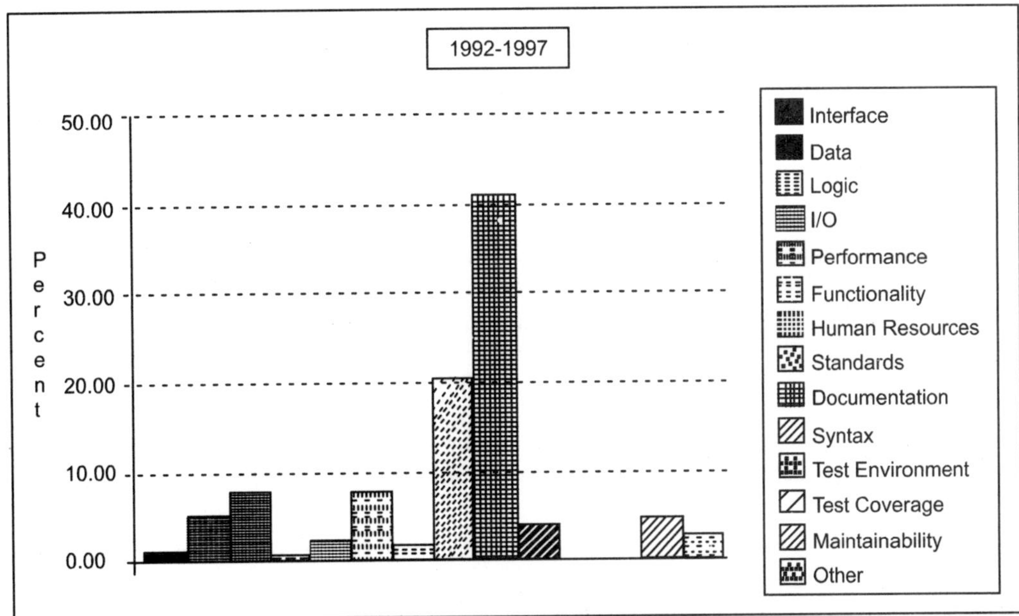

Fig. 2.17: Defect type distribution

(4) Return on Investment

Managers are interested in knowing the return on investment to be derived from software process improvement actions. The Software Inspections Process gathers the data needed to determine this.

The Return on Investment for Software Inspections is defined as Net Savings divided by Detection Cost, where Net Savings is Cost Avoidance less Cost to Repair and Detection Cost is the cost of preparation effort and the cost of conduct effort. The defined measurements collected in the Software Inspections Lab may be combined in complex ways to form this derived metric.

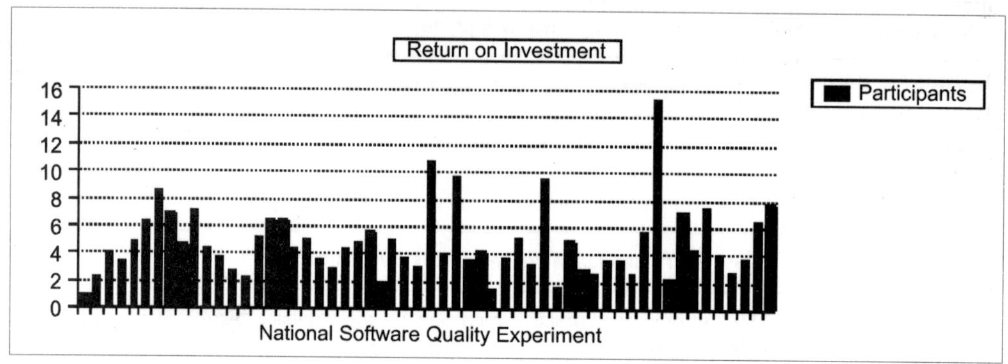

Fig. 2.18: Defect detection and Defect leakage model

The model for Return on Investment bases the savings on the cost avoidance associated with detecting and correcting defects earlier rather than later in the product evolution cycle. A Major Defect that leaks from Development to Test may cost as much as ten times to detect and correct. Some defects, undetected in test, continue to leak from Test to Customer Use and may cost an additional ten times to detect and correct. A Minor Defect may cost two to three times to correct later. IBM Rochester, winner of the Malcolm Baldrige Award, reported that defects leaking from code to test cost nine times more to detect and correct, and defects leaking from test to the field cost thirteen times more. See figure 2.18 Defect Detection and Defect Leakage

Figure 2.18 is a graph showing the Return on Investment Measurements for each organization participating in the National Software Quality Experiment. This graph suggests that the Return on Investment for software inspections ranges from 4:1 to 8:1. For every dollar spent on software inspections, the organization can expect to avoid 4-8 dollars on higher rework cost.

2.16 Defect Tracking

(**Note:** Defect tracking begins by recording a variance from expectations; and will not be considered a true defect until the originator acknowledges the variance as an incorrect condition.)

1. *Defect Recording* – defect recording is used to describe and quantify deviations from requirements/expectations.
2. *Defect Reporting* – reports the status of defects; including severity and location.

3. *Defect Tracking* – monitoring defects from the time of recording until satisfactory resolution has been determined and implemented.

2.17 Defect Tracking Software

Reliable bug tracking software is itself bug-free and stable. Select a product that has a proven track record of success. If possible, talk with actual users to see whether or not the software is meeting their needs.

You want your bug tracking software to be customizable so that it works the way your development team works. But you don't want this task to be so difficult that you have to first take a course to learn how to accomplish this. A good interface is simple and straightforward, and at the same time, intuitive.

Select bug tracking software that fits your budget and works on the hardware configuration you already have in place. If it requires additional, costly hardware to operate, keep looking.

As for features, including the ability to prioritize a reported bug helps managers allocate resources more efficiently. It's important to know additional information about each reported bug, and effective bug tracking software facilitates adding notes. For example, it's important to reproduce the steps that led to the discovery of the bug, the actions that should have happened when the bug was discovered, the actions that actually did happen, and the version that was used at the time of discrepancy. As the bug works its way from team member to team member, the good software tracks that history and allows additional notes to be appended at any time.

Reliable bug tracking software doubles as a management tool. It produces useful reports including work that has already been assigned to each team member. Such a report helps management reprioritize and reassign work when necessary. Also important is a built-in method for notifying specific team members that new work has been assigned to them. As each team member completes work on the bug, they need the ability to update the status of the bug. The bug itself needs to be reassigned to another individual or marked as closed.

Be sure that the bug tracking software you select allows customization of the steps necessary to close an open bug report. Also make sure the software allows you to designate the person(s) who has the authority to close a bug report.

And if the bug tracking software does not allow an easy way to regularly back up its data, find another package. Bug reports are too vital to lose.

Once bug tracking software is installed, don't allow any member of the team to circumvent the software. Regardless of the features, bug tracking software can't keep proper track of bugs if it's not being used properly. Until everybody is using the same tracking system, bugs will continue to run rampant, something you can't afford.

In his white paper Stephen Blair, MetaQuest Software Evaluating, a bug tracking system requires that you understand how specific features, such as configurable workflow and customizable fields, relate to your requirements and your current bug tracking process. This article provides tips and guidelines for evaluating features, and explains how these features fit into a defect tracking process.

Before you start evaluating bug tracking systems, make sure you identify your requirements for the system. Understanding these requirements will help you build a list of features that you can use to guide your evaluations.

To identify your bug tracking requirements, take a look at your current bug tracking process:

- What are the different roles and responsibilities of the people who will use the system?
- What is your workflow for managing and resolving bugs? Identify the steps in the process, and determine who is responsible for each step.
- What information do you need to track for each bug?
- What reports and metrics do you need?
- Do you need to provide different levels of access to different users?

Once you identify your requirements for the system, you can translate the requirements into a feature list. Table 2.5 provides an example of a feature list that could be used to evaluate a bug tracking solution.

Table 2.5: List of Features to Evaluate

Adaptability	E-mail notifications
Change history	Reports
Version control integration	Reports
Customizable fields	Web-based client
Ease of use	Workflow

2.17.1 Adaptability

If you want to track more than just bugs, make sure the bug tracking system can be adapted to track other types of issues (such as support calls, test cases, or purchase orders). A system that is designed specifically for bug tracking can be hard to adapt, so look for a system that provides pre-built templates for tracking different issue types. Also, as you evaluate the various features of the tracking system, look for any hardwired "bug-tracking" terminology or functionality. Fields, queries, reports, notifications, workflow: everything should be adaptable. Otherwise you'll end up trying to fit a round peg into a square hole (for example, trying to fit trouble tickets into bug reports).

For example, if a tool provides a default bug-tracking workflow that you can't replace completely, you won't be able to implement workflows for other issue types.

Evaluation Checklist:

- Pre-built templates for different issue types (support calls, test cases,...)
- No hardwired bug-tracking terminology or functionality

2.17.2 Bug Change Histories

Consider whether you want to track changes to bugs. Some tools maintain change histories (audit trails), which allow you to trace who did what to an issue and when (for example, who raised the priority of a bug).

If the tool provides a change history, look at what information it records. For example, if you change the priority, does the change history simply say "Defect modified" (not so good) or

"Priority modified" (better), or does it say "Priority changed to High" (best)? Some tools offer a sort of compromise, where the tool adds "Defect modified" to the revision history and allows the user to add a comment such as "Changed priority to High after speaking to customer".

A related feature is something called timestamping. In tools that support timestamping, information entered into text fields such as Description, Resolution and Workaround are time and date stamped with the User ID of the individual who entered the text. This time stamping provides a history of the changes to important text fields.

Evaluation Checklist:

- Changes to issues are automatically logged to revision history
- Change history indicates exactly what was changed (for example, Priority changed from Medium to High)
- Change history can be enabled/disabled on a field-by-field basis
- Changes to text fields be timestamped

2.17.3 Customizable Fields

You need to be able to customize the fields used to collect defect information. Otherwise, you'll end up collecting only the information the tool thinks you should track, and using the tool's terminology instead of your own.

Most bug tracking tools come with a predefined set of fields. You probably can use some of these fields as is, and others by simply changing field labels and drop-down list values to match your terminology. For example, if you already classify defects by severity and priority, and the tool includes predefined Severity and Priority fields, you just need to change the severity and priority levels to match those you already use. If you cannot reuse a predefined field, you should be able to delete it, or at least hide it so that users never see it.

To collect all the information you want to track, you may also need to add new fields. The tool should be flexible enough to allow you to put new fields anywhere you want. If you cannot rearrange fields, or if all new fields are put at the bottom of a page or on a separate tab, the usability of even the simplest "bug form" will suffer.

Field relationships

Consider also whether you want to define field relationships. Field relationships can help you keep drop-down lists short and uncluttered. For example, by creating a relationship between the Product and Version fields, you can display only the version numbers of the selected product (instead of displaying all version numbers of all products). Similarly, for software bugs, you can display only the software components and filter out documentation and hardware components.

Some tools also allow you to select a value from a drop-down list based on the values selected from other lists. For example, you could automatically assign bugs based on the selected product and component.

2.17.4 Custom Views and Field Sets

Based on the user's role and the task at hand, do you want to display different sets of fields? The ability to display custom views allows you to reduce UI clutter and present only the fields necessary for the task at hand. For example, a custom view for logging new bugs wouldn't need to include the fields used by QA and Engineering to add information during the resolution process.

Evaluation Checklist:

- Change field labels and drop-down lists to match your company's terminology
- Custom fields—add and remove fields as required
- Control over which fields are required and which are optional
- Customizable field layout
- Add, remove, and rename tabs
- Define field relationships
- Create custom views

2.17.5 Notifications

Notifications are really a workflow feature, because they help you track and manage bugs. For example, notifications can keep team members informed about important changes to bugs, such as changes in priority or addition of new information (such as how to reproduce the problem). Notifications can also help automate the defect management process. For example, you can notify development managers when new bugs are submitted, and developers when bugs are assigned to them.

When evaluating a bug tracking tool, look closely at what kind of notifications you can send. Most bug tracking tools support a fixed, standard set of notifications:

- Bug added
- Bug edited
- Bug status changed
- Bug assigned

Obviously there's a potential for a spam-like deluge of notifications, especially if you enable "Bug edited" notifications. So look for the ability to define notifications for specific changes to specific fields. For example, can you send a notification when someone changes the priority of a bug? Or when your most important customer reports a "must-fix" bug?

If you want to allow customers to submit bugs directly into the system, check if the tool allows you send notifications to the customer (e.g., send the customer a confirmation, notify customer when bug is fixed).

Finally, look at what information goes into a notification message, and how easy (or hard) it is to customize the contents. Some tools offer a predefined list of possible content, such as summary, full details, change history, or all of the above.

Evaluation Checklist:

- Automatic e-mail notifications for comment events (new bugs, changes to bugs, status changes, bug assignments)

- Support for custom events (send notifications for specific changes to specific fields by specific users, for example, notify the developer when a tester modifies the Repro Steps fields)
- Send notifications to users or customers (where customers don't have a user account for the tool)
- Easily customizable notification message contents

2.17.6 Ease-of-Use

Is the interface consistent and easy to navigate? Web-based applications can often be difficult to navigate, especially if they behave more like a sequence of HTML pages than an application. Some Web applications are constantly reloading pages because responding to user input requires a round trip between the Web server and the user's browser. This constant reloading of pages can make an application difficult to work with, because the application doesn't behave the way users expect an application to behave—like a Windows application. When a Web application behaves like a Windows application, it's easier to adopt into your development process. There's less learning curve, and less resistance to change.

Another important consideration is the user interface text; is it user-friendly, simple, and clear?

Finally, and maybe most important, is the interface easy to use? Try evaluating how easy is to perform common tasks, such as logging a new bug or searching for keywords in common text fields. Is it obvious how to do these tasks? And how many mouse clicks does it take? Frequently-used features should never be more than a few mouse clicks away.

Evaluation Checklist:

- Interface is easy to navigate
- Easy to enter new bugs
- Easy access common features (requires only a few mouse clicks)
- User interface text and messages are easy to understand

2.17.7 Security

Security is typically based on user accounts, user groups, and user group permissions. Look for an issue tracking system that provides different levels of permissions:

- Field-level permissions control whether users can edit, or even view fields.
- Bug-level permissions control access to bugs by users.
- Feature-level permissions control access to specific features, such as reporting or user account administration.

Project-level permissions determine which users can access which projects/databases.

There are two approaches to providing field-level security. One approach is to specify on a field-by-field basis which user groups have permission to edit the field. Other tools, such as Census from MetaQuest Software, take a different approach, and allow you to define custom Web views of the bug database, where each custom view includes different fields. For each custom view, you can then specify which user groups that have permission to access the view.

For example, a customer view would include only the fields required to submit a new bug, while a developer view would include all fields. Customers would not be allowed to access the developer view, while developers would be allowed to access either view. Bug-level security is usually accomplished by limiting the available queries.

Evaluation Checklist:

- User groups and user group permissions
- Field-level security
- Bug-level security
- Feature-level security
- Project-level security
- View-level security (define multiple views of a project and then grant access permissions)

2.17.8 Reports and Metrics

An issue tracking system should allow you to quickly gather the information you need for staff meetings (bug listings and printouts), as well as provide more detailed metrics to help you make decisions.

Look for tools that provide both distribution metrics (metrics that break bugs down by category or classification: for example, issue age by severity) and trend metrics (metrics that show changes over time—for example, defect arrival rate). You may also require the ability to build your own custom reports, preferably using an industry standard reporting tool such as Crystal Reports.

Evaluation Checklist:

- Bug listing reports, summary and detailed
- Distribution reports (cross-tab or chart)
- Trend (time-based) reports
- Web-based reporting
- Library of predefined reports
- Export reports and metrics
- Support for industry-standard reporting tools such as Crystal Reports

2.17.9 Workflow

An issue tracking tool should automate and enforce your process for managing and resolving bugs. The tool should provide a configurable workflow that allows you to define the steps in your process and the order of the steps.

Workflow is typically modeled as a series of states, such as New, Fixed, and To be Verified. To support your process, you'll need to be able to add and remove workflow states, as well as define the allowable transitions between states. For example, between Fixed and Closed you may want to add a required Verify Fix state, to ensure that an issue is never closed until after QA verifies the fix.

You should also be able to control which users are allowed to move bugs between states. For example, you may want only members of the QA group to be able to move bugs from Verify Fix to Closed. Granting workflow permissions allows you to enforce accountability and responsibility throughout the process.

While workflow is based primarily on states, you may also want your workflow to depend on other bug attributes, such as product or defect type, or even on user group membership. For example, you may need different workflows for software, hardware, and documentation issues. Finally, you should also expect an issue tracking tool to support different workflows for different projects.

Evaluation Checklist:

- Default workflow
- Configurable workflow: define custom states and transitions
- Enforceable workflow: specify possible transitions and who has permission to make the changes
- Separate workflows for different projects, different issue types

2.17.10 Version Control Integration

The starting point for any worthwhile version control support is the ability to link bugs to source code. Linking bugs to source code means developers can document a bug by linking to the related source files (which is especially important if the bug is deferred). These links will also allow you to track the work done on a bug.

Next, verify the version control operations that you can perform from inside the issue tracking system. You should be able to perform common operations such as checking files in and out, viewing file histories, and getting different versions of a file. The ability to check files in and out is key, particularly for Web-based issue tracking systems. Not all Web-based systems support the check in and check out operation, which limits the usefulness of the version control integration. Web-based check outs/ins help to improve development workflow and save time. If an issue tracking system has both a Windows client and a Web client, make sure you can perform all version control operations through both interfaces.

Evaluation Checklist:

- Link bugs to source code
- Remote, web-based access to Visual SourceSafe databases
- Perform basic version control operations through the issue tracking system
- Web-based check-outs and check-ins

2.17.11 Web-based Client

In addition to evaluating the usability (see Ease-of-Use) of a Web-based client, you should also evaluate the implementation of the client.

Architecture

Web-based clients can be implemented in a number of ways:

Internet Information Server (IIS) applications. An IIS application is a Visual Basic application that lives on a Web server and responds to requests from the browser.

An IIS application uses a combination of ASP and HTML to present its user interface and uses compiled Visual Basic code to process requests and respond to events in the browser.

IIS applications offer good performance. They also offer easy customization and branding, because the user interface is driven by HTML templates stored outside of the DLLs.

Internet Server API (ISAPI) applications. ISAPI was developed by Microsoft to address the resource problems of CGI. ISAPI uses Dynamic Link Libraries (DLLs) that are customized to return specific HTML. The IIS Web server loads the DLL the first time a request is received and then keeps the DLL in memory to service other requests. This minimizes the overhead associated with executing such applications many times.

ISAPI applications offer good performance. However, they are often difficult to customize or brand, because all the HTML that makes up the user interface is emitted by a DLL.

Common Gateway Interface (CGI) applications. CGI is a standard way for a Web server to pass a Web user's request to an application and then forward the results back to the user.

One of the problems of CGI is that every request from the browser starts a new process on the Web server. Consequently, CGI applications are resource hungry, and can impact the performance of your Web server.

Active Server Pages (ASP) applications. ASP is a server-side scripting environment for IIS that combines HTML pages, script commands, and COM components.

ASP performance can be hindered by the fact that ASP is driven by script languages that must be interpreted at run time.

Application Standards

Does the Web-client behave like an application, or like a series of pages? Many Web applications are page-based, like a Web site, and are basically a series of HTML page generated on the server. Every interaction with the user requires a round-trip to the server and a page reload. Something as simple as running a predefined query, or switching to another tab, can require a page reload.

For example, suppose you log on to your issue tracking system to review the defects submitted yesterday. One looks familiar so you decide to do a keyword search for related or duplicate issues. In a page-based tool, this loads a new page, replacing the list of new defects you were looking at. After you type the text you want to search for and click Ok, another page is loaded, this time listing the defects that matched your query. And so it goes, back and forth between different pages as you search, scan lists, and read details.

Contrast this with the behavior of a Web application whose interface follows familiar Windows standards. In this type of Web client, the keyword search, the list of issues, and the issue view/edit form are all part of a unified interface. You don't load another page to define the query, running the query updates the list in place, and the defect you're viewing doesn't disappear just because you ran a query.

Customer Communications

If you want to allow customers to submit bugs or to monitor issue status through a Web-based interface, check that the tool includes a Web-based client that customers can use. The customer submit interface should allow an unlimited number of customers to submit bugs.

Evaluation Checklist:

- Web-based client implemented using best technology
- Web-based client follows familiar desktop UI standards
- Web-based client for customers
- About the Author

The implementation, or coding phase of a software development project should represent only about 20 per cent of the total software cost.

The time spent in testing and integrating a large software product, however, is as much as four times greater than the time spent actually coding the product. Readable, well-structured code can reduce test and integration time while also reducing maintenance costs.

Ways of increasing software code readability are:

- Using a small number of application development tools (such as programming languages, databases, middleware, and source control software).
- Adopting programming style guidelines (such as rules for naming variables, adding comments to source code, and use of control structures).
- Reducing the number of branches and jumps in the code.

EPRI has developed no list of approved software application development tools, and no guidelines or requirements for programming style.

However, individual developers may choose to use programming style guidelines in order to reduce the effort needed to assure quality during test and integration.

Here are examples of guidelines for improving programming style:

- Make identifier names as meaningful as possible. Avoid using names and identifiers that need to be explained using comment statements.
- Use local variables and identifiers for local purposes. Avoiding using global definitions unless absolutely necessary.
- If the programming language does not support a desired feature, do not try to create the feature in an artificial manner. Keep coding simple. Shortcuts, tricky code, and complicated algorithms often conceal errors and drive up maintenance costs.
- Do not create a function without an argument, even if your programming language supports it. A function with no argument is easily confused with a single variable name.
- At the beginning of each subprogram, define arguments and their initial values.
- Use abstraction and information hiding concepts extensively.

- Avoid defining sub-programs whose execution can cause side effects.
- Limit the number of formal arguments to a sub-program to no more than five.
- Use comments at the beginning of each block of code, defining the purpose of the code and the input and output variables.
- Call error messages and user messages from a single routine with the messages in a data file that is loaded upon start of the program. This also makes it easier to translate the messages for other national languages.

2.18 Fault Injection

Fault injection is a testing technique used in computer systems to test both hardware and software. It is the deliberate introduction of faults into a system, and the subsequent examination of the system for the errors and failures that result. It can be performed on either simulations and models or working prototypes or systems in the field. In this manner the weaknesses of interactions can be discovered, but this is a haphazard way of debugging the design errors in a system. It is better used to test the resilience of a fault tolerant system against known faults, and thereby measure the effectiveness of the fault tolerant measures.

There are two main issues in fault injection, and it is along these axes that different fault tolerant techniques may de divided. The first axis is that of simulation versus execution. In the former, a model of the system is developed and faults are introduced into that model. The model is then simulated to find the effects of the fault on the operation of the system. These methods are often slower to test, but easier to change. In the latter, the system itself is deployed, and some mechanism found to cause faults in the system, and its execution is then observed to determine the effects of the fault. These techniques are more useful for analyzing final designs, but are typically more difficult to modify afterwards.

The second axis is that of invasive and non-invasive techniques. The problem with sufficiently complex systems, particularly time dependant ones, is that it may be impossible to remove the footprint of the testing mechanism from the behavior of the system, independent of the fault injected. For example, a real-time communication protocol that ordinarily would meet a deadline for a particular task might miss it because of the extra latency induced by the fault injection mechanism. Invasive techniques are those which leave behind such a footprint during testing. Non-invasive techniques are able to mask their presence so as to have no effect on the system other than the faults they inject.

Fault injection is still a somewhat new technique, however, and there is still development being done to see what kinds of systems this can be applied to, and which systems it is appropriate to test in this manner. While there are some well understood mechanisms for injecting faults into certain kinds of systems, such as distributed systems, other systems still have basic techniques being designed, such as VLSI circuits. Often the method for inserting faults is very application specific, rather than generalized, and therefore comparison of testing methods is difficult. Finally, even when results have been gathered, researchers are still uncertain or divided as to exactly what the results mean, and how they should be used.

Software fault injection is used to inject faults into the operation of software and examine the effects. This is generally used on code that has communicative or cooperative functions so that there is enough interaction to make fault injection useful. All sorts of faults may be injected, from register and memory faults, to dropped or replicated network packets, to erroneous error conditions and flags. These faults may be injected into simulations of complex systems where the interactions are understood though not the details of implementation, or they may be injected into operating systems to examine the effects.

Software simulation are typically of high level description of a system, in which the protocols or interactions are known, but not the details of implementation. These faults tend to be mis-timings, missing messages, replays, or other faults in communication in a system. The simulation is then run to discover the effects of the faults. Because of the abstract nature of these simulations, they may be run at a faster speed that the actual system might, but would not necessarily capture the timing aspects of the final system. This sort of testing would be performed to verify a protocol, or to examine the resistance of an interaction to faults. This would typically be done early in the design cycle so as to flesh out the higher level details before attempting the task of implementation. These simulations are non-intrusive, as they are simulated, but they may not capture the exact behavior of the system.

Software fault injections are more oriented towards implementation details, and can address program state as well as communication and interactions. Faults are mis-timings, missing messages, replays, corrupted memory or registers, faulty disk reads, and almost any other state the hardware provides access to. The system is then run with the fault to examine its behavior. These simulations tend to take longer because they encapsulate all of the operation and detail of the system, but they will more accurately capture the timing aspects of the system. This testing is performed to verify the system's reaction to introduced faults and catalog the faults successfully dealt with. This is done later in the design cycle to show performance for a final or near-final design. These simulations can be non-intrusive, especially if timing is not a concern, but if timing is at all involved the time required for the injection mechanism to inject the faults can disrupt the activity of the system, and cause timing results that are not representative of the system without the fault injection mechanism deployed. This occurs because the injection mechanism runs on the same system as the software being tested.

The main problem with fault injection is knowing what to do with it. Upon first glance, it would seem to be a good tool for debugging a system, and detecting any flaws within it. Once one examines the procedures and the information gained, however, it becomes apparent that fault injection is good at testing known sorts of bugs or defects, but poor at testing novel faults or defects, which are precisely the sorts of defects we would want to discover. Therefore, what emerges is that fault injection is not really suited for debugging and improving the system so much as it is suited for testing the fault tolerant features of the system.[Voas, 95] A known fault in injected and the results examined to see if the system can respond correctly despite the fault.

Along these lines, there are two proposed uses for fault injection. The first is for verification of a system. If a system is designed to tolerate a certain class of faults, or exhibit certain behavior in the presence of certain faults, then these faults can be directly injected into the system to examine their effects. The system will either behave appropriately or not, and it's fault tolerance measured accordingly [Arlat]. For certain classes of ultra-dependable untestable systems in which the occurrence of errors is too infrequent to effectively test the system in the field, fault injection can be a powerful tool for accelerating the occurrence of faults in the system and verifying that the system works properly.

The other proposed use for fault injection is less well understood, because the problem it addresses is poorly understood. Robustness is used in regard to systems these days almost synonymously with fault tolerance, but robustness actually embraces more than this. There is no really good definition of robustness, but it is something along the lines of "the capability of a system to behave correctly in unusual conditions". The difficulty lies in creating unusual conditions so as to test the system for robustness. Fault injection has been proposed as a method to address this problem, by including unusual conditions as well as faults. This would provide us with a metric for measuring the robustness of a system.

There are two difficulties that must be addressed before this use of fault injection can be fully applied. The first is the disparate nature of systems, and the ways in which they can fail or experience faults. Unless two systems are set to accomplish the exact same task, determining the relative robustness of the two systems is a difficult task. A good metric for robustness would be able to resolve this difference. Secondly, it is not yet certain how our metric should be biased. Common practice is to have the test distribution mirror the real world distributions of occurrence of faults. If we are truly testing the system's response to unusual situations, however, it might be better to bias the test towards the less frequently encountered conditions. [Voas, 93] While there is agreement that fault injection can serve as a metric for robustness, the exact mechanisms of doing so are as of yet poorly understood.

2.19 Software Tools and Techniques

Most of the software tools that exist are for testing of actual systems, and not simulation. This is probably due to the difficult task of correctly capturing high level behavior without the implementation being finished, and the relative ease of inserting faults into operating systems due to the debugging facilities provided by modern hardware. Ferrari is a testing system that introduces CPR, memory, and bug faults through CPU traps during normal execution. Ftape is a system that introduces CPU, memory and disk faults through altered drivers and OS modifications [Hsueh]. DOCTOR is a tool for introducing faults into a distributed real time system under synthetic workloads, introducing CPU, memory, and network faults through time-outs, traps and code modification [Han]. Xception causes multiple sorts of faults through hardware exception triggers. ORCHESTRA is a distributed system testbed that tests protocols by inserting faults through the introduction of a Fault Injection Layer between the protocol and the communication layer beneath it [Hsueh]. All of these methods are invasive, due to the fact that they operate on the same system as the hardware they test.

2.20 Software Reliability

Software Reliability is the probability of failure-free software operation for a specified period of time in a specified environment. Software Reliability is also an important factor affecting system reliability. It differs from hardware reliability in that it reflects the design perfection, rather than manufacturing perfection. The high complexity of software is the major contributing factor of Software Reliability problems. Software Reliability is not a function of time—although researchers have come up with models relating the two. The modeling technique for Software Reliability is reaching its prosperity, but before using the technique, we must carefully select the appropriate model that can best suit our case. Measurement in software is still in its infancy. No good quantitative methods have been developed to represent Software Reliability without excessive limitations. Various approaches can be used to improve the reliability of software, however, it is hard to balance development time and budget with software reliability.

2.20.1 Embedded Software and Embedded Disasters

With the advent of the computer age, computers as well as the software running on them, are playing a vital role in our daily lives. We may not have noticed, but appliances such as washing machines, telephones, TVs, and watches are having their analog and mechanical parts replaced by CPUs and software. The computer industry is booming exponentially. With a continuously lowering cost and improved control, processors and software controlled systems offer compact design, flexible handling, rich features and competitive cost. Like machinery replaced craftsmanship in the industrial revolution, computers and intelligent parts are quickly pushing their mechanical counterparts out of the market.

People used to believe that "software never breaks". Intuitively, unlike mechanical parts such as bolts, levers, or electronic parts such as transistors, capacitor, software will stay "as is" unless there are problems in hardware that changes the storage content or data path. Software does not age, rust, wear-out, deform or crack. There is no environmental constraint for software to operate as long as the hardware processor it runs on can operate. Furthermore, software has no shape, color, material, mass. It cannot be seen or touched, but it has a physical existence and is crucial to system functionality.

Without being proven to be wrong, optimistic people would think that once after the software can run correctly, it will be correct forever. A series of tragedies and chaos caused by software proves this to be wrong. These events will always have their place in history.

Tragedies in Therac 25 a computer-controlled radiation-therapy machine in the year 1986, caused by the software not being able to detect a race condition, alerts us that it is dangerous to abandon our old but well-understood mechanical safety control and surrender our lives completely to software controlled safety mechanism.

Software can make decisions, but just as unreliable as human beings. The British destroyer Sheffield was sunk because the radar system identified an incoming missile as "friendly". The defense system has matured to the point that it will not mistaken the rising moon for incoming missiles, but gas-field fire, descending space junk, etc. were also examples that can be misidentified as incoming missiles by the defense system.

Software can also have small unnoticeable errors or drifts that can culminate into a disaster. On February 25, 1991, during the Golf War, the chopping error that missed 0.000000095 second in precision in every 10th of a second, accumulating for 100 hours, made the Patriot missile fail to intercept a scud missile. 28 lives were lost.

Fixing problems may not necessarily make the software more reliable. On the contrary, new serious problems may arise. In 1991, after changing three lines of code in a signaling program which contains millions lines of code, the local telephone systems in California and along the Eastern seaboard came to a stop [Telephone outage].

Once perfectly working software may also break if the running environment changes. After the success of Ariane 4 rocket, the maiden flight of Ariane 5 ended up in flames while design defects in the control software were unveiled by faster horizontal drifting speed of the new rocket.

There are much more scary stories to tell. This makes us wondering whether software is reliable at all, whether we should use software in safety-critical embedded applications. You can hardly ruin your clothes if the embedded software in your washing machine issues erroneous commands; and 50 per cent of the chances you will be happy if the ATM machine miscalculates your money; but in airplanes, heart pace-makers, radiation therapy machines, a software error can easily claim people's lives. With processors and software permeating safety critical embedded world, the reliability of software is simply a matter of life and death. Are we embedding potential disasters while we embed software into systems?

2.20.2 Definition of Software Reliability

According to ANSI, Software Reliability is defined as the probability of failure-free software operation for a specified period of time in a specified environment. Although Software Reliability is defined as a probabilistic function, and comes with the notion of time, we must note that, different from traditional Hardware Reliability, Software Reliability is not a direct function of time. Electronic and mechanical parts may become "old" and wear out with time and usage, but software will not rust or wear-out during its life-cycle. Software will not change over time unless intentionally changed or upgraded.

Software Reliability is an important attribute of software quality, together with functionality, usability, performance, serviceability, capability, installability, maintainability, and documentation. Software Reliability is hard to achieve, because the complexity of software tends to be high. While any system with a high degree of complexity, including software, will be hard to reach a certain level of reliability, system developers tend to push complexity into the software layer, with the rapid growth of system size and ease of doing so by upgrading the software. For example, large next-generation aircraft will have over one million source lines of software on-board; next-generation air traffic control systems will contain between one and two million lines; the upcoming international Space Station will have over two million lines on-board and over ten million lines of ground support software; several major life-critical defense systems will have over five million source lines of software. While the complexity of software is inversely related to software reliability, it is directly related to other important factors in software quality, especially functionality, capability, etc. Emphasizing these features will tend to add more complexity to software.

2.20.3 Software Failure Mechanisms

Software failures may be due to errors, ambiguities, oversights or misinterpretation of the specification that the software is supposed to satisfy, carelessness or incompetence in writing code, inadequate testing, incorrect or unexpected usage of the software or other unforeseen problems. While it is tempting to draw an analogy between Software Reliability and Hardware Reliability, software and hardware have basic differences that make them different in failure mechanisms. Hardware faults are mostly physical faults, while software faults are design faults, which are harder to visualize, classify, detect and correct.

Design faults are closely related to fuzzy human factors and the design process, which we don't have a solid understanding. In hardware, design faults may also exist, but physical faults usually dominate.

In software, we can hardly find a strict corresponding counterpart for "manufacturing" as hardware manufacturing process, if the simple action of uploading software modules into place does not count. Therefore, the quality of software will not change once it is uploaded into the storage and start running. Trying to achieve higher reliability by simply duplicating the same software modules will not work, because design faults cannot be masked off by voting.

A partial list of the distinct characteristics of software compared to hardware is listed below:

- Failure cause: Software defects are mainly design defects.
- Wear-out: Software does not have energy related wear-out phase. Errors can occur without warning.
- Repairable system concept: Periodic restarts can help fix software problems.
- Time dependency and life cycle: Software reliability is not a function of operational time.
- Environmental factors: They do not affect Software reliability, except it might affect program inputs.
- Reliability prediction: Software reliability cannot be predicted from any physical basis, since it depends completely on human factors in design.
- Redundancy: Redundancy cannot improve Software reliability if identical software components are used.
- Interfaces: Software interfaces are purely conceptual other than visual.
- Failure rate motivators: Usually not predictable from analyses of separate statements.
- Built with standard components: Well-understood and extensively-tested standard parts will help improve maintainability and reliability. But in software industry, we have not observed this trend. Code reuse has been around for sometime, but to a very limited extent. Strictly speaking there are no standard parts for software, except some standardized logic structures.

2.20.4 The Bathtub Curve for Software Reliability

Over time, hardware exhibits the failure characteristics shown in Figure 2.19, known as the bathtub curve. Period A, B and C stands for burn-in phase, useful life phase and end-of-life phase. A detailed discussion about the curve can be found in the topic Traditional Reliability.

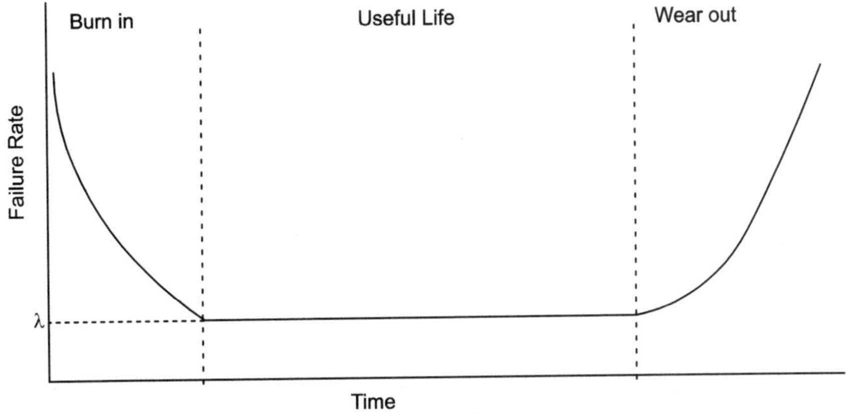

Fig. 2.19: Bathtub curve for hardware reliability

Software reliability, however, does not show the same characteristics similar as hardware. A possible curve is shown in Figure 2.20 if we projected software reliability on the same axes. There are two major differences between hardware and software curves. One difference is that in the last phase, software does not have an increasing failure rate as hardware does. In this phase, software is approaching obsolescence; there are no motivation for any upgrades or changes to the software. Therefore, the failure rate will not change. The second difference is that in the useful-life phase, software will experience a drastic increase in failure rate each time an upgrade is made. The failure rate levels off gradually, partly because of the defects found and fixed after the upgrades.

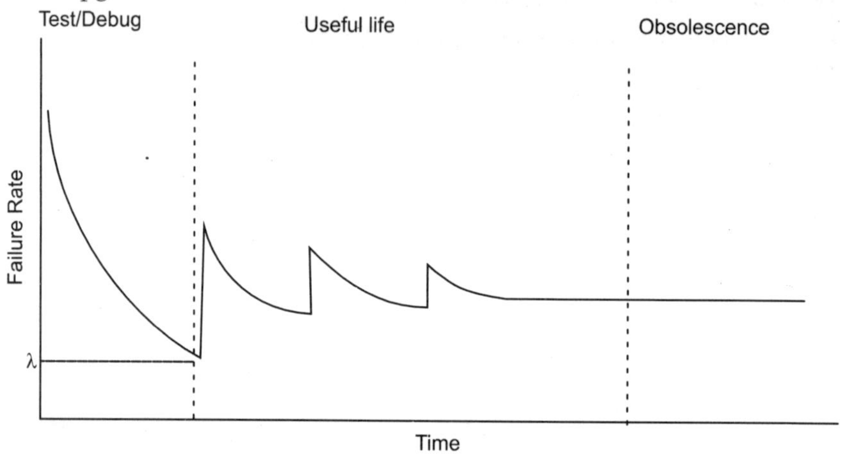

Fig. 2.20: Revised bathtub curve for software reliability

The upgrades in Figure 2.20 imply feature upgrades, not upgrades for reliability. For feature upgrades, the complexity of software is likely to be increased, since the functionality of software is enhanced. Even bug fixes may be a reason for more software failures, if the bug fix induces other defects into software. For reliability upgrades, it is possible to incur a drop in software failure rate, if the goal of the upgrade is enhancing software reliability, such as a redesign or reimplementation of some modules using better engineering approaches, such as clean-room method.

A proof can be found in the result from Ballista project, robustness testing of off-the-shelf software Components. Figure 2.21 shows the testing results of fifteen POSIX compliant operating systems. From the graph we see that for QNX and HP-UX, robustness failure rate increases after the upgrade. But for SunOS, IRIX and Digital UNIX, robustness failure rate drops when the version numbers go up. Since software robustness is one aspect of software reliability, this result indicates that the upgrade of those systems shown in Figure 2.21 should have incorporated reliability upgrades.

Since Software Reliability is one of the most important aspects of software quality, Reliability Engineering approaches are practiced in software field as well. Software Reliability Engineering (SRE) is the quantitative study of the operational behavior of software-based systems with respect to user requirements concerning reliability [IEEE, 95].

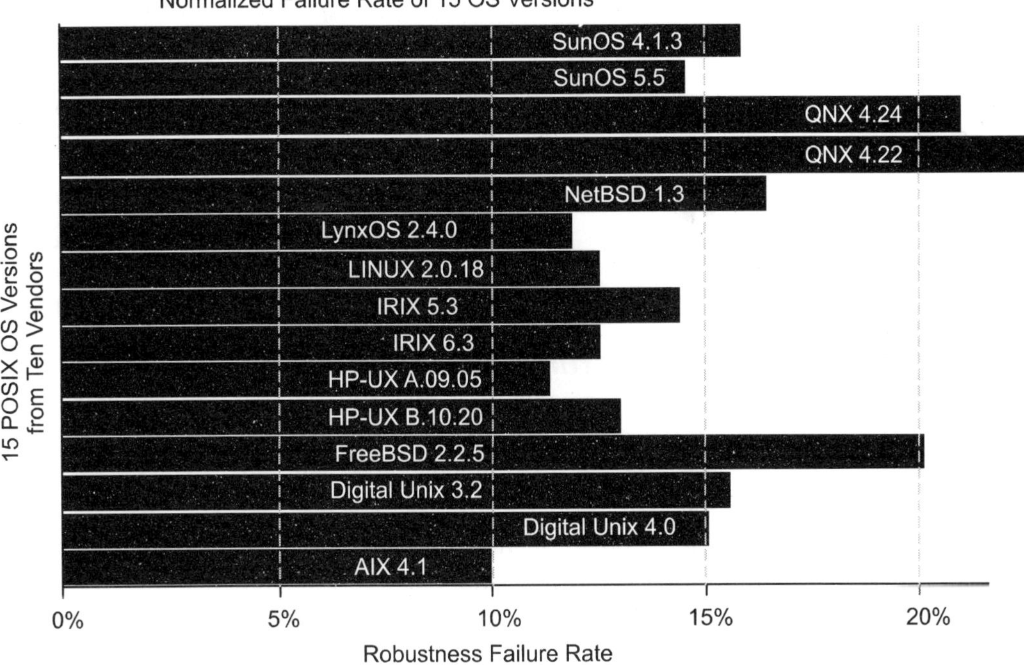

Fig. 2.21: Normalized failure rate of OS versions

2.20.5 Software Reliability Models

A proliferation of software reliability models have emerged as people try to understand the characteristics of how and why software fails, and try to quantify software reliability. Over 200 models have been developed since the early 1970s, but how to quantify software reliability still remains largely unsolved. Interested readers may refer to as many models as there are and many more emerging, none of the models can capture a satisfying amount of the complexity of software; constraints and assumptions have to be made for the quantifying process. Therefore, there is no single model that can be used in all situations. No model is complete or even representative. One model may work well for a set of certain software, but may be completely off track for other kinds of problems.

Most software models contain the following parts: assumptions, factors, and a mathematical function that relates the reliability with the factors. The mathematical function is usually higher order exponential or logarithmic.

Software modeling techniques can be divided into two subcategories: prediction modeling and estimation modeling. Both kinds of modeling techniques are based on observing and accumulating failure data and analyzing with statistical inference. The major differences of the two models are shown in Table 2.6.

Table 2.6: Difference between Software Reliability Prediction Models and Software Reliability Estimation Models

DATA REFERENCE	Uses historical data Uses data from the current software development effort
WHEN USED IN DEVELOPMENT CYCLE	Usually made prior to development or test phases; can be used as early as concept phase. Usually made later in life cycle (after some data have been collected); not typically used in concept or development phases
TIME FRAME	Predict reliability at some future time Estimate reliability at either present or some future time

2.20.6 Issues Prediction Models Estimation Models

Representative prediction models include Musa's Execution Time Model, Putnam's Model and Rome Laboratory models TR-92-51 and TR-92-15, etc. Using prediction models, software reliability can be predicted early in the development phase and enhancements can be initiated to improve the reliability.

Representative estimation models include exponential distribution models, Weibull distribution model, Thompson and Chelson's model, etc. Exponential models and Weibull distribution model are usually named as classical fault count/fault rate estimation models, while Thompson and Chelson's model belong to Bayesian fault rate estimation models.

The field has matured to the point that software models can be applied in practical situations and give meaningful results and, second, that there is no one model that is best in all situations. Because of the complexity of software, any model has to have extra assumptions. Only limited factors can be put into consideration. Most software reliability models ignore the software development process and focus on the results—the observed faults and/or failures. By doing so, complexity is reduced and abstraction is achieved, however, the models tend to specialize to be applied to only a portion of the situations and a certain class of the problems. We have to carefully choose the right model that suits our specific case. Furthermore, the modeling results cannot be blindly believed and applied.

2.20.7 Software Reliability Metrics

Measurement is commonplace in other engineering field, but not in software engineering. Though frustrating, the quest of quantifying software reliability has never ceased. Until now, we still have no good way of measuring software reliability.

Measuring software reliability remains a difficult problem because we don't have a good understanding of the nature of software. There is no clear definition to what aspects are related to software reliability. We cannot find a suitable way to measure software reliability, and most of the aspects related to software reliability. Even the most obvious product metrics such as software size have not uniform definition.

It is tempting to measure something related to reliability to reflect the characteristics, if we cannot measure reliability directly. The current practices of software reliability measurement can be divided into four categories:

2.20.8 Product Metrics

Software size is thought to be reflective of complexity, development effort and reliability. Lines of Code (LOC), or LOC in thousands (KLOC), is an intuitive initial approach to measuring software size. But there is not a standard way of counting. Typically, source code is used (SLOC, KSLOC) and comments and other non-executable statements are not counted. This method cannot faithfully compare software not written in the same language. The advent of new technologies of code reuse and code generation technique also cast doubt on this simple method.

Function point metric is a method of measuring the functionality of a proposed software development based upon a count of inputs, outputs, master files, inquires, and interfaces. The method can be used to estimate the size of a software system as soon as these functions can be identified. It is a measure of the functional complexity of the program. It measures the functionality delivered to the user and is independent of the programming language. It is used primarily for business systems; it is not proven in scientific or real-time applications.

Complexity is directly related to software reliability, so representing complexity is important. Complexity-oriented metrics is a method of determining the complexity of a program's control structure by simplifying the code into a graphical representation. Representative metric is McCabe's Complexity Metric.

Test coverage metrics are a way of estimating fault and reliability by performing tests on software products, based on the assumption that software reliability is a function of the portion of software that has been successfully verified or tested. Detailed discussion about various software testing methods can be found in topic Software Testing.

2.20.9 Project Management Metrics

Researchers have realized that good management can result in better products. Research has demonstrated that a relationship exists between the development process and the ability to complete projects on time and within the desired quality objectives. Costs increase when developers use inadequate processes. Higher reliability can be achieved by using better development process, risk management process, configuration management process, etc.

2.20.10 Process Metrics

Based on the assumption that the quality of the product is a direct function of the process, process metrics can be used to estimate, monitor and improve the reliability and quality of software. ISO-9000 certification, or "quality management standards", is the generic reference for a family of standards developed by the International Standards Organization (ISO).

2.20.11 Fault and Failure Metrics

The goal of collecting fault and failure metrics is to be able to determine when the software is approaching failure-free execution. Minimally, both the number of faults found during testing (i.e., before delivery) and the failures (or other problems) reported by users after delivery are collected, summarized and analyzed to achieve this goal. Test strategy is highly relative to the effectiveness of fault metrics, because if the testing scenario does not cover the full functionality of the software, the software may pass all tests and yet be prone to failure once delivered. Usually, failure metrics are based upon customer information regarding failures found after release of the software. The failure data collected is therefore used to calculate failure density, Mean Time Between Failures (MTBF) or other parameters to measure or predict software reliability.

2.20.12 Software Reliability Improvement Techniques

Good engineering methods can largely improve software reliability. Before the deployment of software products, testing, verification and validation are necessary steps. Software testing is heavily used to trigger, locate and remove software defects. Software testing is still in its infant stage; testing is crafted to suit specific needs in various software development projects in an ad hoc manner. Various analysis tools such as trend analysis, fault-tree analysis, Orthogonal Defect classification and formal methods, etc. can also be used to minimize the possibility of defect occurrence after release and therefore improve software reliability.

After deployment of the software product, field data can be gathered and analyzed to study the behavior of software defects. Fault tolerance or fault failure forecasting techniques will be helpful techniques and guide rules to minimize fault occurrence or impact of the fault on the system. The high cost of correcting software defects that were undetected in the development phase where they were first introduced is shown in the following diagram:

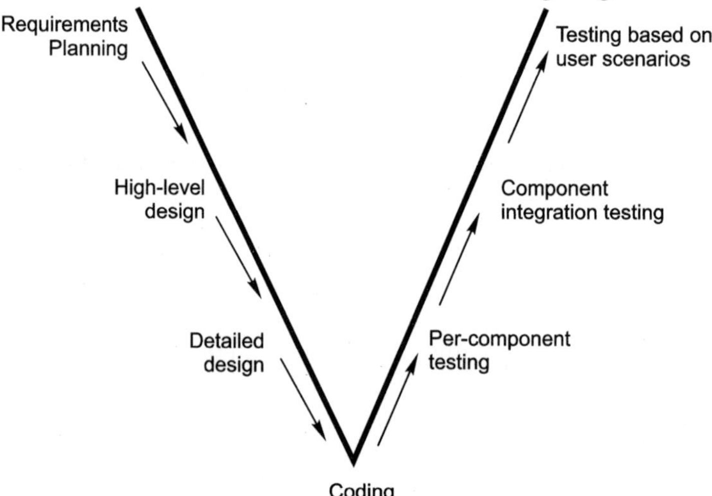

Fig. 2.22: The relationship between implementing and testing a design

Notice that there is mirror-image symmetry between the progressively more detailed stages of designing and implementing a software system versus the progressively more general stages of testing it.

This explains why a schedule is most at risk during the testing phases of a project: the earliest and most fundamental errors may be the last ones to be detected. This discovery can occur long after the errors have had a chance to multiply as they infect the subsequent phases of development. It is well-known that detecting and correcting a design flaw before coding begins is an order of magnitude cheaper than detecting it during component integration testing or system-level testing.

We can see this "cost escalation" effect by adding arrows for bug detection and rework to the diagram:

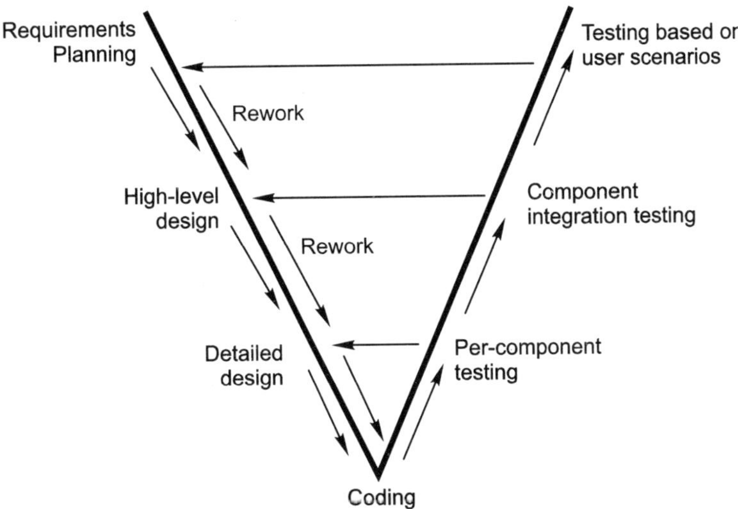

Fig. 2.23: The escalating cost of design errors

Although design errors are the most notoriously expensive, faulty testing also has snowballing costs. Like a design error, a testing error introduces hidden costs that escalate over time. For example, if component-level testing fails to detect a low-level coding error, the cost of this undetected bug multiplies as the bug's sphere of influence increases during system integration. We see this effect when large development teams become paralyzed by their inability to produce stable daily builds and when low-level coding flaws crash a beta test site.

The conventional wisdom sees the "cost escalation" problem of undetected software defects as a justification to spend more time in the design phase: good designs yield good implementations and fewer bugs. The irony is that this "solution" is actually just a tautological restatement of the problem without any real suggestion of how to detect design defects except to extend the schedule.

It is believed that the solution is to provide comprehensive testing at each phase of the development cycle, from requirements planning to high-level design to component design to implementation. Executable specifications are a practical, powerful way of accomplishing this goal.

2.21 Relationship to Other Topics

Software Reliability is a part of software quality. It relates to many areas where software quality is concerned.

2.21.1 Traditional/Hardware Reliability

The initial quest in software reliability study is based on an analogy of traditional and hardware reliability. Many of the concepts and analytical methods that are used in traditional reliability can be used to assess and improve software reliability too. However, software reliability focuses on design perfection rather than manufacturing perfection, as traditional/hardware reliability does.

2.21.2 Software Fault Tolerance

Software fault tolerance is a necessary part of a system with high reliability. It is a way of handling unknown and unpredictable software (and hardware) failures (faults) [Lyu, 95], by providing a set of functionally equivalent software modules developed by diverse and independent production teams. The assumption is the design diversity of software, which itself is difficult to achieve.

2.21.3 Software Testing

Software testing serves as a way to measure and improve software reliability. It plays an important role in the design, implementation, validation and release phases. It is not a mature field. Advance in this field will have great impact on software industry.

2.21.4 Social & Legal Concerns

As software permeates to every corner of our daily life, software related problems and the quality of software products can cause serious problems, such as the Therac-25 accident. The defects in software are significantly different than those in hardware and other components of the system: they are usually design defects, and a lot of them are related to problems in specification. The unfeasibility of completely testing a software module complicates the problem because bug-free software cannot be guaranteed for a moderately complex piece of software. No matter how hard we try, defect-free software product cannot be achieved. Losses caused by software defects causes more and more social and legal concerns. Guaranteeing no known bugs is certainly not a good-enough approach to the problem.

Conclusions

Software reliability is a key part in software quality. The study of software reliability can be categorized into three parts: modeling, measurement and improvement.

Software reliability modeling has matured to the point that meaningful results can be obtained by applying suitable models to the problem. There are many models but no single model can capture a necessary amount of the software characteristics. Assumptions and abstractions must be made to simplify the problem. There is no single model that is universal to all the situations.

Software reliability measurement is naive. Measurement is far from commonplace in software, as in other engineering field. "How good is the software, quantitatively?" As simple as the question is, there is still no good answer. Software reliability cannot be directly measured, so other related factors are measured to estimate software reliability and compare it among products. Development process, faults and failures found are all factors related to software reliability.

Software reliability improvement is hard. The difficulty of the problem stems from insufficient understanding of software reliability and in general, the characteristics of software. Until now there is no good way to conquer the complexity problem of software. Complete testing of a moderately complex software module is infeasible. Defect-free software product cannot be assured. Realistic constraints of time and budget severely limits the effort put into software reliability improvement.

As more and more software is creeping into embedded systems, we must make sure they don't embed disasters. If not considered carefully, software reliability can be the reliability bottleneck of the whole system. Ensuring software reliability is no easy task. As hard as the problem is, promising progresses are still being made toward more reliable software. More standard components, and better process are introduced in software engineering field.

REFERENCES

A. Vizienis and L. Chen. "On the Implementation of N-version Programming for Software Fault Tolerance During Execution." In Proc. *IEEE COMPSAC 77*, pp. 149-155, November 1977.

Albrecht, A.J. "Measuring Application Development Productivity", Proceedings of the Joint IBM/SHARE/GUIDE Application Development Symposium, October 1979, pp. 83-92.

Analytic Models for Rollback and Recovery Strategies in Data Base Systems.

Arlat, J. et al. "Fault Injection for Dependability Validation, A Methodology and Some Applications." *IEEE Transactions on Software Engineering*, February 1990. pp. 166-82.

Basili, V.R. and D.M. Weiss. "A Methodology for Collecting Valid Software Engineering Data," *IEEE Transactions on Software Engineering*, Vol. SE-10, 1984, pp. 728-38.

Boehm, B.W. *Software Engineering Economics*, Englewood Cliffs, N.J.: Prentice-Hall, 1981.

Clark, Jeffrey A.; Pradhan, Dhiraj K. "Fault Injection: A Method for Validating Computer-System Dependability." *Computer*, June 1995. pp. 47-56.

Conte, S.D.; H.E. Dunsmore, and V.Y. Shen. *Software Engineering Metrics and Models*, Menlo Park, Calif.: Benjamin/Cummings, 1986.

Cusumano, M.A. "Objectives and Context of Software Measurement, Analysis and Control," Massachusetts Institute of Technology, Sloan School of Management Working Paper 3471-92, October 1992.

Daskalantonakis, M.K. "A Practical View of Software Measurement and Implementation Experiences Within Motorola," *IEEE Transactions on Software Engineering*, Vol. SE-18, 1992, pp. 998–1010.

DeMarco, T. *Controlling Software Projects*, New York: Yourdon Press, 1982. *Dependability: Basic Concepts and Terminology.*

"Dependable Computing and Fault-Tolerant Systems" *Dependable Computing for Critical Applications*, Vol. 6, Meyer, Schlichting (Editors).

E. Adams. Optimizing Preventive Service of the Software Products.

Fenton, N.E. and S.L. Pfleeger. *Software Metrics: A Rigorous Approach*, 2nd ed., Boston: International Thomson Computer Press, 1997.

Grady, R.B. and D.L. Caswell. *Software Metrics: Establishing a Company-Wide Program*, Englewood Cliffs, N. J: Prentie-Hall, 1986.

Reliability Analysis Center, "Introduction to Software Reliability: A State of the Art Review." Reliability Analysis Center (RAC), 1996.

SOFTWARE TESTING METHODS

3

3.1 Software Testing

Testing is a process used to help identify the correctness, completeness and quality of developed computer software. With that in mind, testing can never completely establish the correctness of computer software. Software Testing is a necessary checking procedure performed by a software company in the final stage of product development to ensure product quality and guarantee customers' satisfaction. A software tester thoroughly tests, step by step, the normal operation of every keypress and function according to specified testing procedures. Software development changes every day, and thousands of companies continually develop and update their products. As a result, software testing will always be an indispensable procedure.

Because of this, in a typical, large company approximately 30-40 per cent of the software engineers are responsible for testing.

There are many approaches to software testing, but effective testing of complex products is essentially a process of investigation, not merely a matter of creating and following rote procedure. One definition of testing is "the process of questioning a product in order to evaluate it", where the "questions" are things the tester tries to do with the product, and the product answers with its behavior in reaction to the probing of the tester. Although most of the intellectual processes of testing are nearly identical to that of review or inspection, the word testing is connoted to mean the dynamic analysis of the product putting the product through its paces.

The quality of the application can and normally does vary widely from system to system but some of the common quality attributes include reliability, stability, portability, maintainability and usability. Refer to the ISO standard ISO 9126 for a more complete list of attributes and criteria.

Software testing determines when a software system can be released and gauges future performance. The context for testing is shown in the software process model in Figure 3.1. Testing is a major source of feedback and provides a basis for interaction with project stakeholders. With the growing complexity of software systems, it is not surprising that a substantial percentage of software development budget (in the range of 30-50%) is spent directly on software testing. And, it becomes apparent that a lot of effort has been put into the development of sound models of testing (Rapps and Weyuker, 1985) and the construction of automated tools supporting testing (Horgan et al., 1994).

Software testing is any activity aimed at evaluating an attribute or capability of a program or system and determining that it meets its required results. Although crucial to software quality and widely deployed by programmers and testers, software testing still remains an art, due to limited understanding of the principles of software. The difficulty in software testing stems from the complexity of software: we cannot completely test a program with moderate complexity. Testing is more than just debugging. The purpose of testing can be quality assurance, verification and validation, or reliability estimation. Testing can be used as a generic metric as well. Correctness testing and reliability testing are two major areas of testing. Software testing is a trade-off between budget, time and quality.

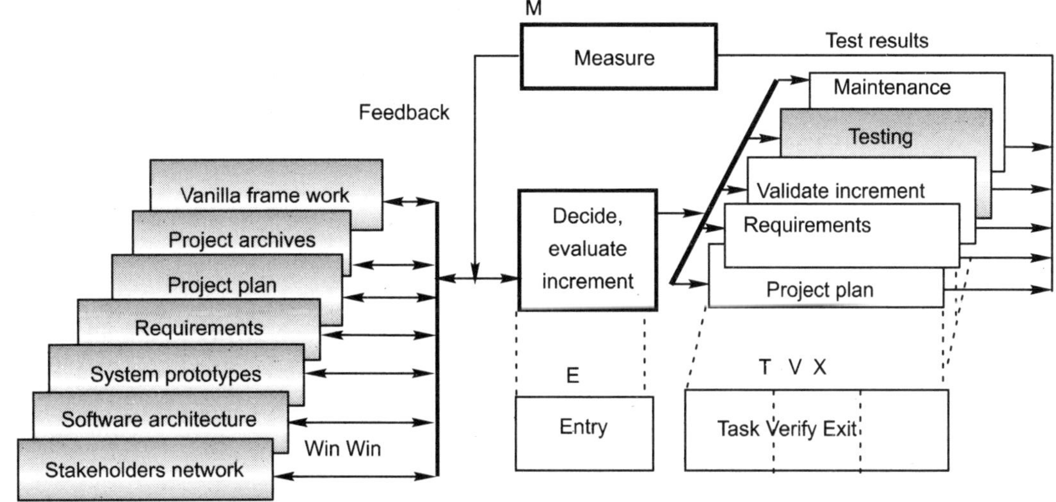

Fig. 3.1: Software testing process

As per Myers, Software Testing is the process of executing a program or system with the intent of finding errors. [Myers, 79] Or, it involves any activity aimed at evaluating an attribute or capability of a program or system and determining that it meets its required results. Software is not unlike other physical processes where inputs are received and outputs are produced. Where software differs is in the manner in which it fails. Most physical systems fail in a fixed (and reasonably small) set of ways. By contrast, software can fail in many bizarre ways. Detecting all of the different failure modes for software is generally infeasible.

Unlike most physical systems, most of the defects in software are design errors, not manufacturing defects. Software does not suffer from corrosion, wear-and-tear—generally it will not change until upgrades, or until obsolescence. So once the software is shipped, the design defects–or bugs–will be buried in and remain latent until activation.

Software bugs will almost always exist in any software module with moderate size, not because programmers are careless or irresponsible, but because the complexity of software is generally intractable—and humans have only limited ability to manage complexity. It is also true that for any complex systems, design defects can never be completely ruled out.

Discovering the design defects in software, is equally difficult, for the same reason of complexity. Because software and any digital systems are not continuous, testing boundary values are not sufficient to guarantee correctness. All the possible values need to be tested and verified, but complete testing is infeasible. Exhaustively testing a simple program to add only two integer inputs of 32-bits (yielding 2^{32} distinct test cases) would take hundreds of years, even if tests were performed at a rate of thousands per second. Obviously, for a realistic software module, the complexity can be far beyond the example mentioned here. If inputs from the real world are involved, the problem will get worse, because timing and unpredictable environmental effects and human interactions are all possible input parameters under consideration.

A further complication has to do with the dynamic nature of programs. If a failure occurs during preliminary testing and the code is changed, the software may now work for a test case that it didn't work for previously. But its behavior on pre-error test cases that it passed before can no longer be guaranteed. To account for this possibility, testing should be restarted. The expense of doing this is often prohibitive.

An interesting analogy parallels the difficulty in software testing with the pesticide, known as the Pesticide Paradox. Every method you use to prevent or find bugs leaves a residue of subtler bugs against which those methods are ineffectual. But this alone will not guarantee to make the software better, because the Complexity Barrier principle states Software complexity (and therefore that of bugs) grows to the limits of our ability to manage that complexity. By eliminating the (previous) easy bugs you allowed another escalation of features and complexity, but this time you have subtler bugs to face, just to retain the reliability you had before. Society seems to be unwilling to limit complexity because we all want that extra bell, whistle, and feature interaction. Thus, our users always push us to the complexity barrier and how close we can approach that barrier is largely determined by the strength of the techniques we can wield against ever more complex and subtle bugs.

Regardless of the limitations, testing is an integral part in software development. It is broadly deployed in every phase in the software development cycle. Typically, more than 5C per cent of the development time is spent in testing.

Testing is usually performed for the following purposes:

3.1.1 To Improve Quality

As computers and software are used in critical applications, the outcome of a bug can be severe. Bugs can cause huge losses. Bugs in critical systems have caused airplane crashes, allowed space shuttle missions to go awry, halted trading on the stock market, and worse. Bugs can kill. Bugs can cause disasters. The so-called year 2000 (Y2K) bug has given birth to a cottage industry of consultants and programming tools dedicated to making sure the modern world doesn't come to a screeching halt on the first day of the next century. In a computerized embedded world, the quality and reliability of software is a matter of life and death.

Quality means the conformance to the specified design requirement. Being correct, the minimum requirement of quality, means performing as required under specified circumstances. Debugging, a narrow view of software testing, is performed heavily to find out design defects by the programmer. The imperfection of human nature makes it almost impossible to make a moderately complex program correct the first time. Finding the problems and get them fixed is the purpose of debugging in programming phase.

3.1.2 For Verification and Validation (V&V)

Just as topic Verification and Validation indicated, another important purpose of testing is verification and validation (V&V). Testing can serve as metrics. It is heavily used as a tool in the V&V process. Testers can make claims based on interpretations of the testing results, which either the product works under certain situations, or it does not work. We can also compare the quality among different products under the same specification, based on results from the same test.

We cannot test quality directly, but we can test related factors to make quality visible. Quality has three sets of factors—functionality, engineering, and adaptability. These three sets of factors can be thought of as dimensions in the software quality space. Each dimension may be broken down into its component factors and considerations at successively lower levels of detail. Table 3.1 illustrates some of the most frequently cited quality considerations.

Table 3.1: Typical Software Quality Factors

Functionality (exterior quality)	Engineering (interior quality)	Adaptability (future quality)
Correctness	Efficiency	Flexibility
Reliability	Testability	Reusability
Usability	Documentation	Maintainability
Integrity	Structure	

Good testing provides measures for all relevant factors. The importance of any particular factor varies from application to application. Any system where human lives are at stake must place extreme emphasis on reliability and integrity. In the typical business system usability and maintainability are the key factors, while for a one-time scientific program neither may be significant. Our testing, to be fully effective, must be geared to measuring each relevant factor and thus forcing quality to become tangible and visible.

Tests with the purpose of validating the product works are named clean tests, or positive tests. The drawbacks are that it can only validate that the software works for the specified test cases. A finite number of tests cannot validate that the software works for all situations. On the contrary, only one failed test is sufficient enough to show that the software does not work. Dirty tests, or negative tests, refers to the tests aiming at breaking the software, or showing that it does not work. A piece of software must have sufficient exception handling capabilities to survive a significant level of dirty tests.

A testable design is a design that can be easily validated, falsified and maintained. Because testing is a rigorous effort and requires significant time and cost, design for testability is also an important design rule for software development.

3.2 Basic Definitions for Software Testing

Software testing is a process of analyzing or operating software for the purpose of finding bugs. Simple as this definition is, it contains a few points that are worth elaboration. The word process is used to emphasize that testing involves planned, orderly activities. This point is important if we're concerned with rapid development, as a well thought-out, systematic approach is likely to find bugs faster than poorly planned testing done in a rush.

According to the definition, testing can involve either "analyzing" or "operating" software. Test activities that are associated with analyzing the products of software development are called static testing. Static testing includes code inspections, walkthroughs, and desk checks. In contrast, test activities that involve operating the software are called dynamic testing. Static and dynamic testing complement one another, and each type has a unique approach to detecting bugs.

The final point to consider in the definition of software testing is the meaning of "bugs". In simple terms, a bug is a flaw in the development of the software that causes a discrepancy between the expected result of an operation and the actual result. The bug could be a coding problem, a problem in the requirements or the design, or it could be a configuration or data problem. It could also be something that is at variance with the customer's expectation, which may or may not be in the product specifications.

Testing involves operation of a system or application under controlled conditions and evaluating the results (e.g. 'if the user is in interface A of the application while using hardware B, and does C, then D should happen'). The controlled conditions should include both normal and abnormal conditions. Testing should intentionally attempt to make things go wrong to determine if things happen when they shouldn't or things don't happen when they should. It is oriented to 'detection'.

Organizations vary considerably in how they assign responsibility for QA and testing. Sometimes they're the combined responsibility of one group or individual. Also common are project teams that include a mix of testers and developers who work closely together, with overall QA processes monitored by project managers. It will depend on what best fits an organization's size and business structure.

Developing a program or system effectively needs to be thoroughly thought out before any raw code is actually written down. One of the most important methods of establishing functional requirements is a storyboard. Prototypes may consist of a storyboard, a sequence and series of screens, showing the end-user a typical scenario of using the program/system.

Software testing is the process of testing the functionality and correctness of software by running it. Software testing is usually performed for one of two reasons:

(1) Defect detection, and

(2) Reliability estimation.

The problem of applying software testing to defect detection is that software can only suggest the presence of flaws, not their absence (unless the testing is exhaustive). The problem of applying software testing to reliability estimation is that the input distribution used for selecting test cases may be flawed. In both of these cases, the mechanism used to determine whether program output is correct (known as an oracle) is often impossible to develop.

"Obviously the benefit of the entire software testing process is highly dependent on many different pieces. If any of these parts is faulty, the entire process is compromised" (Reliable Software Technologies).

Software testing is the most visible activity in the Software Quality Assurance, which is, perhaps, the most critical activity in a software project. It is not a quick glance through application's menus. It is not about catching bugs. It is about making sure that the software product satisfies the customer's needs by preventing bugs. If such happened, that bug appeared, QA is about describing it, locating, fixing, merging the fix and looking for the bug cause.

For Reliability Estimation

Software reliability has important relations with many aspects of software, including the structure, and the amount of testing it has been subjected to. Based on an operational profile (an estimate of the relative frequency of use of various inputs to the program), testing can serve as a statistical sampling method to gain failure data for reliability estimation.

Software testing is not mature. It still remains an art, because we still cannot make it a science. We are still using the same testing techniques invented 20-30 years ago, some of which are crafted methods or heuristics rather than good engineering methods. Software testing can be costly, but not testing software is even more expensive, especially in places that human lives are at stake. Solving the software-testing problem is no easier than solving the Turing halting problem. We can never be sure that a piece of software is correct. We can never be sure that the specifications are correct. No verification system can verify every correct program. We can never be certain that a verification system is correct either.

3.2.1 Software Testing Problems and their Solutions

The following are 5 common problems in the software development process:

- *Poor requirements*—if requirements are unclear, incomplete, too general, and not testable, there will be problems.
- *Unrealistic schedule*—if too much work is crammed in too little time, problems are inevitable.
- *Inadequate testing*—no one will know whether or not the program is any good until the customer complains or systems crash.
- *Featuritis*—requests to pile on new features after development is underway; extremely common.
- *Miscommunication*—if developers don't know what's needed or customer's have erroneous expectations, problems are guaranteed.

3.2.2 What Software Testing Is and Isn't

Informally, software testing is the process of uncovering evidence of defects in software systems. The defect could have been introduced during any phase of development or maintenance and results from one or more bugs mistakes, misunderstandings, omissions, or even misguided intent on the part of the developers. Testing comprises the efforts to find defects. Testing does not include efforts associated with tracking down bugs and fixing them. In other words, testing does not include the debugging or repair of bugs.

Testing is important because it substantially contributes to ensuring that a software application does everything it is supposed to do. Some testing efforts extend the focus to ensure an application does nothing more than it is supposed to do. In any case, testing makes a significant contribution to guarding users against software failures that can result in a loss of time, property, customers, or life.

Testing helps ensure that a product meets requirements, but testing is not quality assurance (QA). Some people mistakenly equate testing and quality assurance. In many organizations, QA is typically responsible for developing test plans and performing system testing. QA might monitor testing during development and keep statistics. Testing is a necessary but insufficient part of any quality assurance process. Quality assurance addresses activities designed to prevent defects as well as to remove those defects that do creep into the product. A project's quality assurance group sets standards that project members should follow in order to build better software. This includes defining the types of documents that should be created to capture design decisions, the processes that guide project activities, and the measures that quantify the results of decisions.

No amount of testing will improve the quality of a computer program. Testing helps in identifying failures so that developers can find bugs and remove them. The more testing we do of a system, the more convinced we might be of its correctness. Yet testing cannot in general prove a system works 100 per cent correctly. Thus, testing's primary contribution to quality is to identify problems that we wish we could have prevented in the first place. The mission of QA is to prevent problems in the first place. That requires processes beyond testing.

Testing can contribute to improved quality by helping to identify problems early in the development process. Fortunately, you can do some testing quite early in the development process—even before code is written. We describe useful techniques in this book, but these techniques require that testers work more closely with developers and that developers work more closely with testers.

One practical consequence of the definition of testing is that test engineers and development engineers need to take fundamentally different approaches to their jobs. The goal of the developer is to create bug-free code that satisfies the software design and meets the customer's requirements. The developer is trying to "make" code. The goal of the tester is to analyze or operate the code to expose the bugs that are latent in the code as it is integrated, configured, and run in different environments. The tester is trying to "break" the code. In this context, a good result of a software test for a developer is a pass, but for that same test a successful outcome for the test engineer is a fail. Ultimately, of course, both the developer and tester want the same thing: a product that works well enough to satisfy their customers.

3.3 Basic Functions of Software Testing

There are three basic functions of software testing:

- Verification
- Validation
- Quality

Validation is the assurance that the final product satisfies the system requirements.

The purpose of validation is to ensure that the system has implemented all requirements, so that each function can be traced back to a particular customer requirement. In other words, validation makes sure that the right product is being built.

Verification is focused more on the activities of a particular phase of the development process. For example, one of the purposes of system testing is to give assurance that the system design is consistent with the requirements that were used as an input to the system design phase. Unit and integration testing can be used to verify that the program design is consistent with the system design. In simple terms, verification makes sure that the product is being built right. We'll see examples of both verification and validation activities in chapter 5.

One additional concept that needs to be defined is quality. Like beauty, quality is subjective and can be difficult to define. We will define software quality in terms of three factors: failures in the field, reliability, and customer satisfaction. A software product is said to have good quality if:

- It has few failures when used by the customer, indicating that few bugs have escaped to the field.
- It is reliable, meaning that it seldom crashes or demonstrates unexpected behavior when used in the customer environment.
- It satisfies a majority of users.

One implication of this definition of quality is that the test group must not only take measures to prevent and detect defects during product development, but also needs to be concerned with the reliability and usability of the product.

3.3.1 Objective behind Software Testing

As per P.D. Coward (1997), the principal objective of software testing is to gain confidence in the software.

Aims:

- Explore dynamic and static testing methods
- Identify and experiment with black and white box testing
- Analyze advantages and limitations of testing methods

3.3.2 Test Deliverables

There are different test deliverables at every phase of the SDLC. These deliverables are provided based on the requirement once before the start of the test phase and there are other deliverables that are produced towards the end/after completion of each test phase. Also there are several test metrics that are collected at each phase of testing. Below are the details of the various test deliverables corresponding to each test phase along with their test metrics.

The standard deliverables provided as part of testing are:

- Test Trace-ability Matrix
- Test Plan
- Testing Strategy
- Test Cases (for functional testing)

- Test Scenarios (for non-functional testing)
- Test Scripts
- Test Data
- Test Results
- Test Summary Report
- Release Notes
- Tested Build
- Test Metrics

There are several test metrics identified as part of the overall testing activity in order to track and measure the entire testing process. These test metrics are collected at each phase of the testing life cycle/SDLC and analyzed and appropriate process improvements are determined and implemented as a result of these test metrics that are constantly collected and evaluated as a parallel activity together with testing both for manual and automated testing irrespective of the type of application. The test metrics can be broadly classified into the following three categories such as:

- *Project Related Metrics*—such as Test Size, # of Test Cases tested per day—Automated (NTTA), # of Test Cases tested per day–Manual (NTTM), # of Test Cases created per day—Manual (TCED), Total number of review defects (RD), Total number of testing defects (TD), etc.
- *Process Related Metrics*—such as Schedule Adherence (SA), Effort Variance (EV), Schedule Slippage (SS), Test Cases and Scripts Rework Effort, etc.
- *Customer Related Metrics*—such as Percentage of defects leaked per release (PDLPR), Percentage of automation per release (PAPR), Application Stability Index (ASI), etc.

3.3.3 Testing Software Changes

1. **Static Testing.** Evaluating changed code and associated documentation at the end of the change process to ensure correct implementation of the change.
2. **Regression Testing.** Testing the whole product to ensure that unchanged functionality performs as it did prior to implementing a change.
3. **Verification.** Reviewing requirements, design and associated document Defect Tracking.

Metric-based defect tracking monitors where defects originate. By identifying the root cause of defects, we can identify patterns which lead to the implementation of a process to control the problem. As an example, while a programmer may be fast, his number of defects may be higher than other team members. It is typical that the person who writes code the fastest, is the one who does the most code for the project. In this situation, the programmer who codes the most, generates the most defects. When programmers are held accountable for their quality, productivity increases as rework decreases. This technique is used by some of the largest software manufacturers. Programmers may only proceed forward when their code meets company defect standards. Monitoring code at this level is typically a luxury that small to mid-sized companies usually do not have the internal resources to apply.

3.3.4 Difficulty in Software Testing

Software testing is probably the most complex task in the software development cycle. It often takes longer to test the software than it does to write the code. The problems discovered during the software testing phase add more time onto the coding phase, resulting in further delays in the product's release, and so this vicious cycle goes.

It's nearly impossible to attribute the problems that arise during the software testing cycle to any single factor. Before going any further, it's important to clarify one point. Software that works, but not the way it is supposed to work, is not considered an error in the coding (also known as a bug). Rather, this situation is the result of an error in the design phase. Software engineers refer to these differences as a "fault" vs. a "failure". Faults can turn into failures, but that's a subject for another time.

So why is software testing such a time-consuming and frustrating process? One factor is the complexity of the software being developed. The more complex the project is, the more there is to test. Also, complex projects typically involve multiple development team members, including those working directly for the company and those working as sub-contractors.

Software testing troubles directly attributable to the human factor include poorly documented code and employee turnover. And if the person who is not properly documenting the project is the same person who leaves the company midway through the project cycle, the problem quickly compounds.

Another software testing difficulty arises when those developing the software are the same ones testing that software. These individuals have a much higher level of understanding about software and computer system. They're not likely to make the same types of mistakes during the software testing phase that end users might make using the finished software. For example, software engineers understand that you never press the power button before you properly close all applications. End users, in their rush to burst out of the office at 5:00 pm just want the computer off, and some won't wait until every application closes properly.

Plenty of software testing applications are available to help during the software testing phase. These products are designed to facilitate and enhance the software testing phase, provided they can be made to work with the software being tested.

The main purpose of software testing is to discover software failures. As failures are discovered, they can be corrected. However, software testing cannot guarantee that the software is problem-free. Testing finds many bugs, but even the most extensive testing processes can't fix failures that are not uncovered. Never rely on software testing as proof that no problems exist. That's considered software verification, an entirely different process.

Regardless of the difficulties involved with software testing, one truth remains. Software failures discovered early on cost far less to correct than those that occur in latter stages of software development, or worse, after the software has been released to the general public.

3.4 Software Testing Life Cycle

The life cycle begins when an application is first conceived and ends when it is no longer in use. It includes aspects such as initial concept, requirements analysis, functional design, internal design, documentation planning, test planning, coding, document preparation, integration, testing, maintenance, updates, retesting, phase-out, and other aspects.

What steps are needed to develop and run software tests?

The following are some of the steps to consider:

- Obtain requirements, functional design, and internal design specifications and other necessary documents.
- Obtain budget and schedule requirements.
- Determine project-related personnel and their responsibilities, reporting requirements, required standards and processes (such as release processes, change processes, etc.).
- Determine project context, relative to the existing quality culture of the organization and business, and how it might impact testing scope, aproaches and methods.
- Identify application's higher-risk aspects, set priorities, and determine scope and limitations of tests.
- Determine test approaches and methods—unit, integration, functional, system, load, usability tests, etc.
- Determine test environment requirements (hardware, software, communications, etc.).
- Determine testware requirements (record/playback tools, coverage analyzers, test tracking, problem/bug tracking, etc.).
- Determine test input data requirements.
- Identify tasks, those responsible for tasks, and labor requirements.
- Set schedule estimates, timelines, milestones.
- Determine input equivalence classes, boundary value analyses, error classes.
- Prepare test plan document and have needed reviews/approvals.
- Write test cases.
- Have needed reviews/inspections/approvals of test cases.
- Prepare test environment and testware, obtain needed user manuals/reference documents/configuration guides/installation guides, set up test tracking processes, set up logging and archiving processes, set up or obtain test input data.
- Obtain and install software releases.
- Perform tests.
- Evaluate and report results.
- Track problems/bugs and fixes.
- Retest as needed.
- Maintain and update test plans, test cases, test environment and testware through life cycle.

3.5 Essential Components of Testing

In a similar vein, rapid testing means testing software faster than you do now, while maintaining or improving your standards of quality. Unfortunately, there is no simple way to achieve rapid testing. Figure 3.2 shows a somewhat simplistic sketch that represents rapid testing as a structure that is built on a foundation of four components. If any of these components is weak, the effectiveness of testing will be greatly impaired. As illustrated in the figure, the four components that must be optimized for rapid testing are people, integrated test process, static testing, and dynamic testing. We'll briefly examine each of the four components.

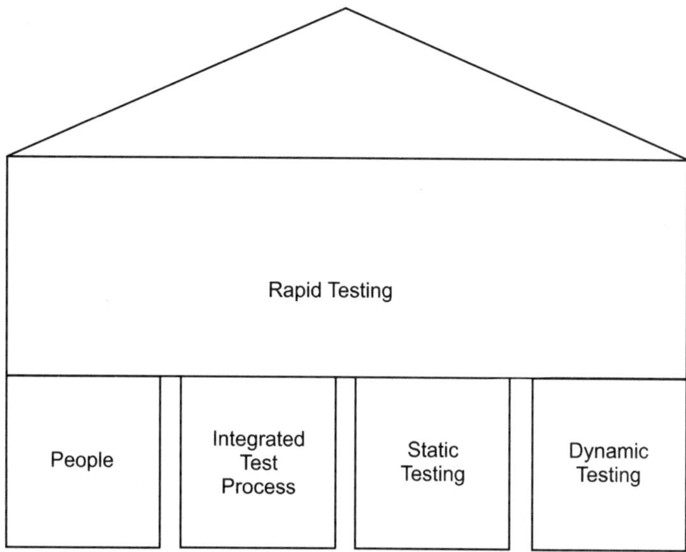

Fig. 3.2: Essential components of rapid testing

3.5.1 People

As every test manager knows, the right people are an essential ingredient to rapid testing. There are several studies that show productivity differences of 10:1 or more in software developers. The same is true with test engineers—not everyone has the skills, experience, or temperament to be a good test engineer. Rapid testing particularly needs people who are disciplined, flexible, who can handle the pressure of an aggressive schedule, and who are able to be productive contributors through the early phases of the development life cycle.

3.5.2 Integrated Test Process

No matter how good your people may be, if they do not have a systematic, disciplined process for testing, they will not operate at maximum efficiency. The test process needs to be based on sound, fundamental principles, and must be well integrated with the overall software development process.

3.5.3 Static Testing

Static testing is defined as test activities associated with analyzing the products of software development. Static testing is done for the purpose of validating that a work product such as a design specification properly implements all the system requirements, and verifying the quality of the design. Static testing is one of the most effective means of catching bugs at an early stage of development, thereby saving substantial time and cost to the development. It involves inspections, walkthroughs, and peer reviews of designs, code, and other work products, as well as static analysis to uncover defects in syntax, data structure, and other code components. Static testing is basically anything that can be done to uncover defects without running the code. In the experience of the authors, it is an often-neglected tool. Static testing will be discussed in chapter 7 of this book.

3.5.4 Dynamic Testing

Often when engineers think of testing, they are thinking of dynamic testing, which involves operating the system with the purpose of finding bugs. Whereas static testing does not involve running the software, dynamic testing does. Generally speaking, dynamic testing consists of running a program and comparing its actual behavior to what is expected. If the actual behavior differs from the expected behavior, a defect has been found. As we'll see in later chapters, dynamic testing will be used to perform a variety of types of tests such as functional tests, performance tests, and stress tests. Dynamic testing lies at the heart of the software testing process, and if the planning, design, development, and execution of dynamic tests are not performed well, the testing process will be very inefficient. Dynamic testing is not only performed by the test team; it should be a part of the development team's unit and integration testing as well. Dynamic testing is discussed in chapter 8 of this book.

3.5.5 Requirements Analysis

When analyzing software requirements, the goals of the test team and the development team are somewhat different. Both teams need a clear, unambiguous requirements specification as input to their jobs. The development team wants a complete set of requirements that can be used to generate a system functional specification, and that will allow them to design and code the software. The test team, on the other hand, needs a set of requirements that will allow them to write a test plan, develop test cases, and run their system and acceptance tests.These requirements are discussed in chapter 4 of this book in detail.

A very useful output of the requirement analysis phase for both development and test teams is a requirements traceability matrix. A requirements traceability matrix is a document that maps each requirement to other work products in the development process such as design components, software modules, test cases, and test results. It can be implemented in a spreadsheet, word processor table, database, or Web page.

3.5.6 Test Planning

By test planning we mean determining the scope, approach, resources, and schedule of the intended testing activities. Efficient testing requires a substantial investment in planning, and a willingness to revise the plan dynamically to account for changes in requirements, designs, or code as bugs are uncovered. It is important that all requirements be tested or, if the requirements have been prioritized, that the highest priority requirements are tested. The requirements traceability matrix is a useful tool in the test planning phase because it can be used to estimate the scope of testing needed to cover the essential requirements.Test Planning methods are discussed in detail in chapter 10 of this book.

Ideally, test planning should take into account static as well as dynamic testing, but since the waterfall test process described in Figure 3.3 and Table 3.2 is focused on dynamic testing, we'll exclude static testing for now. The activities of the test planning phase should prepare for the system test and acceptance test phases that come near the end of the waterfall, and should include:

- Definition of what will be tested and the approach that will be used.
- Mapping of tests to the requirements.
- Definition of the entry and exit criteria for each phase of testing.
- Assessment, by skill set and availability, of the people needed for the test effort.
- Estimation of the time needed for the test effort.
- Schedule of major milestones.
- Definition of the test system (hardware and software) needed for testing.
- Definition of the work products for each phase of testing.
- An assessment of test-related risks and a plan for their mitigation.

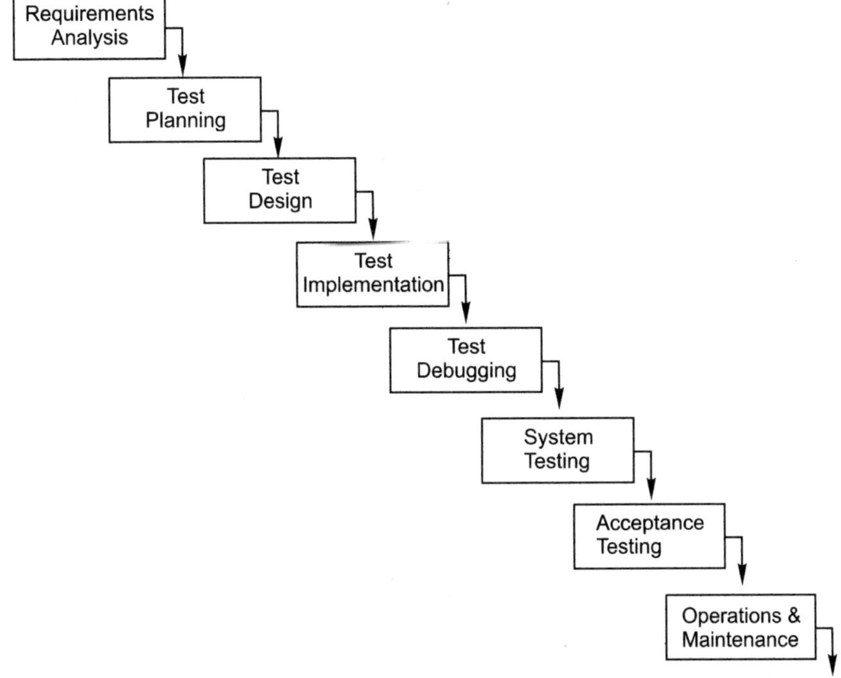

Fig. 3.3: Waterfall test process.

The work products or outputs that result from these activities can be combined in a test plan, which might consist of one or more documents.

3.5.7 Test Design, Implementation, and Debugging

Dynamic testing relies on running a defined set of operations on a software build and comparing the actual results to the expected results. If the expected results are obtained, the test counts as a pass; if anomalous behavior is observed, the test counts as a fail, but it may have succeeded in finding a *bug*. The defined set of operations that are run constitute a test case, and test cases need to be designed, written, and debugged before they can be used.

Table 3.2: Test Plan Input and Output for the Water Fall Model

Activity	Inputs	Outputs
Requirements analysis	Requirements definition, requirements specification	Requirements traceability matrix
Test planning	Requirements specification, requirements trace matrix	Test plan—test strategy, test system, effort estimate and schedule
Test design	Requirements specification, requirements trace matrix, test plan	Test designs—test objectives, test input specification, test configurations
Test implementation	Software functional specification, requirements trace matrix, test plan, test designs	Test cases—test procedures and automated tests
Test debugging	"Early look1 build of code, test cases, working test system	Final test cases
System testing	System test plan, requirements trace matrix, "test-ready" code build, final test cases, working test system	Test results—bug reports, test status reports, test results summary report
Acceptance testing	Acceptance test plan, requirements trace matrix, beta code build, acceptance test cases, working test system	Test results
Operations and maintenance	Repaired code, test cases to verify bugs, regression test cases, working test system	Verified bug fixes

A test design consists of two components:

- Test architecture and
- Detailed test designs.

The test architecture organizes the tests into groups such as functional tests, performance tests, security tests, and so on. It also describes the structure and naming conventions for a test repository. The detailed test designs describe the objective of each test, the equipment and data needed to conduct the test, the expected result for each test, and traces the test back to the requirement being validated by the test. There should be at least a one-to-one relationship between requirements and test designs.

Detailed test procedures can be developed from the test designs. The level of detail needed for a written test procedure depends on the skill and knowledge of the people that run the tests. There is a tradeoff between the time that it takes to write a detailed, step-by-step procedure, and the time that it takes for a person to learn to properly run the test. Even if the test is to be automated, it usually pays to spend time up front writing a detailed test procedure so that the automation engineer has an unambiguous statement of the automation task.

Once a test procedure is written, it needs to be tested against a build of the product software. Since this test is likely to be run against "buggy" code, some care will be needed when analyzing test failures to determine if the problem lies with the code or with the test.

Guidelines for Software Testing:

- Determine when to stop testing.
- Assign the responsibility of your test program to a tester (not yourself).
- Describe the expected results for every test case.
- Avoid non-reproducible or on-the-fly testing.
- Write test cases for invalid as well as valid input conditions.
- Inspect the result of each test thoroughly.

Testing the product spec isn't something that all software testers have the luxury of doing. Sometimes you might come into a project midway through the development cycle after the specification is written and the coding started. If that's the case, don't worry—you can still use the techniques overviewed here to test the final specification.

3.6 Black-Box and White-Box Testing

Two terms that software testers use to describe how they approach their testing are black-box testing and white-box testing. Figure 3.4 shows the difference between the two approaches. In black-box testing, the tester only knows what the software is supposed to do—he can't look in the box to see how it operates. If he types in a certain input, he gets a certain output. S/he doesn't know how or why it happens, just that it does.

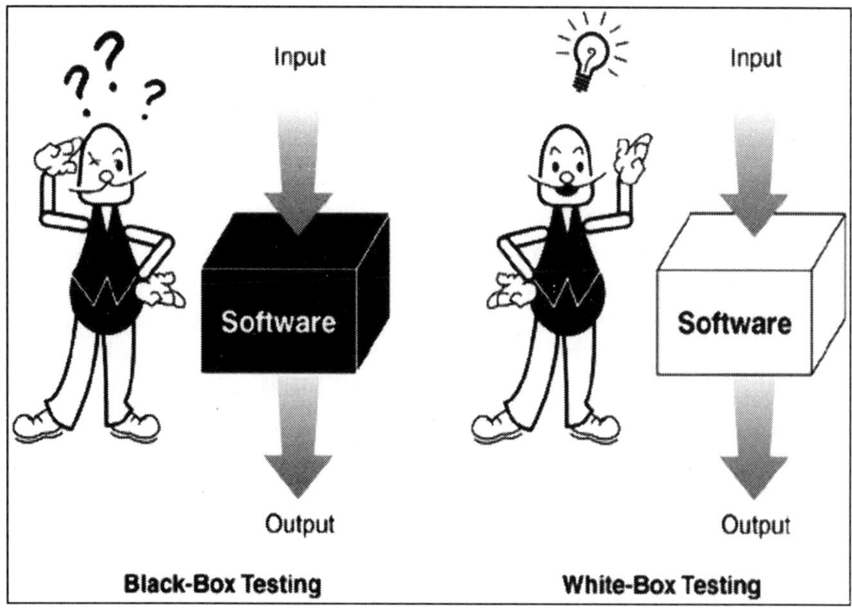

Fig. 3.4: Black and White box Testing

3.7 History of Testing

The first formal technical conference devoted to software testing was held in June 1972 at the University of North Carolina. Although that certainly was not the first time a program was tested, it was the first time that researchers who were primarily concerned with the practicalities of software quality assembled to discuss the whole range of issues involved.

Subsequent to that meeting there have been many International Software Engineering Conferences, and a spate of smaller workshops and symposia devoted either fully or in part to questions of program testing. At the Oregon Conference on Computing in the 1980s, testing technology was considered as a formal part of software engineering technology, probably for the first time.

The history of testing goes back to the beginnings of the computing field; the programs that ran on the earliest machine were "tested". In fact, there is even an early paper by Turing indicating that "testing is the empirical form of software quality assurance, while proving is the theoretical way". Results of both approaches have varied widely. Some software has performed excellently, and other software has done quite badly. There are plenty of "doom and gloom" anecdotes such as the famous missing comma in the Venus probe software, the structural faults that led to the detection of the moon as an incoming ICBM, and the like. Perhaps expectedly, many of the successes are not so well known or discussed.

3.7.1 The Direction for the Future

There is a steadily increasing need for effective software quality assurance at affordable prices. The need arises from various sectors of industry, all of which need practical methods for assuring quality (minimizing the chance of a latent error) without having the costs of doing so go off the scale. At the end of this section are some practical guidelines on what the costs to do this might actually be.

The one obstacle to the widespread adoption of software testing is its negative reward structure. The objective of a dedicated software tester is to find errors and report them to somebody, but that attitude and perspective may be at odds with the software implementors and/or their managers. Hence, in many cases it is found necessary to consider special organizational setups both to isolate this negativity (or to turn it around as a positive force) and to maximize any benefits of synergy.

As more and more experience with testing is gained, an increasingly strong set of intuitions and guidelines on handling the software quality assurance problem is being developed as well as ideas on how to get the most out of what is currently known about the techniques for achieving software quality. Knowing how to choose among the many technical alternatives is the responsibility of the well-informed quality assurance manager.

3.8 Software Quality Testing

This section provides a high-level overview and perspective on software testing technology as it is practiced today and as it may be practiced in the near future. Of all of the areas within computer science, none has received more attention in the past decade than the issue of software quality. Software quality lies at the foundation of many (or even all) of the problems facing the computing community; the issue of quality determines whether particular solutions to problems that involve a computer are, or are not accepted. Certainly, there are sufficiently many examples of systems (i.e. software solutions) that have failed to meet minimum levels of acceptability; there are, in addition, a few instances of genuine success.

What is the difference between the successes and the failures? The answer is manifold: it not only involves the application of good software engineering techniques and the use of modern programming practices, software design methodologies, and more reliable high-level languages, but also must take into account the software engineering methods used (whatever they are) to assure the quality of the delivered software system. Quality is assured primarily through some form of software testing; a number of instances of formal program verification exist, but in relative terms the total amount of software that has been processed with this theoretically important but costly method is very small. Very often, what passes for software quality assurance with testing has not been called that at all: instead, it was termed advanced debugging, interface testing, or acceptance testing, and so forth.

Now, however, there is growing agreement on the role of testing as a software quality assurance discipline, as well as on the terminology, technology, and phenomenology of, and the expectations about testing. This section presents some intuitive descriptions of each of these categories.

3.8.1 Basics of Testing

A quality analysis oriented test of a computer program consists of:

- Running the program with a controlled set of inputs.
- Observing the run-time effect the inputs have on the program.
- Examining the program outputs to determine their acceptability.

One usually attends to these items informally during the program debugging process, whereas, during formal program testing, one thinks less in terms of making the program do something and more in terms of showing precisely what the program does. One way to distinguish between formal testing and a less formal debugging activity is to examine the tools used. Debugging relies on the program production tools (i.e., compilers, debugging packages that examine a program's internal operation), whereas testing may involve other kinds of tools.

In addition to the process of running programs under controlled and observable circumstances (a process called dynamic testing), a second stage called static testing is ordinarily included. Static testing may include manual code inspections, structured walkthroughs, or the use of automated tools that analyze software by looking for certain kinds of common errors (those not caught during the normal program production process). Contemporary testing technology advocates combinations of static and dynamic quality analysis processes.

The input data used to make a program demonstrate its own features are called a test case or test data. Individual programs can be tested, a process called unit testing.

Whole systems of software can also be tested in an activity called system testing. Normally, system testing is divided into a set of individual activities that are larger than unit testing but smaller than full system testing. Testing can be done from either the black box or the white box perspective, depending on whether the internal operation of the program is being observed during the testing process. Normally, black box testing is reserved only for the system level; most programs are fully unit tested using white box methods.

During white box testing, the tester observes the extent to which test cases exercise program structure. The resulting coverage is used as an indicator of the likelihoods of any remaining undiscovered errors. Note that input/output relationships still have to be examined in detail for appropriateness.

One of the more common strategies for testing involves declaring in a minimum level of testing coverage, ordinarily expressed as a percentage of the elemental segments that are exercised in aggregate during the testing process. This is called C1 coverage, where C1 denotes the minimum level of testing coverage so that every logically separate part of the program has been exercised at least once during the set of tests. Unit testing usually requires at least 85-90 per cent C1 coverage.

At the system level it is possible to define similar measures of coverage that relate to the extent to which subroutines and invocations to them are exercised. Many different strategies exist for governing the process of multiple unit testing and/or system-level testing.

An underlying premise of structurally motivated and measured testing is that at a minimum, it is necessary to know that all of the functions in a software system have been exercised at least once. It is not reasonable to accept (or release, or approve) any software system unless it is known that every part of it has been exercised. Although this criterion cannot be guaranteed (in formally provable terms) to force discovery of all errors, it can be shown to be a practically effective method for systematically analyzing large and complex software systems (see below).

3.9 Typical Testing Applications

Much of contemporary testing technology arises from the need to examine the quality of software that is embedded in products sold directly to consumers or that otherwise affects the public. This factor was not predicted as the major motivating force in the past, perhaps because nobody expected that there would be such widespread use of software. It is valuable to take a look at some typical application areas and identify for each of them the primary areas of concern for software quality.

• **Instrumentation Systems.** The use of computers, and especially microcomputers, in instrumentation has been increasing rapidly in the past five years. For example, many oscilloscope, data display, signal analysis, and communication link analyzers are more effective and can have more capabilities and flexibility with embedded microcomputers. The instrument manufacturers have found, however, that they are poorly equipped to deal with the software component in such instruments. In a typical instrumentation system, the software is coded at the assembly language level, a choice usually dictated by economies of program storage space and execution time. It seems well understood now that the cost to repair or modify such systems is very large, particularly if it must be done after product introduction and/or if the production run is large. As a consequence, the instrument manufacturers are generally providing fairly basic levels of software quality assurance through testing, with the effort level based on the relative cost to repair the software in the field.

• **Process Control Systems.** Computers are finding increasing application in process control, particularly for those systems that have rapid real-time response requirements that cannot ordinarily be met by human controllers. Examples of systems that fall into this category range from nuclear reactors to petroleum plants to automated assembly lines. The cost of failure of such computer-based control systems ranges from politically unacceptable to economically undesirable. Largely as a function of the potential impact of a failure caused by software, organizations responsible for these kinds of systems are "betting" on a number of techniques. In many cases, triple modular redundancy is provided at the hardware level to reduce the chances of a hardware failure to vanishingly small probability. Corresponding methods of multiple implementation of software control processes have also been used effectively, particularly in very critical applications.

• **Appliances.** As with instrumentation systems, most appliance-based software is written at a very low level, sometimes even in direct machine code. The cost of failure, or the impact on the organization, as the result of a deficiency in software is ordinarily measured by a combination of direct and indirect costs. Direct costs include the costs of repair, as well as the cost to provide legal protection in the event of software failure. The indirect costs involve such factors as product image, organizational image, and reputation.

• **Automotive Computers.** Everyone has been talking for some time about the revolution in automotive electronics, in which many of the current mechanically implemented control functions have been replaced by full digital control. While this has been slower to occur than many had thought, recent model cars do contain computers, and they are used in a more than peripheral fashion. Announcements appeared for several retrofits based on dash computers, in many instances similar to previously available "rally-style" computers in function but not in technology. For this class of application, software reliability can affect the driver and passengers only in an indirect manner. An unanswered question, however, is extent of liability assumed by the supplier of the software/hardware combination.

• **Telephony.** Computers are increasingly the central feature of complex telephone switching equipment, both for the public network and for privately maintained in-house systems. In addition to the switching function is the data transfer function represented by the new value-added data transmission networks. For all of these applications, the implications of software failure are generally less severe than those previously noted, being intrinsically restricted to the loss of communication and/or the effect of an errant call. For value-added data switching networks, however, the implications of a failure are not so clear cut. While the telephone companies themselves have devoted substantial effort to systematically testing computerized switching systems and substantial experience has been gained in effectiveness evaluation of switched data networks, much quality assurance work remains to be done.

• **Military Systems.** Because military systems typically involve the risk of human life, substantial emphasis has always been placed on the software quality issue. Modern concepts of third party verification and validation of software projects had their origin in the military community. Notwithstanding this head start, however, contemporary technology seems to be passing up military systems in favor of developing techniques more applicable to the popular languages and/or the popular computers. Much of research and development activity in the area of program verification has been focused on military applications software. Full verification and validation for military style software is a very expensive proposition. Estimates range from \$10 to \$25 per statement and higher for "the full treatment". A number of companies have been active in this field for some time with measurable effectiveness. After all, strategic systems that employ computers have experienced no failures, although this may have been the result of luck.

3.10 Benefits of Systematic Testing

Apart from all of these motivating forces, additional benefits may accrue as the result of instituting a systematic testing discipline. Some of these are:

- By focusing attention on the issues of software quality, programmers as well as program testers are made conscious of the need for error-free software.
- The processes involved in analyzing computer programs from the perspective of a program tester almost automatically ensure that the more flagrant kinds of errors will be detected.
- The systematic testing process, even if it does not identify significant errors, still acts as a backup to other techniques such as design reviews, structured walkthroughs and so on.
- Instituting a systematic testing activity provides a framework in which new quality assurance technologies can be applied as soon as they become available.

As subsequent sections will show, contemporary technology does permit general kinds of statements about testing activity, how it should be organized, and what should be expected of it.

3.11 Testing by the Software Developer

Software testing entails running software products under known conditions with defined inputs and documented outcomes that can be compared to their predefined expectations. It is a time consuming, difficult, and imperfect activity. As such, it requires early planning in order to be effective and efficient.

Test plans and test cases should be created as early in the software development process as feasible. They should identify the schedules, environments, resources (personnel, tools, etc.), methodologies, cases (inputs, procedures, outputs, expected results), documentation and reporting criteria. The magnitude of effort to be applied throughout the testing process can be linked to complexity, criticality, reliability, and/or safety issues (e.g., requiring functions or modules that produce critical outcomes to be challenged with intensive testing of their fault tolerance features). Descriptions of categories of software and software testing effort appear in the literature, for example:

- NIST Special Publication 500-235, Structured Testing: A Testing Methodology Using the Cyclomatic Complexity Metric;
- NUREG/CR-6293, Verification and Validation Guidelines for High Integrity Systems; and
- IEEE Computer Society Press, Handbook of Software Reliability Engineering.

Software test plans should identify the particular tasks to be conducted at each stage of development and include justification of the level of effort represented by their corresponding completion criteria.

Software testing has limitations that must be recognized and considered when planning the testing of a particular software product. Except for the simplest of programs, software cannot be exhaustively tested.

Generally it is not feasible to test a software product with all possible inputs, nor is it possible to test all possible data processing paths that can occur during program execution. There is no one type of testing or testing methodology that can ensure a particular software product has been thoroughly tested. Testing of all program functionality does not mean all of the program has been tested. Testing of all of a program's code does not mean all necessary functionality is present in the program. Testing of all program functionality and all program code does not mean the program is 100% correct. Software testing that finds no errors should not be interpreted to mean that errors do not exist in the software product; it may mean the testing was superficial.

An essential element of a software test case is the expected result. It is the key detail that permits objective evaluation of the actual test result. This necessary testing information is obtained from the corresponding, predefined definition or specification. A software specification document must identify what, when, how, why, etc. is to be achieved with an engineering (i.e., measurable or objectively verifiable) level of detail in order for it to be confirmed through testing. The real effort of effective software testing lies in the definition of what is to be tested rather than in the performance of the test.

A software testing process should be based on principles that foster effective examinations of a software product. Applicable software testing tenets include:

- The expected test outcome is predefined;
- A good test case has a high probability of exposing an error;
- A successful test is one that finds an error;
- There is independence from coding;
- Both application (user) and software (programming) expertise are employed;
- Testers use different tools from coders;
- Examining only the usual case is insufficient.

Test documentation permits its reuse and an independent confirmation of the pass/fail status of a test outcome during subsequent review.

Once the prerequisite tasks (e.g., code inspection) have been successfully completed, software testing begins. It starts with unit level testing and concludes with system level testing. There may be a distinct integration level of testing. A software product should be challenged with test cases based on its internal structure and with test cases based on its external specification. These tests should provide a thorough and rigorous examination of the software product's compliance with its functional, performance, and interface definitions and requirements.

3.12 Typical Tasks: Testing by the Software Developer

Test Planning:

- Structural Test Case Identification
- Functional Test Case Identification
- Trace ability Analysis

Testing:

- Unit (Module) Tests to Detailed Design
- Integration Tests to High Level Design
- System Tests to Software Requirements
- Unit (Module) Test Execution
- Integration Test Execution
- Functional Test Execution
- System Test Execution
- Acceptance Test Execution
- Test Results Evaluation
- Error Evaluation/Resolution
- Final Test Report

3.13 Software Testing Strategies

Software testing encompasses a rich spectrum of testing strategies. These include:

- Dynamic versus static testing,
- White (glass) box testing versus black box testing.

3.13.1 Static and Dynamic Testing

Two other terms used to describe how software is tested are static testing and dynamic testing. Static testing refers to testing something that's not running—examining and reviewing it. Dynamic testing is what you would normally think of as testing—running and using the software.

The best analogy for these terms is the process you go through when checking out a used car. Kicking the tyres, checking the paint, and looking under the hood are static testing techniques. Starting it up, listening to the engine, and driving down the road are dynamic testing techniques.

3.13.2 White (glass) Box Testing versus Black Box Testing

In white-box testing (sometimes called clear-box testing), the software tester has access to the program's code and can examine it for clues to help him with his testing—he can see inside the box. Based on what he sees, the tester may determine that certain numbers are more or less likely to fail and can tailor his testing based on that information.

With black-box testing, the software tester doesn't know the details of how the software works.

Think about the Windows Calculator. If you type 3.14159 and press the sqrt button, you get 1.772453102341. With black-box testing, it doesn't matter what gyrations the software goes through to compute the square root of pi. It just does it. As a software tester, you can verify the result on another "certified" calculator and determine if the Windows Calculator is functioning correctly.

There is a risk to white-box testing. It's very easy to become biased and fail to objectively test the software because you might tailor the tests to match the code's operation.

Glass and black box testing are just instances of the fundamental classes of approaches to software testing. Dynamic testing is sometimes called software testing or simply dynamic analysis. Dynamic analysis requires that software be executed with test data. It relies on the use of probes inserted into a program. A probe is a statement inserted into a program. Probes can either be a simple output statement to track the values of variables during program execution or a probe makes calls to analysis routines that keep track of the number of times elements of a program are executed. The key objective of dynamic analysis is to experiment with the behavior of the software in order to detect errors. As stated by Myers (1976) "testing is the process of executing a program with the intent of finding errors". As the error detection is a main thrust of software testing, it triggers interest in developing adequate test data sets (test sets) so that they sensitize (activate) errors. Similarly, one has to allocate a certain amount of time (testing time) to complete testing, especially in large software systems and develop different testing strategies which tend to implement a sound trade-off between coverage of testing and amount of time allocated to testing.

3.13.3 Functional Prototypes

This is one of the most useful methods for making sure the programmer understands just what a program is intended to do. A functional prototype is a very limited version of the final program which gives some idea of the appearance of the final product, but with a lot of functions missing. Displaying a simple storyboard to a client or bug tester is necessary, as they will be able to comment on whether the "expected input" takes the "observed output" resulting from running the program. This will also force the programmer to think through many of the details of what the program is meant to do.

3.13.4 Test Sets

Creating workable and effective sets of tests is intellectually challenging. Testing can almost never be exhaustive, and it may even be possible that not all programming flaws are evaluated even after very stringent testing has been covered. In the real "commercial" world, a significant source of program defects is created by people running tests and not checking the results carefully; the programmers run the tests, but do not take enough care in reviewing the results to see that the tests showed unexpected flaws in the programs.

Tests must be convincing, and must demonstrate a successful performance of the program. In a commercial setting, there are many methodologies used to produce a set of tests. One of the necessary tests that should be first evaluated covers the main function of the program. The programmer must decide on a set of tests that enable him/her to see if the code achieves its desired outcome.

All conditions of the program need to be thoroughly checked, including:

- case, loop, and if/then/else structures
- boundary conditions (e.g., with **`"IF $i<100 THEN ... "`**, make sure that 99, 100, and 101 values for $i are properly dealt with)
- exercises of all parts of the code (by designing a rigorous set of tests)

Naturally, sets of tests will assess the same parts of the program repeatedly. Known as "equivalence partitioning" for tests, it may seem like duplication, but it is standard economical testing. Perhaps part of the code works in one scenario, but not another—this needs to be carefully checked. The first thing a programmer needs to understand is that testing will demonstrate the presence of bugs, but it will not demonstrate the absence of bugs. Semantic errors fall into this category—that is, errors in the logic of the program, that the compiler or interpreter is unable to help you with.

Testings falls into two broad categories:

- Defect testing
- Acceptance testing

3.13.5 Regression (Defect) Testing

This type of test tries to detect all the defects the program may have. All parts of the program should be tested, and if the programmer feels that one part of the code may not properly deal with unexpected input, more rigorous tests should be performed on that area of the code. One key point to remember in this is that nobody knows a program better than the programmer himself. The programmer will know the area of the program that is most likely defective, so a designed set of tests on that area should be practiced before a Beta release is produced.

Regression testing stems from defect testing, and is the process of testing changes within the programming environment to make sure the older program still works with the new implemented changes. Regression testing is a normal part of the program development process and, in the commercial world, is performed by code testing specialists. Test department coders develop code test scenarios and exercises that will test new units of code after they have been written. These test cases form what becomes the test bucket. Before a new version of a software product is released, the old test cases are run against the new version to make sure all the old capabilities still work. The reason they might not work is that changing or adding new code to a program can easily introduce errors into code that was not supposed to be changed, and thus will obscure test results. Recursive regression testing is a must.

3.13.6 Acceptance Testing

Acceptance testing is done in conjunction with defect testing, and runs an agreed set of sets with an agreed output. These should demonstrate that the code does an agreed task well enough for the programmer and client to be satisfied. In the commercial world, acceptance tests are part of the contract for defining what the customer insists on before money ever changes hands.

3.13.7 Structural Prototyping

Prototyping of this nature is relatively simple. Structural prototyping is a stripped-down version of a program that shows a structure, in skeleton form, of the complete version. All major aspects of the code are written, but routines and sub-programs are written only as stubs, comments/statements within the program that show the programmer that the actual routine has been called or executed.

Maintaining effective code that is easily interpreted by the programmer and other developers (and allows further extensions to be added easily) requires three code characteristics:

- Understandability
- Adaptability
- Cohesion

Understandability means that programs that are easier to understand are considered to be better designed than ones that do the same task but are harder to understand. A key to developing stable code is a good functional prototype that allows the general idea of the program to be observed before code writing takes place. It may also be necessary to note that better code is clear and neatly presented, spaced out where necessary with comments to let the reader understand what is going on.

Adaptability refers to how easy it is to modify areas of the code to perform alternate tasks. This is directly linked to understandability. The more understandable the code, the easier it is to adapt.

Cohesion refers to a routine or sub-program that does one clear task which is apparent to the reader and programmer. A well-defined task should give a clear indication of what the program is intended to do; this includes well-chosen names for variables, constants, headers, etc. As small as this concept may seem, it allows any coder to pick up the source and quickly scan through and understand what the program is about.

3.14 Signs to Observe

Whether you are checking the source for bugs or testing the executable for flaws, all of the above tests need to be considered and exercised. It's most common that bugs present themselves in boundary structure conditions. When designing a set of tests, it cannot be stressed enough that boundaries need to be checked on both sides of their "walls". Other flaws that should be checked before releasing a beta include the malpractice of dealing with format control bugs such as %s. The programmer must employ capable input routines/parameters to correctly deal with user-supplied input, ensuring that all possible scenarios have been considered before adopting the most suitable code to perform the given command.

This includes identifiers themselves, avoiding use of getenv(), strcpy(), and sprint() wherever possible in exchange for more secure methods like strncpy() or snprintf(); the "n" refers to the number of bytes allowed to be copied to a buffer. Avoid common mistakes often used by sloppy programmers to get user-supplied environment variables from the terminal or environment. Establish your own method of setting or checking the environment, and make it insusceptible to malformed data that could lead to unexpected outcomes such as spawning a shell—a definite security risk, and one that is often observed in many UNIX environments. (Early ZGV [a console graphics viewer] releases were always victim to getenv ('HOME') problems.)

Another way to use acceptance testing to expose flaws is to use the proper data set meant to be sent to the program, but to send extensive data to a particular input command, such as sending 1024 bytes to a 512-byte buffer, causing an overflow.

Sometimes, when a program appears to have decreased its efficiency in terms of speed or processing of the data, it may be directly linked to a heap or stack overflow caused by corrupt data being entered. At this stage, vital tests need to be conducted by the bug tester.

Let's take a real life example of a program that I exposed with a flaw not long ago, the WinSMTPD mailer/pop3d daemon, versions 1.06f and 2.X.

After acceptance testing this program, everything worked well. All the desired tasks of the program were fulfilled, and the smptd and pop3d servers performed their tasks efficiently.

Now, here is where defect testing came into play:

To start an SMTP transaction, the client needs to send a "**HELO %s**" call, where the format string "%s" is your hostname. WinSTMPD only allowed a fixed buffer of 170 bytes before the expected output became unexpected. When I sent 150 bytes after the HELO field, the program noticeably paused before proceeding to function as normal. That told me that one of two things had happened:

- It had been poorly coded in terms of speed, OR
- It didn't deal with boundary tests, with excessive data being entered.

As it turned out, WinSTMPD was vulnerable to a stack overflow. By sending 170+ bytes to the HELO field, I got:

```
WINSMTP caused a general protection fault
in module WINSMTP.EXE at 0003:00002359.
Registers:
EAX=461e0001 CS=42e7 EIP=00002359 EFLGS=00000246
EBX=00807fe0 SS=4207 ESP=00007e36 EBP=00004141
ECX=00010283 DS=4207 ESI=0000544c FS=05c7
EDX=58600000 ES=461e EDI=00001547 GS=0000
Bytes at CS:EIP:
cb 49 73 49 63 6f 6e 69 63 00 00 58 4c 6f 63 00
Stack dump:
41414141 41414141 41414141 41414141 41414141 41414141
41414141 41414141 41414141 41414141 41414141 41414141
41414141 41414141 41414141 41414141
```

Obviously, this isn't what the programmer had in mind when performing an SMTP transaction. The 41414141 that appears on the stack is "A" binary value, which I had filled the buffer with. From this general protection fault, we as bug testers and programmers are able to ascertain that this 16-bit program (judged by the leading 0s within the memory registers) has successfully overwritten the EBP register (+4 bytes for EIP), and as ethical programmers/bug testers, that's all we need to know to fix this bug. If there were, say, an unethical cracker out there, loading up the stack with malicious data could allow arbitrary code to be executed from the stack, and anything is possible from there. This is why it is important to test for bugs, and especially to check the boundaries and the data that is allowed to be sent by the client/user.

Data sets and tests computed to the program/system are effectively system calls executed by active processes. These include different kinds of programs (e.g., programs that run as daemons and those that do not), programs that vary widely in their size and complexity, and programs with different purposes. Spawns or fork()s by applications are tested when the maximum process limit is exhausted by various resource-depleting exploits; this too needs to be prepared for when making a heavily-used program. Normal computed data can be "synthetic" or "live". Synthetic traces are collected in production environments by running a prepared script, often called a driver program. The program options are chosen solely for the purpose of exercising the program (acceptance testing), not to meet any real user's requests. Live normal data traces of programs are computed during normal usage of a production computer system (manual specificities of code testing and boundary testing). Both methods are often put to test when processing en masse software applications.

3.15 Organising for the Testing

Test management is also concerned with both test resource and test environment management.

Key elements of test management include:

(1) Test organisation : The set-up and management of a suitable test organisational structure and explicit role definition. The project framework under which the testing activities will be carried out is reviewed, high level test phase plans prepared and resource schedules considered. Test organisation also involves the determination of configuration standards and the definition of the test environment.

(2) Test planning : The requirements definition and design specifications facilitate in the identification of major test items and these may necessitate the test strategy to be updated. A detailed test plan and schedule is prepared with key test responsibilities being indicated.

(3) Test specifications : Required for all levels of testing and covering all categories of test. The required outcome of each test must be known before the test is attempted.

(4) Unit, integration and system testing : Configuration items are verified against the appropriate specifications and in accordance with the test plan. The test environment should also be under configuration control and test data and results stored for future evaluation.

(5) Test monitoring and assessment : Ongoing monitoring and assessment of the integrity of the development and construction. The status of the configuration items should be reviewed against the phase plans and test progress reports prepared providing some assurance of the verification and validation activities.

(6) Product assurance : The decision to negotiate the acceptance testing programme and the release and commissioning of the service product is subject to the 'product assurance' role being satisfied with the outcome of the verification activities. Product assurance may oversee some of the test activity and may participate in process reviews.

A common criticism of construction programmes is that insufficient time is frequently allocated to the testing and commissioning of the building systems together with the involvement and subsequent training of the Facilities Management team. Testing and commissioning is often considered by teams as a secondary activity and given a lower priority particularly as pressure builds on the programme towards completion.

Sufficient time must be dedicated to testing and commissioning as ensuring the systems function correctly is fairly fundamental to the project's success or failure. Traditionally the responsibility for testing and commissioning is buried deep within the supply chain as a sub-contract of a sub-contract. It is possible to gain greater control of this process and the associated risk through the use of specialists such as Systems Integration who can be appointed as part of the professional team.

The time necessary for testing and commissioning will vary from project to project depending upon the complexity of the systems and services that have been installed. The Project Sponsor should ensure that the professional team and the contractor consider realistically how much time is needed.

If a testing activity is going to be instituted, some appropriate questions are:

- When should the program-testing methodology be applied?
- How should the testing group be organized?
- How much effort should be applied to the testing activity?
- What outcomes can be expected from the testing group?

Some answers to these and related questions are given in the paragraphs below.

3.15.1 Recommended Time for Testing

As already indicated, program testing is an activity that requires that the computer software be relatively stable. Testing as discussed here is a post-development process, or it could be interpreted as an "acceptance test" process. A software system can be considered reasonably stable:

- When the structure of the system is well determined, that is, all of the major sub-systems and most of the modules are defined at the time of first release of a working prototype.

It is important to delay the formal testing process until after the program is debugged because too many changes tend to complicate things by shifting the burden of testing to one of retesting. Most typical applications of software-testing technology advocate testing at least at the following three levels (or stages) of software development:

- After individual modules have been completed and thoroughly tested by their programmers (unit testing).
- During integration of individual modules into sub-systems or during integration of sub-systems into the final system (development testing).
- During final integration (hardware/software integration) (system testing).

A tradeoff exists between the onset of formal testing and the quality ultimately achieved, although this relationship is not yet thoroughly documented. It appears necessary to plan for program testing fairly early in the software development process. By doing so the software engineer is thereby assured of a sufficiently good set of test cases with which to begin formal testing. Most of the time, programmers devise tests that exercise the working features of the program, rather than tests that identify errors. Hence, the testing process must concentrate on those features that were not exercised previously.

Organizational Schemes. Precisely how the testing team is organized and how it fits into the software life cycle are important questions that need to be addressed early. As already suggested, current thinking advocates the beginning of formal test procedures immediately after module development. The question remains, however, whether the testing should be done by a programmer, by a separate group in the organization, by an independent group (either within the organization or outside), or by somebody else. Some of the factors to be investigated in choosing the organizational structure for the testing team are:

- To whom does the testing team report? If the test team reports to the ultimate buyer, then its independence is not in question. If software is supplied by a sub-contractor, then the testing team should report to the prime contractor. In general, it is important that the testing team have adequate freedom to ensure that it can deliver its report without interference.
- How is the budgeting done? Testing budgets could be set as a function of total system implementation costs or as a fixed percentage of staff time, or be based on the size of the software system (e.g., a fixed dollar amount of testing per statement).

3.16 Psychological View of Testing

Characteristics of good Software Test

Recapitulating all those deliberations of this chapter, we receive the following properties of a software test:

- it is destructive.
- it is a comparison of what is and what should be.
- its goal is to find faults.
- it cannot prove the absence of bugs.
- it cannot find all bugs.
- it is extremely influenced by psychology.
- a lot of self-control is necessary for it.
- it has to be repeatable and reproducible.
- it is hard to define its ending condition.

Positive and negative psychological view has a great impact on quality of software and software testing.

3.16.1 The Negative Side

As with many human-based methodologies, the overall effectiveness of program-testing activity can be influenced by the attitudes held about testing. The prevailing attitude, and one that should be resisted as much as possible, views testing in the following ways:

- Testing is a dirty business, involving cleaning up someone else's mess and not involving any of the "fun" of creating programs.

- Testing is unimaginative and lacks the sense of adventure and opportunity for self-expression ordinarily associated with software production.
- Testing is menial work and involves handling too many details.
- Testing is too difficult, because of the complexity of programs, the difficulty of the logic of programs, and deficiencies in technology.
- Testing is not important, is under-funded, and generally involves too much work in too little time.
- The tools associated with testing are primitive and difficult to use.
- The techniques of testing are not rigorous. Too much ad hoc thinking is required; there is too little systematic knowledge to rely upon; too often every new activity is another "special case"; and there are too few generally accepted principles with demonstrated value.
- Testing has a negative reward structure; finding mistakes requires a critic's mentality.

All of these factors, or any one of them in the extreme, can change a successful program testing activity into a fiasco.

3.16.2 The Positive Side

It is possible to make the following claims about the psychology of testing:

- Testing is a challenge because it is a complicated problem that requires significant creativity at all times and because it rewards discipline.
- Testing is significant because software creators will appreciate having their oversights discovered, because managers will then feel more confident in the product, and because program testers can take pride in the software.
- Testing is interesting because the technology is imperfectly understood (and therefore represents an opportunity for innovation), because insights gained can be used in developing automated tools, and because many different approaches will be valued.

This positive view, unfortunately, has been apparent only in a few instances. Fortunately, this situation is changing in many areas of the computing community.

How can it be determined if a test environment is appropriate?

This is a difficult question in that it typically involves tradeoffs between 'better' test environments and cost. The ultimate situation would be a collection of test environments that mimic exactly all possible hardware, software, network, data, and usage characteristics of the expected live environments in which the software will be used. For many software applications, this would involve a nearly infinite number of variations, and would clearly be impossible. And for new software applications, it may also be impossible to predict all the variations in environments in which the application will run. For very large, complex systems, duplication of a 'live' type of environment may be prohibitively expensive.

In reality judgements must be made as to which characteristics of a software application environment are important, and test environments can be selected on that basis after taking into account time, budget, and logistical constraints. Such judgements are preferably made by those who have the most appropriate technical knowledge and experience, along with an understanding of risks and constraints.

For smaller or low risk projects, an informal approach is common, but for larger or higher risk projects (in terms of money, property, or lives) a more formalized process involving multiple personnel and significant effort and expense may be appropriate.

In some situations it may be possible to mitigate the need for maintenance of large numbers of varied test environments. One approach might be to coordinate internal testing with beta testing efforts. Another possible mitigation approach is to provide built-in automated tests that run automatically upon installation of the application by end-users. These tests might then automatically report back information via the internet, about the application environment and problems encountered.

3.17 Software Testing Management Guidelines

Presented below are general guidelines on the size, difficulty, cost, and expected outcomes of a formal software testing activity. Naturally, such estimates must be used carefully. Estimates are based on experience in testing software written in a high level language.

3.17.1 Size of Testing Budget

A common way to express the size of the testing activity is as a percentage of the total software development costs. For High Level Language coded systems, experience suggests that budgets in the range of 25 to 45 per cent of the total development cost for the software are appropriate. Here, total development cost is intended to include all of those costs up to the time when the first release of the software is made. Naturally enough, the amount of effort devoted to the formal testing activity is a function of how critical the system is. The higher percentage figure is what appears to be minimally adequate for the highest-priority software system. Examples of systems that fall into this class are those that are man-rated and those that have a large production run (with value far exceeding the total software development cost). A second rule-of-thumb that has been found useful in the past is to provide insurance based on the expected cost of failure. For a product with an embedded computer, for example, it would be reasonable to allocate 5 to 10 per cent of the total cost to repair the first (set of?) software failure(s), in the field if necessary, solely with a well-organized search for errors through systematic testing. The attitude to have is that there are errors in the software and the only question is whether they are going to be found before or after issuance of the product. Note that this attitude allows for a product to be issued with a known error if the cost to repair it at the time it is found is too large (e.g., when the program is "burned" into ROM), or when the impact of it is judged too small to warrant changes until the "next model".

3.17.2 Size of the Testing Problem

It is possible to estimate the total difficulty of the testing activity for software systems written in an HLL from past experience in analyzing software. Naturally there is a rather wide variance in these properties, depending on both the kind of problem being solved and the style of programming. To appreciate the numbers, it is important to understand the precise meanings of some testing-related terminology:

(1) A statement in a program is either a declaration or an action statement, and may run to more than one line of text.

(2) A segment is a logically independent piece of program text that corresponds to the actions the program takes as the consequence of a program decision (including the

decision to make a subroutine invocation). Hence a program with no logic has one segment each; IF statement contributes two segments, and so forth.

(3) A test is one transfer of control to the software system (regardless of the part being examined) and the consequential actions the system takes. This corresponds (in effect) to a single subroutine invocation.

Note that a subroutine with no logical statements—the so-called straight-line program—has one segment consisting of all the statements of the program, and at least one test would be required. Coverage is measured (in the C1 measure) by the percentage of segments that are exercised at least once in aggregate, that is, over all of the tests run. Typical programs will have a number of segments approximately equal to between 5 and 25 per cent of the number of statements. (That is, each segment corresponds typically to about 5 to 20 statements.) A good "middle" figure is 10 per cent: Multiply the number of statements by 0.1 and you get the number of segments.

The number of tests required to achieve an 85 per cent C1 coverage level also tends to be a constant. For typical HLL-coded programs, each test exercises between 5 and 50 statements. This figure should not be misinterpreted; achieving 85 per cent C1 coverage may involve some tests that exercise only a few statements and others that exercise as much as 50 per cent of the program.

The 85 per cent C1 coverage figure was chosen because it represents a reasonably attainable goal in practice with a large software system. It is important to appreciate that, in most cases, bringing the figure to 100 per cent, if it is possible at all, would increase the number of tests required substantially.

3.17.3 The Results of Testing

The most important questions is, given 85 per cent coverage of segments in a complex HLL-coded program, what is the likelihood of finding errors of varying severity? It is difficult to quote a precise figure, since the number of errors found is a function of the skill of the program testing team, the quality of the software (or lack of it), and the amount of prior testing that has been performed. For a typical situation in which software has been fully unit-tested by the programmers, but which has not been systematically tested by a separate group, one can expect a latent defect count (see below) at a rate of 0.5 to 5.0 per cent of the number of statements. This suggests that a 1000 statement program, when declared "finished" by the programmer, may have as many as 100 defects of varying levels of severity. Such defects fall into two classes: fatal and non-fatal defects. Approximately 15 to 20 per cent of the defects are fatal. The implication is that the total number of fatal errors is as much as 1 per cent of the total number of statements. (This may or may not be a comforting fact, depending on one's point of view.)

3.17.4 System Test

A set of finished, debugged tests can be used in the next phase of the waterfall test process, system test. The purpose of system testing is to ensure that the software does what the customer expects it to do. There are two main types of system tests: function tests and performance tests.

Functional testing requires no knowledge of the internal workings of the software, but it does require knowledge of the system's functional requirements. It consists of a set of tests that determines if the system does what it is supposed to do from the user's perspective.

Once the basic functionality of a system is ensured, testing can turn to how well the system performs its functions. Performance testing consists of such things as stress tests, volume tests, timing tests, and recovery tests. Reliability, availability, and maintenance testing may also be included in performance testing.

In addition to function and performance tests, there are a variety of additional tests that may need to be performed during the system test phase; these include security tests, installability tests, compatibility tests, usability tests, and upgrade tests.

3.18 Types of Testing Methods

The following definitions have been derived from BS 7925-1 British Computer Society Specialist Interest Group in Software Testing (BCS SIGIST).

3.18.1 Acceptance Testing

A kind of Formal testing conducted to enable a user, customer or other authorized entity to determine whether to accept a system or component. Acceptance testing is high up on the V model, a counterpart to the requirements specification process. There are two types: Business Acceptance and User Acceptance. Historically this element of testing comes at the end of the development lifecycle. However, with an understanding of risk, it is apparent that closer and more timely appreciation is needed.

Acceptance Test

When system testing is completed, the product can be sent to users for acceptance testing. If the users are internal to the company, the testing is usually called alpha testing. If the users are customers who are willing to work with the product before it is finished, the testing is beta testing. Both alpha and beta tests are a form of pilot tests in which the system is installed on an experimental basis for the purpose of finding bugs.

Another form of acceptance test is a benchmark test in which the customer runs a predefined set of test cases that represent typical conditions under which the system is expected to perform when placed into service. The benchmark test may consist of test cases that are written and debugged by your test organization, but which the customer has reviewed and approved. When pilot and benchmark testing is complete, the customer should tell you which requirements are not satisfied or need to be changed in order to proceed to final testing.

The final type of acceptance test is the installation test, which involves installing a completed version of the product at user sites for the purpose of obtaining customer agreement that the product meets all requirements and is ready for delivery.

Maintenance

Maintenance of a product is an often challenging task for the development team and the test team. Maintenance for the developer consists of fixing bugs that are found during customer operation and adding enhancements to product functionality to meet evolving customer requirements. For the test organization, maintenance means verifying bug fixes, testing enhanced functionality, and running regression tests on new releases of the product to ensure that previously working functionality has not been broken by the new changes.

Even though the acceptance test and maintenance activities are important, they will not be discussed in detail in this book. The basic principles of regression testing and bug verification apply well to these phases of the life cycle. For a detailed treatment of software maintenance from a testing perspective, Lewis (2000) offers a great deal of information.

3.18.2 Ad hoc Testing

It is carried out using no recognised test case design technique closely linked to Error Guessing. However, the phrase ad hoc has connotations of being much more on whim of the tester.

Certainly in exploratory testing there is a need for ad hoc measures. It is in exploratory testing that a tester can get "a feel" for the application, without the confines of a strict testing regime.

3.18.3 Alpha Testing

Simulated or actual operational testing at an in-house site not otherwise involved with the software developers.

Alpha testing is typically done for two reasons:

(1) to give confidence that the software is in a suitable state to be seen by customers (but not necessarily released).

(2) to find bugs that may only be found under operational conditions. Any other major defects or performance issues should have been discovered by this stage.

Historically, companies may have gone through many cycles of Alpha testing. However as development life cycles have decreased, these have decreased. Also the timing has been pushed much closer to the release date.

A subtle distinction can be made between alpha testing, its sibling beta testing and acceptance testing. Alpha/Beta testing can be seen as "does the software work", whereas acceptance testing is more for the customer to say, "are we willing to pay for the software?" Alpha testing is high up on the V model, mapping against the requirements process function.

Ideally, Alpha testing should be conducted with as much independence as possible from Development and the personnel that did the system or other forms of testing up to that point. Independence can bring a fresh view point to the party. "Workarounds" used in system testing can become cast in stone if the root cause of the problem is not dealt with. In the worse case, the software can be released, without the workaround, so all the user sees is a defect.

However, in the real world, not many organisations have the resources for an independent system test and an independent Alpha test team. Consequently testers have to wear both hats. An alternative is to co-opt personnel closer to the customer, such as consultants and implementors to do the testing.

Due to its very nature of testing an entire system, Alpha testing traditionally occurred very late in the cycle. Depending on the development model used, the "when" can happen at different points.

In the traditional Waterfall model Alpha testing took place very late in the project. Unfortunately in many cases, time for testing is squeezed very tightly at the end of the development. Thus compromises in the quality of testing are made.

In the iterative model, particularly the RUP, a large emphasis is placed on risk mitigation and constant builds, followed by Smoke testing. At all times the implementors, consultants and customers can be seen as stakeholders. For instance at the end of the elaboration phase, it should be demonstrable that the core architecture of the system is stable and performs as expected. Thus, during the transition period the stakeholders will have seen the software numerous times and there should not be too many surprises when the software is shown in the Alpha form. Indeed in the RUP Alpha testing has a far lower priority than achieving life cycle milestones.

Alpha testing is usually undertaken at the developing organisations site. Both manual and automated techniques can be used for Alpha testing. Performance testing especially can be automated. Testing types that can be used included documentation, installability and operational testing. A large degree of regression testing should also occur, especially on high risk areas of the system.

3.18.4 Beta Testing

Beta testing is an Operational testing at a site not otherwise involved with the software developers. Having a close relation to Alpha Testing, Beta is also very high up on the V Model diagram, mapping against the Requirement specification.

The positioning, however, is closer to market than that of Alpha Testing due to the increased independence of the testers. The reasons are however the same:

(1) to give confidence that the software is in a suitable state to be seen by customers (but not necessarily released).

(2) to find bugs that may only be found under operational conditions. Any other major defects or performance issues should have been discovered by this stage.

The distinction between Alpha/Beta/Released software has become blurred in recent years. A certain Seattle base company has as very extensive Beta testing programme for all of its products. Some malicious people have even suggested that the first release of any product by this company is really a Beta version and that the last stages of testing is actually done by users.

Implementors and consultants from the developing organisation, customers, end users and interested technical people in general are all candidates to be Beta Testers. How the testers are selected depends/should depend on the software and the environment into which it is to be released. For example if the project is a very large system for a government department, then the beta testers are/should be drawn from the team implementing the system and experienced end-users. Conversely, a mass market graphics product may be tested by many hundreds of artists, drawn from a panel.

Usually, beta testing takes place on the customer site. In the case of large-scale market products, software can be sent out on CD or downloaded. For a product like Office it would be impossible to test every new piece of functionality against all possible test environments, let alone regression test. Thus only by many users using the software in a real world setting are obscure defects found.

Testing should take place once the developing organisation is happy that the required amount of risk has been mitigated. In real terms, this means the software will not crash and only small defects are left to be found. Defects which found in system testing that were considered too minor or not cost effective to fix may still be present in the beta release.

In the real world commercial pressures will often determine the beta release. For example if a release date has been sent to the press, embarassment will ensue if it slips. Thus beta testing may start before the software is ready.

Even at this late stage in the process, functionality delivered in the beta release may not be what is in the final product. However, if major modifications are needed, then something has gone seriously wrong with that organisations development processes.

The organisation generates a build of the software, with the production standards of a released product. Ideally the software should be packaged with the documentation and other artifacts, that are also to be delivered. Installation documentation and the basic operational documentation is especially important in this respect.

3.18.5 Black-Box Testing

The essence of black-box testing is that the software is exercised by the tester with no reference to the internal workings of the component. This means that it is further defined by the kind of tests that can be planned. Typical test techniques for black-box testing include boundary value analysis and equivalence partitioning. Other black-box techniques include *State Transition Testing, Cause-Effect Graphing* and *Syntax Testing.*

Once all the carefully planned tests have been completed, one can indulge in some Error Guessing. This is in addition to the functional and structural testing and is based on the testers knowledge and experience of the system, to identify errors.

Test design specification and test case specification are prescribed in IEEE829:1998 Standard for Software Test Documentation. IEEE829 is an attempt to date collate together all the various test documentation and standardise them.

Test Design Specification is written to show which test cases are to be included in the test case suite. The Test Case Specification is at the individual case level. The document details how a particular case will test a requirement. Note a requirement may be tested by more than one test case. Conversely, a test case may cover more than one requirement.

Of course, the need for such documentation is not universally accepted. For instance, companies implementing the Rational Unified Process (RUP) might decide that this level of ceremony is not necessary in their development cycle. If they do decide it is necessary, it might grow as development passes through the phases, inception or construction. However if they are following the Rational prescriptions they are likely to be using Unified Modelling Language (UML).

There are two reasons for Black-box testing. Firstly, for the documentatary process. Thus anyone can see what is to be tested and after the event it can be used for auditing purposes. This might be the case in safety critical software or that requires regulatory approval. An example is medical monitoring software.

Secondly, for the focus it brings to the test process. Many test phases miss this stage out, or do not follow through thoroughly on the documentation. However, they run the risk of missing important test cases or not testing requirements.

A negative aspect is that it takes a large amount of time. Additionally the amount of documentation can seem onerous and overboard. Thus in many test programmes, people just start writing tests without forethought.

In an *ideal world* the test case specification documents would be drawn up by a team of test analysts. A senior analyst would draw up the Test Design Specification. These would then be seamlessly passed on to a team of test engineers and test technicians to actually execute the test suite.

In the *real world*, the roles of test analyst and test engineer are just rolled into one. An individual tester will often decide which tests to run, against which requirements (if the organisation maps tests back to requirements). He or she will then proceed to execute the tests themselves.

Black box testing can be used within the development team and at their offices. However if the organisation is using the RUP or an agile methodology they might draw these up (if they do at all) in conjunction with the customer or other stakeholders, at their own site.

In a traditional waterfall cycle the specifications would be drawn up as the development was taking place. Ready for the test phase at the end of the development cycle. Now that the waterfall is out of fashion, this is seen as a high risk strategy.

The worst case scenario (quite common) is that the documents are drawn up, using an expensive process. They are then left to gather dust. As the project continues, changes are made to the requirements, but the test spec's are ignored.

The Test Design spec should have in the document, which features to be tested and success/fail criteria. Criteria for determining input values for tests are laid out. The input values themselves are not detailed.

For a test specification, the following are needed:

- input values and existing data.
- the predicted outcome and any change in the state of the software.
- any special procedures.

The documents need to be up-to-date, so that they mirror the requirements. Thus everyone can see what is to be tested and how, at any given time. Finally there has to be a mechanism for the beta testers to log incidents or defects.

3.18.6 Installability Testing

There are two related areas: Documentation testing and Conversion testing.

Installability to me, means ensuring that everything the customer does, runs smoothly. This runs from taking delivery of the code and other artifacts through to the end-users being able to log on.

Experts believe that Installability testing should be done with as much independence as possible. Additionally the testers should be as close as possible to the customer. Ideally I would want someone from support or an implementor to test. Otherwise, if independence from development is lost, work arounds and inside knowledge will not expose bugs. Customers may even take part, if they are in a beta testing programme, usually at the developers site. However, it might even be done outside by the customers site.

Although Installability probably is fairly high up on the V Model, this does not mean that testing has to start late in the life cycle. As soon as the organisation is able, it should be reviewing or inspecting the documentation that is to be sent with the product. This might include installation guides, manuals and deliverables. Typos and other simple faults will be trapped by this process.

The install shield procedures and other processes (such as unpacking a .tar file) can be tested long before release. If the installation is considered to be high risk the central processes might be tested early on in the cycle.

Both manual and automated testing can be conducted. The more mundane and repeatable elements of the process are candidates for automation. Manual testers can then concentrate on the more complex elements.

As with all testing, expected outcomes should be compared with the actual outcome. The expected outcome should be derived from a requirement. Ideally this would be explicitly declared. In many cases they are only implied.

Each test case should have the following:

- The start/entry state
- The requirement which is to be tested
- Actions and inputs
- The expected outcome

The test case outlined above is very concise. However if many organisations are beta-testing, then many more scenarios, not necesarrily specified will be tested. An important issue is that of complexity of the environments into which the software is to be installed.

For example, compare a specialist piece of medical software and a release of office. The medical software, will likely be installed into an environment that is highly regulated and controlled. Other elements to which it will connect will also have been rigourously tested. Requirements will probably have been tightly controlled. Thus the developing organisation, can with reasonable confidence use the above methodology to test installability. In addition, they know it will be tested by the medical authorities to make sure it is safe.

Microsoft on the other hand, cannot be sure into which environment, business users will install Office. Home users, installing the shrink wrapped product create an infinite range of environments, even if they have good housekeeping on their PCs. So whilst Microsoft can test against the most common environments and lay down requirements, it must be nigh or impossible to cover more than the surface, with the methodology shown above. (Not that I am sticking up for them, you understand.)

3.18.7 Integration Testing

Testing performed to expose faults in the interfaces and in the interaction between integrated components. The above definition only refers to "integrated components". This is known as "integrtion testing in the small". Thus checking that widget A, when integrated with widget B generates a bleep, after a given input, constitutes integration testing. "Integration testing in the large" refers to the whole systems being joined. For example checking that a Payroll system interacts as required with the Human Resources system.

Integration testing connects with many other designs and techniques. Including Black Box Testing, Alpha and Beta Testing.

Purpose

There are three main reasons to conduct Integrated testing:

(1) To find faults that could not have been found in the component testing because they only become apparent when components are integrated. (Rather they should only be found at integration.)

(2) To generate credible information about the software under test, so that technical and business decisions can be made.

(3) Confirm that as the system grows risk of failure is being diminished.

As integration testing covers such a broad length of the V model, it is not surprising that a large range of people should be conducting it. From the developer who joins 2 widgets together to make a tiny sub-system, to the systems integrator who has to join the systems up on the customer site. Almost all integration will take place at the developing organisation's site.

Once the components or sub-systems, to be integrated have themselves been fully component tested if any are not ready to be integrated, this is not necessarily a problem as their functionality can be simulated.

Integration testing can either be conducted incrementally or non-incrementally. The non-incremental approach is also known as "big-bang" testing. This approach is very unfashionable due to the level of risk that one takes in hoping that the system will perform as expected.

Incrementally, testing can be split into top-down testing and bottom-up testing. Middle-out is another variation.

In top-down testing, higher level modules are tested. If lower modules required to make-up the system are not yet available then, stubs are used to simulate their activity.

Conversely, Bottom-up testing tests the lower levels first. If the higher level modules required to make up the system are not yet available then drivers are used to simulate their activity.

It is a testing method that can be undertaken on the now integrated system are both functional and non-functional.

3.18.8 Interface Testing

Integration testing is where the interfaces between system components are tested. Integration of "components" can take place at many stages of the life cycle. The process can be "in the small" or "in the large". The size refers to component. In the small means integration of the smallest components, to make sub-assemblies. At the other extreme, in the large, is the integration of entire systems. BS 7925-1 however, seems only to concentrate on the smaller of the two. Interface testing is primarily interested in the interaction between two or more components.

3.18.9 Load Testing

In load testing the software under test in subjected to various levels of "load", to test its behaviour. Load testing is not defined in BS7925-1. It can mean different things depending on to whom you are speaking. It is most definitely a non-functional test. The aspect of behaviour that concerned is that of performance.

The testing has to be conducted within a structured framework otherwise its results are open to question.

Various elements need to be considered before engaging in Load Testing. Planning Load Testing is like any other activity. Good quality is the result of planning and foresight, enabling the test to be ran over and over again.

Objectives: What do we hope to achieve? This question has to be answered in relation to the specified requirements of the Software Under Test (SUT). The tester needs to know how the SUT (a) should behave under, (b) a given load.

For example for a large site it may be accepted as a business risk that the SUT will run slower at high loads. However, this needs confirming, otherwise the business runs the risk of the SUT due to underestimating the effect of higher loads.

Which aspect of the system is to bear the specified load? The answer ranges from a single component to a Web Services system made up of many third party applications. As the SUT becomes larger, it becomes more complex. Consequently, the load testing suite becomes more complex.

For example, it is decided a website checkout facililty needs testing. This can be tested in isolation as a component or as part of the system. If it can only be tested once the integration has taken place and a fault occurs, was the problem with the cart or somewhere else in the system.

Iterative development styles suit load testing, as they successively build up a full system. The RUP with its inception etc. phases, gives many opportunities. During the Inception and Elaboration phases the core architecture can be assessed. In construction smaller components can be tested as they added incrementally and then as an integrated whole system.

The Sequential or Waterfall method is less suited, due to its single big-bang approach to integration. Thus after months or even years of development, can the system as a whole be load tested. The problem is that it is difficult to establish what you are testing and the causes of failure.

How is the load on the SUT to be generated? Multiple users or a small number of users generating large numbers of transactions? The important factor is to replicate the situation the SUT will meet in the real world. For example a bank system, processing payments will have one user processing a lot of data. Whereas a consumer website may have millions of users conducting one or two transactions a day.

Should the data be increased as the test progresses, or at a steady sustained level for a long period?

Should the load be of a single type or multiple? For example in our checkout example; a certain percentage of the transactions should be of the user dropping out of the transaction. Again this mirrors the real world.

Testers looking at load testing may want to consider using Monte Carlo simulations. Here data is randomly generated according to a set of rules, i.e. we do not know which transaction is coming next, but it has a 1 in 5 chance of being a dropout from the checkout.

An important point, often overlooked is that the load may spike. Advertising may make the SUT suddenly very attractive to users. The classic example of failure to realise this, was the Victoria's Secrets affair. Here a fashion show of lingerie, during the half time break in the Super Bowl was heavily promoted. Consequently millions of Americans logged on, and lo and behold the servers crashed under the strain.

Expected Outcomes: The tester has to be aware of what to expect. Should this not be the case, then raise it with the analyst. Just because load testing is non-functional, we still need to know what to expect.

Logging: As the test progresses we need to know what exactly (a) the load being applied and (b) the behaviour exhibited. This has two benefits, firstly we can keep track of any deterioration of performance as the load increases.

Tools: Due to the large amount of transactions, many Load Testing can only realistically be undertaken with Computer Aided Software Tools (CAST). Load Runner and Rational Robot are the front runners for this type of testing.

3.18.10 Top-down Testing

An approach to integration testing where the component at the top of the component hierarchy is tested first, with lower level components being simulated by stubs. Tested components are then used to test lower level components. The process is repeated until the lowest level components have been tested.

3.18.11 Bottom-up Testing

An approach to integration testing where the lowest level components are tested first, then used to facilitate the testing of higher level components. The process is repeated until the component at the top of the hierarchy is tested.

3.18.12 Systematic Testing

Under the term systematic testing all testing activities will be subsumed that examine the behaviour of software under specific conditions with particular results expected. Whereas the objectives behind scenario testing ask for the integration of users into the testing exercise, systematic tests can be performed solely by software engineers and/or user representatives. There are three objectives that are particularly relevant for user-oriented testing, which are discussed in the following.

3.18.13 Task-oriented Testing

Task-oriented testing is performed to examine whether a piece of software actually fulfils pre-defined tasks. These tasks may either be stated in the requirements specification document, as in software development projects, or may be implied by third parties as, for instance, in consumer reports. The primary quality characteristic under investigation in task-oriented testing is functionality. The testing environment is normally the working place of the evaluator and is in principle not relevant to the interpretation of results. Task-oriented testing can be carried out during the software development process at any stage of the software life-cycle as well as with any off-the-shelf software product. The costs of task-oriented testing are comparatively small and the investment in man/hours depends on the number of tasks tested. Apart from the technical environment of the evaluator (hardware and software) no extra investment in testing equipment or instruments is normally necessary.

3.18.14 Menu-oriented Testing

Menu-oriented testing is carried out to test each program feature or function in sequence. It is prominent in many glass and black box testing techniques. The software is examined in great detail; the evaluator follows every possible path of program execution, considering each individual function as it is sequentially offered in the menu bar. Thus, while in both scenario and task-oriented testing only those functions that are necessary to perform the test tasks are performed, in menu-oriented testing each function of the software is executed at least once. As with task-oriented testing, menu-oriented testing can be performed at any stage of the software life cycle as well as with off-the-shelf products. The costs of menu-oriented testing mainly lie in the recruitment of excellent evaluation personnel, who are capable of the ad hoc generation of metrics and data.

3.18.15 Benchmark Testing

Benchmark testing examines the performance of systems. The notion of performance can be applied either to individual functions, to system modules or to the system as a whole. In the strict technical sense, a benchmark test is a measurement of system performance which cannot be affected by variables resulting from human involvement. Typical reporting instruments applied for benchmark tests are checklists that cover the quality characteristic, the benchmark, measurement technique and results. If a benchmark involves the execution of more than one function, it is useful to construct a standard way of calling the procedures for testing purposes.

3.18.16 Systematic Testing and Adequacy Evaluation

All of the types of systematic testing described here are potentially of interest in the context of adequacy evaluation. Task-oriented testing can indicate whether a product does in fact do what a user wants it to do. Menu-oriented testing can be used to ensure that little used, but perhaps nonetheless important, functionalities are not forgotten. Benchmark testing can be used to check whether a product meets a user's minimum requirements.

3.18.17 Performance Testing

Performance testing is the "testing conducted to evaluate the compliance of a system or component with specified performance requirements" [IEEE].

Performance testing is a sub-set of non-functional requirements testing. Other techniques that appear in this area include: conformance testing, conversion testing, documentation testing, penetration testing, recovery testing, serviceability testing, storage testing. However as with most things, one man's performance test is another man's stress test.

Test techniques include load testing and stress testing. The reason to include these as part of performance testing, is that they evaluate how the behaviour is modified at under various levels of usage.

To establish that the system or component under test will behave as we expect, under the conditions we expect. Note that we are not setting out to blindly "hammer" to system into submission or destruction. The end result should be that management can have confidence in the software. Additionally they will have enough information to base business related decisions on.

Performance testing is usually done within the developing organisation. Although, it may be contracted out to a specialist test lab or consultancy. Contracting out is popular due to the heavy investment required in tools and training.

In terms of testing roles, performance testing can be split. Typically this is split between a test analysis and test automation. Thus the test analyst will decide which tests are to be run. Test automators or engineers will actually create the scripts and configure the tools. In addition, more junior staff may act as technicians to execute them. Technicians are used because, once the test suite is written it can become a mundane task to automate them.

Performance testing is generally done at the developing site or a specialist facility. The timing of performance testing depends on the model or methodologies being used. In the case of the Waterfall, perfomance testing will take place at the very end of the development lifecycle. In the worst case scenario, imagine a system that has tested without fault in functional testing with a single user. When a load of 3 concurrent users is simulated, it crashes with due to continous data locks etc. Huge amounts of time are required to fix high profile defects, at or near release time.

In incremental testing, the system is built up by adding components or sub-systems one at a time. As each component is added, the system can be tested to see if it meets requirements. Of course, the individual components or sub-systems can be tested for performance by themselves.

In the case of the Rational Unified Process (RUP), performance may take place during the very earliest phase of Inception. It is Inception that the business risk is mitigated. Also one possible core architecture is put forward. Simple performance testing might be done to confirm that the architecture is suitable (in a very coarse grained manner). This would be the case for such systems generating large numbers of transactions.

Performance testing requires huge numbers of users, data and transactions. Such requirements mean that manual testing is unfeasible. Automated testing is really the only way to go. Of course there are many tools available on the market, for instance Loadrunner.

Types of tools include, data preparation, execution. They are generally known as Computer Aided Software Testing (CAST) Tools.

The difficulty with performance testing is replicating the real world environment, especially the randomness of individual events, whilst maintaining the predictability of the big picture. Various statistical methods are available to help in this process. Experts favourite is Monte Carlo scenario modelling. In a Monte Carlo simulation, they follow the rules of the casino. Thus if we shake a dice once, we do not know if it will be a 1 through to a 6. However if we roll it 6 million times, they will get a million ones, a million twos, etc.

3.18.18 Portability Testing

"Testing aimed at demonstrating the software can be ported to specified hardware or software platforms". Portability can be considered in the same group as compatibility testing, conversion testing, installability testing and recovery testing. This group of test techniques all occur at the top of the V model and are concerned with the system as a whole. On large projects, sub-systems may also be tested using these techniques.

Portability is definitely a black box technique as it is conducted without reference to the code level. The best definition of portability could be "A software unit is portable (exhibits portability) across a class of environments to the degree that the cost to transport and adapt it to a new environment in the class is less than the cost of redevelopment".

Our old friends *risk* and *complexity* appear again. The sheer range of potential environment, in which we expect software to operate can be bewildering. Even bespoke software that is to run only on Windows, will have to be tested against the various flavours, e.g. 2000 and XP. These can have radically different effects on the behaviour of software. Especially if the software utilises the Windows operating system functionality.

It is this portability that we are testing. Does the system behave as we want it to in these different environments?

Ideally, an independent team of system testers, will cover all the scenarios, across all environments that the software is expected to operate. In a highly regulated with tight controls on testing, this may be mandated. Examples may be the nuclear or aeronautical industries. Here the software will have to be tested to the *n*th degree in every environment in which it may operate.

However, this is not possible in many cases. A product such as Office is expected to operate with many different operating systems. Against this we have to combine in the different hardware. Thus the software is extensively tested in house. However due to the complexity of the software and the range of environments, extensive beta testing may be required, therefore the testers are in effect the users. In many cases, it is at this stage that faults are found.

Where: At the site of the developing organisation. However as described above, many portability derived faults will only appear under operational conditions in beta testing.

When: Even though portability testing is high up on the V-model, early consideration should be given to it. Decisions about which environments and hardware configurations will need to be made early on in the process. These decisions may have an effect on the central core architecture.

If the organisation is using the Rational Unified Process, (RUP®), they may decide to test portability (if considered an risk that has to be mitigated early), in the Inception or Elaboration phases. Thus they can see if the chosen central architecture is suitable, therefore mitigating a large element of risk.

How: Portability testing, as with virtually all other techniques requires two things:- requirements and predicted outcomes.

Requirements should state in which environments the software is designed to work in, and the behaviours they need to exhibit, whilst in each environment. Note that the behaviour may differ according to the environment. For example, it may appear different to the User depending on whether a PC or an Apple is displaying the user interface. Environmental details may include the operating system, type of hardware and database platforms.

The predicted outcome should be derived from the behaviour detailed in the specification for the environment in question.

3.18.19 Progressive Testing

"Progressive testing involves testing of new features after regression testing of previous features." [Beizer].

Why: Simply because if we are adding new features to our software, we need to make sure that their behaviour is as we expect. This is such an oxymoron, that most people would regard this as testing per se. Thus Progressive testing as a phrase, is heard much less than its opposite regression testing.

Who: As progressive testing is all pervasive, everyone sooner or later will become involved. Either as a developer conducting small scale component testing or the customer user acceptance testing.

Where: Again progressive testing will take place anywhere that the new features are to be exercised. This might be at the developers desk through to the customer site.

In an ideal world, I suppose that we would follow Beizer's definition. Thus we would make sure, that previously introduced features are still behaving properly, first. However in the real world, the temptation is to concentrate on the new stuff first. Regression testing is usually relegated to second place.

How: As shown above, progressive testing is buried so far into the software quality cycle, it is difficult to pinpoint particular techniques. Far better, then to point to particular techniques on which to build. In addition to the ones above, see incremental testing and intergration testing.

3.18.20 Recovery Testing

Testing aimed at verifying the system's ability to recover from varying degrees of failure.

3.18.21 Regression Testing

Retesting of a previously tested program following modification to ensure that faults have not been introduced or uncovered as a result of the changes made.

Requirements-based testing

It includes designing tests based on objectives derived from requirements for the software component (e.g., tests that exercise specific functions or probe the non-functional constraints such as performance or security).

If you read the rest of this site, or indeed any testing literature, requirements-based testing is axiomatic. I believe this because of the very nature of testing. We are ensuring that the software meets the needs of the people we have developed it for, i.e. the customer. The representation of the customers needs are captured in "requirements". It does not matter if those requirements turn out to be functional or non-functional, they still need to be tested.

When we look at the various other types of testing (for a full listing) we find that test cases are almost invariably involve requirements to a lesser or greater degree. So even if we state up front that we are going to use requirements based testing, we will pretty quickly drill down to say we are for instance, black box or stress testing.

Virtually everybody in the organisation needs to be involved if requirements testing is to be a success. Not just the testers. The project management needs to build a culture of accurately capturing requirements and ensuring they are met. Analysts have to be accurate in the capturing of requirements. Additionally they need to have an awareness of the risk and other issues related to individual or groups of requirements. If there are separate designers, then testability becomes an issue, which should be built in to the system, and act as a guide to the requirements.

The culture of testing against requirements, should also be pervasive, throughout the organisation. So every physical site which is involved in developing the software should be used to help the testing.

This test is needed throughout the whole length of the software development life cycle. No matter which model or framework is being used.

How: Successful development of software that is bug free (to a level satisfactory in a business sense), is dependant on good requirement capture and representation of those requirements. How that occurs is outside the scope of this article. However we as testers are reliant on them.

Analysis is then needed, to ensure that the risk associated with each requirement will be mitigated following the testing cycle.

An individual test case, I suggest, requires:

- The requirement to be satisfied
- The state of the software before any input data setup inputs predicted outcome.

3.18.22 Security Testing

"Security testing is for testing whether the system meets its specified security objectives." BS 7925-1 British Computer Society Specialist Interest Group in Software Testing (BCS SIGIST).

The latest fashionable technique is penetration testing, where the tester tries to simulate attempts to break system security as a real intruder would. In most cases security is a non-functional requirement. The exception of course is where the purpose of the software is security itself.

We all hope that unfriendly people or organisations will not be able to abuse our software or the data that is held or generated by it. Depending on the type of people or organisation our customers are, and the uses to which they are going to put the software should dictate the amount of security testing we do.

Three events, have put security testing into the spotlight:- September 11th, moving business online and large virus attacks. Notwithstanding the events mentioned every system will have some level of security requirement, and will therefore need testing.

Thus, a military communications system will require stringent security testing. At a more personal level, any system that will hold delicate personal information, should for privacy reasons be secure.

Even fairly inoccous software can be exploited to either do something it should not or be used to break into another system. A good example is the humble Excel product. Many viruses take advantage of buffer overruns to spread themselves or use it as a gateway to the operating system and ultimately take over the users machine.

The definition above only mentions the system. However awareness of security should begin even earlier in component testing. It is at this stage many of the chinks in armour defects will be found. For example buffer overruns. Websites may find the potential for hot sql injection intrusions. The growing use of web services, with the reliance on opening individual components or sub-systems up for all to use, will make this level of testing even more crucial. Thus we can start our list of with developers or whoever is conducting unit testing.

Especially in high risk systems, analysts need to be ensuring, security, is built into the system design and processes. Additionaly testability needs to be high in this particular area.

Ideally the software though is tested by an independent test team of system testers. In the case of penetration testing, an outside consultancy is brought in to try simulate an attack. However constraints on resources mean that, independence in many cases suffers.

Testing that software is secure can take place anywhere, including the developers own site. At the other extreme is for the penetration tester or "intruder" to be sitting on a different continent using the telecoms network and internet to try and break into an online transaction site.

This type of testing is resorted to throughout the whole software development life cycle for the developing organisation and accepting customer. In addition regular security testing should be undertaken to make sure the software is still secure.

This testing can be done perhaps more than any other form, security testing is associated with risk. Thus if security is of such importance, i.e. to the police or military, then awareness and practice has to be pervasive amongst the stakeholders. If the organisation has a mature development culture and are at level 3 or above in the CMMI they should have a strategy for risk mitigation.

3.18.23 Smoke Testing

It is a simple test case suite, designed to give confidence in an integrated build of a system or sub-system. It may also be referred to as a health check or reality check.

The phrase is derived from the testing of hardware. For example a computer would be ran until it literally started smoking.

As the software is incrementally integrated, smoke testing confirms the stability of the Software Under Test (SUT).

An integrated build of software is a complex thing. Defects related to interfaces, bottlenecks and usability may only come to light at integration. Every time a build is constructed, with additional components or sub-systems, new opportunities for failure arise.

When testing at the system level, the test team needs to have confidence in the stability of the overall SUT. A successful run of the smoke test, generates this confidence. Often a smoke test, is considered an entry criteria for system testing.

An effect of smoke testing, is the early discovery of major defects, that make the SUT unreleasable. (Known universally as a showstopper.) A lot of time is saved, by not testing on an unstable platform. Smoke testing also has an element of regression testing. The smoke test, confirms (in simple terms) that previously tested and integrated code is still functioning as it should.

Smoke testing is the first stage of integration testing. Also closely related is incremental testing. In both of these, an essential element is the joining together of all available components and sub-systems. If the organisation is implementing an iterative based framework, smoke testing is used too extensively. An example is the Rational Unified Process (RUP) which seeks to progressively mitigates risks. Smoke testing can aid this process, by generating confidence in both the SUT and the build process.

Personnel involved in Smoke Testing are usually close to the build process or in the configuration arena. This is due to two reasons. First, confirmation that the build is stable, has to be made as quickly as possible. Second is the large degree of automation.

The suite itself, would be designed by a tester or test analyst. Automation or writing the scripts may be done by a test automater or engineer. Actual execution of the test suite, is a test technician role. The repetivity of the activity makes it extremely mundane.

Where: As close as possible to the build environment. The vast majority of smoke testing is at the developing organisations site.

When: The testing should be done after every build. At Microsoft this means every night, the entire product is rebuilt, and a Smoke Test ran against it. A small product, at release time may be rebuilt 2-3 times a day.

How: The reliance on a new build to be existing, means implicitly that the organisation is testing incrementally or iteratively. As the project progresses, the SUT grows with the addition of new or altered code. (Not necessarily new features though.)

The test suite consequently grows in an incremental fashion. Ideally as potential areas of high risk are identified, they are mitigated in the SUT. Analysis is required to establish if additional test cases are required, to confirm that they have indeed been mitigated.

Automated tests are used extensively, due to the repetitive nature of the testing. Winrunner is a popular choice for such a task. If performance is an issue, LoadRunner, might be used to confirm that no performance issues, such as bottlenecks have been introduced.

3.18.24 Statement Testing

Statement Testing is a test case design technique for a component in which test cases are designed to execute statements as per BS 7925-1 British Computer Society Specialist Interest Group in Software Testing (BCS SIGIST).

Statement Testing is a structural or white box technique, because it is conducted with reference to the code. Statement testing comes under Dynamic Analysis.

In an ideal world every statement of every component would be fully tested. However, in the real world this hardly ever happens. In statement testing every possible statement is tested. Compare this to Branch testing, where each branch is tested, to check that it can be traversed, whether it encounters a statement or not.

In the diagram below, statement testing would have 1 test, as only the left hand branch has a statement on it. The alternative branch along the 2nd arrow does not have a statement and does not need to be tested.

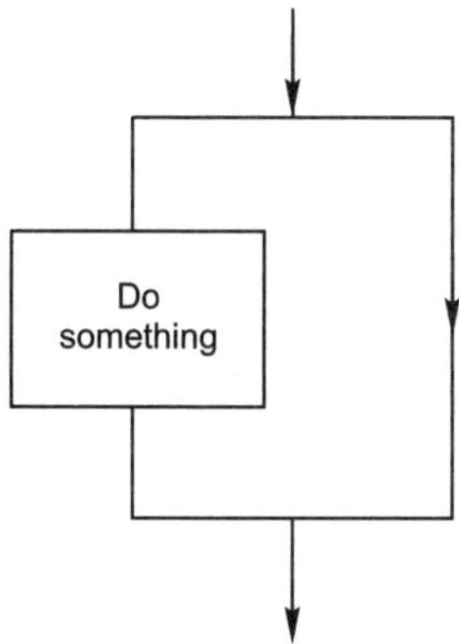

Why: This testing is done:

(1) To find faults

(2) Give credible information about the state of the component, on which business decisions can be taken.

Who: Ideally an independent person or body, to the one that wrote the code. Usually, however it is conducted by the developer.

Where: As close as possible to the point where the code was written. This testing is done as a part of component testing.

How: In each test case, the following should be specified:

(1) Inputs to the component

(2) Statement to be executed

(3) Expected outcome.

A metric statement coverage is available to measure how much of the code has been executed.

3.18.25 Static Testing

Static testing is performed usually as part of Component Testing Inspections and reviews are the most important forms of static testing. Inspections or "Fagan" inspections are the most formal technique. Whilst walkthrough reviews are most informal. Any document can be reviewed or inspected.

Why: The usual suspects apply here, to generate credible info about the state of the software, confidence and identify faults or incidents. An additional consideration is cost. In Boris Beizers well-known analysis, the longer a fault stays in the product as it goes through the life cycle, by a factor of 10 at each stage. This has become a cliche somewhat, but is not without foundation. If the fault can be found by the developer or colleague it will cost tens or hundreds of pounds. If a customer finds the fault, thousands of pounds may be the cost.

Who: Ideally by a independent individual or team. The reviewer should understand domain or jargon of the text reviewed. Thus code is reviewed by developers. Requirements gathering documents by analysts. This avoids the risk that, the author will be blind to errors and faults.

Where: As close as possible to where the document was written. There is a balancing act between geographical and organisational proximity versus independence of the reviewing team. Almost certainly at the developing organisations site.

When: As soon as possible after the document or code is written. However there should be some element of entry criteria into the review process.

How: Static testing is usually labour intensive, however tools do exist to help the tester. Tools can be used to check the syntax of the code. Thus unclosed instances and unoptimized sql can be highlighted.

In an informal process the developer or analyst may just pass his work across to a colleague. In the Inspection process developed by Fagan there are entry and exit criteria, logging incidents, process improvement and fault resolution and fault eradication.

No matter which process is undertaken, faults or incidents must be recorded either electronically or on paper.

3.18.26 Statistical Testing

It is a test case design technique in which a model is used of the statistical distribution of the input to construct representative test cases.

3.18.27 Stress Testing

It is a testing conducted to evaluate a system or component at or beyond the limits of its specified requirements. [IEEE]

Stress testing is quite distinct from Load Testing. Here the aim is to discover how the system will behave when it is pushed beyond the non-functional requirements. This situation will typically occur when the customer pushes too hard. The developing organisation may only support up to the load requirements. However they do need to know when it is likely to happen. This sort of testing is essential for safety critical software.

Indeed Stress testing is often used inform the decision about setting safe load instructions for end-users

Load testing, however sets out to confirm that the system does operate within defined parameters when set within the requirements levels.

An essential element of stress testing is to log everything. This is because a number of steps would have gone to before a failure occurs. Additionally you need to know exactly the state and environment the application was operating in at the time of the failure. Typical metrics include how many concurrent users there were or transactions trying to take place.

If a database is used, ensure transactions add, amend or delete records continously. Doing so enables checking on record locks, memory leakage or if the database is growing at too fast a rate.

3.18.28 Path Testing

Path testing is a test case design technique in which test cases are designed to execute paths of a component as per BS 7925-1 British Computer Society Specialist Interest Group in Software Testing (BCS SIGIST).

Testing paths through a component is largely a **white box** test technique. This is because the tester needs access to the code. Typically path testing would be conducted towards full component testing.

Why: Components are the building blocks of software. If we cannot be sure about their internal workings how can we expect to trust a system that is built from them?

Only by identifying and executing the different paths or routes through the component, can we be sure that all the behaviour the component will exhibit has been tested. This does not necessarily mean that all the paths must be tested. Only those that will (a) satisfy us that the requirements of the components have been met, and (b) enable us to give credible technical and business information to stakeholders for confidence.

Who: Ideally someone with independence from the person who designed and/or coded the component. However this is quite rare and it usually ends up with the developer who did the coding. Not satisfactory, but this is the real world.

Where: Invariabliy at the developing organisations home site.

When: Execution of the tests should be as close as possible to the completion of the code.

How: Path testing is primariliy a dynamic analysis activity. Tests can be either manual or automated. Various tools are available including static analyzers and run time analysis tools. The tester needs to be aware of the various paths through the component. From this he can decide the paths to be tested. (Assuming the 100% path coverage is not the target.) The decision on which paths to test should be derived from the requirements. With experience an element of risk assessment can be entered.

All the paths required to ensure the components behaviour is functionally correct. In addition as many alternative paths should be tested. Commonly the first paths not to be tested are those useful in negative testing. This however runs the risk of not exposing serious defects, when the user takes a path that he should not.

The more life or business critical the component or software, the more paths will be tested. Thus a component for the Space Shuttle will probably have 100 per cent path coverage.

In the long-run, though path testing has to be part of a wider culture of testability. Analysts and designers need to be aware of complexity. If they continue to demand complex objects, then path testing becomes ineffective due to the number of paths a tester is required to traverse.

3.18.29 Performance Testing

System performance is generally assessed in terms of response time and throughput rates under differing processing and configuration conditions. To attack the performance problems, there are several questions to be asked first:

- How much application logic should be remotely executed?
- How much updating should be done to the database server over the network from the client workstation?
- How much data should be sent to each in each transaction?

According to Hamilton, the performance problems are most often the result of the client or server being configured inappropriately.

The best strategy for improving client-sever performance is a three-step process. First, execute controlled performance tests that collect the data about volume, stress, and loading tests. Second, analyze the collected data. Third, examine and tune the database queries and, if necessary, provide temporary data storage on the client while the application is executing.

3.18.30 Other Software Testing Types

The following are the other different types of software testing.

Compatibility Testing. Testing to ensure compatibility of an application or Web site with different browsers, OSs, and hardware platforms. Compatibility testing can be performed manually or can be driven by an automated functional or regression test suite.

Conformance Testing. Verifying implementation conformance to industry standards. Producing tests for the behavior of an implementation to be sure it provides the portability, interoperability, and/or compatibility a standard defines.

Functional Testing. Validating an application or Web site conforms to its specifications and correctly performs all its required functions. This entails a series of tests which perform a feature by feature validation of behavior, using a wide range of normal and erroneous input data. This can involve testing of the product's user interface, APIs, database management, security, installation, networking, etc. Functional testing can be performed on an automated or manual basis using black box or white box methodologies.

Load Testing. Load testing is a generic term covering Performance Testing and Stress Testing.

Performance Testing. Performance testing can be applied to understand your application or WWW site's scalability, or to benchmark the performance in an environment of third party products such as servers and middleware for potential purchase. This sort of testing is particularly useful to identify performance bottlenecks in high use applications. Performance testing generally involves an automated test suite as this allows easy simulation of a variety of normal, peak, and exceptional load conditions.

Regression Testing. Similar in scope to a functional test, a regression test allows a consistent, repeatable validation of each new release of a product or Web site. Such testing ensures reported product defects have been corrected for each new release and that no new quality problems were introduced in the maintenance process. Though regression testing can be performed manually an automated test suite is often used to reduce the time and resources needed to perform the required testing.

Smoke Testing. A quick-and-dirty test that the major functions of a piece of software work without bothering with finer details. Originated in the hardware testing practice of turning on a new piece of hardware for the first time and considering it a success if it does not catch on fire.

Stress Testing. Testing conducted to evaluate a system or component at or beyond the limits of its specified requirements to determine the load under which it fails and how. A graceful degradation under load leading to non-catastrophic failure is the desired result. Often Stress Testing is performed using the same process as Performance Testing but employing a very high level of simulated load.

Unit Testing. Functional and reliability testing in an Engineering environment. Producing tests for the behavior of components of a product to ensure their correct behavior prior to system integration.

Unit Testing. The most 'micro' scale of testing; to test particular functions or code modules. Typically done by the programmer and not by testers, as it requires detailed knowledge of the internal program design and code. Not always easily done unless the application has a well-designed architecture with tight code; may require developing test driver modules or test harnesses.

Incremental Integration Testing. Continuous testing of an application as new functionality is added; requires that various aspects of an application's functionality be independent enough to work separately before all parts of the program are completed, or that test drivers be developed as needed; done by programmers or by testers.

Integration Testing. Testing of combined parts of an application to determine if they function together correctly. The 'parts' can be code modules, individual applications, client and server applications on a network, etc. This type of testing is especially relevant to client/server and distributed systems.

Functional Testing. Black-box type testing geared to functional requirements of an application; this type of testing should be done by testers. This doesn't mean that the programmers shouldn't check that their code works before releasing it (which of course applies to any stage of testing).

System Testing. Black-box type testing that is based on overall requirements specifications; covers all combined parts of a system.

End-to-end Testing. Similar to system testing; the 'macro' end of the test scale; involves testing of a complete application environment in a situation that mimics real-world use, such as interacting with a database, using network communications, or interacting with other hardware, applications, or systems if appropriate.

Sanity Testing or Smoke Testing. Typically an initial testing effort to determine if a new software version is performing well enough to accept it for a major testing effort. For example, if the new software is crashing systems every 5 minutes, bogging down systems to a crawl, or corrupting databases, the software may not be in a 'sane' enough condition to warrant further testing in its current state.

Regression Testing. Re-testing after fixes or modifications of the software or its environment. It can be difficult to determine how much re-testing is needed, especially near the end of the development cycle. Automated testing tools can be especially useful for this type of testing.

Acceptance Testing. Final testing based on specifications of the end-user or customer, or based on use by end-users/customers over some limited period of time.

Load Testing. Testing an application under heavy loads, such as testing of a web site under a range of loads to determine at what point the system's response time degrades or fails.

Stress Testing. Term often used interchangeably with 'load' and 'performance' testing. Also used to describe such tests as system functional testing while under unusually heavy loads, heavy repetition of certain actions or inputs, input of large numerical values, large complex queries to a database system, etc.

Performance Testing. Term often used interchangeably with 'stress' and 'load' testing. Ideally 'performance' testing (and any other 'type' of testing) is defined in requirements documentation or QA or Test Plans.

Usability Testing. Testing for 'user-friendliness'. Clearly this is subjective, and will depend on the targeted end-user or customer. User interviews, surveys, video recording of user sessions, and other techniques can be used. Programmers and testers are usually not appropriate as usability testers.

Install/uninstall Testing. Testing of full, partial, or upgrade install/uninstall processes.

Recovery Testing. Testing how well a system recovers from crashes, hardware failures, or other catastrophic problems.

Failover Testing. Typically used interchangeably with 'recovery testing'.

Security Testing. Testing how well the system protects against unauthorized internal or external access, willful damage, etc; may require sophisticated testing techniques.

Compatability Testing. Testing how well software performs in a particular hardware/software/operating system/network etc. environment.

Exploratory Testing. Often taken to mean a creative, informal software test that is not based on formal test plans or test cases; testers may be learning the software as they test it.

Ad-hoc Testing. Similar to exploratory testing, but often taken to mean that the testers have significant understanding of the software before testing it.

Context-driven Testing. Testing driven by an understanding of the environment, culture, and intended use of software. For example, the testing approach for life-critical medical equipment software would be completely different than that for a low-cost computer game.

User Acceptance Testing. Determining if software is satisfactory to an end-user or customer.

Comparison Testing. Comparing software weaknesses and strengths to competing products.

Mutation Testing. A method for determining if a set of test data or test cases is useful, by deliberately introducing various code changes ('bugs') and retesting with the original test data/cases to determine if the 'bugs' are detected. Proper implementation requires large computational resources.

3.19 Estimation of Software Test

Estimating the required testing effort is part of the project planning process. Proper allocation of resources can then take place, ensuring they are used in the most effective manner possible.

In the wider scheme, estimating can be used to reduce risk. The rationale is that due to insufficient resources or the wrong kind of resources, major defects may not be found leading to a potential failure of the project.

As estimating is a predictive science, the obvious time is before you actually start the project. The less obvious time is once the project has actually started. An even less obvious time to consider estimation is when the project is over. This is because you can use lessons learnt from the just completed project for the next one.

The danger is that the estimate document is done as part of some "box ticking" exercise and is then put on the shelf and forgotten about. In this instance, the exercise may never actually have taken place.

The development methodology can make a difference in the times that the estimations take place. Additionally the depth to which the estimation takes place. The traditional Waterfall method would demand that the process takes place months, even years before the testing is due to take place. There are a number of risks with this. Firstly the estimate can become a document that is never revisited to take account of changes in the project. Secondly, as the project progresses, the time allotted for requirements capture and development etc. increase. However updating the estimate is not updated. As a consequence the time allotted for testing constantly declines.

The most common iterative development environment is that of the Rational Unified Process (RUP). A risk driven process where the aim is to mitigate risk at the earliest possible opportunity. Iterations, within phases (Inception, Elaboration, Construtction and Transition) are the control mechanism to ensure that this happens. Testing in the RUP is present in all phases. However the degree to which it takes place, and the type of testing, change, depending on the phase. At the start of the project in Inception, a coarse estimate can be made of resources required as part of the business case. In planning each phase or iteration, a finer estimation can be made. This constant estimating over different phases can demand a large amount of historical data about previous projects.

Estimating and consequent allocation of resources can be a highly emotive or political subject. Who actually makes that decision can be in a powerful position.

Does the organisation use a top-down or a bottom-up approach? In the top-down approach, estimation is undertaking by senior management at the project level. Time and other resources are allocated from this high level estimate. In the bottom-up approach, testers at the lower level indicate how long they estimate their area will take, an aggregate is then taken. Both approaches have their advantages and disadvantages. In most cases a compromise is made between the two. For example a project manager will allocate a month for testing. This is then split down to finer elements. Testing staff can then feed back up their comments, after estimates and allocations may be amended.

3.19.1 Influencing Factors

A number of factors have an impact on the estimation process:

- **Tester Skill Level Technical Skill of the Tester:** An inexperienced tester without training, will take longer to find all the defects in code than an experienced tester. A test team where experience of testers are at the extremes will skew the estimate greatly.
- **Test Tool Knowledge:** Does everyone on the team know how to use the tools available to them? Otherwise time and training resources will be required.
- **Maturity of Organization:** A good measure of the maturity of an organisation is against the Capability Maturity Model for Integration (CMMI). At the lower levels of maturity testing is either not at all or is merely repeated, no metrics are collected. Estimates in this scenario, will have a wide variability. It is highly likely that the actual time to test will not be near the estimate. And at the other extreme highly optimised organisations, quality awareness is pervasive throughout the organisation. Defects are found at the documentation stage through inspections. Metrics are collected. For these highly optimiezed organisations, estimation should be very accurate.
- **Test Requirements Scope:** What kind of testing is required. Manual, automated or both? Is a large amount of regression testing is to be done? Are non-functional tests (load, performance or usability) to be undertaken?
- **Domain Knowledge:** How much the Test Team knows about the subject matter of the application, e.g. e-brokers will have excellent domain or business knowledge if they are testing an insurance application. None if they are testing a satellite communication system.
- **Test Team Organisation:** At the team level, organisation can have an effect. For example if their is a hierachial, linear structure or more like a matrix. Additionally, are the testers encouraged to interact with analysts or developers, also involved in the project.
- **Number of Builds Planned:** If a number have to be ran each time a build is generated, the test effort will increase dramatically. Automation could reduce this, only if the build number is high enough.
- **Process:** Does the team/organization have documented or defined processes. If everyone is allowed to do their own thing, it has to be translated for their colleagues. Junior testers will face a very long and steep learning curve.
- **Risk:** What are the risk levels for failure? A failure in aircraft control software is going to be much greater than for a failure in a game. Consequently the testing for aviation is much more rigorous.
- **Regulatory Control:** Does the organisation have to conform to a particular industry or customer standard? Examples include IEEE 829:1998 Software Test Documentation. The UK Ministry of Defence and the US Defense Department enforce their own standards on suppliers.
- **Physical Location:** Are the testers in close proximity to each other? Is the Test Team close to the developers? Efficient communication is very important, and location can be a large barrier to be factored in.

- **Language:** Is everyone speaking the same language? As ever more development tasks are being sent offshore, language difficulties can affect the estimate.

3.19.2 How to Estimate

Over the years many attempts have been made to devise a method of accurately estimating.

- **Guess:** Of course this is the easiest and quickest way. However invariably you leave the project open to many nasty surprises. A huge contingency will be needed. Lastly any one making a decision based on a guessed estimate, are themselves on very shaky ground. Organisations in this position would be considered very immature. They are also most likely to run into difficulties when deadlines approach.
- **Tester/Developer Ratio:** The number of testers required for a project is set based on a ratio. Thus for every 3 developers we shall have 1 tester. The ratio can be defined at many levels, e.g. the same for all projects, split into project types or at the individual level. The higher up the project chain the ratio is set, the less accurate it will be at the individual level.

To refine the process, the complexity, type and risk factors of the project/s will need to be examined. More risk and complexity indicates a need for a higher tester/developer ratio. Allegorically Microsoft reckon on two testers for every one developer. This would be considered high for most organisations.

The life cycle will also play a part. In the Waterfall approach, the organisation will need a sudden increase in the ratio when it comes to the integration phase. The RUP on the other hand requires a much more steady increase of the ratio as the project passes through the phases.

Lastly the demarcation lines between Unit Testing, System Testing and Integration Testing need to be set. e.g. is the unit testing to be done by the "developers"? If so the tester/developer ratio can be lower.

- **Project Staff Ratio:** The ratio is between the tester and all other types of project member, not just the developers. The greater complexity of calculation, i.e. involving analysts and project management staff, requires higher levels of metrics to be factored in. In addition, more information is required about configuration management, reviews and project administration.
- **Test Procedure Method:** The number of test procedures required to guarantee full coverage of the project. To employ this technique, the organisation would need to be structured enough to collect accurate metrics about its developments.

Size of developments can be calculated from function points, lines of code or number of test procedures. Also needed are the personnel hours for the project and the individual areas.

To estimate the next project's required resources, calculate how long on average previous tasks took. Count the number of test procedures and multiply by the average. This will give total hours e.g. 4,800. Divide by the time allocated e.g. 8 months or 1,600 hour. Thus 3 full time testers.

- **Task Planning Method:** Again Task Planning requires a very structured organisation, as it requires a history of accurately recorded metrics. In this case, how long it takes to undertake a particular task.

Instead of the procedures, the base is that of testing tasks such as automation of testing, start up procedures, planning etc.

A total number of hours for the project is calculated (Possibly using the Test Procedures method). The hours are then apportioned according to the historical percentage for a project type of the current one. This gives a number of hours for each task.

The next stage is to adjust the figures to take account of project specific details. Tasks that are not to be done, are removed, and the total hours re-calculated. The hours are then divided to show how many testers are required.

There is no simple answer for this. The 'best approach' is highly dependent on the particular organization and project and the experience of the personnel involved.

For example, given two software projects of similar complexity and size, the appropriate test effort for one project might be very large if it was for life-critical medical equipment software, but might be much smaller for the other project if it was for a low-cost computer game. A test estimation approach that only considered size and complexity might be appropriate for one project but not for the other.

Following are some approaches to consider:

- **Implicit Risk Context Approach**

A typical approach to test estimation is for a project manager or QA manager to implicitly use risk context, in combination with past personal experiences in the organization, to choose a level of resources to allocate to testing. In many organizations, the 'risk context' is assumed to be similar from one project to the next, so there is no explicit consideration of risk context. (Risk context might include factors such as the organization's typical software quality levels, the software's intended use, the experience level of developers and testers, etc.) This is essentially an intuitive guess based on experience.

- **Metrics-Based Approach**

A useful approach is to track past experience of an organization's various projects and the associated test effort that worked well for projects. Once there is a set of data covering characteristics for a reasonable number of projects, then this 'past experience' information can be used for future test project planning. (Determining and collecting useful project metrics over time can be an extremely difficult task.) For each particular new project, the 'expected' required test time can be adjusted based on whatever metrics or other information is available, such as function point count, number of external system interfaces, unit testing done by developers, risk levels of the project, etc. In the end, this is essentially 'judgement based on documented experience', and is not easy to do successfully.

- **Test Work Breakdown Approach**

Another common approach is to decompose the expected testing tasks into a collection of small tasks for which estimates can, at least in theory, be made with reasonable accuracy. This of course assumes that an accurate and predictable breakdown of testing tasks and their estimated effort is feasible. In many large projects, this is not the case. For example, if a large number of bugs are being found in a project, this will add to the time required for testing, retesting, bug analysis and reporting. It will also add to the time required for development, and if development schedules and efforts do not go as planned, this will further impact testing.

• **Iterative Approach**

In this approach for large test efforts, an initial rough testing estimate is made. Once testing begins, a more refined estimate is made after a small percentage (e.g., 1%) of the first estimate's work is done. At this point testers have obtained additional test project knowledge and a better understanding of issues, general software quality, and risk. Test plans and schedules can be refactored if necessary and a new estimate provided. Then a yet-more-refined estimate is made after a somewhat larger percentage (e.g. 2%) of the new work estimate is done. Repeat the cycle as necessary/appropriate.

• **Percentage-of-Development Approach**

Some organizations utilize a quick estimation method for testing based on the estimated programming effort. For example, if a project is estimated to require 1000 hours of programming effort, and the organization normally finds that a 40 per cent ratio for testing is appropriate, then an estimate of 400 hours for testing would be used. This approach may or may not be useful depending on the project-to-project variations in risk, personnel, types of applications, levels of complexity, etc.

Successful test estimation is a challenge for most organizations, since few can accurately estimate software project development efforts, much less the testing effort of a project. It is also difficult to attempt testing estimates without first having detailed information about a project, including detailed requirements, the organization's experience with similar projects in the past, and an understanding of what should be included in a 'testing' estimation for a project (functional testing? unit testing? reviews? inspections? load testing? security testing?).

With agile software development approaches, test effort estimations may be unnecessary if pure test-driven development is utilized. In general, agile-based projects by their nature will not be heavily dependent on large testing efforts, since they emphasize the construction of releasable software in very short iteration cycles. Therefore test effort estimates may not be as difficult and the impact of inaccurate estimates will be minimized.

3.20 Zero-Defect Software Development (ZDSD)

Not to be taken as meaning "bug-free," Zero-Defect Software Development (ZDSD) is a practice of developing software that is maintained in the highest quality state throughout the entire development process. "Defects" are aspects of the evolving software that would not be suitable for the final product as-is. This broad definition includes bugs as well as unwanted deviations from the desired final outcome. Defects in the development of a computer game would include unpolished artwork, an unacceptably low frame rate on the target system, levels that aren't fun enough, or any number of unfinished features.

The basic tenet of ZDSD is this: Maintain your product in what you believe to be a defect-free state throughout the development process. This sounds simple, but it is a rare practice. The most common approach is to delay major testing until the final QA phase of software development, where defects are often discovered for the first time. Most bugs are not detected or fixed until long after their introduction. The longer a defect remains, the harder it is to fix. On large software products, each stage of development that a defect survives will increase the cost of fixing the defect by ten to fifty times. A defect introduced in the design phase can cost hundreds of times more to fix in the testing phase than it would if fixed immediately after its introduction.

By focusing on product quality throughout the development life cycle, you will actually complete products faster than if you didn't pay attention to quality until the end of the project. The general rule of software quality is counter-intuitive: Improving quality actually reduces development time. This is because you eliminate all the time spent fixing bugs and reworking code, which can account for as much as 50 per cent of development costs on a large project. The typical programmer writes between eight and twenty lines of code a day; the rest of the day is usually spent on debugging. ZDSD shortens schedules by eliminating most debugging time. Extensive studies done at NASA, IBM, and elsewhere have shown that better QA leads to shorter schedules. An IBM study concluded that software projects that make quality a top priority typically have the shortest schedules, the highest productivity, and even the best sales.

Here are the ten basic rules of ZDSD:

(1) **Test your product every day as you develop it, and fix defects as soon as you find them.**

Apply the daily build and smoke test. At the end of every day you work on your project, build the current version of your software, and test it for basic functionality. Microsoft enforces this policy religiously, using large teams to build each project on a daily basis. A programmer whose code breaks the build may be called in the middle of the night and must go back to work to fix the problem immediately. For developers working on small projects, this is far easier. At the end of each day, test your program for at least ten minutes. Make a list of anything you would consider a "defect," and resolve to fix all defects before implementing any new features. Once you find a defect, fixing it becomes your number one priority, and you avoid writing any new code until the defect is 100 per cent eliminated.

(2) **Review your code regularly.**

When most people think of QA, they think of testing, but testing is actually one of the least cost-effective strategies for finding bugs. The most rigorous testing will typically find less than 60 per cent of all bugs in a program, and there are certain types of bugs that testing will rarely find. Studies conducted at many large software organizations have concluded that code inspections are far more cost-effective than testing. A NASA study found that code reading detected almost twice as many defects per hour as testing. Whenever you've added a few hundred lines of new code to your project, set aside an hour or two to read over your work and look for mistakes. One hour of code review is equivalent to two or more hours of methodical testing. As you gain experience, keep a list of the types of defects you find, and run down your list whenever reviewing new code. To find even more defects, have someone else read your code as well.

(3) **Rewrite poor-quality modules.**

When you discover an obscure new bug, do you ever pray, "Oh no! Please don't let it be in that module!" We all have monster modules of legacy code that were written when we weren't such seasoned programmers as we are today. Don't fear them; rewrite them. Often a better approach will only become clear when an inferior solution has already been implemented. This is certainly true for John Carmack, who coded dozens of different approaches when writing the Quake engine before discovering one that met his criterion. Defects will not be distributed evenly across your code. You will typically find that 20 per cent of your routines are responsible for 80 per cent of your errors. In my programs it is normally the modules that interact with the hardware or with third-party drivers, especially DirectX, that are the most buggy. Raise your standards for those modules that seem to produce a never-ending supply of bugs, and take the time to rewrite them from scratch. You may find that other intermittent bugs disappear completely as a result.

(4) **Assume full responsibility for every bug.**

95 per cent of all software defects are caused by the programmer. Only 1 per cent of defects are hardware errors, and the remaining 4 per cent are caused by the compiler, the OS, or other software. Never dismiss a potential bug; find out the exact cause of any anomaly. When a Mars probe suffered serious software glitches during its mission, it was learned that the same glitch had occurred only once during testing on earth, but the engineers dismissed it as a temporary hardware hiccup. Unless your hardware drinks soda, it does not hiccup.

(5) **Handle change effectively.**

You will always think of great new features to add after you have started coding. Carefully consider how each change will impact your pre-existing code. Poor integration of unanticipated features is a major cause of defects.

(6) **Rewrite all prototyping code from scratch.**

Sometimes you may quickly prototype a new feature to see if it will be viable. Often this is done by sacrificing code quality in the name of rapid development. If you eventually decide to keep the feature, it is very tempting to simply tack on some basic error checking to the prototyping code. Don't fall into this trap. If you weren't writing the code originally with quality as a priority, scrap the prototyping code, and re-implement the feature from scratch. Rapidly prototyped features that slip into the final product are a major source of bugs because they are not subject to the same quality standards as the rest of the code.

(7) **Set QA objectives at the beginning of every project.**

Studies have shown that developers who set reasonable QA goals will usually achieve them. Decide in advance if your product must be fast, small, feature-rich, intuitive, scalable, etc. Then prioritize those objectives. When designing the interface code for Dweep, I decided that my top three priorities were to make the interface beginner-intuitive, fast, and fun, in that order. Consequently, Dweep's interface isn't as graphically rich as other games, but it is easier to use and is extremely fast and responsive, and I was pleased with the results. Whenever you have to make a design decision, keep your objectives in mind. If you do not set clear QA goals, then you are doomed to accept the results of random chance.

(8) **Don't rush debugging work.**

Fully 50 per cent of all bug fixes are done incorrectly the first time, often introducing new bugs in the process. Never experiment by simply changing "x-1" to "x+1" to see if that will do the trick. Take the time to understand the source of the bug. Many years ago when I was a boy scout and had to put out a campfire, the Scoutmaster would sometimes test my thoroughness by asking me to put my hand in the ashes. I learned very quickly how to put out a fire so well that I had complete confidence it was 100 per cent extinguished. When you find a defect, it means your code is on fire. As long as the defect remains, any new code you write will add fuel to that fire. Whenever you find a defect, drop everything to fix it, and don't move on until you are 100 per cent confident that your fix is correct. If you don't take the time to do it right the first time, when will you find the time to do it over?

(9) Treat the quality of your code at the same level of importance as the quality of your product.

Rate your code on a scale of one to ten for overall quality. The first time I did this, I rated my 30,000-line project as a four. I rewrote the worst of the code until I reached an eight overall. It was one of the best investments of time I ever made because I was then able to add new features at double my previous rate. The quality of your code is highly indicative of the quality of your product. You may find as I have that your best-selling products also receive your highest ratings for code quality.

(10) Learn from every bug; each one represents a mistake that you made.

Learn why you made each mistake, and see if you can change something about your development practices to eliminate it. Over the years I have adopted many simple coding practices that allow me to avoid common bugs that used to plague me. There are many types of bugs that I now never encounter because my coding style makes it physically impossible for me to introduce them.

Each of these rules represents a simple concept, but their combined benefits are significant. You will achieve higher progress visibility, avoiding the situation of being "99 per cent done" for the last 80 per cent of your development time. Higher quality will make your products easier to maintain and less expensive to support. You will spend less time debugging old code and more time writing new code. And most importantly, it actually takes less time to write high-quality code than it does to write low-quality code, so you will save a great deal of time on overall development. If you have never developed products with a zero-defect philosophy from day one, its adoption can reduce your development time for new products by 30 per cent or more while simultaneously improving product quality.

3.21 Disaster Management

What if the software is so buggy it can't really be tested at all?

The best bet in this situation is for the testers to go through the process of reporting whatever bugs or blocking-type problems initially show up, with the focus being on critical bugs. Since this type of problem can severely affect schedules, and indicates deeper problems in the software development process (such as insufficient unit testing or insufficient integration testing, poor design, improper build or release procedures, etc.) managers should be notified, and provided with some documentation as evidence of the problem.

How can it be known when to stop testing?

This can be difficult to determine. Many modern software applications are so complex, and run in such an interdependent environment, that complete testing can never be done. Common factors in deciding when to stop are:

- Deadlines (release deadlines, testing deadlines, etc.)
- Test cases completed with certain percentage passed
- Test budget depleted
- Coverage of code/functionality/requirements reaches a specified point

- Bug rate falls below a certain level
- Beta or alpha testing period ends

What if there isn't enough time for thorough testing?

Use risk analysis to determine where testing should be focused.

Since it's rarely possible to test every possible aspect of an application, every possible combination of events, every dependency, or everything that could go wrong, risk analysis is appropriate to most software development projects. This requires judgement skills, common sense, and experience. (If warranted, formal methods are also available.) Considerations can include:

- Which functionality is most important to the project's intended purpose?
- Which functionality is most visible to the user?
- Which functionality has the largest safety impact?
- Which functionality has the largest financial impact on users?
- Which aspects of the application are most important to the customer?
- Which aspects of the application can be tested early in the development cycle?
- Which parts of the code are most complex, and thus most subject to errors?
- Which parts of the application were developed in rush or panic mode?
- Which aspects of similar/related previous projects caused problems?
- Which aspects of similar/related previous projects had large maintenance expenses?
- Which parts of the requirements and design are unclear or poorly thought out?
- What do the developers think are the highest-risk aspects of the application?
- What kinds of problems would cause the worst publicity?
- What kinds of problems would cause the most customer service complaints?
- What kinds of tests could easily cover multiple functionalities?
- Which tests will have the best high-risk-coverage to time-required ratio?

What if the project isn't big enough to justify extensive testing?

Consider the impact of project errors, not the size of the project. However, if extensive testing is still not justified, risk analysis is again needed and the same considerations as described previously in 'What if there isn't enough time for thorough testing?' apply. The tester might then do ad hoc testing, or write up a limited test plan based on the risk analysis.

A software architecture is also a simplified model of the finished end product— its primary function is to define the software components and their relationships to each other so that the whole can be seen to be a consistent, complete, and correct representation of what the user had in mind—especially for the computer-human interface. It is also used to ensure that the components fit together and relate in the desired way.

It is necessary to distinguish between the architecture of the user's world and the engineered software architecture. The former represents and addresses problems and solutions in the user's world. It is principally captured in the computer-human-interfaces (CHI) of the engineered system. The engineered system represents the engineering solutions—how the engineer proposes to develop and/or select and combine the components of the technical infrastructure to support the CHI. In the absence of an architect, there is an unfortunate tendency to confuse the two architectures, since the engineer thinks in terms of software, but the user may be thinking in terms of solving a problem of getting people from point A to point B in a reasonable amount of time and with a reasonable expenditure of energy, or of getting needed information to customers and staff.

3.22 Software Qualities

Internal—software product qualities primarily affect the software development organization.

Maintainability, reusability, modularity, etc.

External—software product qualities can be directly visible by customer or client.

Dependability—Does the software do what it is intended to do. For example, correctness, reliability, robustness, safety, etc.

Usefulness. For example, user-friendliness, usability.

Dependability Properties

- Correctness—A program or system is correct if it is consistent with its specification
- Reliability—A statistical approximation to correctness. Roughly speaking, reliability is a measure of the likelihood of correct function for some "unit" of behavior.
- Safety is concerned with depend.bmp preventing certain undesirable behaviors called hazards.

3.23 Software Test Plan

Software testing entails running software products under known conditions with defined inputs and documented outcomes that can be compared to their predefined expectations. It is a time consuming, difficult, and imperfect activity. As such, it requires early planning in order to be effective and efficient.

Test plans and test cases should be created as early in the software development process as feasible. They should identify the schedules, environments, resources (personnel, tools, etc.), methodologies, cases (inputs, procedures, outputs, expected results), documentation and reporting criteria. The magnitude of effort to be applied throughout the testing process can be linked to complexity, criticality, reliability, and/or safety issues (e.g., requiring functions or modules that produce critical outcomes to be challenged with intensive testing of their fault tolerance features).

Software test plans should identify the particular tasks to be conducted at each stage of development and include justification of the level of effort represented by their corresponding completion criteria.

Software testing has limitations that must be recognized and considered when planning the testing of a particular software product. Except for the simplest of programs, software cannot be exhaustively tested. Generally it is not feasible to test a software product with all possible inputs, nor is it possible to test all possible data processing paths that can occur during program execution. There is no one type of testing or testing methodology that can ensure a particular software product has been thoroughly tested. Testing of all program functionality does not mean all of the program has been tested. Testing of all of a program's code does not mean all necessary functionality is present in the program. Testing of all program functionality and all program code does not mean the program is 100 per cent correct. Software testing that finds no errors should not be interpreted to mean that errors do not exist in the software product; it may mean the testing was superficial.

An essential element of a software test case is the expected result. It is the key detail that permits objective evaluation of the actual test result. This necessary testing information is obtained from the corresponding, predefined definition or specification. A software specification document must identify what, when, how, why, etc. is to be achieved with an engineering (i.e., measurable or objectively verifiable) level of detail in order for it to be confirmed through testing. The real effort of effective software testing lies in the definition of what is to be tested rather than in the performance of the test.

A software testing process should be based on principles that foster effective examinations of a software product. Applicable software testing tenets include:

- The expected test outcome is predefined;
- A good test case has a high probability of exposing an error;
- A successful test is one that finds an error;
- There is independence from coding;
- Both application (user) and software (programming) expertise are employed;
- Testers use different tools from coders;
- Examining only the usual case is insufficient;

Test documentation permits its reuse and an independent confirmation of the pass/fail status of a test outcome during subsequent review.

Once the prerequisite tasks (e.g., code inspection) have been successfully completed, software testing begins. It starts with unit level testing and concludes with system level testing. There may be a distinct integration level of testing. A software product should be challenged with test cases based on its internal structure and with test cases based on its external specification. These tests should provide a thorough and rigorous examination of the software product's compliance with its functional, performance, and interface definitions and requirements.

Even simple software presents testers with obstacles, as the sidebar "A Sample Software Testing Problem" shows. To get a clearer view of some of software testing's inherent difficulties, we can approach testing in four phases:

- Modeling the software's environment
- Selecting test scenarios
- Running and evaluating test scenarios
- Measuring testing progress

These phases offer testers a structure in which to group related problems that they must solve before moving on to the next phase.

Phase 1: Modeling the Software's Environment

A tester's task is to simulate interaction between software and its environment.

Testers must identify and simulate the interfaces that a software system uses and enumerate the inputs that can cross each interface.

This might be the most fundamental issue that testers face, and it can be difficult, considering the various file formats, communication protocols, and third-party (application programming interfaces) available. Four common interfaces are as follows:

- Human interfaces include all common methods for people to communicate with software. Most prominent is the GUI but older designs like the command line interface and the menu-driven interface are still in use. Possible input mechanisms to consider are mouse clicks, keyboard events, and input from other devices. Testers then decide how to organize this data to understand how to assemble it into an effective test.
- Software interfaces, called APIs, are how software uses an operating system, database, or runtime library. The services these applications provide are modeled as test inputs. The challenge for testers is to check not only the expected but also the unexpected services. For example, all developers expect the operating system to save files for them. The service that they neglect is the operating system's informing them that the storage medium is full. Even error messages must be tested.
- File system interfaces exist whenever software reads or writes data to external files. Developers must write lots of error-checking code to determine if the file contains appropriate data and formatting. Thus, testers must build or generate files with content that is both legal and illegal, and files that contain a variety of text and formatting.
- Communication interfaces allow direct access to physical devices (such as device drivers, controllers, and other embedded systems) and require a communication protocol.

To test such software, testers must be able to generate both valid and invalid protocol streams. Testers must assemble—and submit to the software under test—many different combinations of commands and data, in the proper packet format.

Next, testers must understand the user interaction that falls outside the control of the software under test, since the consequences can be serious if the software is not prepared. Examples of situations testers should address are as follows:

- Using the operating system, one user deletes a file that another user has open.
- What will happen the next time the software tries to access that file?
- A device gets rebooted in the middle of a stream of communication. Will the software realize this and react properly or just hang?
- Two software systems compete for duplicate services from an API. Will the API correctly service both?
- Each application's unique environment result in a significant number of user interactions to test.

Considerations

When an interface presents problems infinite size or complexity, testers face difficulties. They must carefully select values for any variable input, and they decide how to sequence inputs. In selecting values, testers determine the values of individual variables and assign interesting combinations when a program accepts multiple variables as input.

Testers most often use the boundary partitioning technique for selecting values for variables at or around boundaries.

For example, testing the minimum, maximum, and zero values for a signed integer a commonly accepted idea as well as surrounding each of these partitions example, 1 and –1 (which surround the boundary). The values between boundaries are treated as the same number; whether use 16 or 16,000 makes no difference software under test.

A more complex issue is choosing for multiple variables processed simultaneously that could potentially affect each Testers must consider the entire cross product of value combinations. For two integers, we consider both positive, both negative, positive and one zero, and so forth.

In deciding how to sequence inputs, have a sequence generation problem. Testers treat each physical input and abstract as symbols in the alphabet of a formal language and define a model of that language. Model lets testers visualize the set of possible tests to see how each test fits the big picture.

The most common model is a graph or diagram, although with many variations. Other popular models include regular expressions and grammars, tools from language theory. Less-used models are stochastic processes and genetic algorithms. This is a representation that describes how event symbols are combined to syntactically valid words and sentences.

These sentences are sequences of input that can be applied to the software under test.

For example, consider the input *Filemenu. Open*, which invokes a file selection box; filename, which represents the selection (with mouse clicks, perhaps) of an existing file, and *ClickOpen* and *ClickCancel*, which represent button presses. The sequence Filemenu.Open filename *ClickOpen* is legal, as are many others. The sequence *ClickCancel Filemenu.Open* is impossible because the cancel button cannot be pressed until the dialog box has been invoked. The model of the formal language can make such a distinction between sequences.

3.24 Black Box or White Box Testing

An easy way to start up a debate in a software testing forum is to ask the difference between black box and white box testing. These terms are commonly used, yet everyone seems to have a different idea of what they mean.

Black box testing begins with a metaphor. Imagine you're testing an electronics system. It's housed in a black box with lights, switches, and dials on the outside. You must test it without opening it up, and you can't see beyond its surface. You have to see if it works just by flipping switches (inputs) and seeing what happens to the lights and dials (outputs). This is black box testing. Black box software testing is doing the same thing, but with software. The actual meaning of the metaphor, however, depends on how you define the boundary of the box and what kind of access the "blackness" is blocking.

An opposite test approach would be to open up the electronics system, see how the circuits are wired, apply probes internally and maybe even disassemble parts of it. By analogy, this is called white box testing, but already the metaphor is faulty. It is just as hard to see inside a white box as a black one. In the interests of logic, some people prefer the term "clear box" testing, but even a clear box keeps you from probing the internals of the system. It might be even more logical to call it "no box" testing. But the metaphor operates beyond logic. Since "white box" testing is the most common term, I'll use it here.

To help understand the different ways that software testing can be divided between black box and white box techniques, Five-Fold Testing System elaborated below is useful. It lays out five dimensions that can be used for examining testing:

- People (who does the testing)
- Coverage (what is tested)
- Risks (why are you testing)
- Activities (how you are testing)
- Evaluation (how do you know if you've found a bug)

Let's use this system to understand and clarify the characteristics of black box and white box testing.

3.24.1 People: Who does the testing?

Some people know how software works (developers) and others just use it (users). Accordingly, any testing by users or other nondevelopers is sometimes called "black box" testing. Developer testing is called "white box" testing. The distinction here is based on what the person knows or can understand.

3.24.2 Coverage: What is tested?

If we draw the box around the system as a whole, "black box" testing becomes another name for system testing. And testing the units inside the box becomes white box testing. This is one way to think about coverage.

Another is to contrast testing that aims to cover all the requirements with testing that aims to cover all the code. These are the two most commonly used coverage criteria. Both are supported by extensive literature and commercial tools. Requirements-based testing could be called "black box" because it makes sure that all the customer requirements have been verified. Code-based testing is often called "white box" because it makes sure that all the code (the statements, paths, or decisions) is exercised.

3.24.3 Risks: Why are you testing?

Sometimes testing is targeted at particular risks. Boundary testing and other attack-based techniques are targeted at common coding errors. Effective security testing also requires a detailed understanding of the code and the system architecture. Thus, these techniques might be classified as "white box".

Another set of risks concerns whether the software will actually provide value to users. Usability testing focuses on this risk, and could be termed "black box".

3.24.4 Activities: How you are testing?

A common distinction is made between behavioral test design, which defines tests based on functional requirements, and structural test design, which defines tests based on the code itself. These are two design approaches. Since behavioral testing is based on external functional definition, it is often called "black box", while structural testing—based on the code internals—is called "white box". Indeed, this is probably the most commonly cited definition for black box and white box testing.

Another activity-based distinction contrasts dynamic test execution with formal code inspection. In this case, the metaphor maps test execution (dynamic testing) with black box testing, and maps code inspection (static testing) with white box testing.

We could also focus on the tools used. Some tool vendors refer to code-coverage tools as white box tools, and tools that facilitate applying inputs and capturing inputs—most notably GUI capture replay tools—as black box tools. Testing is then categorized based on the types of tools used.

3.24.5 Evaluation: How do you know if you've found a bug?

There are certain kinds of software faults that don't always lead to obvious failures. They may be masked by fault tolerance or simply luck. Memory leaks and wild pointers are examples. Certain test techniques seek to make these kinds of problems more visible. Related techniques capture code history and stack information when faults occur, helping with diagnosis. Assertions are another technique for helping to make problems more visible. All of these techniques could be considered white box test techniques, since they use code instrumentation to make the internal workings of the software more visible. These contrast with black box techniques that simply look at the official outputs of a program.

To summarize, black box testing can sometimes describe user-based testing (people); system or requirements-based testing (coverage); usability testing (risk); or behavioral testing or capture replay automation (activities). White box testing, on the other hand, can sometimes describe developer-based testing (people); unit or code-coverage testing (coverage); boundary or security testing (risks); structural testing, inspection or code-coverage automation (activities); or testing based on probes, assertions, and logs (evaluation).

3.25 What is Rapid Testing?

As the stakes grow higher in the software marketplace, pressure grows to develop more products at a faster pace. This places increasing demands on software developers and on software testers not only to produce faster, but also to make products that are of good enough quality that the customer will be satisfied with them.

There are therefore two major demands placed on today's software test engineer:

- We need to test quickly to meet aggressive product delivery schedules.
- We need to test well enough that damaging defects don't escape to our customers.

The challenge is to satisfy each of these needs without sacrificing the other.

The term "rapid testing" in this book is used as a complement to the notion of "rapid development". As Steve McConnell has pointed out, rapid development means different things to different people. To some people, it's rapid prototyping. To others, it's a combination of

CASE tools, intensive user involvement, and tight time boxes. Rather than identify rapid development with a specific tool or method, McConnell (1996, p. 2) makes the following definition:

> Rapid development is a generic term that means the same thing as "speedy development" or "shorter schedules". It means developing software faster than you do now. A "rapid development project", then, is any project that needs to emphasize development speed.

3.25.1 Developing a Rapid Testing Strategy

If you were to analyze your current software development process for ways to improve testing efficiency, where in the process would you look? Would you start by looking at the way you conduct test planning? At the means and contents of your automation? What about your defect tracking system?

Our approach in this book will be to look at every phase of the software process from the viewpoint of the test engineer to see if there is a way to speed up testing while maintaining or improving quality. The image we have in mind is one of you sitting in the "test engineer's swivel chair", turning to look at every aspect of the development process to see if you can prevent defects from escaping that phase of the process, or to see if you can extract information from that phase that will speed up your test effort.

Before we can take a detailed look at each phase of the software development process from the testing perspective, we need to lay some groundwork. In this chapter we define basic terms and concepts of software testing, and provide an overview of the software development process. Then we examine each phase of a typical development process to see how the efficiency and speed of testing can be improved. When examining each development phase, we bear the following questions in mind:

- Is there any action that the test team can take during this phase that will prevent defects from escaping?
- Is there any action that the test team can take during this phase that will help manage risk to the development schedule?
- Is there any information that can be extracted from this phase that will allow the test team to speed up planning, test case development, or test execution?
- If a test process is designed around the answers to these questions, both the speed of testing and the quality of the final product should be enhanced.

3.26 Extreme Programming

One of the very best coding/testing techniques is *Extreme Programming*. It's not a magic bullet—nothing is, and while it won't prevent all bugs, it's the best way I've seen yet to reduce their number before the code is released into the wild. The technique is simple—Write the tests before you write the feature. This technique works like this:

- Consider the functionality of the code you want to write. Decide what you want it to do, and what you don't want it to do.

- Pick one thing you either want, or don't want your code to do, and code a test around it. The test must be fully automated—able to tell by itself whether it was successful or not.
- Write enough code for your application in order that the test will compile. If after doing this, all your tests succeed, including the new one, return to step one. If the test fails, continue.
- Write enough code that the new test succeeds. Ensure also that all previous tests still succeed.
- Return to step one.

The advantages of this system are legion. Testing first means more testable code.

Writing tests for previously written code can be a total nightmare. Often, it's impossible to write an automated test for something vital, because the code you're testing isn't built so that it can be tested. By writing the test first, you ensure that everything you need to test can be tested, easily and automatically. Those parts of a system that are really difficult to test automatically (GUI for example) are more likely to be properly separated from things that can be tested.

Often, you will find this leading to cleaner design of your code overall.

3.26.1 Testing first can prevent over-engineering

You know that you have finished programming when you run out of things to test. Because at each step, you have only done what was necessary in order to cause the test you wrote to succeed, this means that you haven't coded anything into your application that is not necessary.

Note that when programming incrementally like this, you must always take time to refactor your code, in order to make sure you don't end up with an unreadable mass of spaghetti.

3.26.2 Testing first leads to more maintainable code

When you make a modification to something you haven't looked at for half a year, you still have all the tests that convinced you then that it was working six months ago. If they still run, that means that you are as convinced now that the code works as you were before. You have a complete set of regression tests as an integral part of the coding process, not as some tacked-on-as-an-afterthought test suite.

This means that you can allow more people to modify more of your program, provided that they also follow the "test-first" rule, and that they make sure that all tests are green before they check any code in.

3.26.3 Testing first can help you program

Often, by the time you've finished writing the test, you've already worked out the best way to code the feature. Because you've already thought of what could go wrong, and written code to test it, when it comes to write the feature, you've already thought through how you are going to implement it, and what pitfalls you might have to avoid.

Try it some time. If you're stuck how to code something, change your mindset, and try to think of how you'd automate a test to see if it was successful. You'll find that when you do that, you'll have solved your problem indirectly.

Testing first forces programmers to think defensively because the way that you determine when you've finished coding is "can I think of anything more that needs testing?", programmers are forced to continually ask themselves, "What could I do to break this?" These questions are asked right at the time the programmer is closest to the code in question, not sometime later during quality control or security audit sessions. You're much more likely to notice an unchecked buffer or too-trusted input in this state.

3.27 Testing Terminologies

- Failure—the manifested inability of a system or component to perform a required function within specified limits (external incorrect behavior and symptoms)
- Error—Invalid execution state resulting from a fault
- Fault—missing or incorrect code (cause)

Classification of Testing Techniques

- Statistical Testing—Used to test a program's performance and reliability.
- Defect Testing—Used to find areas of non-conformance to the system specification.
- Functional Testing (Black box testing)
  - Test cases are generated based on software specification
  - Views program as a black box
- Structure Testing (White box testing)
  - Test cases are generated based on internal structure of the software
  - Views program as a white box

Dependability Properties

- Correctness — Consistency of implementation with specification
- Reliability — Likelihood of correct functioning
- Robustness — Acceptable behavior in unusual circumstances
- Safety — Absence of unacceptable behaviors

Software Testing and Analysis

- Robust
- Safe
- Robust but not safe: catastrophic failures can occur
- Correct but not safe or robust: the specification is inadequate

Reliable

Reliable but not correct: failures occur, rarely correct

Safe but not correct: annoying failures can occur

Correctness

- Correctness is a consistency relation
  - Meaningless without a specification
- Absolute correctness is nearly impossible to establish
  - seldom a cost-effective goal for a non-trivial software product
- Approximations are difficult to define and measure e.g., faults per 1000 lines of code

Correctness and Specification

- Example: for a "correct" language interpreter, we require:
  - Precise grammar (e.g., BNF)
  - Precise semantics
- Hoare-style proof rules, or denotational semantics, or operational semantics from model implementation (bugs and all)
- Few application domains are well enough understood for full specifications

Reliability

- Quantifiable: Mean time between failures, availability, etc.
  - describes behavior, not the product itself, e.g. fewer bugs, higher reliability
- Still relative to a specification
  - but perhaps a simple one
- Relative to a usage profile
  - often difficult to obtain in advance
  - may not be static, or even well-defined

Reliability Examples

- Telephone switch availability
  - well-defined: minutes of down-time per year
  - based on accessible, stable usage profiles
- Word processor reliability
  - Crashes per hour? Per session? Per document?
  - Inaccessible, poorly defined usage profile (several classes of users and use); may be meaningless

Fault density: a static measure

- Reliability is about execution; faults are in code (a static measure)
- Faults/ kLOC
  - May be counted, e.g. in acceptance test phase
- Problems
  - Count reflects only known faults, not total
  - Unclear what is a single fault

Robustness

- Beyond correctness: A property of specifications and implementations both
  - A robust system has specified behavior in unexpected and severe conditions
- Orthogonal to reliability
  - concerned with unusual conditions
- Often concerned with partial
  - Count reflects only known faults, not total
  - Unclear what is a single fault
  - Relation to observable quality is not clear
  - concerned with unusual conditions
- Often concerned with partial functionality
  - graceful degradation

Failure and Robustness

- Fail soft: Maintaining partial functionality
  - example: "POTS" service when extra phone services unavailable
- Fail safe: Avoiding unsafe behavior
  - may not provide any useful functionality
  - establish a "safe" state
  - example: engine shut-off in case of self-diagnosed error
- how reliable are programs with the 1999 bug?

Traffic Signal: Robustness

- Specification completeness
  - behavior when a light is disabled
  - behavior when central schedule unavailable
  - self-check and fault recovery
- Negative properties
  - never allow conflicting directions
  - no traffic waits forever

Word Processor: Robustness

- Specification completeness
  - behavior when file system full, memory exhausted, etc. (environment problems)
  - acceptable response to user error
  - crash recovery
- Negative properties
  - never enter "vulnerable" state where crash is

Software Safety

- Not concerned with maintaining function
  - Simple, incomplete, often redundant specifications of hazard prevention
- Adaptation of system safety
  - An established engineering field
- May depend on reliability, or conflict with it
  - Preventing bad things from happening (robustness/negative specifications)

Safety vs. Reliability

- Interdependent when safety depends on continued (perhaps degraded) function
  - example: flight control of fly-by-wire aircraft
- Conflicting when function does not contribute to safety
  - example: an automobile that does not start is safe, but unreliable
  - example: the safest torpedo never explodes

Fail-soft and Fail-safe

- Elaborate negative requirement: never signal green to conflicting lanes
- If North/South green inoperable, use blinking yellow in its place
  - (USA: blinking yellow => proceed with caution)
- If North/South red inoperable, blink red East/West, yellow North/South
  - (USA: blinking red => stop before proceeding)

Why negative properties?

- Formal descriptions are incomplete
  - positive specifications may not rule out dangerous behaviors
- Implementations are imperfect
  - and more complexity => more errors
  - a redundant, simple specification may facilitate stronger assurance of critical properties

Safety property examples from non-critical applications

- Language interpreter (ex. Java, safe TCL) Prohibit unsafe I/O
- e.g., cannot sneak through a firewall
  - Require predictable type-state (Java)
- to support the file & network safety assurances
- includes predictable behavior for all errors
- Unix ftp ignores world-readable.netrc
- Operating system: Memory protection prevents system crash

3.28 Special Systems Tests

There are other tests that are in a special category, since they do not focus on the normal running of the system. Six tests are essential

3.28.1 Peak Load Testing

There are critical times in many systems, particularly online systems. For example, in a banking system, analysts want to know what will happen if all tellers sign on at their terminals at the same time before the start of the business day. Will the system handle them one at a time without incident, will it attempt to handle all of them at once and be so confused that it "locks up" and must be restarted, or will terminal addresses be lost? The only sure way to find out is to test for it. The same situations can arise when tellers sign out during lunch periods and at the end of the day, so testing is looking at real situations.

3.28.2 Storage Testing

Analysts specify a capacity for the system when it is designed and constructed. Capacities are measured in terms of the number of records that a disk will handle or a file can contain. These capacities are linked to disk space and the size of indices, record keys, and so on, but they too must be tested. If the documentation for a new system to be run on a microcomputer claims that a disk file can store up to 10,000 records, each 393 bytes long, the claim must be verified before implementation.

Storage testing often requires entering data (see the discussion that follows on live versus synthetic data) until the capacity is reached. Comparing the actual and claimed capacities will verify the accuracy of the documentation on the one hand and allow a judgment about actual capacity at the same time. Many, many systems are never tested in this way. Users find out too late that claims made during installation are not true: there is not enough storage capacity for transactions and master file records.

3.28.3 Performance Time Testing

When analysts are developing a design, their concerns are more on reports, inputs, files, and processing sequences than on performance time, although this changes with experience. During simple unit and systems testing, relatively small sets of data are used to find errors or cause failures. Therefore, users frequently find out how slow or fast the response time of the system is only after it has been installed and loaded up with data. That may be too late. (Systems are rarely too fast for users.)

Performance time testing is conducted prior to implementation to determine how long it takes to receive a response to an inquiry, make a backup copy of a file, or send a transmission and receive a response. It also includes test runs to time indexing or resorting of large files of the size the system will have during a typical run or to prepare a report.

A system that runs well with only a handful of test transactions may be unacceptably slow when fully loaded. And the time to know about this is prior to implementation, when adjustments can be more easily made. Once files are fully loaded and the user is relying on the system for daily activities, it is difficult to pull it back and begin large scale changes. The user needs the system and the analyst will not want to risk the loss of live data.

3.28.4 Recovery Testing

Analysts must always assume that the system will fail and data will be damaged or lost. Even though plans and procedures are written to cover these situations, they also must be tested. By creating a failure or data loss event where the users are forces to reload and recover from a backup copy, analysts can readily determine whether recovery procedures are adequate. The best-designed plans usually are adjusted or augmented after this test.

3.28.5 Procedure Testing

The aim of procedure testing will be to ensure that the whole system fits together as planned. This will involve the clerical procedures that preceded input; the actual machine processes themselves; and the output procedures that follow. Overall timings and the ability of staff to handle the anticipated volumes will be under scrutiny.

3.28.6 Software Defect Analysis Metrics

Defect			
UI-GUI	5%	Other Defect Domains	3%
Process	12%	Customer Operations	31%
Database	1%	Incomplete	6%
Server Process	35%	Vendor Code	60%
Server Process Database	47%		
	100%		100%

3.29 Software Testing Tools

Are they really useful? There's no easy answer to this question. Software testing is a crucial part of the development process, and tools definitely help with this oftentimes overwhelming task. But to be useful, software testing tools must support the testing process.

What does this mean? It means you need to start by understanding the different phases of software testing. For example, do you understand the difference between black box and white box testing? Black box confirms only that the software meets its stated requirements and functions accordingly. White box testing looks at the actual software code to ensure paths, conditions, code statements and branches are written properly.

Do you know which software testing tools work best for unit testing, integration testing or system testing? Each of these testing processes addresses a different aspect or view of the software. Starting to understand that software testing tools are not a "one size fits all" solution?

Some rounds of software testing are better accomplished using humans, not software testing tools. Do you know which ones? Functional testing, alpha testing, acceptance testing and usability testing fall into this category. To confuse matters even a bit further, you've got to make sure you're using the right type of human for the different "human" software testing processes.

Software testers work closely with developers throughout all stages of development and use software testing tools. End users are those individuals for whom the software has been created. Beta testers are humans with more technical backgrounds (generally) who get involved in software testing just before the software is ready to be released into production. They look for last minute bugs and functionality issues. User acceptance testing ensures the resulting software is "user friendly" and satisfies the end users' needs; also important before the software goes into production.

There are even more phases of software testing that go on during the software development lifecycle. Determining which of the phases are better accomplished using software testing tools and which are better left to human intervention takes effort. In larger development houses, the IT department has a pretty good grasp on this. And they're the ones who ultimately decide which of the hundreds of software testing tools on the market are best for their development/testing teams; definitely not an easy task.

Software testing tools are themselves software. As such, each of these testing tools undergoes the whole development, testing, maintenance and upgrade cycles that other types of software do. So before making purchasing decisions, it's best to try out these products, talk with existing users, research the product's track record, and know how much configuration you'll need to do to get the product up and running.

And remember, software testing tools can't work miracles. They cannot make poorly designed software better. They can't do anything about unrealistic development schedules. And most importantly, software testing tools will never work properly if management or others are allowed to continually change software specifications after development has begun.

To be useful, software testing procedures must encompass all aspects of the software testing process. It's vitally important that the procedures define the people who will be involved in the testing process, the skill set of each team member, and their availability for the duration of the testing cycle. For the software cycle to remain on track, the software testing procedure must also delineate a carved-in-stone testing schedule including dates of important milestones.

To be effective and useful, software testing procedures require much more information. Procedures must define guidelines for creating test cases. Include in this section the processes for running these test cases, and the creation, testing and maintenance of testing scripts. Also include here a thorough explanation of all other approaches that will be used during the software testing phase. In addition to a discussion of the specific processes for software testing, be sure to define the specific parts of the software to be tested during the stated timeframe.

Software testing procedures must also define the hardware and software resources that are needed to keep the testing process on track and the length of time each will be needed. If the resources are not available, it won't be possible to meet project deadlines.

One aspect of software testing procedures that can be difficult to agree on is a definition of acceptable testing results. It's imperative, however that a firm decision be made here. No software testing procedure should ever begin without a clear understanding of what results are and are not acceptable.

Finally, there needs to be a process for reporting the results of the software testing phase, including the reporting of bugs. Software testers are not responsible for fixing software problems; only reporting them. However, they are responsible for verifying that previously reported bugs have been fixed. It's imperative that this process also be detailed in software testing procedures. Equally important is discussion of and procedures for regression testing. Software testers need to ensure that new fixes, and any software changes and enhancements do not adversely affect previously tested parts of the software.

Software testing is a critical component of the software development cycle. And software testing procedures are critical to the success of the testing phase. Software remains in a perpetual state of change which is why software testing, whether manual or automated, is so vital to a software product's success. Typically, 30-40% of the software engineers employed at larger software development companies work on software testing and each of these individuals needs to understand his or her role in this ongoing process. Software testing procedures help ensure that they do.

Interoperability refers to the ability of two or more systems (computers, communication devices, networks, software, and other information technology components) to interact with one another and exchange data according to a prescribed method in order to achieve predictable results. (ISO ITC-215)

When you're introducing a new hardware or software item or system into an existing environment, interoperability is essential. The technology environment is continually growing and diversifying into various areas such as PDAs, cell phones, MP3 Players, DVD devices, etc. PCTest has assembled a test laboratory composed of elements from all these industries and more. Our Interoperability Testing is a fundamental component in modern logic-based product development. Our engineers understand the difference between incompatibilities with the standards and functionality issues, and they will actively take a proactive role supporting your developers in discussing any possible design changes that they see may be helpful.

Performance testing as it applies to networks, websites and web-based applications involves load testing. Other performance testing for software and hardware involves benchmarking.

Load testing is employed to determine if your system (application) and servers (website) are equipped to handle the network traffic anticipated at deployment, as well as increased network traffic in the future.

What happens when your server or website is hit by a large number of users at the same time? Will it still function as intended? The basic purpose of load and performance testing an application and/or website is to accomplish the following:

- To measure the effects on user experience as total user load is increased
- To measure the average page response time and determine if the performance is acceptable at both average and maximum user loads
- To quantify the upper limit of the hardware being accessed by the application to determine whether the current system is capable of handling the anticipated future loads
- Capacity of your current system
- Router/firewall problems

- A broken web server, application server or database server
- Load balancing problems
- Bandwidth problems
- Server capacity problems
- Performance (average page response time) problems

3.30 Bench Mark

A benchmark is a standard of excellence or achievement used to compare and measure similar products. It is a technique for identifying measurable successes of others and applying them to your own organization. The benchmarking process compares an organization's practices, processes and outcomes to standards of excellence in a systematic way. It is a process that can also be used to design a new system or model.

To gain insight into your application's behavior and bring about consistent performance, you need to quantify what is frequently only subjective or anecdotal information. Benchmarking programs provide the ability to set acceptability standards based on real world comparisons (such as a competing product or recognized industry standard) and track performance against those standards through each new release.

Benchmarking helps in accomplishing the following:

- Fine-tune your product and/or its operating environment
- Optimize response time and resource usage
- Verify marketing claims or set price points
- Compare the performance of a product to a competing software or industry standard
- Set and improve production standards
- Identify areas of improvement opportunities
- Performance issues
- System limitations
- Realistic comparison against known standards

3.31 Areas of Improvement Opportunities

If you are developing a hardware or software solution, we will test your product using many of the industry recognized benchmark tools and compare the results to your own previous versions or your competitors' products. Let PCTest help you evaluate the performance of your application under situations of stress.

Functionality testing is employed to verify whether your product meets the intended specifications and functional requirements laid out in your development documentation.

As competition in the software and hardware development arena intensifies, it becomes critical to deliver products that are virtually bug-free. Functionality testing helps your company provide products with a minimum amount of issues to an increasingly sophisticated pool of end users. Gone are the days when users will quietly find their own workarounds for bug-filled technology. Potential purchasers of your products may find professional and consumer review sites online where honest and often brutal product reviews and bug reports deter them from buying your software. PCTest will help ensure that your product functions as intended, keeping your service and support calls to a minimum. Let our trained professionals find functional issues and bugs before your end users do.

3.32 Types of Functional Testing Techniques

Ad Hoc—Takes advantage of individual testing talents and intelligence based upon consideration of product goals, level of user capabilities and possible areas and features that may create confusion. The tester will generate test cases on the spur of the moment, as quickly as possible, as ideas occur to them. This kind of testing generally finds most bugs in new software in the shortest possible time.

Exploratory—The tester designs and executes tests while learning the product. Test design is organized by a set of concise patterns designed to assure that testers don't miss anything important.

Combination—The tester performs a sequence of events using different paths to complete tasks. This can uncover bugs related to order of events that are difficult to find using other methods.

Scripted—The tester uses a test script that lays out the specific functions to be tested. A test script can be provided by the customer/developer or constructed by PCTest, depending on the needs of your organization.

Competitive Analysis is a process of gathering and analyzing information about your competitors, their practices, products, strengths and weaknesses and business trends in order to assess your position in the market and improve your products and marketing strategies.

In today's market, you must know what your competitors are doing and what to do to stay ahead of the competition. Many businesses believe they are providing a good product to their customers, but do not have reliable information showing how customers perceive their product or how it compares to the competition.

A Competitive Analysis performed by an unbiased third party is an invaluable tool because it can help you identify ways to attract new customers, as well as keep the ones you have satisfied with your products. PCTest's Competitive Analysis can help you determine the following:

- Strengths and weaknesses: How your product stacks up against the competition and in what areas they have an edge over your product and in what areas your product is superior.
- Identify your competition: Verify who are your primary and secondary competitors are.
- Improvements: How and in what areas your product, processes, and practices must be improved to meet market demands or to stay ahead of the competition.
- Marketing: What improvements you need to make in your marketing approach—you may want to highlight why your product is ahead of the competition, or the unique features that consumers desire.

Competitive Analysis gives you a realistic view of your competition. It also gives you the opportunity to identify improvement in areas like manufacturing processes, customer services, and marketing claims. It can help you compare products prior to making your marketing and promotional decisions, thus saving you both time and money. PCTest's Competitive Analysis will help you accomplish the following:

- Have a realistic view of your competition.
- Foresee market changes and demands.
- Identify ways to attract customers from your competitors.
- Discover opportunities for improvement in your business practices.
- Identify necessary changes in your processes to meet market demands.
- Identify necessary changes in your processes to reduce costs.
- What products compete with yours.
- What advantages your products have over the competition.
- What disadvantages your products have when compared to the competition.
- The readiness of a new product in the market.
- A realistic view of customers' perception of your product against the competition.

PCTest evaluates features and functions of your products and those of the competition. Each evaluation covers a wide range of criteria, which are then classified in categories and subcategories. The results of the evaluations are kept in a proprietary secure web-based tool kit accessible only to you on-line.

Staffing: PCTest will assign a Project Leader and Competitive Analysis Engineers to test and evaluate your product. The PCTest Project Leader's primary responsibility is to ensure that our testing meets your requirements and is executed according to the agreements. We will also provide you with up-to-date progress, status, and findings. In addition to managing the testing process, the Project Leader will provide technical expertise and will work with you to make any required changes to the test plan as issues arise.

Scope: Before the Competitive Analysis is started, PCTest Engineers will collaborate with you to define the scope of the analysis—which of your products and which of your competitors and their products will be included in the test.

Test Case Scenarios: PCTest will work with you to develop evaluation profiles to ensure all features and functions are included.

Competitive Analysis Report: At the conclusion of testing your product, you will receive a detailed on-line Competitive Analysis Report from the PCTest Project Leader and the PCTest Engineers.

3.33 Testing Automation

Software testing can be very costly. Automation is a good way to cut down time and cost. Software testing tools and techniques usually suffer from a lack of generic applicability and scalability. The reason is straight-forward. In order to automate the process, we have to have some ways to generate oracles from the specification, and generate test cases to test the target software against the oracles to decide their correctness. Today we still don't have a full-scale system that has achieved this goal. In general, significant amount of human intervention is still needed in testing. The degree of automation remains at the automated test script level.

The problem is lessened in reliability testing and performance testing. In robustness testing, the simple specification and oracle doesn't crash, doesn't hang suffices. Similar simple metrics can also be used in stress testing.

3.34 The Time Per Ending Testing Process

Testing is potentially endless. We cannot test till all the defects are unearthed and removed — it is simply impossible. At some point, we have to stop testing and ship the software. The question is when.

Realistically, testing is a trade-off between budget, time and quality. It is driven by profit models. The pessimistic, and unfortunately most often used approach is to stop testing whenever some, or any of the allocated resources—time, budget, or test cases—are exhausted. The optimistic stopping rule is to stop testing when either reliability meets the requirement, or the benefit from continuing testing cannot justify the testing cost [Yang 95]. This will usually require the use of reliability models to evaluate and predict reliability of the software under test. Each evaluation requires repeated running of the following cycle: failure data gathering—modeling—prediction. This method does not fit well for ultra-dependable systems, however, because the real field failure data will take too long to accumulate.

3.35 Alternatives to Testing

Software testing is more and more considered a problematic method toward better quality. Using testing to locate and correct software defects can be an endless process. Bugs cannot be completely ruled out. Just as the complexity barrier indicates: chances are testing and fixing problems may not necessarily improve the quality and reliability of the software. Sometimes fixing a problem may introduce much more severe problems into the system, happened after bug fixes, such as the telephone outage in California and eastern seaboard in 1991. The disaster happened after changing 3 lines of code in the signaling system.

In a narrower view, many testing techniques may have flaws, for example Coverage testing. Is code coverage, branch coverage in testing really related to software quality? There is no definite proof. As early as in, the so-called "human testing"—including inspections, walkthroughs, reviews—are suggested as possible alternatives to traditional testing methods. advocates inspection as a cost-effect alternative to unit testing. The experimental results suggests that code reading by stepwise abstraction is at least as effective as on-line functional and structural testing in terms of number and cost of faults observed.

Using formal methods to "prove" the correctness of software is also an attracting research direction. But this method cannot surmount the complexity barrier either. For relatively simple software, this method works well. It does not scale well to those complex, full-fledged large software systems, which are more error-prone.

In a broader view, we may start to question the utmost purpose of testing. Why do we need more effective testing methods anyway, since finding defects and removing them does not necessarily lead to better quality. An analogy of the problem is like the car manufacturing process. In the craftsmanship epoch, we make cars and hack away the problems and defects. But such methods were washed away by the tide of pipelined manufacturing and good quality engineering process, which makes the car defect-free in the manufacturing phase. This indicates that engineering the design process (such as clean-room software engineering) to make the product have less defects may be more effective than engineering the testing process. Testing is used solely for quality monitoring and management, or, "design for testability". This is the leap for software from craftsmanship to engineering.

Other White Box Techniques

Other white box testing techniques include:

1. Condition testing exercises the logical conditions in a program.
2. Data flow testing selects test paths according to the locations of definitions and uses of variables in the program.

REFERENCES

Ballista COTS Software Robustness Testing Harness homepage.

Beizer, Boris. *Black-box Testing: Techniques for Functional Testing of Software and Systems*. Publication info: New York: Wiley, c1995. Physical description: xxv, 294 p.: ill.

Boris Beizer. *Software Testing Techniques*. Second edition. 1990.

Cem Kaner. Testing Computer Software. 1993.

Dick Hamlet. "Foundations of Software Testing: Dependability Theory" Proceedings of the second ACM SIGSOFT symposium on foundations of software engineering, 1994, pp. 128-39.

Filippos I. Vokolos, and Elaine J. Weyuker. "Performance Testing of Software Systems". Proceedings of the first international workshop on Software and Performance, 1998, pp. 80-87.

Harry Koehnemann, and Timothy Lindquist. "Towards Target-level Testing and Debugging Tools for Embedded Software" Conference proceedings on TRI-Ada '93, 1993, p. 288.

Hetzel, William C. *The Complete Guide to Software Testing*, 2nd ed. Publication info: Wellesley, Mass. : QED Information Sciences, 1988. Physical description: ix, 280 p. ill.

IEEE Standard Glossary of Software Engineering Terminology (IEEE Std 610.12-1990), IEEE Computer Soc., Dec. 10, 1990.

Joe W. Duran and Simeon C. Ntafos. "An Evaluation Random Testing", *IEEE Transactions on Software Engineering*, Vol. SE-10, No. 4, July 1984, pp. 438-43.

John D. Musa. "Software-reliability-engineered Testing Practice" (tutorial); Proceedings of the 1997 International Conference on Software Engineering, 1997, pp. 628-29.

John DeVale, Philip Koopman & David Guttendorf. "The Ballista Software Robustness Testing Service". Proceedings of TCS'99, Washington DC.

Kropp, N.P., Koopman, P.J. and Siewiorek, D.P. "Automated Robustness Testing of off-the-shelf Software Components". Twenty-eighth Annual International Symposium on Fault-Tolerant Computing (Cat. No.98CB36224).

Michael R. Lyu. *Handbook of Software Reliability Engineering*. McGraw-Hill Publishing, 1995.

Myers, Glenford J. *The Art of Software Testing*, Publication info: New York : Wiley, c1979. Physical description: xi, p. 177 : ill.

Norman Parrington and Marc Roper. *Understanding Software Testing*, Published by John Willey & Sons, 1989.

Philip Koopman and John DeVale. "Comparing the Robustness of POSIX Operating Systems". Proceedings of FTCS'99, 15-18 June 1999, Madison, Wisconsin.

Richard A. DeMillo. "Progress toward Automated Software Testing", Proceedings of the 13th International Conference on Software Engineering , 1991, p. 180.

Technical Report, Department of Computer Science, University of Maryland, College Park, 1985.

Victor R. Basili and Richard W. Selby, Jr. "Comparing the Effectiveness of Software Testing Strategies".

William E. Howden. *Functional Program Testing and Analysis*. McGraw-Hill, 1987.

William E. Perry. *A Standard for Testing Application Software,* 1990.

Yang, M.C.K. and Chao, A. "Reliability-estimation and Stopping-rules for Software Testing, based on Repeated Appearances of Bugs", *IEEE Transactions on Reliability,* vol. 44, no. 2, pp. 315-21, 1995.

SOFTWARE REQUIREMENT AND SPECIFICATION

4

4.1 Requirements

One of the most reliable methods of ensuring problems, or failure, in a large, complex software project is to have poorly documented requirements specifications. Requirements are the details describing an application's externally-perceived functionality and properties. Requirements should be clear, complete, reasonably detailed, cohesive, attainable, and testable. A non-testable requirement would be, for example, 'user-friendly' (too subjective). A testable requirement would be something like 'the user must enter their previously-assigned password to access the application'. Determining and organizing requirements details in a useful and efficient way can be a difficult effort; different methods are available depending on the particular project.

Care should be taken to involve all of a project's significant 'customers' in the requirements process. 'Customers' could be in-house personnel or out, and could include end-users, customer acceptance testers, customer contract officers, customer management, future software maintenance engineers, salesmen, etc. Anyone who could later derail the project if their expectations aren't met should be included if possible.

Organizations vary considerably in their handling of requirements specifications. Ideally, the requirements are spelled out in a document with statements such as 'the product shall.....'. 'Design' specifications should not be confused with 'requirements'; design specifications should be traceable back to the requirements.

In some organizations requirements may end up in high level project plans, functional specification documents, in design documents, or in other documents at various levels of detail. No matter what they are called, some type of documentation with detailed requirements will be needed by testers in order to properly plan and execute tests. Without such documentation, there will be no clear-cut way to determine if a software application is performing correctly.

'Agile' methods such as Extreme Programming (XP) use methods requiring close interaction and cooperation between programmers and customers/end-users to iteratively develop requirements. In the XP 'test first' approach developments create automated unit testing code before the application code, and these automated unit tests essentially embody the requirements.

4.2 Software Requirements Analysis

Software requirements analysis is the activity of eliciting, analyzing, and recording requirements for software systems. It shares much in common with requirements analysis for more general kinds of systems, but has its own specific approaches.

The purpose of analysis activity is to transform candidate technical requirements into formal requirements by ensuring that they express the needs of the customer.

Analysis is an iterative activity. The process steps will likely to be repeated several times, with consultation between customers, end users and developers during each iteration and communication through the steps.

- **Eliciting Requirements:** Requirements elicitation is the task of communicating with customers and users to determine what are their requirements.
- **Analyzing Requirements:** The true analysis part of requirements analysis locates places where requirements are unclear, incomplete, ambiguous, or contradictory. Requirements analysts work with customer representatives to resolve these issues, sometimes preparing tradeoff studies to compare alternatives.
- **Recording Requirements:** The classic Waterfall process records requirements in large natural-language documents. Processes based on the Unified Modeling Language record requirements as use cases. Extreme programming records requirements as user stories.

4.3 Purpose of User Requirements

Definition

The purpose of defining user requirements as described in this step is to prepare for writing an accurate and complete Statement of Work. The Statement of Work is a key element of the Software Contract Package. When user requirements are well understood from the start of a project, customer satisfaction with the resulting software will be higher.

Describe Users

Identify the characteristics of the intended users of the software:

- Names of industries, specific businesses and job functions.
- Minimum computer skills and equipment that users will have.
- Specialized technical knowledge or expertise that users will possess.
- Specialized equipment that is owned or operated by the intended users.
- Different job functions or levels of experience that differentiate the various sets of expected users. These groupings or types of expected users are known as the "user classes" for the software.
- Approximate numbers of the various types of users expected for the software.
- How often users are expected to use the software.
- The tasks that the users will accomplish with the software.

- Viewed broadly, a user is anyone who is affected by or who may affect the software product. User roles are the kinds of persons who will be affected by the system: those who use the software directly, those who use the results produced, and those who never see the system, but have information influencing its design (such as regulators and lawyers). Considering this broad list of user classes suggests features and functions that need to be included.

Information Technology departments at customer companies are another important group to consider. For example, including steps to participate in customer internal software development processes may be important to ensure acceptance of the completed software within their systems.

Gather Initial Requirements

- Get the users involved very early in the concept discussions to understand what they need the software to do. These are the initial functional requirements.
- Discuss the software requirements with funders and end-users. Be sure to cover:
    - Key features and functions that the software must perform, including graphical interface, management reports, and human factors (usability)
    - Benefits to the customer including savings that could be obtained
    - Approximate cost for the development
    - Any commercial software products that provide overlapping or competing capabilities.

4.4 High Level Requirements

The user/sponsor views the system's analyst (SA) as the user's representative and provide all input through the SA. Direct interaction with programmer/tester is generally discouraged as the chance of mutual misunderstanding is very high. The user requirements' specification should be a joint product of the user and system analyst: the user brings his/her/their needs and wish list, the system analyst brings knowledge of what is likely to prove doable within cost and time constraints. When the user needs are translated into a set of high level requirements it is also the best time to write the first version of the acceptance test, which should, thereafter, be religiously kept up to date with the requirements. That way, the user will be absolutely clear about what s/he is getting. It is also a safeguard against untestable requirements, misunderstandings, and requirements creep.

The development of the first level of requirements is not a purely analytical exercise and should also involve both the system analyst and engineer. If any compromises are to be made to meet constraints like cost, schedule, power, or space, the system analyst must ensure that the final product and overall look and feel do not stray very far from the user's intent. The system analyst should focus on developing a design that optimizes the constraints but ensures a workable and reliable product. The system analyst is primarily concerned with the comfort and usability of the product; the engineer is primarily concerned with the producibility and utility of the product.

The provision of needed services to the user is the true function of an engineered system. However, as systems become ever larger and more complex, and as their emphases move away from simple hardware and software components, the narrow application of traditional systems development principles is found to be insufficient—the application of the more general principles of systems, hardware, and software system architecture to the design of (sub) systems is seen to be needed. An system architecture is also a simplified model of the finished end product—its primary function is to define the parts and their relationships to each other so that the whole can be seen to be a consistent, complete, and correct representation of what the user had in mind—especially for the computer-human-interface. It is also used to ensure that the parts fit together and relate in the desired way.

4.5 Requirements Testing

Requirements testing is used:

- To ensure that system performs correctly.
- To ensure that correctness can be sustained for a considerable period of time.
- System can be tested for correctness through all phases of SDLC but in case of reliability the programs should be in place to make system operational.

The objective of requirements testing is:

- Successful implementation of user requirements.
- Correctness maintained over considerable period of time. Processing of the application complies with the organization's policies and procedures.
- Secondary users needs are fulfilled:
  - Security officer
  - DBA
  - Internal auditors
  - Record retention
  - Comptroller

Implementing Requirement Analysis

Test conditions created

These test conditions are generalized ones, which become test cases as the SDLC progresses until system is fully operational. Test conditions are more effective when created from user's requirements. If there are any errors in the documents those will get incorporated in Test conditions that are created from these documents and testing would not be able to find those errors. Test conditions if created from other sources (other than documents), error trapping is effective.

- Functional Checklist created.
- Every application should be Requirement tested.
- Should start at Requirements phase and should progress till operations and maintenance phase.
- The method used to carry requirement testing and the extent of it is important.

Example:

- Creating test matrix to prove that system requirements as documented are the requirements desired by the user.
- Creating checklist to verify that application complies to the organizational policies and procedures.

4.6 What is a Specification?

A specification can be defined as "a statement of needs to be satisfied by the procurement of external resources". It is also known as an operational requirement, statement of requirement, statement of service requirement and output-based specification.

Its purpose is to present prospective suppliers with a clear, accurate and full description of the organisation's needs, and so enable them to propose a solution to meet those needs. The supplier's response to the requirement is evaluated to arrive at, depending upon the procurement strategy, either the supplier to be awarded the contract, or those suppliers invited to take part in negotiations.

The requirements in the specification subsequently become incorporated in the contract with the successful supplier.

4.6.1 Functional Specifications

Functional specifications are a key part of many development processes and came into vogue with the development of the waterfall process. While it is a development process aspect, it is critically necessary for software functional test. A functional specification often describes the external view of an object or a procedure indicating the options by which a service could be invoked. The testers use this to write down test cases from a black box testing perspective.

The advantage of having a functional specification is that the test generation activity could happen in parallel with the development of the code. This is ideal from several dimensions. Firstly, it gains parallelism in execution, removing a serious serialization bottleneck in the development process. By the time the software code is ready, the test cases are also ready to be run against the code. Secondly, it forces a degree of clarity from the perspective of a designer and an architect, so essential for the overall efficiencies of development. Thirdly, the functional specifications become documentation that can be shared with the customers to gain an additional perspective on what is being developed.

4.6.2 Reviews and Inspection

Software inspection, which was invented by Mike Fagan in the mid-70's at IBM, has grown to be recognized as one of the most efficient methods of debugging code.

Today, 20 years later, there are several books written on software inspection, tools have been made available, and consulting organizations teach the practice of software inspection. It is argued that software inspection can easily provide a ten times gain in the process of debugging software. Not much needs to be said about this, since it is a fairly well-known and understood practice.

Review Requirements with Users

Review the initial requirements with end-users and funders to obtain their approval of:

- What tasks the users want to use the software to do.
- Key features and functions.
- Reports and results the software should produce.
- Other software that needs to interface to this software.
- User interface description.
- Other key requirements of users and funders.

VERIFICATION AND VALIDATION

5

5.1 Precision and Accuracy

Precision and Accuracy are two qualities of a software's working which look similar but are quite different. Let us see how:

Precision

Precision is the degree of refinement in the performance of an operation, or the degree of perfection in the instruments and methods used to obtain a result. An indication of the uniformity or reproducibility of a result. Precision relates to the quality of an operation by which a result is obtained, and is distinguished from accuracy, which relates to the quality of the result.

Accuracy

Accuracy is the degree of conformity with a standard (the "truth"). Accuracy relates to the quality of a result, and is distinguished from precision, which relates to the quality of the operation by which the result is obtained.

The goal of the testing activity is to find as many errors as possible before the user of the software finds them. We can use testing to determine whether a program component meets its requirements. To accomplish its primary goal (finding errors) or any of its secondary purposes (meeting requirements), software testing must be applied in a systematic fashion. Testing involves operation of a system or application under controlled conditions and evaluating the results.

5.2 Verification and Validation

Verification and Validation (V&V) is a Software Testing activity to enhance quality of the software being built. It is planned and conducted systematically throughout the software life cycle.

Verification is the checking or testing of items, including software, for conformance and consistency with an associated specification. Software testing is just one kind of verification, which also uses techniques such as reviews, analysis, inspections and walkthroughs.

Validation is the process of checking that what has been specified is what the user actually wanted. Validation activity may begin when most or all software functions as per customer expectations. Validation testing provides final accurance that the software meets all functional, behavioural and performance requirements. Usually Black-box testing is used for this activity.

Schulmeyer and Mackenzie (2000) define verification and validation (V&V) as follows: "Verification is the assurance that the products of a particular phase in the development process are consistent with the requirements of that phase and the preceding phase".

The Quality System regulation is harmonized with ISO 8402:1994, which treats "verification" and "validation" as separate and distinct terms. On the other hand, many software engineering journal articles and textbooks use the terms "verification" and "validation" interchangeably, or in some cases refer to software "verification, validation, and testing (VV&T)" as if it is a single concept, with no distinction among the three terms.

Software verification provides objective evidence that the design outputs of a particular phase of the software development life cycle meet all of the specified requirements for that phase. Software verification looks for consistency, completeness, and correctness of the software and its supporting documentation, as it is being developed, and provides support for a subsequent conclusion that software is validated. Software testing is one of many verification activities intended to confirm that software development output meets its input requirements. Other verification activities include various static and dynamic analyses, code and document inspections, walkthroughs, and other techniques.

Software validation is a part of the design validation for a finished device, but is not separately defined in the Quality System regulation. FDA considers software validation to be "confirmation by examination and provision of objective evidence that software specifications conform to user needs and intended uses, and that the particular requirements implemented through software can be consistently fulfilled." In practice, software validation activities may occur both during, as well as at the end of the software development life cycle to ensure that all requirements have been fulfilled. Since software is usually part of a larger hardware system, the validation of software typically includes evidence that all software requirements have been implemented correctly and completely and are traceable to system requirements. A conclusion that software is validated is highly dependent upon comprehensive software testing, inspections, analyses, and other verification tasks performed at each stage of the software development life cycle. Testing of device software functionality in a simulated use environment, and user site testing are typically included as components of an overall design validation program for a software automated device.

Software verification and validation are difficult because a developer cannot test forever, and it is hard to know how much evidence is enough. In large measure, software validation is a matter of developing a "level of confidence" that the device meets all requirements and user expectations for the software automated functions and features of the device. Measures such as defects found in specifications documents, estimates of defects remaining, testing coverage, and other techniques are all used to develop an acceptable level of confidence before shipping the product. The level of confidence, and therefore the level of software validation, verification, and testing effort needed, will vary depending upon the safety risk (hazard) posed by the automated functions of the device.

5.3 Verification Techniques

In the development of an software system, it is important to be able to determine if the system meets specifications and if its outputs are correct. This is the process of verification and validation (V&V) and its planning must start early in the development life cycle. Both aspects are necessary as a system meeting its specifications does not necessary mean it is technically correct and vice versa. There are many different V&V techniques which are applicable at different stages of the development life cycle. The results of V&V forms an important component in the safety case, which is a document used to support certification. Certification is usually pursued due to either legal reasons or economic advantages. The certification process also starts from the beginning of the life cycle and requires cooperation between the developer and regulatory agency from the very start. Though V&V does not prove that the system is safe or dependable, and there is always a limit to how much testing is enough testing. In addition, certification does not prove that a system is correct, so it does not eliminate the developer's legal and moral obligations. Therefore, extreme care should be taken in the development of embedded systems to make sure that the right amount of time is spent on V&V, and also that certification not be used to prove that a system is correct.

Verification, validation, and certification are essential in the life cycle of any safety critical embedded system. The development of any system is not complete without rigorous testing and verification that the implementation is consistent with the specifications. Verification and validation (V&V) have become important, especially in software, as the complexity of software in systems has increased, and planning for V&V is necessary from the beginning of the development life cycle. Over the past 20 to 30 years, software development has evolved from small tasks involving a few people to enormously large tasks involving many people. Because of this change, verification and validation has similarly also undergone a change.

Previously, verification and validation was an informal process performed by the software engineer himself. However, as the complexity of systems increased, it became obvious that continuing this type of testing would result in unreliable products. It became necessary to look at V&V as a separate activity in the overall software development life cycle. The V&V of today is significantly different from the past as it is practised over the entire software life cycle. It is also highly formalized and sometimes activities are performed by organizations independent of the software developer. [Andriole, 86] In addition, V&V is very closely linked with certification because it is a major component in support of certification.

While the terms verification and validation are used interchangably in papers and texts, there are distinct differences in their terminology. According to the *IEEE Standard Glossary of Software Engineering Terminology*, verification is defined as "The process of evaluating a system or component to determine whether the products of a given development phase satisfy the conditions imposed at the start of that phase." Validation, on the other hand, is defined as "The process of evaluating a system or component during or at the end of the development process to determine whether it satisfies specified requirements." So verification simply demonstrates whether the output of a phase conforms to the input of a phase as opposed to showing that the output is actually correct. Verification will not detect errors resulting from incorrect input specification and these errors may propagate without detection through later stages in the development cycle. It is not enough to only depend on verification, so validation is necessary to check for problems with the specification and to demonstrate that the system is operational. Finally, certification is "A written guarantee that a system or compnent complies with its specified requirements and is acceptable for operational use."

5.3.1 Primary Goal of Software Validation

A documented requirements specification represents the user's needs and intended uses from which the product is developed. A primary goal of software validation is to then demonstrate that all completed software products comply with all documented software and system requirements. The correctness and completeness of both the system requirements and the software requirements should be addressed as part of the design validation process for the device. Software validation includes confirmation of conformance to all software specifications and confirmation that all software requirements are traceable to the system specifications. Confirmation is an important part of the overall design validation to ensure that all aspects of the medical device conform to user needs and intended uses.

The IEEE Standard for Software Verification and Validation (IEEE Std 1012-1998) contains information on software integrity levels, the V&V process, the Software V&V reporting, administrative, and documentation requirements, and an outline of the software verification and validation plan.

V&V can be performed by the same organization performing the design, development, and implementation but sometimes it is performed by an independent testing agency. This is called independent verification and validation (IV&V). These agencies usually need to be accredited by a higher organization, to be sure that their results are dependable. For example, in the United Kingdom, the National Measurement Accreditation Service has begun to accredit companies for testing computer software used in safety-critical systems. The first company was accredited in 1994. The testing methods approved includes a suite of in-house procedures including static and dynamic testing techniques. [Storey, 96]

V&V is a very time consuming process as it consists of planning from the start, the development of test cases, the actual testing, and the analysis of the testing results. It is important that there are people specifically in charge of V&V that can work with the designers. Since exhaustive testing is not feasible for any complex system, an issue that occurs is how much testing is enough testing. Sure, the more testing the better but when do the cost and time of testing outweigh the advantages gained from testing. The amount of time and money spent on V&V will certainly vary from project to project. In many organizations, testing is done until either or both time and money runs out. Whether this method is effective or not, it is a technique used by many companies.

5.3.2 Certification Process

Verification and validation are part of the long certification process for any embedded system. There are different reasons why a product needs certification. Sometimes certification is required for legal reasons. For example, before an aircraft is allowed to fly, it must obtain a license. Being certified would also be important for commercial reasons like having a sales advantage. One of the main reasons for certification is to show competence in specific areas. Certification are usually carried out by government agencies or other organizations with a national standing.

5.3.3 Benefits of Software Validation

Software validation is a critical tool used to assure the quality of device software and software automated operations. Software validation can increase the usability and reliability of the device, resulting in decreased failure rates, fewer recalls and corrective actions, less risk to patients and users, and reduced liability to device manufacturers. Software validation can also reduce long-term costs by making it easier and less costly to reliably modify software and revalidate software changes. Software maintenance can represent a very large percentage of the total cost of software over its entire life cycle. An established comprehensive software validation process helps to reduce the long-term cost of software by reducing the cost of validation for each subsequent release of the software.

5.4 Coding Standards

The best applications are coded properly. This sounds like an obvious statement, but by 'properly', it is meant that the code not only does its job well, but is also easy to add to, maintain and debug.

This "maintainable code" is a popular talking point among those involved with PHP and probably with other languages as well. There's nothing worse than inheriting an application or needing to make changes to code that requires a lot of energy to decipher—you end up trawling through lines and lines of code that doesn't make its purpose or intentions clear. Looking through unfamiliar code is much easier if it is laid out well and everything is neatly commented with details that explain any complicated constructs and the reasoning behind them.

When we learn a new language, we usually begin to code in a specific style. In most cases, we'll write in a style that we want, not one that has been suggested to us. But once we start to code using a particular style, like a spoken language dialect, it will become second nature—we'll use that style in everything we create. Such a style might include the conventions we use to name variables and functions ($userName, $username or $user_name for example), and how we comment our work. Any style should ensure that we can read our code easily.

However, what happens when we start to code bigger projects and introduce additional people to help create a large application? Conflicts in the way you write your code will most definitely appear.

5.4.1 Coding Standards Document

A coding standards document tells developers how they must write their code. Instead of each developer coding in their own preferred style, they will write all code to the standards outlined in the document. This makes sure that a large project is coded in a consistent style—parts are not written differently by different programmers. Not only does this solution make the code easier to understand, it also ensures that any developer who looks at the code will know what to expect throughout the entire application.

Coding standards are great—but how do you decide which standards you want to apply, and how they will be defined? When you formulate your ideal coding style, you should think about these points:

- Can you actually read the code? Is it spaced out clearly?
- Do you separate blocks of code into 'paragraphs' so that different sections are easily defined?
- Are you using indentation to show where control structures (if, else, while and other loops) begin and end, and where the code within them is?

- Are your variable naming conventions consistent throughout the code and do they briefly describe that data that they'll contain?
- Are functions named in accordance with what they do?
- If you come back to the code in a few weeks or months, will you be able to work out what's happening without needing to look at every line?
- How are you commenting the work?
- Have you used complex language functions/constructs that are quicker to write but affect readability?

Once you've considered those points, you can begin to draft your coding standards. Consult with your team members (if any) and compare how they code to your own style—you shouldn't force total change upon everyone. Compromise and incorporate elements of everyone's style. If someone has been coding in a specific way for a long-time, it will take a while for that developer to change to the new method. Developers will likely adopt the style gradually, just as an accent develops over time.

5.4.2 Create Maintainable Code

As we said at the beginning of this discussion, you want to create maintainable code. If you stop developing a project, return to it several months later, or hand development over to someone else, you (and other developers) want to be able to understand what's going on in the code. We keep mentioning 'readability', but what actually constitutes "readable code"? The answer to this question will obviously differ for each programmer, but I believe there are some common fundamentals, which we'll discuss now. I've used PHP to outline various styles here, but similar ideas will apply to other languages:

```
// Method 1
if (condition)
function1($a, $b, $c);
for ($i < 7 && $j > 8 || $k == 4)
a($i);
// Method 2
if (condition)
{
 get_user($id, $username, $key);
}
For (($i < 7) && (($j < 8) || ($k == 4)))
{
display_graph($value);
}
```

Here are two ways we might write the same code—you can see the difference between easily readable code and complex, but more quickly written code. Even if you don't know much PHP, you probably noted that the second snippet is much tidier and easier to understand. I've named functions using a verb (get, display), used variable names that describe the data they contain, and used brackets to help show what the condition is. Not only that, but

I've also included the braces for the control structures and used indentation to show which code appears under each structure.

Your own idea of readable code might differ slightly from this, but I'd bet that every PHP coder could easily understand what's going on in the second example. The first example, however, takes extra time to comprehend. Sacrificing extra lines and whitespace will make a noticeable difference to the layout of the code. As you develop coding standards, try to ensure that they allow anyone to work out the code in future.

5.4.3 Why Standard is Important?

Though at initial stages it seems like a burden to follow standard, its advantages become visible once the software grows to few thousand lines spanning few hundred files. Some of the advantages are:

- Programmer feels comfortable with the code written by others, as it is similar to what he himself would have written.
- Person joining the group at later stage can pickup the code easily (once he is familiar with the standards).

If care is taken to define the standard in such a way that it avoids problematic C++ idioms, then silly mistakes can be avoided. The problem with having standard is that it takes time to get acquainted with it. And if care is not taken during this transition period, then the resulting code will be a mix of standard and programmer's natural style. This can be avoided by having regular code review sessions.

Coding standards increase productivity in the development process, make code easier to maintain, and keep code from being tied to one person or team. But where should standards come from? How extensive should they be, and more importantly, who should enforce them? Here are the short answers to these questions:

5.4.4 Who Dictates the Coding Standards?

You can choose from many industry coding standards. Some companies—Microsoft and Sun Microsystems, for example—offer guidelines. Some coding standards, such as Hungarian Notation, are the product of one person's labor (in this case, Dr. Charles Simonyi, a Hungarian software developer at Microsoft).

Certain coding standards are language specific. Standards for Visual Basic dictate that you should prefix all textboxes with "txt" and all buttons with "cmd." Sun Microsystems offers coding standards for Java. Once you've settled on a coding standard, take the language-specific suggestions and add your own. For example, you might decree that variable and function names should be descriptive, or that the behavior of particular functions must be clearly commented. (The recommended mantra is "Document, document, document: every class, every method, every few lines of code".)

While it's important to have coding standards, it's equally important not to have superfluous coding standards. Imagine, if you will, a standard that dictates that the first character of a variable name must indicate the application in which it resides, the second character must indicate the module, and the third character must indicate the data type. Excessive coding standards such as this can impede the creative process and become a hindrance to development.

You should not have more coding standards than will fit on one or two pages. It makes it very hard to name your variable if you have to consult a chart to do so. The first step in enforcing coding standards is to keep those standards easily accessible. Ideally, you should have a laminated cheat sheet pinned up in each developer's cube.

During peer code review sessions, someone's job must include being code standards bad cop. However, automated tools offer another option to managers looking to enforce standards.

Some of the best tools on the market are made by Parasoft. Parasoft produces language-specific tools that automatically enforce more than 300 coding standards. The products include a Rule Wizard feature, which allows developers to create and implement their own custom rules.

One of the standards enforced by Parasoft products requires that one-character variable names be used only for their conventional purpose, such as b for a byte, c for a chart, f for a float. If this standard is violated, the output would look like this:

```
package examples.rules.naming;
public class CVN {
void method () {
int b = 1; // VIOLATION
 }
 }
```

5.4.5 Programming Style

Programming style (also called coding standards or code convention) is a term that describes conventions for writing source code in a certain programming language.

Programming style is often dependent on the choice of programming language one is writing in. C style will vary from BASIC style, and so on.

5.4.6 Characteristics of Styles

Good style, being a subjective matter, is difficult to concretely categorize; however, there are a number of general characteristics. With the advent of software that formats source code automatically, the focus on how source code looks should yield to a greater focus on naming, logic, and higher techniques. As a practical point, using a computer to format source code saves time, and it is possible to then enforce company-wide standards without religious debates.

(1) Appropriate Variable Names

Appropriate choices for variable names is seen as the keystone for good style. Poorly-named variables make code harder to read and understand.

For example, consider the following pseudocode snippet:

```
get a b c
if a < 12 and b < 60 and c < 60
    return true
           else
   return false
```

Because of the choice of variable names, the function of the code is difficult to work out. However, if the variable names are made more descriptive,

```
get hours minutes seconds
if hours < 12 and minutes < 60 and seconds < 60
 return true
else
 return false
```

the code's intent is easier to discern, namely, "Given a 24-hour time, true will be returned if it is in the morning and false otherwise."

(2) Indent Style

Indent style, in programming languages that use braces or indenting to delimit logical blocks of code, such as C, is also a key to good style. Using a logical and consistent indent style makes one's code more readable. Compare:

```
if(hours < 12 && minutes < 60 && seconds < 60){
 return true;
}else{
 return false;
}
```

or

```
if(hours < 12 && minutes < 60 && seconds < 60)
{
 return true;
}
else
{
 return false;
}
```

with something like

```
if(hours<12&&minutes<60&&seconds<60){return true;}
else{return false;}
```

The first example is much easier to read because it is indented well, and logical blocks of code are grouped and displayed together more clearly.

(3) Boolean Values in Decision Structures

Some programmers think decision structures such as the above, where the result of the decision is merely computation of a Boolean value, are overly verbose and even prone to error. They prefer to have the decision in the computation itself, like this:

```
return hours < 12 && minutes < 60 && seconds < 60;
```

The difference is often purely stylistic and syntactic, as modern compilers produce identical object code for both forms.

(4) Looping and Control Structures

The use of logical control structures for looping adds to good programming style as well. It helps someone reading code to understand the program's sequence of execution (in imperative programming languages). For example, in pseudocode:

```
count = 0
while count < 5
print count * 2
count = count + 1
endwhile
```

The above snippet obeys the two aforementioned style guidelines, but the following use of the "for" construct makes the code much easier to read:

```
for count = 0, count < 5, count=count+1
print count * 2
```

In many languages, the often used "for each element in a range" pattern can be shortened to:

```
for count = 0 to 5
print count *
```

(5) Spacing

Free-format languages often completely ignore white space. Making good use of spacing in one's layout is therefore considered good programming style.

Compare the following examples of C code.

```
into                                                     count;
for(count=0;count<10;count++){printf("%d",count*count+count);}
```

with

```
int count;
for (count = 0; count < 10; count++)
{
printf("%d", count * count + count);
}
```

In the C-family languages, it is also recommended to avoid using tab characters in the middle of a line as different text editors render their width differently.

Python uses indentation to indicate control structures, so correct indentation is required. By doing this, the need for bracketing with curly braces ({ and }) is eliminated, and readability is improved while not interfering with common coding styles. However, this frequently leads to problems where code is copied and pasted into a Python program, requiring tedious reformatting. Additionally, Python code is rendered unusable when posted on a forum or webpage that removes white space.

5.5 General Principles of Software Validation

As per guidance issued by FDA an integration of software life cycle management and risk management activities is recommended. Based on the intended use and the safety risk associated with the software to be developed, the software developer should determine the specific approach, the combination of techniques to be used, and the level of effort to be applied. While this guidance does not recommend any specific life cycle model or any specific technique or method, it does recommend that software validation and verification activities be conducted throughout the entire software life cycle.

Where the software is developed by someone other than the device manufacturer (e.g., off-the-shelf software) the software developer may not be directly responsible for compliance with FDA regulations. In that case, the party with regulatory responsibility (i.e., the device manufacturer) needs to assess the adequacy of the off-the-shelf software developer's activities and determine what additional efforts are needed to establish that the software is validated for the device manufacturer's intended use.

This section lists the general principles that should be considered for the validation of software.

(1) Requirements

A documented software requirements specification provides a baseline for both validation and verification. The software validation process cannot be completed without an established software requirements specification.

(2) Defect Prevention

Software quality assurance needs to focus on preventing the introduction of defects into the software development process and not on trying to "test quality into" the software code after it is written. Software testing is very limited in its ability to surface all latent defects in software code. For example, the complexity of most software prevents it from being exhaustively tested. Software testing is a necessary activity. However, in most cases software testing by itself is not sufficient to establish confidence that the software is fit for its intended use. In order to establish that confidence, software developers should use a mixture of methods and techniques to prevent software errors and to detect software errors that do occur. The "best mix" of methods depends on many factors including the development environment, application, size of project, language, and risk.

(3) Time and Effort

To build a case that the software is validated requires time and effort. Preparation for software validation should begin early, i.e. during design and development planning and design input. The final conclusion that the software is validated should be based on evidence collected from planned efforts conducted throughout the software lifecycle.

(4) Software life cycle

Software validation takes place within the environment of an established software life cycle. The software life cycle contains software engineering tasks and documentation necessary to support the software validation effort. In addition, the software life cycle contains specific verification and validation tasks that are appropriate for the intended use of the software. This guidance does not recommend any particular life cycle models—only that they should be selected and used for a software development project.

(5) Plans

The software validation process is defined and controlled through the use of a plan. The software validation plan defines "what" is to be accomplished through the software validation effort. Software validation plans are a significant quality system tool. Software validation plans specify areas such as scope, approach, resources, schedules and the types and extent of activities, tasks, and work items.

(6) Procedures

The software validation process is executed through the use of procedures. These procedures establish "how" to conduct the software validation effort. The procedures should identify the specific actions or sequence of actions that must be taken to complete individual validation activities, tasks, and work items.

(7) Software Validation After a Change

Due to the complexity of software, a seemingly small local change may have a significant global system impact. When any change (even a small change) is made to the software, the validation status of the software needs to be re-established. Whenever software is changed, a validation analysis should be conducted not just for validation of the individual change, but also to determine the extent and impact of that change on the entire software system. Based on this analysis, the software developer should then conduct an appropriate level of software regression testing to show that unchanged but vulnerable portions of the system have not been adversely affected. Design controls and appropriate regression testing provide the confidence that the software is validated after a software change.

(8) Validation Coverage

Validation coverage should be based on the software's complexity and safety risk—not on firm size or resource constraints. The selection of validation activities, tasks, and work items should be commensurate with the complexity of the software design and the risk associated with the use of the software for the specified intended use. For lower risk devices, only baseline validation activities may be conducted. As the risk increases additional validation activities should be added to cover the additional risk. Validation documentation should be sufficient to demonstrate that all software validation plans and procedures have been completed successfully.

(9) Independence of Review

Validation activities should be conducted using the basic quality assurance precept of "independence of review". Self-validation is extremely difficult. When possible, an independent evaluation is always better, especially for higher risk applications. Some firms contract out for a third-party independent verification and validation, but this solution may not always be feasible. Another approach is to assign internal staff members that are not involved in a particular design or its implementation, but who have sufficient knowledge to evaluate the project and conduct the verification and validation activities. Smaller firms may need to be creative in how tasks are organized and assigned in order to maintain internal independence of review.

(10) Flexibility and Responsibility

Specific implementation of these software validation principles may be quite different from one application to another. The device manufacturer has flexibility in choosing how to apply these validation principles, but retains ultimate responsibility for demonstrating that the software has been validated.

Software is designed, developed, validated, and regulated in a wide spectrum of environments, and for a wide variety of devices with varying levels of risk. FDA regulated medical device applications include software that:

- is a component, part, or accessory of a medical device;
- is itself a medical device; or
- is used in manufacturing, design and development, or other parts of the quality system.

In each environment, software components from many sources may be used to create the application (e.g., in-house developed software, off-the-shelf software, contract software, shareware). In addition, software components come in many different forms (e.g., application software, operating systems, compilers, debuggers, configuration management tools, and many more). The validation of software in these environments can be a complex undertaking; therefore, it is appropriate that all of these software validation principles be considered when designing the software validation process. The resultant software validation process should be commensurate with the safety risk associated with the system, device, or process.

Software validation activities and tasks may be dispersed, occurring at different locations and being conducted by different organizations. However, regardless of the distribution of tasks, contractual relations, source of components, or the development environment, the device manufacturer or specification developer retains ultimate responsibility for ensuring that the software is validated.

5.5.1 Activities and Tasks

Software validation is accomplished through a series of activities and tasks that are planned and executed at various stages of the software development life cycle. These tasks may be one time occurrences or may be iterated many times, depending on the life cycle model used and the scope of changes made as the software project progresses.

Validation through Defined User Requirements

A very important key to software validation is a documented user requirements specification that defines:

- the "intended use" of the software or automated equipment; and
- the extent to which the device manufacturer is dependent upon that software or equipment for production of a quality medical device.

The device manufacturer (user) needs to define the expected operating environment including any required hardware and software configurations, software versions, utilities, etc. The user also needs to:

- document requirements for system performance, quality, error handling, startup, shutdown, security, etc.;
- identify any safety related functions or features, such as sensors, alarms, interlocks, logical processing steps, or command sequences; and
- define objective criteria for determining acceptable performance.

The validation must be conducted in accordance with a documented protocol, and the validation results must also be documented. Test cases should be documented that will exercise the system to challenge its performance against the pre-determined criteria, especially for its most critical parameters. Test cases should address error and alarm conditions, startup, shutdown, all applicable user functions and operator controls, potential operator errors, maximum and minimum ranges of allowed values, and stress conditions applicable to the intended use of the equipment. The test cases should be executed and the results should be recorded and evaluated to determine whether the results support a conclusion that the software is validated for its intended use.

A device manufacturer may conduct a validation using their own personnel or may depend on a third party such as the equipment/software vendor or a consultant. In any case, the device manufacturer retains the ultimate responsibility for ensuring that the production and quality system software:

- is validated according to a written procedure for the particular intended use; and
- will perform as intended in the chosen application.

The device manufacturer should have documentation including:

- defined user requirements;
- validation protocol used;
- acceptance criteria;
- test cases and results; and
- a validation summary that objectively confirms that the software is validated for its intended use.

For some off-the-shelf software development tools, such as software compilers, linkers, editors, and operating systems, exhaustive black-box testing by the device manufacturer may be impractical. Without such testing—a key element of the validation effort—it may not be possible to validate these software tools. However, their proper operation may be satisfactorily inferred by other means. For example, compilers are frequently certified by independent third-party testing, and commercial software products may have "bug lists", system requirements and other operational information available from the vendor that can be compared to the device manufacturer's intended use to help focus the "black-box" testing effort. Off-the-shelf operating systems need not be validated as a separate program. However, system-level validation testing of the application software should address all the operating system services used, including maximum loading conditions, file operations, handling of system error conditions, and memory constraints that may be applicable to the intended use of the application program.

5.5.2 Available Tools, Techniques, and Metrics

There are an abundance of verification and validation tools and techniques. It is important that in selecting V&V tools, all stages of the development cycle are covered. For example, Table 5.1 lists the techniques used from the requirements analysis stage through the validation stage. Sources such as the Software Engineer's Reference Book (McDermid, 1992), Standard for Software Component Testing (British Computer Society, 1995), and standards such as DO-178B and IEC 1508 are useful in selecting appropriate tools and techniques.

Table 5.1: Use of Testing Methods throughout the Development Life Cycle

Static	Dynamic
Requirements analysis and functional specification	
• walkthroughs	
• design reviews	
• checklists	
Top-level design	
• walkthroughs	
• design reviews	
• checklists	
• formal proofs	
• fagan inspection	
Detailed design	
• walkthroughs	
• design reviews	
• control flow analysis	
• data flow analysis	
• symbolic execution	
• checklists	
• fagan inspection	
• metrics	
Implementation	
• static analysis	•functional testing
	• boundary value analysis
	• probabilistic testing
	• process simulation
	• structured-based testing
	• error guessing

(Contd...)

Static	Dynamic
	• error seeding
Integration testing	
• walkthroughs	functional testing
• design reviews	time and memory tests
• sneak circuit analysis	boundary value analysis
	• performance testing
	• stress testing
	• probabilistic testing
	• error guessing
Validation	
	• functional testing

There are many organizations and companies that perform independent verification and validation. For example, NASA has a Software Independent Verification & Validation Facility which provides IV & V technical analyses for NASA programs, industries, and other government agencies. [NASA, 99]

With all the work dealing with the Y2K problem, many Y2K companies have embraced a new role as IV & V companies. One such example is SEEC. SEEC has an IV & V Workbench which is a comprehensive, integrated solution that includes year 2000 remediation. The workbench brings together powerful tool and processes such as the SEEC COBOL Analyst 2000 and SEEC Smart Change 2000 for verification and the SEEC COBOL Slicer and SEEC/Test Director for validation.

5.6 Structured Walkthrough

A 'walkthrough' is an informal meeting for evaluation or informational purposes. Little or no preparation is usually required. A structured walkthrough is an in-depth, technical review of some aspect of a software system. Walkthroughs can be used at any time, during any phase of a software project. Thus, all or any part of the software requirements, the architectural design specifications, the detailed design specifications, the test plan, the code, supporting documents, or a proposed maintenance modification can be reviewed at any stage of evolution.

A walkthrough team consists of four to six people. The person whose material is being reviewed is responsible for providing copies of the review material to members of the walkthrough team in advance of the walkthrough session, and team members are responsible for reviewing the material prior to the session. During the walkthrough the reviewee "walks through" the material while the reviewers look for error, request clarifications, and explore problem areas in the material under review.

It is important to emphasize that the material is reviewed, and not the reviewee. Thus, everyone's work should be reviewed in turn, and high-level managers should not attend walkthrough sessions. The focus of a walkthrough is on detection of errors and not on corrective actions. A designated secretary for the session records action items to be pursued by the reviewee following the review session. The reviewee is responsible for follow-up and for informing the reviewers of corrective actions taken.

Design inspections are conducted by teams of trained inspectors who work from checklists of items to examine. Special forms are used to record problems encountered. A typical design inspection team consists of a moderator/secretary, a designer, an implementor, and a tester. The designer, implementor, and tester may or may not be the people responsible for actual design, implementation, and testing of the product being inspected. Team members are trained for their specific roles and typically conduct two 2-hour sessions per day.

In one experiment, 67 per cent of the errors found in a software product during product development were found using design and code inspection prior to unit testing. Another experimenter reported 70 per cent error removal using inspections. Many software developers report similar results. Formal design and code inspections are thus an effective mechanism for error detection and removal.

A structured walkthrough is a group review of any product of software development prior to its release into the project life-cycle. It is also referred to as a peer group review, team debugging or ego-less programming. Walkthroughs can take place at various stages in a project. During analysis, such items as E-R diagrams and DFDs might be subject to review. During the design phase a review of structure charts might be considered. At the implementation phase, walkthroughs of programs and the associated documentation are essential. Yourdon (1978) has maintained that structured walkthroughs have a number of tangible and intangible benefits:

(1) Correctness

Organisation that subject all systems to stringent walkthroughs reportedly reduce the program error-rate from an average of three to five defects per hundred lines of code to a more manageable average of three to five defects per thousand lines of code.

(2) Standards

Walkthroughs are a useful way of establishing and enforcing standards for the analysis, design coding, testing and documentation of computer systems.

(3) Readability

Walkthroughs improve the readability of programs and systems documentation, thereby aiding the process of software maintenance.

(4) Training

Walkthroughs have the effect of passing on good organisational practices to new company personnel.

(5) Insurance

Walkthroughs disseminate information about systems throughout the organisation, thus offsetting the problems of high staff turnover.

A structured walkthrough is usually a group effort, with several people serving different roles within the team. A team might consist of a presenter, a coordinator, a scribe, a maintenance critic, a standards critic, and one or more user representatives.

(1) The presenter is normally the creator of the purduct being reviewed. His or her role is to lead the team through an examination of product.

(2) The coordinator organises all the activities that should occur prior to a walkthrough. For example, the coordinator must ensure that each team member receives a copy of the product to be reviewed prior to the walkthrough.

(3) The scribe records the proceedings, and eventually forwards a report to management summarising the team's findings.

(4) The maintenance critic inspects the product for any source of future maintenance problems.

(5) The standards critic ascertains that the product adheres to organisational standards.

(6) User representatives verify that the product performs as requested.

Even though each member has a primary role, all team members are equally accountable in terms of examining the quality of the system and offering comments and criticisms. The responsibility of the team is to gtive an accurate appraisal of the product being reviewed. The participants should identify defects, but they should not attempt to correct them. Correction is the sole responsibility of the presenter.

During the walkthrough, participants are required to remain as objective as possible. In particular, they should remember to evaluate only the product itself, and not the preson presenting it. A walkthrough can easily degenerate into heated and destructive argument if criticims becomes personal. Moreover, the participants should remember that in system development there are many 'correct' solutions to the same problem. Participants should therefore not try to impose their own preferred solution on the problem under consideration

5.6.1 Walkthrough Report

The outcome of the walkthrough is the walkthrough report prepared by the scribe. This report comes in two parts: a summary and an issues list.

On the summary, all participants sign the report to indicate that they are in agreement with the decisions made. At the bottom of the summary the final verdict is given. The product is accepted as is with minor revisions or its is rejected. Rejection can be broken down into three categories:

The second page of the report, the issues list, details all the problems that need attention. As the problems are corrected, they are checked off this list by the team member assigned to monitor progress.

Table Outline of a Software Verification Plan:

1. Requirements to be verified
2. Design verification plan
3. Source-code test plan
4. Test completion criteria
5. Document verification plan
6. Tools and techniques to be used

5.7 Inspections

Inspections, like walkthroughs, can be used throughout the software life cycle to assess and improve the quality of the various work products. Inspection teams consist of one to four members who are trained for their tasks. The inspectors work from checklists of inspection items. Inspections are conducted in a similar manner to walkthroughs, but more structure is imposed on the sessions, and each participant has a definite role to play.

An inspection is more formalized than a 'walkthrough', typically with 3-8 people including a moderator, reader, and a recorder to take notes. The subject of the inspection is typically a document such as a requirements spec or a test plan, and the purpose is to find problems and see what's missing, not to fix anything. Attendees should prepare for this type of meeting by reading thru the document; most problems will be found during this preparation. The result of the inspection meeting should be a written report. Thorough preparation for inspections is difficult, painstaking work, but is one of the most cost effective methods of ensuring quality. Employees who are most skilled at inspections are like the 'eldest brother' in the parable in 'Why is it often hard for organizations to get serious about quality assurance?'. Their skill may have low visibility but they are extremely valuable to any software development organization, since bug prevention is far more cost-effective than bug detection.

Design and code inspections were first described by Fagan. In Fagan's experiment, three separate inspections were performed: one following design, but prior to implementation; one following implementation, but prior to unit testing; and one following unit testing. The inspection following unit testing was not considered to be cost-effective in discovering errors; therefore, it is not recommended.

According to Fagan, an inspection team consists of four persons, who play the roles of moderator, designer, implementer, and tester. Items to be inspected in a design inspection might include completeness of the design with respect to the user and functional requirements, internal completeness and consistency in definition and usage of terminology, and correctness of the interfaces between modules. Items to be inspected in a code inspection might include subprogram interfaces, decision logic, data referencing, computational expressions, I/O statements, comments, data flow, and memory usage.

Actual items examined under the category of subprogram interfaces, for example, might include:

(1) Are the numbers of actual parameters and formal parameters in agreement?

(2) Do the type attributes of actual and formal parameters match.

(3) Do the dimensional units of actual and formal parameters match?

(4) Are the numbers, attributes, and ordering of arguments of built-in functions correct?

(5) Are constants passed as modifiable arguments?

(6) Are global variable definitions and usage consistent among modules?

The actual items in the checklist will depend on the implementation language. In a language that enforces separate compilation, many of the error conditions listed above will be checked by type checking across the compilation interfaces. In FORTRAN systems, on the other hand, none of the conditions listed above are checked by the compiler or linker. They are thus candidates for inspection.

In Fagan's initial experiment, the inspection team conducted two 2-hour sessions per day and expended 25 hours per person (100 person-hours total). Of the errors found during development, 67 per cent were found before any unit testing was performed. During the first

7 months of operation, 38 per cent fewer errors were found in the inspected program than in a similar program produced by a control group using informal walkthroughs. The difference in productivity between the project team using inspections and the control group was negligible. It should be noted that the productivity data included training time for the inspectors.

In a subsequent experiment, Fagan found that 82 per cent of all errors discovered during development of a software product were found during design and code inspections. The savings in programmer resources on the project was 25 per cent of estimated cost because most errors were found before unit testing. It was also observed that the inspection rate was approximately five-times faster for applications programs than for systems programs.

Subsequent experiments have reported 70 per cent and greater error removal during design and code inspections (JON, 78). Given these results, it is difficult to understand why inspections are not routinely used on every software project. Inspections and walkthroughs are particulary valuable for real-time systems, where debugging of execution sequences is difficult due to the non-repeatability of error situations.

An interesting aspect of inspections is the observation that different programmers tend to make different kinds of characteristic errors. Errors found during an inspection can be cycled back to the programmers who make them, and with this feedback, programmers tend to eliminate those types of errors from their subsequent work, thus improving quality and productivity.

In his paper, Fagan contrasts walkthroughs and inspections, and observes a number of advantages for inspection teams: inspectors have definite roles to play; the moderator, rather than the reviewee, directs the effort; an error checklist is utilized; and detailed error feedback is provided to individual programmers. On the other hand, we observe that walkthroughs improve project team communication and project morale by involving team members in the walkthrough process. In addition, walkthroughs are an excellent educational medium for new team members. Balanced use of both inspections and walkthroughs is recommended.

5.8 Certification

Software certification is an endorsement of the correctness of the program, an issue that is rising in importance for information systems applications. There is an increasing dependence on the purchase or lease of commercial software rather than on its on-house development. However, before analysts are willing to approve the acquisition of a package, they often require certification of the software by the developer or an unbiased third party.

For example, selected accounting firms are now certifying that a software packing in fact does what the vendor claims it does and in a proper manner. To so certify the software, the agency appoints a team of specialists who care fully examine the documentation for the system to determine what the vendor claims the system does and how it is accomplished. Then they test the software against those claims. If no serious discrepancies or failures are encountered, they will certify that the software does what the documentation claims. They do not, however, certify that the software is the right package for a certain organization. That responsibility remains with the organization and its item of analysts.

Certification can be applied to either organizations or individuals, tools or methods, or systems or products. Certification of organizations aims at assuring that the organization achieves a certain level of proficiency and that they agree to certain standards or criterias. This however, is not applicable to all areas because while it is easy to measure the procedures of a company, it is much harder to measure the competence with which they are performed. So certification is usually applied to areas such as quality assurance and testing as opposed to design. Certification may also apply to individuals where workers must be certified in order to be a certain profession. This usually applies to workers such as doctors, lawyers, accountants, and civil engineers.

Tools or methods may also be certified. For example, although DO-178B does not specifically define the tools that must be used, it does give certain requirements of tools used to gain certification. Finally, systems or products may also be certified. In certification, there is always the issue of whether artifacts or methodology be certified. This becomes an issue in the certification of products containing software. Because software testing is so difficult, certification must be based on the process of development and on the demonstrated performance. This is a case where the methodology (development process) is certified instead of the artifact (software).

Even though certification does not occur until the end of a system development cycle, the planning starts from the very beginning. Because certification is a complicated process between the developer and the regulatory agency, the certification liason between the parties must be established early on in the process. Next, the developer should submit a verification plan for approval by the regulatory agency. After the submission, discussion takes place between the developer and regulatory agency to resolve areas of misunderstanding and disagreement. Changes to the methods used have to be approved by the regulatory body to ensure that certification will not be affected. Throughout the entire development life cycle of the product, documentation must be continually submitted to show that the certification plan is satisfied. The regulating authority will also hold a series of reviews to discuss the submitted material. At the end, if the terms of the certification plan have been satisfied, then a certificate or license is issued.

The safety case is an important document used to support certification. It contains a set of arguments supported by analytical and experimental evidence concerning the safety of a design. It is created early in the development cycle and is then expanded as issues important to safety come up. In the safety case, the regulatory authority will look to see that all potential hazards have been identified, and that appropriate steps have been taken to deal with them. In addition, the safety case must also demonstrate that appropriate development methods have been adopted and that they have been performed correctly. Items that should be included in the safety case includes, but are not limited to the following: specification of safety requirements, results of hazard and risk analysis, verification and validation strategy, and results of all verification and validation activities. The CONTESSE Test Handbook, which is applicable in the United Kingdom, lists a number of items that should be included in a safety case. [Storey, 96]

A potential problem with certification is that manufacturers use it to avoid its legal and moral obligations. An important aspect of certification is that it does not prove that the system is correct. Certification only proves that a system has met certain standards set by the certifying agency. The standards show that a product has met certain guidelines, but it does not mean that the system is correct. Any problem with the system is ultimately the responsibility of the designer and manufacturer, not the certification agency.

5.9 Software Metrics

Metrics are a set of measurements that quantify results. Performance metrics quantify the units performance. Project metrics tell you whether the project is meeting its goals. Business metrics define the business' progress in measurable terms.

Metrics are a system of parameters or ways of quantitative and periodic assessment of a process that is to be measured, along with the procedures to carry out such measurement and the procedures for the interpretation of the assessment in the light of previous or comparable assessments. Metrics are usually specialized by the subject area, in which case they are valid only within certain domain and cannot be directly benchmarked or interpreted outside it.

The following elements must be known for a metric to be fully defined. Common software metrics include:

- order of growth
- source lines of code
- cyclomatic complexity
- function points
- bugs per line of code
- code coverage
- number of lines of customer requirements
- number of classes and interfaces
- Robert Cecil Martin's software package metrics
- Cohesion
- Coupling

Effective management of the software development process requires effective measurement of that process. Software metrics are numerical data related to software development. Metrics strongly support software project management activities. They relate to the four functions of management as follows:

(1) **Planning**—Metrics serve as a basis of cost estimating, training planning, resource planning, scheduling, and budgeting.

(2) **Organizing**—Size and schedule metrics influence a project's organization.

(3) **Controlling**—Metrics are used to status and track software development activities for compliance to plans.

(4) **Improving**—Metrics are used as a tool for process improvement and to identify where improvement efforts should be concentrated and measure the effects of process improvement efforts.

A metric quantifies a characteristic of a process or product. Metrics can be directly observable quantities or can be derived from one or more directly observable quantities. Examples of raw metrics include the number of source lines of code, number of documentation pages, number of staff-hours, number of tests, number of requirements, etc. Examples of derived metrics include source lines of code per staff-hour, defects per thousand lines of code, or a cost performance index.

The term indicator is used to denote a representation of metric data that provides insight into an ongoing software development project or process improvement activity. Indicators are metrics in a form suitable for assessing project behavior or process improvement. For example, an indicator may be the behavior of a metric over time or the ratio of two metrics. Indicators may include the comparison of actual values versus the plan, project stability metrics, or quality metrics. Examples of indicators used on a project include actual versus planned task completions, actual versus planned staffing, number of trouble reports written and resolved over time, and number of requirements changes over time.

Indicators are used in conjunction with one another to provide a more complete picture of project or organization behavior. For example, a progress indicator is related to requirements and size indicators. All three indicators should be used and interpreted together.

5.9.1 Metrics Set

The metrics to be collected provide indicators that track ongoing project progress, software products, and software development processes.

The defined indicators are consistent with the Software Engineering Institute's Capability Maturity Model (CMM). Table 5.2 shows the indicator categories, the management insight provided, and the specific indicators for recommended metrics. Depending upon the nature of the project, specific contractual requirements, or management preference, a project may choose to collect additional metrics or to tailor the recommended set.

Table 5.2: Recommended Metrics Set for a Project

Indicator Category	**Management Insight**	**Indicators**
Progress	Provides information on how well the project is performing with respect to its schedule.	Actual vs. planned task completions durations.
Effort	Provides visibility into the contributions of staffing on project costs, schedule adherence, and product quality.	Actual vs. planned staffing profiles.
Cost	Provides tracking of actual costs against estimated costs and predicts future costs.	Actual vs. planned costs.
Review Results	Provides status of action items from life-cycle review.	Status of action items.
Trouble Reports	Provides insight into product and process quality and the effectiveness of the testing.	Stains of trouble reports Number of trouble reports opened, closed, etc. during reporting period.
Requirements Stability	Provides visibility into the magnitude and impact of requirements changes.	Number of requirements changes/classification Distribution of requirements over releases.

(Contd...)

Indicator Category	Management Insight	Indicators
Size Stability	Provides insight into the completeness and stability of the requirements and into the ability of the staff to complete the project within the current budget and schedule.	Size growth Growth releases.
Size Stability	Provides insight into the completeness and stability of the requirements and into the ability of the requirements and into the ability of the staff to complete the project within the current budget and schedule.	Size growth Distribution of size over releases.
Computer Resource Utilization	Provides information on how well the project is meeting its computer resource utilization goals/requirements.	Actual vs. planned profiles of computer resource utilization.
Training	Provides information on the training program and staff skills.	Actual vs. planned number of personnel attending classes.
Cost	Provides tracking of actual costs against estimated costs and predicts future costs.	Actual vs. planned costs.
Cost and schedule variances	Review results provides status of action items from life-cycle review. Trouble Reports Provides insight into product and process quality and the effectiveness of the testing. Requirements stability provides visibility into the magnitude and impact of requirements changes.	Status of trouble reports. Number of trouble reports opened, closed, etc. during reporting period.
Number of requirements changes/ clarifications	Distribution of requirements over releases.	Size stability provides insight into the completeness and stability of the requirements and into the ability of the staff to complete the project within the current budget and schedule.
Distribution of size over releases.	Computer Resource Utilization.	Provides information on how well the project is meeting its computer resource utilization goals/requirements. Actual vs. planned profiles of computer resource utilization

Training Provides information on the training program and staff skills, Actual vs. planned number of personnel attending classes

5.9.2 Chart Construction Summary

Charts are prepared for the standard metrics. All charts require titles, legends, and labels for all axes. They should clearly and succinctly show the metrics of interest, with no excessive detail to detract the eye. Do not overuse different line types, patterns, or color, or added dimensionality unless used specifically to differentiate items. Overlayed data is preferable to multiple charts when the different data are related to each other and can be meaningfully depicted without obscuring other details.

Tracking Chart

The most common type of chart is the tracking chart. This chart is used extensively for the Progress indicator, and is used in similar forms for many of the other indicators. For task progress, it depicts the cumulative number of planned and actual task completions (or milestones) against time. For other indicators, it may show actual versus planned staffing profiles, actual versus planned software size, actual versus planned resource utilization or other measures compared over time.

There are many ways to modify the tracking chart. A horizontal planned line representing the cumulative goal can be drawn at the top, multiple types of tasks can be overlaid on a single tracking chart (such as design, code, and integration), or the chart can be overlaid with other types of data.

It is recommended that tracked quantities be shown as a line chart, and that replanned task progress be shown as a separate planning line. The original planned baseline is kept on the chart, as well as all replanning data if there is more than a single replan.

The following sections provide brief descriptions of the different metrics categories with samples of the required charts. Individual projects may enhance the charts for their situations or have additional charts for the categories. The sample charts are designed for overhead presentations and are available as templates from the professor.

5.9.3 Progress

Progress indicators provide information on how well the project is performing with respect to planned task completions and keeping schedule commitments. Tasks are scheduled and then progress is tracked to the schedules. Metrics are collected for the activities and milestones identified in the project schedules. Metrics on actual completions are compared to those of planned completions to determine whether there are deviations to the plan. The difference between the actual and planned completions indicates the deviations from the plan.

Each project identifies tasks for which progress metrics will be collected.

The completion criteria for each task must be well defined and measurable. The project should establish range limits (thresholds) on the planned task progress for the project. The thresholds are used for management of software development risk.

Figure 5.1 depicts the cumulative number of planned and actual completions (or milestones) over time. Note that this chart is generic, and each project will substitute specific tasks (units, milestones, SLOCs, etc.). Additionally, each project is expected to produce multiple progress charts for different types of tasks, different teams, etc.

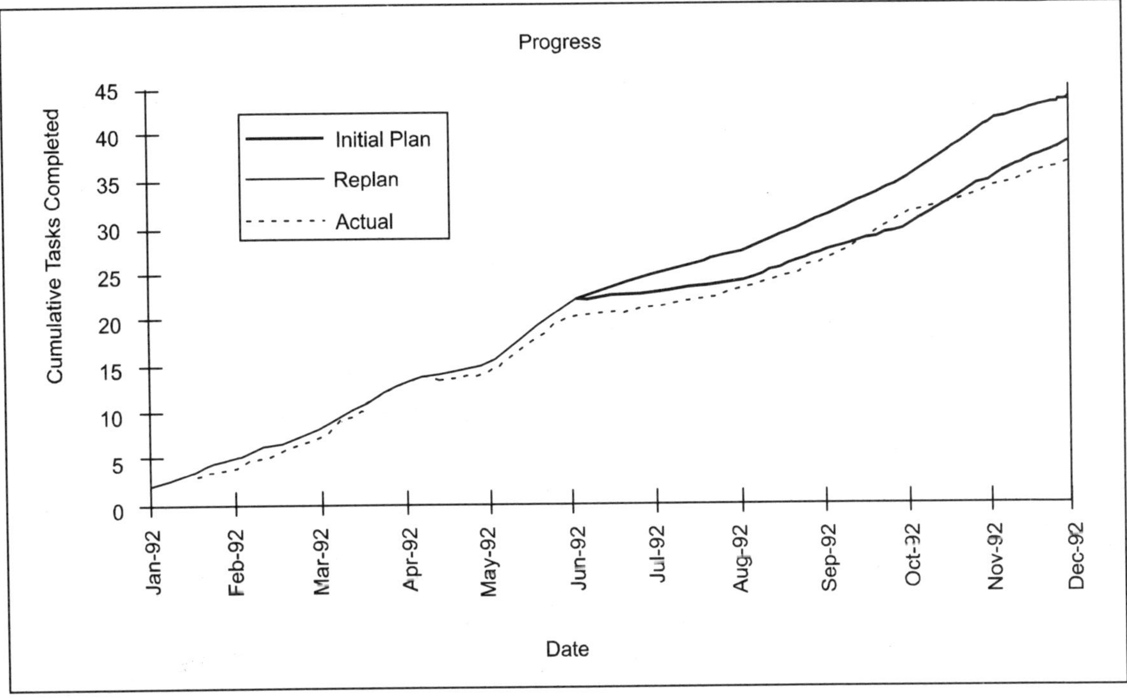

Fig. 5.1: Progress Indicator

5.9.4 Effort

Effort indicators allow the software manager to track personnel resources. They provide visibility into the contribution of staffing to project costs, schedule adherence, product quality and the amount of effort required for each activity. Effort indicators include trends in actual staffing levels, staffing profile by activity or labor category, or a profile of unplanned staff loses.

Effort indicators may be used by all levels of project software management to measure the actual profile against the plan. Each level of management forms a profile for its area of control and monitors the actual profile against the plan.

Determining the number of staff needed at any one time is an important function performed by software management. By summing the number of staff during each reporting period, the composite staffing profile for the project can be determined.

These indicators are applied during all life-cycles phases, from project inception to project end. Effort metrics are to be collected and reported at least on a monthly basis.

The effort and cost metrics are related. By convention, effort metrics are non-cumulative expenditures of human resources, and cost metrics are cumulative levels of effort as tracked by earned value. Thus, cost metrics are a cumulative depiction of effort.

Figure 5.2 shows a sample plot of monthly actual versus planned effort.

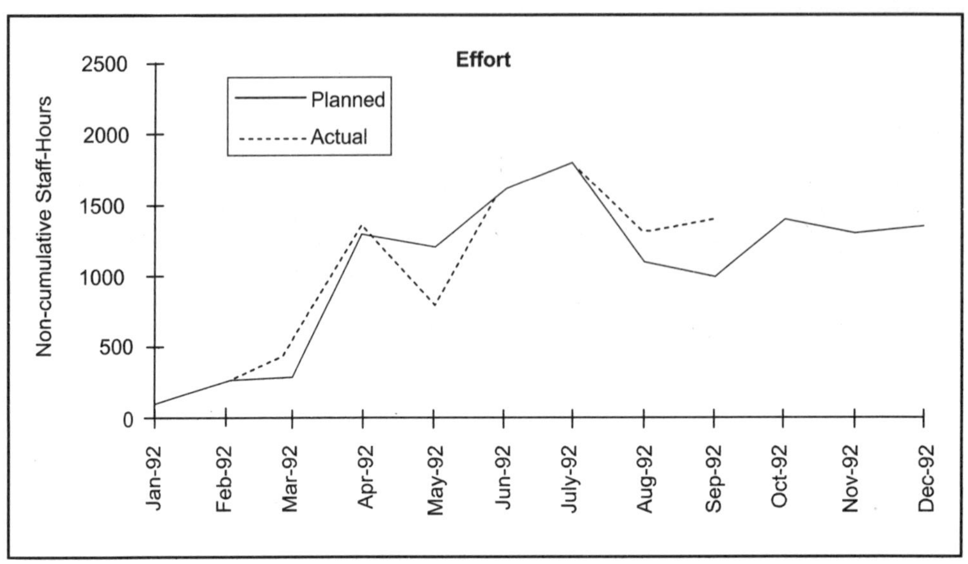

Fig. 5.2: Effort Indicator

5.9.5 Cost

Cost management is an important activity for the success of a project, and labor is the primary component of software development cost. Managers must define the work in their area, determine the skill level required to perform the work, and use productivity estimates and schedule constraints to determine budgeted costs over time.

Use staff-hours to measure cost, rather than dollars. The dollars per staff-hour varies over time and by labor category, and the conversion is made only by Finance. Cost is related to the effort indicator, with cost defined as an accumulation of effort expenditures. (The total project cost also includes non-labor costs, but they are not tracked here.) Only those projects using earned value can report the earned value quantities.

A Work Breakdown Structure (WBS) is established to define the structures that will be used to collect the costs. The WBS identifies separate elements for requirements, design, documentation, code and unit test, integration, verification, and system testing. Costs can also be segregated by component, function, or configuration item. Work packages are derived from the WBS. Costs are allocated to work packages using an earned value method. This system allows managers to track the actual costs and measure them against the budget for their respective areas of responsibility.

Figure 5.3 is a sample Cost Indicator Chart. The actual and budgeted quantities are derived from an earned value system, and are shown in terms of staff-hours.

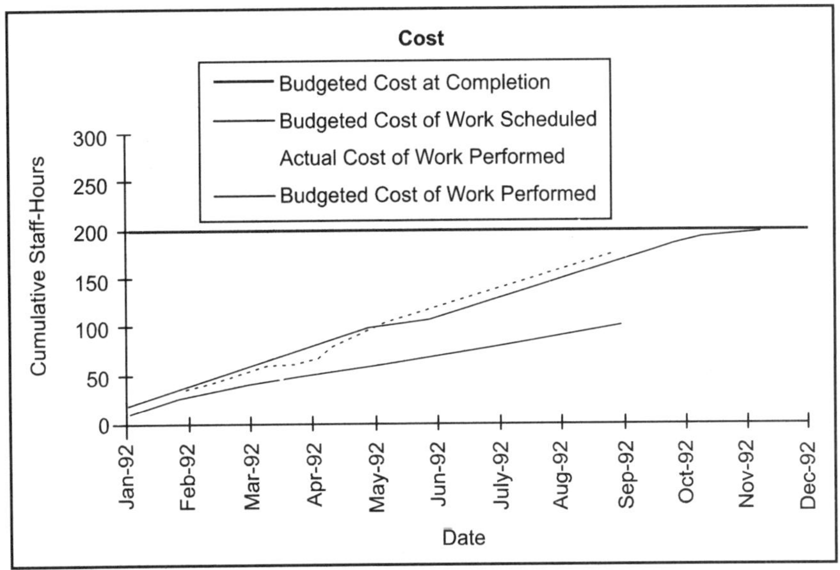

Fig. 5.3: Cost Indicator

5.9.6 Review Results

Review Results indicators provide insight into the status of action items from life cycle reviews. The term Action Item (AI) refers to inspection defects and customer comments. Reviews include the following:

- Formal inspections of software documents or code
- Formal customer milestones, e.g. SSR, PDR, CDR, or TRR
- Informal peer evaluations of products, e.g. walkthroughs, technical reviews, or internal PDRs

5.9.7 Management Reviews

- Process reviews, e.g. SQA audits, SEI CMM assessments, or the causal analysis from formal inspections.

There are standards for some reviews, as well as procedures for conducting them. For example, formal inspections result in assertion logs that document the minor and major defects uncovered by the inspection process. Therefore, standard review result indicators for formal inspections are:

1. Counts of minor/major defects
2. Rates of defect detection (e.g., assertions per inspection meeting minute, defects per inspected document page, or defects per KSLOC of code inspected)
3. Defect status (e.g., age of open defects, number of open/closed defects, and breakdown by defect categories).

A customer-conducted review such as a Preliminary Design Review (PDR) generates AIs that must be closed before approval of the Software Design Document. Therefore, standard review result indicators for a PDR are the number of comments written and their status (open, closed, and age).

Review metrics record the AIs identified in the review findings and track them until they are resolved. These metrics provide status on both products and processes. Review results are not to be used to evaluate the performance of individuals.

Review Results are collected and reported at least monthly at every stage of the software life cycle, but preferably weekly for key AIs.

Figure 5.4 depicts the cumulative counts of AIs written and closed by reporting period.

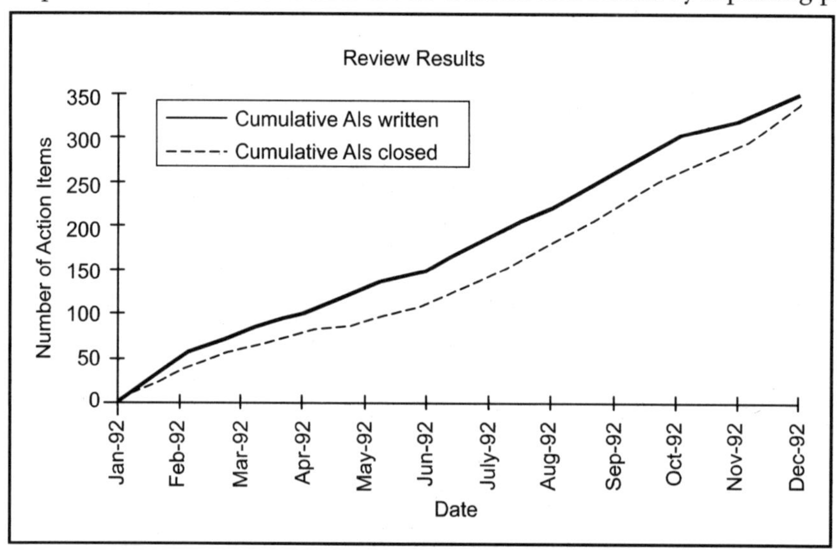

Fig. 5.4: Review Results Indicator

5.9.8 Trouble Reports

TR indicators provide managers with insight into the quality of the product, software reliability, and the effectiveness of testing. They also provide information on the software development process. The terms defect and problem will be used interchangeably herein. Monthly tracking of TR indicators shows the project's trends in the following areas:

1. The rate at which TRs are being written and resolved.
2. The type and severity of the TRs.
3. Relationship between the number of TRs and the number of test cases passed or the number of test steps passed.
4. The TR density (the number of TRs per unit size).
5. The number of defects in each software application/unit.

TR indicators are applicable only in the following life cycle stages (and each release of the software within these stages, and during the informal and formal test segments of these stages) (1) application test and integration, (2) system test, (3) acceptance test. Thus the TR indicators are applicable only to defects during the operation or execution of a computer program. Due to the shortness of testing periods, and the dynamics involved between the test team and the implementation team that analyzes the TRs and fixes the defects, the TR indicators are generally evaluated on a weekly basis.

The terms open and closed are defined as follows:

- **Open:** The problem has been reported.
- **Closed:** The investigation is complete and the action required to resolve the problem has been proposed, implemented, and verified to the satisfaction of all concerned. In some cases, a TR will be found to be invalid as part of the investigative process and closed immediately.

Figure 5.5 shows the cumulative count of total, open, and closed TRs over time (weekly periods).

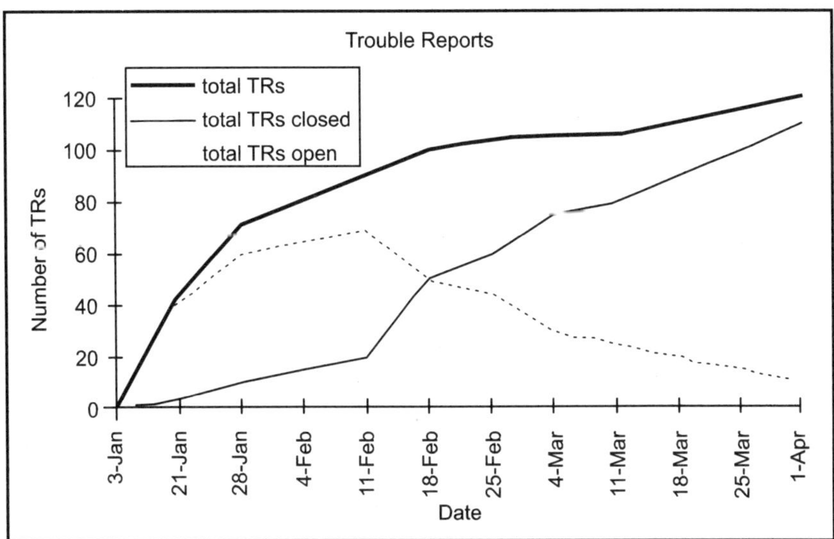

Fig. 5.5: TR Indicator

5.9.9 Requirements Stability

Requirements Stability provides an indication of the completeness, stability, and understanding of the requirements. It indicates the number of changes to the requirements and the amount of information needed to complete the requirements definition. A lack of requirements stability can lead to poor product quality, increased cost, and schedule slippage.

Requirements stability indicators are in the form of trend charts that show the total number of requirements, cumulative changes to the requirements, and the number of TBDs over time. A TBD refers to an undefined requirement. Based on requirements stability trends, corrective action may be necessary.

Requirements stability is applicable during all life-cycles phases, from project inception to the end. The requirements stability indicators are most important during requirements and design phases. Requirements stability metrics are collected and reported on a monthly basis.

Figure 5.6 shows an example of the total number of requirements, the cumulative number of requirements changes, and the number of remaining TBDs over time. It may be desirable to also show the number of added, modified and deleted requirements over time.

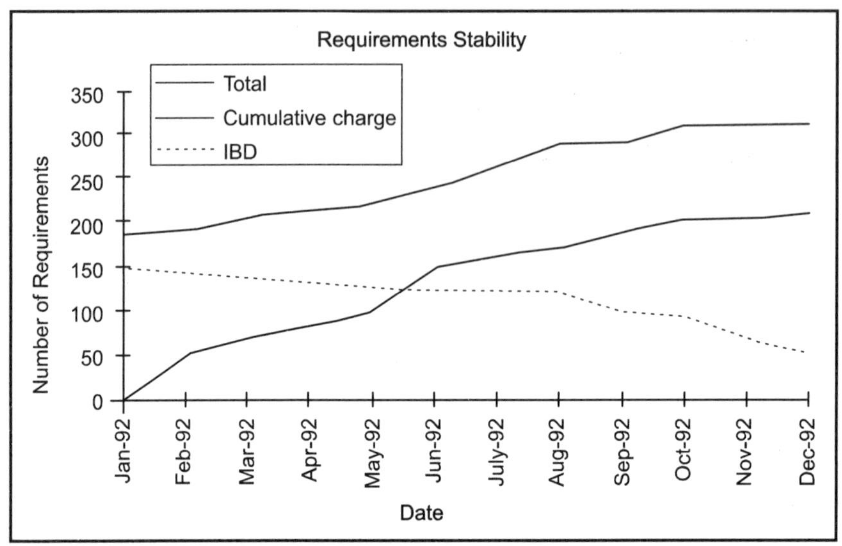

Fig. 5.6: Requirements Stability Indicator

5.9.10 Size Stability

Software size is a critical input to project planning. The size estimate and other factors are used to derive effort and schedule before and during a project.

The software manager tracks the actual versus planned software product size. Various indicators show trends in the estimated code size, trends by code type, the variation of actual software size from estimates or the size variation by release.

Size stability is derived from changes in the size estimate as time goes on. It provides an indication of the completeness and stability of the requirements, the understanding of the requirements, design thoroughness and stability, and the capability of the software development staff to meet the current budget and schedule. Size instability may indicate the need for corrective action.

Size metrics are applicable during all life-cycle phases. Size metrics are collected and reported on a monthly basis, or more often as necessary.

Figure 5.7 shows an example of planned and currently estimated software size per release over time. Besides showing re-allocation of software content between releases, this also shows the growth in the total estimated size.

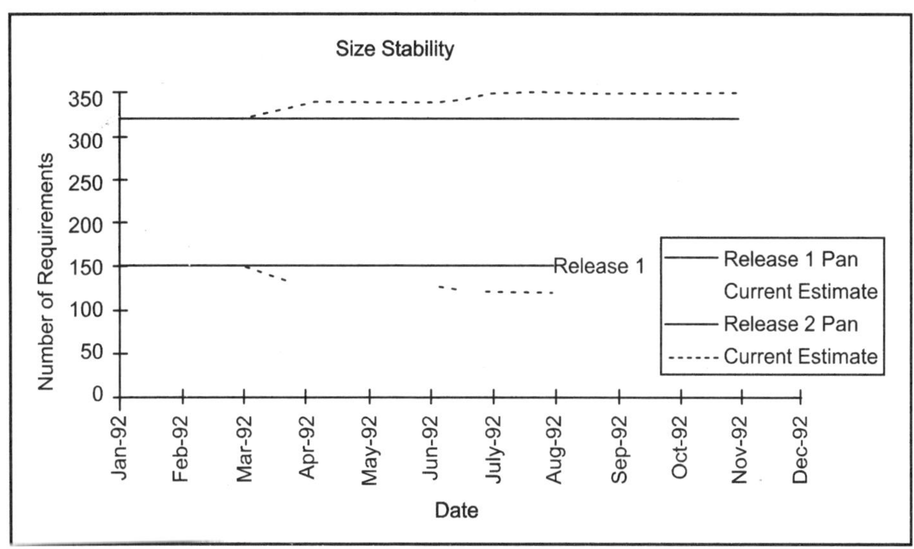

Fig. 5.7: Size Indicator

5.9.11 Computer Resource Utilization

Computer Resource Utilization indicators show whether the software is using the planned amount of system resources. The computer resources are normally CPU time, I/O, and memory. For some software, the constraints of computer resources significantly affect the design, implementation, and testing of the product. They can also be used to replan, re-estimate, and guide resource acquisition.

Computer resource utilization is planned during the requirements activity and reviewed during the design activity. Resources are monitored from the start of implementation activity to the end of the life cycle.

For memory utilization, the unit of data is the byte, word, or half-word. For CPU time, the unit of data is either MIPS (millions of instructions per second), or the percentage of CPU time used during a peak period. For I/O time, the unit of data is the percentage of I/O time used during a peak period. Resource Utilization data is collected and reported at least monthly, with the period between collection and reporting becoming shorter as the software system nears completion and a better picture of software performance can be seen. Note that the resource utilization is normally an estimate until integration occurs, at which time the actual data is available.

Figure 5.8 shows an example of CPU and memory use as a per cent of available and the maximum allowed.

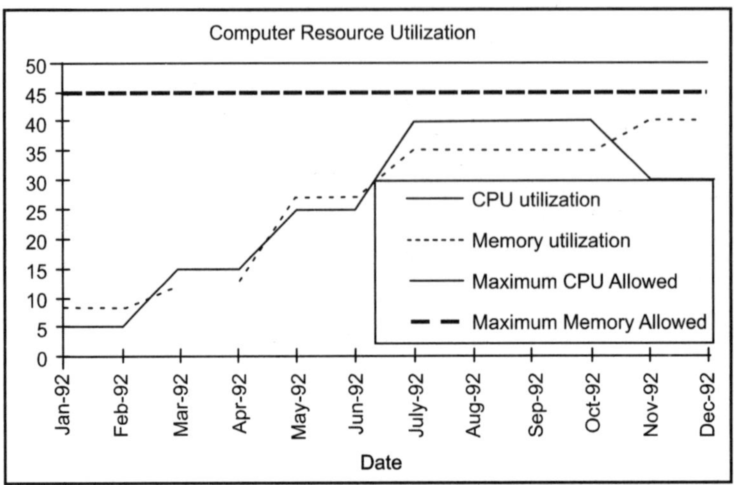

Fig. 5.8: Computer Resources Indicator

5.9.12 Training

Training indicators provide managers with information on the training program and whether the staff has necessary skills. A trained staff is a commitment. The manager must ensure that the staff has the skills needed to perform their assigned tasks. The objective of the training indicator is to provide visibility into the training process, to ensure effective utilization of training, and to provide project software managers with an indication of their staff's skill mixture.

The manager should investigate the deviations in the number of classes taught from the number of classes planned, and the deviation of the number of staff taught to the planned number. The quality of the training program should also be determined from completed course evaluation sheets. The number of waivers requested and approved for training should also be tracked.

Fig. 5.9 shows a sample graph of the total monthly attendance of personnel attending training classes. It represents the sum of the number of personnel attending all classes.

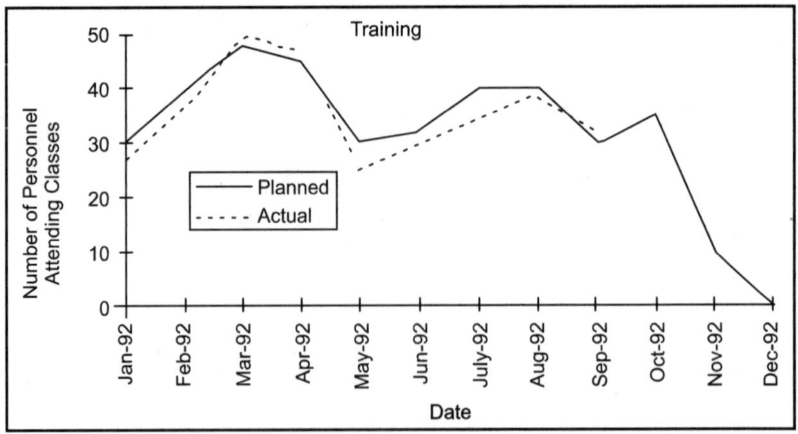

Fig. 5.9: Training Indicator

5.9.13 Overview of Project Procedures

Metrics are planned at project conception, used to track project status and recorded at the end of the project.

When starting a software development project, determine the list of software metrics. Use the goal-question-measure paradigm to select appropriate measurements for the project. To do this, first establish goals for the project, develop questions to be answered by measurement, and then collect the data needed. Document the software metrics to be collected for the project in the project plan. During a project, collect and report the metrics. Use the collected metrics data to track project status. At the end of a project, utilize the data for postmortem reporting.

Use automated data collection and analysis tools whenever possible to collect the metrics data for your project. Some tools that can aid in this process include Amadeus for code measurement, TR statusing tools, requirements management tools, etc. Excel spreadsheets are useful for generating metrics reports.

5.10 Software Package Metrics

This section describes various software package metrics as described by Robert Cecil Martin in his *Agile Software Development: Principles, Patterns, and Practices* (2002).

The term software package, as it is used here, refers to a group of related classes (in the field of object-oriented programming).

- *Number of Classes and Interfaces*: The number of concrete and abstract classes (and interfaces) in the package is an indicator of the extensibility of the package.
- *Afferent Couplings (Ca)*: The number of other packages that depend upon classes within the package is an indicator of the package's responsibility.
- *Efferent Couplings (Ce)*: The number of other packages that the classes in the package depend upon is an indicator of the package's independence.
- *Abstractness (A)*: The ratio of the number of abstract classes (and interfaces) in the analyzed package to the total number of classes in the analyzed package. The range for this metric is 0 to 1, with A=0 indicating a completely concrete package and A=1 indicating a completely abstract package.
- *Instability (I)*: The ratio of efferent coupling (Ce) to total coupling ($Ce + Ca$) such that $I = Ce / (Ce + Ca)$. This metric is an indicator of the package's resilience to change. The range for this metric is 0 to 1, with $I=0$ indicating a completely stable package and $I=1$ indicating a completely instable package.
- *Distance from the Main Sequence (D)*: The perpendicular distance of a package from the idealized line $A + I = 1$.
- This metric is an indicator of the package's balance between abstractness and stability. A package squarely on the main sequence is optimally balanced with respect to its abstractness and stability. Ideal packages are either completely abstract and stable (x=0, y=1) or completely concrete and instable (x=1, y=0). The range for this metric is 0 to 1, with $D=0$ indicating a package that is coincident with the main sequence and $D=1$ indicating a package that is as far from the main sequence as possible.

- *Package Dependency Cycles*: Package dependency cycles are reported along with the hierarchical paths of packages participating in package dependency cycles.

5.11 Source Lines of Code (SLOC)

Source lines of code (SLOC) is a software metric used to measure the amount of code in a software program. SLOC is typically used to estimate the amount of effort that will be required to develop a program, as well as to estimate productivity or effort once the software is produced.

5.11.1 Measuring SLOC

There are two major types of SLOC measures: physical SLOC and logical SLOC. Specific definitions of these two measures vary, but the most common definition of physical SLOC is a count of "non-blank, non-comment lines" in the text of the program's source code. Logical SLOC measures attempt to measure the number of "statements", but their specific definitions are tied to specific computer languages (one simple logical SLOC measure for C-like languages is the number of statement-terminating semicolons). It is much easier to create tools that measure physical SLOC, and physical SLOC definitions are easier to explain. However, physical SLOC measures are sensitive to logically irrelevant formatting and style conventions, while logical SLOC is less sensitive to formatting and style conventions. Unfortunately, SLOC measures are often stated without giving their definition, and logical SLOC can often be significantly different from physical SLOC.

Consider this snippet of C code as an example of the ambiguity encountered when determining SLOC:

```
for (i=0; i<100; ++i) printf("hello"); /* How many lines of code is this? */
```

Depending on the programmer and/or coding standards, the above "line of code" could be, and usually is, written on many separate lines:

```
for (i=0; i<100; ++i)
{
 printf("hello");
} /* Now how many lines of code is this? */
```

Even the "logical" and "physical" SLOC values can have a large number of varying definitions. Robert E. Park (while at the Software Engineering Institute) et al. developed a framework for defining SLOC values, to enable people to carefully explain and define the SLOC measure used in a project. For example, most software systems reuse code, and determining which (if any) reused code to include is important when reporting a measure.

5.11.2 Origins of SLOC

At the time that people began using SLOC as a metric, the most commonly used languages, such as FORTRAN and assembler, were line-oriented languages. These languages were developed at the time when punch cards were the main form of data entry for programming. One punch card usually represented one line of code. It was one discrete object that was easily counted. It was the visible output of the programmer so it made sense to managers to count lines of code as a measurement of a programmer's productivity. Today, the most commonly used computer languages allow a lot more leeway for formatting. One line of text no longer necessarily corresponds to one line of code.

5.11.3 Usage of SLOC Measures

SLOC measures are somewhat controversial, particularly in the way that they are sometimes misused. Experiments have repeatedly confirmed that effort is highly correlated with SLOC, that is, programs with larger SLOC values take more time to develop. Thus, SLOC can be very effective in estimating effort. However, functionality is less well correlated with SLOC: skilled developers may be able to develop the same functionality with far less code, so one program with less SLOC may exhibit more functionality than another similar program. In particular, SLOC is a poor productivity measure of individuals, since a developer can develop only a few lines and yet be far more productive in terms of functionality than a developer who ends up creating more lines (and generally spending more effort). Good developers may merge multiple code modules into a single module, improving the system yet appearing to have negative productivity because they remove code. Also, especially skilled developers tend to be assigned the most difficult tasks, and thus may sometimes appear less "productive" than other developers on a task by this measure.

SLOC is particularly ineffective at comparing programs written in different languages unless adjustment factors are applied to normalize languages. Various computer languages balance brevity and clarity in different ways; as an extreme example, most assembly languages would require hundreds of lines of code to perform the same task as a few characters in APL. The following example shows a comparison of a "Hello World" program written in C, and the same program written in COBOL — a language known for being particularly verbose.

```
C COBOL
#include <stdio.h>
int main(void) {
 printf("Hello World");
}
000100 IDENTIFICATION DIVISION.
000200 PROGRAM-ID. HELLOWORLD.
000300
000400*
000500 ENVIRONMENT DIVISION.
000600 CONFIGURATION SECTION.
000700 SOURCE-COMPUTER. RM-COBOL.
000800 OBJECT-COMPUTER. RM-COBOL.
000900
001000 DATA DIVISION.
001100 FILE SECTION.
001200
100000 PROCEDURE DIVISION.
100100
```

```
100200 MAIN-LOGIC SECTION.
100300 BEGIN.
100400 DISPLAY " " LINE 1 POSITION 1 ERASE EOS.
100500 DISPLAY "Hello world!" LINE 15 POSITION 10.
100600 STOP RUN.
100700 MAIN-LOGIC-EXIT.
100800 EXIT.
```

Lines of code: 4 (excluding whitespace) Lines of code: 17 (excluding whitespace)

Another increasingly common problem in comparing SLOC metrics is the difference between auto-generated and hand-written code. Modern software tools often have the capability to auto-generate enormous amounts of code with a few clicks of a mouse. For instance, GUI builders automatically generate all the source code for a GUI object simply by dragging an icon onto a workspace. The work involved in creating this code cannot reasonably be compared to the work necessary to write a device driver, for instance.

There are several cost, schedule, and effort estimation models which use SLOC as an input parameter, including the widely-used Constructive Cost Model (COCOMO) series of models by Barry Boehm et al. and Galorath's SEER-SEM. While these models have shown good predictive power, they are only as good as the estimates (particularly the SLOC estimates) fed to them. Many have advocated the use of function points instead of SLOC as a measure of functionality, but since function points are highly correlated to SLOC (and cannot be automatically measured) this is not a universally held view.

The following list provides rough estimates of the average number of lines of code required to build one function point in various programming languages:

```
Programming Language LOC/FP (Average)
Assembly language 300
COBOL 100
FORTRAN 100
Pascal 90
Ada 70
Object-oriented languages 30
Fourth-generation languages (4GL) 20
Code generators 15
```

According to Andrew Tanenbaum, the SLOC values for various operating systems in Microsoft's Windows NT product line are as follows:

```
Year Operating System SLOC (Million)
1993 Windows NT 3.1 6
1994 Windows NT 3.5 10
1996 Windows NT 4.0 16
2000 Windows 2000 29
2002 Windows XP 40
```

David A. Wheeler studied the Red Hat distribution of the GNU/Linux operating system, and reported that Red Hat Linux version 7.1 (released April 2001) contained over 30 million physical SLOC. He also determined that, had it been developed by conventional proprietary means, it would have required about 8,000 person-years of development effort and would have cost over $1 billion (in year 2000 U.S. dollars).

A similar study was later made of Debian GNU/Linux version 2.2 (also known as "Potato"); this version of GNU/Linux was originally released in August 2000. This study found that Debian GNU/Linux 2.2 included over 55 million SLOC, and if developed in a conventional proprietary way would have required 14,005 person-years and cost $1.9 billion (USD) to develop. Later runs of the tools used report that the following release of Debian had 104 million SLOC, and as of year 2005, the newest release is going to include over 213 million SLOC.

```
Operating System SLOC (Million)
Red Hat Linux 6.2 17
Red Hat Linux 7.1 30
Debian 2.2 56
Debian 3.0 104
Debian 3.1 213
Sun Solaris 7.5
Linux kernel 2.6.0 6.0
Programs for counting lines of code
```

There are many applications available for programmatically counting lines of code within source.

5.11.4 SLOC and Relation to Security Faults

"Measuring programming progress by lines of code is like measuring aircraft building progress by weight."—Bill Gates.

A number of experts have claimed a relationship between the number of lines of code in a program and the number of bugs that it contains. This relationship is not simple, since the number of errors per line of code varies greatly according to the language used, the type of quality assurance processes, and level of testing, but it does appear to exist. More importantly, the number of bugs in a program has been directly related to the number of security faults that are likely to be found in the program.

This has had a number of important implications for system security and these can be seen reflected in operating system design. Firstly, more complex systems are likely to be more insecure simply due to the greater number of lines of code needed to develop them. For this reason, security focused systems such as OpenBSD grow much more slowly than other systems such as Windows and Linux. A second idea, taken up in both OpenBSD and many Linux variants, is that separating code into different sections which run with different security environments (with or without special privileges, for example) ensures that the most security critical segments are small and carefully audited.

5.11.5 Advantages

(a) **Scope for Automation of Counting:** Since Line of Code is a physical entity; manual counting effort can be easily eliminated by automating the counting process. Small utilities may be developed for counting the LOC in a program. However, a code counting utility developed for a specific language cannot be used for other languages due to the syntactical and structural differences among languages.

(b) **An Intuitive Metric:** Line of Code serves as an intuitive metric for measuring the size of software due to the fact that it can be seen and the effect of it can be visualized. Function Point is more of an objective metric which cannot be imagined as being a physical entity, it exists only in the logical space. This way, LOC comes in handy to express the size of software among programmers with low levels of experience.

5.11.6 Disadvantages

(a) **Lack of Accountability:** Lines of code measure suffers from some fundamental problems. Some think it isn't useful to measure the productivity of a project using only results from the coding phase, which usually accounts for only 30% to 35% of the overall effort.

(b) **Lack of Cohesion with Functionality:** Though experiments have repeatedly confirmed that effort is highly correlated with LOC, functionality is less well correlated with LOC. That is, skilled developers may be able to develop the same functionality with far less code, so one program with less LOC may exhibit more functionality than another similar program. In particular, LOC is a poor productivity measure of individuals, since a developer can develop only a few lines and still be more productive than a developer creating more lines of code.

(c) **Adverse Impact on Estimation:** As a consequence of the fact presented under point (a), estimates done based on lines of code can adversely go wrong, in all possibility.

(d) **Developer's Experience:** Implementation of a specific logic differs based on the level of experience of the developer. Hence, number of lines of code differs from person to person. An experienced developer may implement certain functionality in fewer lines of code than another developer of relatively less experience does, though they use the same language.

(e) **Difference in Languages:** Consider two applications that provide the same functionality (screens, reports, databases). One of the applications is written in C++ and the other application written a language like COBOL. The number of function points would be exactly the same, but aspects of the application would be different. The lines of code needed to develop the application would certainly not be the same. As a consequence, the amount of effort required to develop the application would be different (hours per function point). Unlike Lines of Code, the number of Function Points will remain constant.

(f) **Advent of GUI Tools:** With the advent of GUI-based languages/tools such as Visual Basic, much of development work is done by drag-and-drops and a few mouse clicks, where the programmer virtually writes no piece of code, most of the time. It is not possible to account for the code that is automatically generated in this case. This difference invites huge variations in productivity and other metrics with respect to different languages, making the Lines of Code more and more irrelevant in the context of GUI-based languages/tools, which are prominent in the present software development arena.

(g) **Far from OO Development:** Line of Code makes no meaning in the case of Object-Oriented development where everything is treated in terms of Objects and classes. Since object is a true representation of data and functionality and so is a Function Point, FPA remains more relevant for Object-Oriented software development.

(h) **Problems with Multiple Languages:** In today's software scenario, software is often developed in more than one language. Very often, a number of languages are employed depending on the complexity and requirements. Tracking and reporting of productivity and defect rates poses a serious problem in this case since defects cannot be attributed to a particular language subsequent to integration of the system. Function Point stands out to be the best measure of size in this case.

(i) **Lack of Counting Standards:** There is no standard definition of what a line of code is. Do comments count? Are data declarations included? What happens if a statement extends over several lines? — These are the questions that often arise. Though organizations like SEI and IEEE have published some guidelines in an attempt to standardize counting, it is difficult to put these into practice especially in the face of newer and newer languages being introduced every year.

5.12 Function Point

A function point is a unit of measurement to express the amount of business functionality an information system provides to a user. Function points are an ISO recognized software metric to size an information system based on the functionality that is perceived by the user of the information system, independent of the technology used to implement the information system. Function Points were defined in 1977 by Alan Albrecht at IBM.

The method of measuring the size of an information system and expressing it in a number of function points is called Function Point Analysis. The method is kept up to date by worldwide cooperating FPA user groups like NESMA and IFPUG.

Function Point Analysis

Function Point Analysis (FPA) is an ISO recognized method to measure the functional size of an information system. The functional size reflects the amount of functionality that is relevant to and recognized by the user in the business. It is independent of the technology used to implement the system.

The unit of measurement is "function points". So, FPA expresses the functional size of an information system in a number of function points (for example: the size of a system is 314 fp's).

The functional size may be used:

- to budget application development or enhancement costs
- to budget the annual maintenance costs of the application portfolio
- to determine project productivity after completion of the project

5.13 Cohesion

Cohesion is a measure of how well the lines of source code within a module work together to provide a specific piece of functionality. Cohesion is an ordinal type of measurement and is usually expressed as "high cohesion" or "low cohesion" when being discussed. Modules with high cohesion tend to be preferable because high cohesion is associated with several desirable traits of software including robustness, reliability, reusability, and understandability whereas low cohesion is associated with undesirable traits such as being difficult to maintain, difficult to test, difficult to reuse, and even difficult to understand.

Cohesion is usually contrasted with coupling. High cohesion often correlates with low coupling, and vice versa. The software quality metrics of coupling and cohesion were defined by Wayne P. Stevens, Glenford J. Myers, and Larry L. Constantine from source code analysis they conducted on several programming projects while at IBM, all in an effort to identify the characteristics of "good" programming practices.

5.13.1 High Cohesion

In object-oriented programming, it is good to assign responsibilities to classes in a way that keeps cohesion high. The likelihood of reuse is increased and complexity kept manageable.

Cohesion is a measure of how strongly related and focused the responsibilities of a single class are. Cohesion is decreased if:

- The responsibilities (methods) of a class have little in common.
- Methods carry out many varied activities, often using varied data.

Disadvantages of low cohesion (or "weak cohesion") are:

- Difficult to understand.
- Difficult to maintain, because it is constantly affected by changes.
- Difficult to reuse a class because most applications won't need a random set of operations * attached to a class.

5.13.2 Types of Cohesion

Cohesion is a qualitative measure meaning that the source code text to be measured is examined using a rubric to determine a cohesion classification. The types of cohesion, in order of lowest to highest, are as follows:

(1) Coincidental cohesion

Coincidental cohesion is when parts of a module are grouped arbitrarily; the parts have no significant relationship (e.g., a module of frequently used functions).

(2) Logical cohesion

Logical cohesion is when parts of a module are grouped because of a slight relation (e.g., using control coupling to decide which part of a module to use, such as how to operate on a bank account).

(3) Temporal cohesion

Temporal cohesion is when parts of a module are grouped by when they are processed—the parts are processed at a particular time in program execution (e.g., a function which is called after catching an exception which closes open files, creates an error log, and notifies the user).

(4) Procedural cohesion

Procedural cohesion is when parts of a module are grouped because they always follow a certain sequence of execution (e.g., a function which checks file permissions and then opens the file).

(5) Communicational cohesion

Communicational cohesion is when parts of a module are grouped because they operate on the same data (e.g., a method updateStudentRecord which operates on a student record, but the actions which the method performs are not clear).

(6) Sequential cohesion

Sequential cohesion is when parts of a module are grouped because the output from one part is the input to another part (e.g., a function which reads data from a file and processes the data).

(7) Functional cohesion

Functional cohesion is when parts of a module are grouped because they all contribute to a single well-defined task of the module (a perfect module).

Since cohesion is a ranking type of scale, the ranks do not indicate a steady progression of improved cohesion. Studies by various people including Larry Constantine and Edward Yourdon as well as others indicate that the first two types of cohesion are much inferior to the others and that modules with communicational cohesion or better tend to be much superior than lower types of cohesion. The seventh type, functional cohesion, is considered the best type.

However, while functional cohesion is considered the most desirable type of cohesion for a software module, it may not actually be achievable. There are many cases where communicational cohesion is about the best that can be attained in the circumstances. However the emphasis of a software design should be to maintain module cohesion of communicational or better since these types of cohesion are associated with modules of lower lines of code per module with the source code focused on a particular functional objective with less extraneous or unnecessary functionality, and tend to be reusable under a greater variety of conditions.

5.14 Coupling

In computer science, coupling or dependency is the degree to which each program module relies on each other module.

Coupling is usually contrasted with cohesion. Low coupling often correlates with high cohesion, and vice versa. The software quality metrics of coupling and cohesion were invented by Larry Constantine, original developer of Structured Design (see also SSADM).

5.14.1 Low Coupling

Coupling can be "low" (also "loose" and "weak") or "high" (also "tight" and "strong"). Low coupling means that one module does not have to be concerned with the internal implementation of another module, and interacts with another module with a stable interface (see Information hiding). With low coupling, a change in one module will not require a change in the implementation of another module. Low coupling is a sign of a well-structured computer system.

However, in order to achieve maximum efficiency, a highly coupled system is sometimes needed. In modern computing systems, performance is often be traded for lower coupling; the gains in the software development process are greater than the value of the running performance gain.

Low-coupling/high-cohesion is a general goal to achieve when structuring computer programs, so that they are easier to understand and maintain. The concepts are usually related: low coupling implies high cohesion and vice versa. In the field of object-oriented programming, the connection between classes tends to get lower (low coupling), if we group related methods of a class together (high cohesion).

In object-oriented programming, coupling is a measure of how strongly one class is connected to another.

Coupling is increased between two classes A and B if:

- A has an attribute that refers to (is of type) B.
- A calls on services of a B object.
- A has a method which references B (via return type or parameter).
- A is a subclass of (or implements) B.

Disadvantages of high coupling include:

- A change in one class forces a ripple of changes in other classes.
- Difficult to understand a class in isolation.
- Difficult to reuse or test a class because dependent class must also be included.

One measure to achieve low coupling is functional design: it limits the responsibilities of modules. Modules with single responsibilities usually need to communicate less with other modules, and this has the virtuous side-effect of reducing coupling and increasing cohesion in many cases.

5.14.2 Types of Coupling

The types of coupling, in order of lowest to highest coupling, are as follows:

(1) **Data coupling:** Data coupling is when modules share data through, for example, parameters. Each datum is an elementary piece, and these are the only data which are shared (e.g., passing an integer to a function which computes a square root).

(2) **Stamp coupling:** (Data-structured coupling) : Stamp coupling is when modules share a composite data structure, each module not knowing which part of the data structure will be used by the other (e.g. passing a student record to a function which calculates the student's GPA).

(3) **Control coupling:** Control coupling is one module controlling the logic of another, by passing it information on what to do (e.g., passing a what-to-do flag).

(4) **External coupling:** External coupling occurs when two modules share an externally imposed data format, communication protocol, or device interface.

(5) **Common coupling:** Common coupling is when two modules share the same global data (e.g., a global variable).

(5) **Content coupling:** Content coupling is when one module modifies or relies on the internal workings of another module (e.g., accessing local data of another module).

In object-oriented programming, sub-class coupling describes a special type of coupling between a parent class and its child. The parent has no connection to the child class, so the connection is one way (i.e. the parent is a sensible class on its own). The coupling is hard to classify as low or high; it can depend on the situation.

Example

In the first instances of the IBM PC, BIOS, some developers used low level but undocumented internal functions to optimize their programs, instead of the public API. This approach had the advantage of bringing higher performance, but as a result the programs were more complex, more difficult to maintain, and the internal functions could change on a subsequent BIOS version.

Known uses

Dependency is also common in talking about software package management. One software package, in order to work or to be fully functional, may depend on other software packages and thus must also be installed, and their specific versions must be known if backward compatibility is broken between versions. The Advanced Packaging Tool package format, as well as some versions of the RPM package format, include dependency information between packages. This is convenient for updating software but can lead to dependency hell.

Build systems like make are also dependency driven in the sense that a more complex object, like a program, only gets linked together once all its dependencies, i.e. the objects it is built of, have been compiled.

High cohesion and low coupling are attributes of good design.

5.15 Verification Techniques

There are many different verification techniques but they all basically fall into 2 major categories—dynamic testing and static testing.

(1) **Dynamic testing**—Involves the execution of a system or component. Basically, a number of test cases are chosen, where each test case consists of test data. These input test cases are used to determine output test results. Dynamic testing can be further divided into three categories:

- Functional testing,
- Structural testing, and
- Random testing.

(a) **Functional testing**—Testing that involves identifying and testing all the functions of the system as defined within the requirements. This form of testing is an example of black-box testing since it involves no knowledge of the implementation of the system.

(b) **Structural testing**—Testing that has full knowledge of the implementation of the system and is an example of white-box testing. It uses the information from the internal structure of a system to devise tests to check the operation of individual components. Functional and structural testing both choose test cases that investigate a particular characteristic of the system.

(c) **Random testing**—Testing that freely chooses test cases among the set of all possible test cases. The use of randomly determined inputs can detect faults that go undetected by other systematic testing techniques. Exhaustive testing, where the input test cases consists of every possible set of input values, is a form of random testing. Although exhaustive testing performed at every stage in the life cycle results in a complete verification of the system, it is realistically impossible to accomplish. [Andriole, 86]

(2) **Static testing**—Testing that does not involve the operation of the system or component. Some of these techniques are performed manually while others are automated. Static testing can be further divided into 2 categories—techniques that analyze consistency and techniques that measure some program property.

(a) **Consistency techniques**—Techniques that are used to ensure program properties such as correct syntax, correct parameter matching between procedures, correct typing, and correct requirements and specifications translation.

(b) **Measurement techniques**—Techniques that measure properties such as error proneness, understandability, and well-structuredness. [Andriole, 86]

5.15.1 Other Validation Techniques

There are also numerous validation techniques, including

- formal methods,
- fault injection, and
- dependability analysis.

Validation usually takes place at the end of the development cycle, and looks at the complete system as opposed to verification, which focuses on smaller sub-systems.

(1) **Formal Methods**—Formal methods is not only a verification technique but also a validation technique. Formal methods means the use of mathematical and logical techniques to express, investigate, and analyze the specification, design, documentation, and behavior of both hardware and software.

(2) **Fault Injection**—Fault injection is the intentional activation of faults by either hardware or software means to observe the system operation under fault conditions.

(a) **Hardware Fault Injection**—Can also be called physical fault injection because we are actually injecting faults into the physical hardware.

(b) **Software Fault Injection**—Errors are injected into the memory of the computer by software techniques. Software fault injection is basically a simulation of hardware fault injection.

(3) **Dependability Analysis**—Dependability analysis involves identifying hazards and then proposing methods that reduces the risk of the hazard occuring.

Hazard Analysis—Involves using guidelines to identify hazards, their root causes, and possible countermeasures.

Risk Analysis—Takes hazard analysis further by identifying the possible consequences of each hazard and their probability of occuring. [Kopetz, 97]

Requirements Analysis: To detect and report requirements errors that may have surfaced during the software requirements and design process.

Software Architecture—To detect and report errors that occured during the development of the software architecture.

Source Code—To detect and report errors that developed during source coding.

Outputs of the Integration Process—To ensure that the results of the integration process is complete and correct.

Test Cases and their Procedures and Results—To ensure that the testing is performed accurately and completely.

Low-level Testing—To verify the implementation of software low-level requirements.

The standard includes a plan that outlines the information necessary for the certification of the software and the software verification plan. A section also details tool qualification. This is necessary when processes in the standard are eliminated, reduced, or automated by using a software tool without following the software verification process.

5.16 Correctness Proof

The notion of correctness is of great importance to the users of software who, it can be assumed, want software which produces the 'right' results. It has not proved straightforward to make the informal notion of correctness more concrete, however, and a variety of definitions have been used since the 1950s.The way that correctness is defined has implications for the techniques that are adopted in software development.

In a survey of the software engineering literature, Stuart Shapiro identified two major approaches to ensuring the correctness of software, one based on the notion of testing completed programs, and the other hoping to guarantee the correctness of software by using formal techniques based on mathematics and logic during the development process. This paper analyses a number of definitions of software correctness, and examines their different implications for the techniques of proof and testing. The various approaches are characterized using a framework taken from philosophical accounts of scientific methodology.

5.16.1 Checking Computations

It was not obvious how the results produced by the first electronic computers should be checked. Computers enabled calculations to be carried out that could not be performed by hand, so there was no possibility of a direct manual check of the results produced. At a conference held in Cambridge in 1949, a number of papers explicitly considered the problems involved in checking the calculations performed by automatic computers.

J.C.P. Miller identified a number of possible sources of error in computations: errors made in the mathematical solution to the problem being addressed, errors arising in the coding of the problem, and errors made by the machine when executing the program. Mathematical sources of errors, although significant, were familiar from the pre-electronic days of computation, and errors introduced by malfunctioning electronic circuitry raised issues of reliability which were relatively easily dealt with by traditional means.

Coding, or programming, errors, on the other hand, were a new category of error, and turned out to be more significant than expected. In 1949 Miller wrote that such errors could be expected, in time, to become infrequent, but in 1951, in the first programming text book to be published, Maurice Wilkes and his colleagues at Cambridge reported that such mistakes are much more difficult to avoid than might be expected. Programming errors are design errors: unlike hardware errors, they are not caused by mechanical or electronic failure, and so cannot be removed by increasing the reliability of any device.

A variety of techniques for preventing such errors were considered, including the inspection of programs to reveal common mistakes, the inclusion of additional code to check the results being obtained, and the automation of the programming process itself. Another technique that was soon adopted was the use of library subroutines: these contain reusable code to perform various common tasks, and because of their frequent use were found more likely to be free from errors than new code. It is noteworthy that there is no mention at this time of the modern notion of testing, which involves repeatedly executing the program with particular data values for which the expected results are known. Wilkes refers to the amount of machine time that could be lost running erroneous programs; as machine time was in this period a scarce resource, testing was simply too expensive and it was natural to emphasize techniques of error avoidance. At this time, then, the notion of correctness was applied to the computations carried out by a machine. Correct computations are those which produce correct results, although it may not always be easy to tell which these are: "It cannot therefore be assumed that if a program apparently operates correctly it is giving correct results, and careful numerical checks must always be applied". The coding process emerged as a significant source of errors, and the desirability of reducing the number of coding errors was recognized. Correctness was recognized to be a product of many factors, however, including the algorithm used, the coding of it for a particular machine, any library routines utilized, and the physical machine itself.

5.16.2 Correctness and Proof

The development of high-level programming languages, and in particular the publication of the Algol 60 report, made explicit a new concept of a computer program: from this point on it became natural to think of programs as expressions in a formal language, rather than as instructions given to a particular machine to perform some computation. Initially, there was an expectation that the use of high-level languages like FORTRAN and Algol would get rid of programming errors. This turned out to be an illusion: one early programmer recalls that the only place where we made a mistake . . . was believing that when FORTRAN came along we wouldn't make any mistakes in coding, and cites a survey which indicated that FORTRAN programs typically had to be compiled up to 50 times before they were correct. During the 1960s it was widely believed that the failure to be able reliably to produce correct software was causing severe problems for the software industry.

This addressed the issue of the correctness of programs from the perspective of an individual programmer, and asked how programmers can have confidence that the results of a program are the results that were intended, particularly in cases where the results cannot be directly checked. Dijkstra considered and rejected approaches to correctness based on testing, a position, encapsulated in his famous remark that—[p]rogram testing can be used to show the presence of bugs, but never to show their absence. The argument hinged on the fact that for all but the most trivial programs, the tests carried out would exercise only a small subset of the program's possible behaviours, and the observation that the successful execution of a set of tests implied nothing about the program's behaviour in untested cases. Dijkstra's alternative approach to the problem of correctness was to make a connection between the new activity of programming and the established canons of mathematical proof.

He is careful to state that mathematical proofs are not guarantees of the truth of the results proved. Nevertheless, the methodology of proof is taken to be the best available model of how the correctness of assertions can be assured, and Dijkstra's plan is to apply the lessons learned from proof to the development of programs in the attempt to increase our epistemological confidence in the results of programs. But how is this analogy to be exploited? Dijkstra spells out his intended analogy in detail: The analogy between proof construction and program construction is, again, striking. In both cases the available starting points are given (ax-ioms and existing theory versus primitives and available library programs); in both cases the goal is given (the theorem to be proved versus the desired performance); in both cases the complexity is tackled by division into parts (lemmas versus subprograms and procedures).

When worked out in detail, the appeal to mathematical standards of rigour in connection with programming proved to be highly attractive. An important aspect of this derives from the understanding, established by the Algol 60 report, that programs could be thought of as expressions in a formal language. For Dijkstra, the process by which a programmer becomes assured of the correctness of a program is text-based: a programmer should examine the source code of a program, and arrive at a conviction of what the program is doing in much the same way as a mathematician reads a proof and comes to accept the truth of the result that is proved. As a result of these and similar arguments, correctness became understood not as a property of individual computations, but as a property of source code, of programs understood as expressions in a formal language. Concurrently with this change, the activity of testing was given less importance in methodological discussions.

Refinement: A Proof Theory for Programs

Initial attempts at applying standards of proof to programming soon made it apparent that it was rather difficult to argue mathematically about the correctness of existing programs: the arguments needed to prove the correctness even of very trivial programs proved to be long and tedious.

In 1968, Dijkstra published a paper entitled 'A constructive approach to the problem of program correctness'. Rather than proving the correctness of an existing program, constructive approaches aimed to develop programs in such a way that their correctness would be an automatic consequence of the development method used. The idea of the constructive approach is to develop program and its proof simultaneously. If this is done, programmers can hope to end up with a program that has been proved to be correct, and thus avoid the need to verify existing code retrospectively. The constructive approach was brought to wider notice in 1971 by Niklaus Wirth in a paper which introduced the terminology of stepwise refinement: 'refinement' refers to the process by which an initial version of a program, written in such as simple way as to be 'obviously' correct, could be transformed into a more concrete version, and the label was chosen to emphasize the iterative, step-by-step nature of the development process that was proposed. The notion on refinement completes the analogy between traditional logic and programming are here rather striking. Classical logic is concerned with truth: the cardinal semantic property of sentences in logic is their truth value, and the most important relationship between sentences in proof theory, namely inference, is explained as being a relation that preserves truth.

The notion of truth does not apply straightforwardly to programs, of course, as they are in the imperative rather than the indicative mood. However, Dijkstra and Wirth view the correctness of a program as its most important semantic property, and in developing the constructive approach, refinement emerges as a relationship between programs which preserves correctness. A development using stepwise refinement can, therefore, be seen as formally the equivalent of a proof where, rather than deriving logical consequences from a set of hopefully self-evident axioms, we derive fully implemented programs from initial versions which are assumed to be, or are 'obviously', correct. Thus the methodology of stepwise refinement provides a realization of Dijkstra's ideal of bringing mathematical standards of rigour to programming by defining a way in which the activity of programming can itself be viewed as a proof-like process. As with mathematics, the 'proofs' can be carried out with greater or lesser degrees of formality, but in either case the approach derives from the understanding of programs as linguistic entities to which the basic notion of correctness can be applied.

5.16.3 Program Specifications

Stepwise refinement places the emphasis in development on program texts, beginning with an 'obviously correct' version of a program. This judgment is dependent on some understanding of what the program is meant to achieve, however, and this insight became formalized in the notion of a program's specification. Atypical statement of the role of the specification is the following: To determine whether a program is correct, we must have some way of specifying what it is intended to do; we cannot speak of the correctness of a program in isolation, but only of its correctness with respect to some specifications. After all, even an incorrect program performs some computation correctly, but not the same computation that the programmer had in mind. In this model, the production of a requirements specification is a crucial first step in the process of developing a software system. In 1976, Boehm made the link between specification and correctness explicit: without a good requirements specification, testing is impossible, because there is nothing to test against.

According to this view, then, there are two distinct types of entity relevant to correctness, namely specifications and programs. A program is said to be correct with respect to a specification if its behaviour is in accordance with the requirements defined in the specification. Many processes have been described for bridging the gap between specification and program, using a wide variety of design notations, both textual and graphical.

The 'axioms' in the theory are the specification; from the specification other expressions are 'deduced', by correctness preserving refinement steps, culminating in the production of 'conclusions' in the form of executable programs in the target programming language. The relationship between expressions in a software development is not deduction, but the formal structure is identical to a logical theory: this can be expressed by saying that software engineering views software development as being a quasi-deductive activity.

Viewing software development as quasi-deductive seems to leave little place for the activity of testing, however. The relationship between these two approaches can best be understood by drawing on accounts of scientific methodology developed in the philosophy of science, which relate the notions of theory and experiment. In the next section these ideas will be applied to software development, using a typology developed by Imre Lakatos.

5.16.4 Lakatos's Typology

Lakatos models scientific and mathematical theories as deductive systems which relate axioms to 'basic statements': these are the 'final conclusions' drawn by the theory. In scientific theories, the basic statements are those which make some testable, empirical assertion. Applying this terminology to the quasi-deductive systems used in software engineering, the basic statements would be the executable programs which are the end points of a software development.

These 'confront reality' by being run and tested. Lakatos identifies two basic types of theory, which he terms 'Euclidean' and 'quasi-empirical'. These are distinguished by the place where truth values are 'injected' into the system. Euclidean theories inject truth at the top, by assuming the existence of true axioms and deducing valid conclusions from them; quasi-empirical theories inject falsity at the bottom, by testing the basic statements. A failed test forces some modifications at 'higher' points in the theory.

It is implicit in much of what has been said in previous sections that the standard view of software engineering is that it is a Euclidean system, in Lakatos' sense. Correctness is injected at the top of the system, in the form of a fixed specification of what the system is to do. The task of software development is understood to be that of systematically developing from this a program which implements the specified functionality, by means of a number of development steps which preserve correctness, in the sense that the consequent of each step is consistent with the given specification. The hope is that the success of this programme would make the activity of testing obsolete: I should like to point out that the constructive approach to program correctness sheds some new light on the debugging problem.

Many debugging aids that are en vogue now are invented as a compensation for the shortcomings of a programming technique that will be denounced as obsolete in the near future. In practice, however, software engineering practice does not follow a rigorous Euclidean methodology, and testing still plays a central role. Even advocates of formal methods do not recommend that formally developed programs be put into service without a period of operational testing. In part, this stems from a recognition that current Euclidean software technology and techniques are fallible, in that development steps are not guaranteed to preserve correctness.

A pragmatic view of this situation, such as the one taken by Shapiro would be that the use of formal methods and testing on the same project simply represents a belt and braces approach to verification, based on the observation that neither technique on its own is sufficient to guarantee correctness. Proponents of an Euclidean approach, however, have articulated a distinctive view of the role of testing in these methods: its purpose is not to assess directly the correctness of the software, but rather, by checking consistency between the specification and the program, to assess whether the development process has been correctly carried out. The recommended response to a failed test is not to correct the final artefact, but rather to modify and make less fallible the process that led to it. Although this position appears to give a role to testing in software engineering, it is firmly rooted in a belief in the possibility, if not practicability, of Euclidean methods which guarantee the correctness of programs, and failed tests are not given the role that they would have in a quasi-empirical theory, i.e. an inductive view of testing. By contrast with this, the traditional view of testing was that programmers should keep running, testing and modifying a program until it passes all its tests.

A passed test represents an injection of correctness at the bottom of the system, a confirmation that the program was behaving as required. As Lakatos points out, the belief that correctness can be injected at the bottom of a deductive system is tantamount to a belief in inductive methods, and the comparison between induction and the traditional account of testing has been made in the software engineering literature. The thought is that successful tests are singular statements of a program's correctness; from a set of such statements, we want to be able to infer that the program as a whole will give correct results at all times in the future.

Although this belief underlies much informal, small-scale programming practice, positive statements of an inductive principle are rare in the software engineering literature, no doubt because of the prominence of Dijkstra's early attack on the position, quoted above. One notable attempt was made by Goodenough and Gerhart to characterize the 'logic of testing'; they proved a 'fundamental theorem of testing' which states that in some cases, a test is a proof of correctness. The idea underlying this theorem was to partition the input space of a program in such a way that the successful completion of one test would imply that the program would function correctly for all other inputs from a given partition. This attempt foundered, however, on the impossibility in practice of finding a partition of the testing space with the required formal properties.

Quasi-empirical Software Development

An alternative view of software engineering would characterize it as a quasi-empirical discipline, in which failed tests represent injections of incorrectness at the bottom of the quasi-deductive system. This has suggested to a number of writers an analogy between the testing of programs and the refutation of scientific theories: for example, Fetzer writes that it might be said that that programs are conjectures, while executions are attempted and all too frequently successful refutations (in the spirit of Popper), and Dasgupta has articulated the thesis that design problem solving, which includes the design of programs, is a special instance of (and is indistinguishable from) the process of scientific discovery.

There is a significant body of work in software engineering research which adopts a broadly quasi-empirical approach. One salient characteristic of this tradition is that it accepts the inherent fallibility of software. In 1971, Bauer wrote in an overview of the then young field of software engineering that the aim of the discipline was to obtain economically software that is reliable and works efficiently on real machines. It is noteworthy that Bauer refers not to the correctness of the software, but rather its reliability; a later paper surveying approaches to the study of reliability made the point explicitly: Our position is that it is neither necessary nor economically feasible to get 100 per cent reliable (totally error-free) software in large, complex systems. Rather than trying to ensure the absolute correctness of software, software engineers who accept the inevitability of errors in software have been concerned with techniques for developing fault-tolerant systems and for statistical characterizations of the reliability of software.

A further characteristic that we might expect to find in quasi-empirical software engineering is 'bold hypotheses, followed by dramatic refutations', as in Popperian rhetoric about fallible science. Much current practice can in fact be interpreted in this way. For example, many writers have commented on the fact that software products are full of errors, and rapidly evolve with subsequent versions correcting some of the faults in earlier ones and also adding new functionality, a situation familiar to users of many commercial software packages. Traditional software engineering views this as a problem, feeling that a mature engineering profession ought to be able to do better. It is precisely what would be expected, however, if software engineering was in fact a quasi-empirical discipline. In passing, it is worth noting that a recent school in software engineering has characterized itself as 'empirical', and is based on the belief that the most important thing to understand is the relationship between various process characteristics and product characteristics.

In terms of the characterization proposed in this paper, this school would seem to fall squarely in the Euclidean tradition, but to emphasize the external, managerial aspects of the development process rather than the internal properties of software-related artifacts. What is being proposed appears to be an empirical study of a Euclidean process, not an empirical approach to development itself.

5.16.5 Correctness and the User

In Euclidean approaches, failed tests must be interpreted as indicating a problem in the development process, on the assumption that correctness has been injected at the start of the process in the form of the specification. However, the very possibility of such a correctness-injection can also be questioned, as it was for example by Douglas Ross in 1968: The most deadly thing in software is the concept, which almost universally seems to be followed, that you are going to specify what you are going to do, and then do it. And that is where most of our troubles come from. The projects that are called successful, have met their specifications. But those specifications were based upon the designers' ignorance before they started the job. Implicit in this is a distinct definition of correctness: it is not adequate to view correctness as a relationship between a program and its specification, but rather it takes the form of a relationship between a program and its users. These two notions of correctness are widely discussed in the software engineering literature, and terminology has been introduced to describe the process of checking the correctness of a program in both senses.

The process of checking that a program meets its specification is known as verification whereas the process of checking that a software engineering artifact either specification or program meets the actual requirements of its users is known as validation. In a quasi-empirical approach, failed tests can be taken as evidence of errors in process, but more fundamentally they can indicate problems with the specification. Quasi-empirical software development would be a process which involved the future users of a program, as the response to a failed test might routinely involve revisions to the specification established with regard to the users' requirements. Such approaches have been consistently recommended in the history of software engineering, in a stream of work running parallel to the main, Euclidean tradition.

Examples include approaches involving ideas such as 'evolutionary prototyping' and more recently 'extreme programming', which emphasize the ongoing involvement of users throughout a development. Recent work in the philosophy of science has described a model in which scientific knowledge is not articulated as part of a deductive structure, but rather emerges in the course of an unpredictable process in which scientists explore the resistances provided by non-human actors. Examples of this approach include the actor network and Pickering's notion of the 'mangle'. It appears that this work can be directly applied to characterize certain approaches to software engineering.

REFERENCES

Andriole, Stephen J., (editor). *Software Validation, Verification, Testing, and Documentation*, Princeton, NJ: Petrocelli Books, 1986.

Kopetz, Herman. Real-Time Systems: Design Principles for Distributed Embedded Applications, Boston, MA: Kluwer Academics Publishers, 1997.

NASA Software Independent Verification & Validation Facility, http://www.ivv.nasa.gov, accessed May 5, 1999.

RTCA-DO-178B. "Software Considerations in Airborne Systems and Equipment Certification", December 1992.

Rushby, John. "Formal Methods and the Certification of Critical Systems", SRI-CSL Technical Report, November 1993.

Storey, Neil. *Safety Critical Computer Systems*, Harlow, England: Addison-Wesley, 1996.

The ISO Information Exchange, http://www.iso-9000.co.uk/index.html, accessed May 7, 1999.

FURTHER READING

(1) Andriole, Stephen J., (editor). *Software Validation, Verification, Testing, and Documentation*, Princeton, NJ: Petrocelli Books, 1986.

(2) Neumann, B. de, (editor). *Software Certification*, London, New York: Elsevier Applied Science, 1986.

(3) "Design Control Guidance for Medical Device Manufacturers", Center for Devices and Radiological Health, Food and Drug Administration, March 1997.

(4) "Do It by Design: An Introduction to Human Factors in Medical Devices", Center for Devices and Radiological Health, Food and Drug Administration, March 1997.

(5) Electronic Records; Electronic Signatures Final Rule, 62 Federal Register 13430 (March 20, 1997).

(6) "Glossary of Computerized System and Software Development Terminology", Division of Field Investigations, Office of Regional Operations, Office of Regulatory Affairs, Food and Drug Administration, August 1995.

(7) "Guidance for the Content of Pre-market Submissions for Software Contained in Medical Devices", Office of Device Evaluation, Center for Devices and Radiological Health, Food and Drug Administration, May 1998.

(8) "Guidance for Industry, FDA Reviewers and Compliance on Off-the-Shelf Software Use in Medical Devices", Office of Device Evaluation, Center for Devices and Radiological Health, Food and Drug Administration, September 1999.

(9) "Guideline on General Principles of Process Validation", Center for Drugs and Biologics, & Center for Devices and Radiological Health, Food and Drug Administration, May 1987.

(10) Medical Devices; Current Good Manufacturing Practice (CGMP) Final Rule; Quality System Regulation, 61 Federal Register 52602 (October 7, 1996).

(11) "Reviewer Guidance for a Pre-Market Notification Submission for Blood Establishment Computer Software", Center for Biologics Evaluation and Research, Food and Drug Administration, January 1997.

(12) *Student Manual 1*, Course INV545, Computer System Validation, Division of Human Resource Development, Office of Regulatory Affairs, Food and Drug Administration, 1997.

(13) Technical Report, Software Development Activities, Division of Field Investigations, Office of Regional Operations, Office of Regulatory Affairs, Food and Drug Administration, July 1987.

International and National Consensus Standards

1. ANSI / ANS-10.4-1987, Guidelines for the Verification and Validation of Scientific and Engineering Computer Programs for the Nuclear Industry, American National Standards Institute, 1987.
2. ANSI / ASQC Standard D1160-1995, Formal Design Reviews, American Society for Quality Control, 1995.
3. ANSI / UL 1998:1998, Standard for Safety for Software in Programmable Components, Underwriters Laboratories, Inc., 1998.
4. AS 3563.1-1991, Software Quality Management System, Part 1: Requirements. Published by Standards Australia [Standards Association of Australia], 1 The Crescent, Homebush, NSW 2140.
5. AS 3563.2-1991, Software Quality Management System, Part 2: Implementation Guide. Published by Standards Australia [Standards Association of Australia], 1 The Crescent, Homebush, NSW 2140.
6. IEC 60601-1-4:1996, Medical electrical equipment, Part 1: General requirements for safety, 4. Collateral Standard: Programmable electrical medical systems. International Electrotechnical Commission, 1996.
7. IEC 61506:1997, Industrial process measurement and control—Documentation of application software. International Electrotechnical Commission, 1997.
8. IEC 61508:1998, Functional safety of electrical/electronic/programmable electronic safety-related systems. International Electrotechnical Commission, 1998.
9. IEEE Std 1012-1986, Software Verification and Validation Plans, Institute for Electrical and Electronics Engineers, 1986.
10. IEEE Standards Collection, Software Engineering, Institute of Electrical and Electronics Engineers, Inc., 1994. ISBN 1-55937-442-X.
11. ISO 8402:1994, Quality management and quality assurance—Vocabulary. International Organization for Standardization, 1994.
12. ISO 9000-3:1997, Quality management and quality assurance standards—Part 3: Guidelines for the application of ISO 9001:1994 to the development, supply, installation and maintenance of computer software. International Organization for Standardization, 1997.
13. ISO 9001:1994, Quality systems—Model for quality assurance in design, development, production, installation, and servicing. International Organization for Standardization, 1994.
14. ISO 13485:1996, Quality systems—Medical devices—Particular requirements for the application of ISO 9001. International Organization for Standardization, 1996.
15. ISO/IEC 12119:1994, Information technology—Software packages—Quality requirements and testing, Joint Technical Committee ISO/IEC JTC 1, International Organization for Standardization and International Electrotechnical Commission, 1994.
16. ISO/IEC 12207:1995, Information technology—Software life cycle processes, Joint Technical Committee ISO/IEC JTC 1, Subcommittee SC 7, International Organization for Standardization and International Electrotechnical Commission, 1995.
17. ISO/IEC 14598:1999, Information technology—Software product evaluation, Joint Technical Committee ISO/IEC JTC 1, Subcommittee SC 7, International Organization for Standardization and International Electrotechnical Commission, 1999.
18. ISO 14971-1:1998, Medical Devices—Risk Management—Part 1: Application of Risk Analysis. International Organization for Standardization, 1998.
19. Software Considerations in Airborne Systems and Equipment Certification. Special Committee 167 of RTCA. RTCA Inc., Washington, D.C. Tel: 202-833-9339. Document No. RTCA/DO-178B, December 1992.

Production Process Software References

20. "The Application of the Principles of GLP to Computerized Systems," Environmental Monograph #116, Organization for Economic Coopération and Development (OECD), 1995.

21. George J. Grigonis, Jr., Edward J. Subak, Jr. and Michael Wyrick. "Validation Key Practices for Computer Systems Used in Regulated Operations", *Pharmaceutical Technology*, June 1997.

22. Guide to Inspection of Computerized Systems in Drug Processing, Reference Materials and Training Aids for Investigators, Division of Drug Quality Compliance, Associate Director for Compliance, Office of Drugs, National Center for Drugs and Biologics, & Division of Field Investigations, Associate Director for Field Support, Executive Director of Regional Operations, Food and Drug Administration, February 1983.

23. Daniel P. Olivier. "Validating Process Software", *FDA Investigator Course: Medical Device Process Validation*, Food and Drug Administration.

24. *GAMP Guide for Validation of Automated Systems in Pharmaceutical Manufacture*, Version V3.0, Good Automated Manufacturing Practice (GAMP) Forum, March 1998: Volume 1, Part 1: User Guide.

BLACK-BOX TESTING

6

6.1 Black-box Testing

Black-box and white-box are test design methods. Black-box test design treats the system as a "black-box", so it doesn't explicitly use knowledge of the internal structure. Black-box test design is usually described as focusing on testing functional requirements. Synonyms for black-box include:

- Behavioral,
- Functional,
- Opaque-box, and
- Closed-box.

A Simple Black box Specification

Fig. 6.1: A Simple representation of Black box

Black-Box Testing is testing technique having no knowledge of the internal functionality/structure of the system. This testing technique treats the system as black-box or closed-box. Tester will only know the formal inputs and projected results. Tester does not know how the program actually arrives at those results. Hence tester tests the system based on the functional specifications given to him. That is the reason black-box testing is also considered as functional testing. This testing technique is also called as behavioral testing or opaque box testing or simply closed box testing. Although black-box testing is a behavioral testing, Behavioral test design is slightly different from black-box test design because the use of internal knowledge is not illegal in behavioral testing.

Black-box and white-box are test design methods. Black-box test design treats the system as a "black-box", so it doesn't explicitly use knowledge of the internal structure. Black-box test design is usually described as focusing on testing functional requirements. Synonyms for black-box include: behavioral, functional, opaque-box, and closed-box. White-box test design allows one to peep inside the "box", and it focuses specifically on using internal knowledge of the software to guide the selection of test data. Synonyms for white-box include: structural, glass-box and clear-box.

While black-box and white-box are terms that are still in popular use, many people prefer the terms "behavioral" and "structural". Behavioral test design is slightly different from black-box test design because the use of internal knowledge isn't strictly forbidden, but it's still discouraged. In practice, it hasn't proven useful to use a single test design method. One has to use a mixture of different methods so that they aren't hindered by the limitations of a particular one. Some call this "gray-box" or "translucent-box" test design, but others wish we'd stop talking about boxes altogether.

It is important to understand that these methods are used during the test design phase, and their influence is hard to see in the tests once they're implemented. Note that any level of testing (unit testing, system testing, etc.) can use any test design methods. Unit testing is usually associated with structural test design, but this is because testers usually don't have well-defined requirements at the unit level to validate.

Tests are designed to answer the following questions:

(1) How is the function's validity tested?

(2) What classes of input will make good test cases?

(3) Is the system particularly sensitive to certain input values?

(4) How are the boundaries of a data class isolated?

(5) What data rates and data volume can the system tolerate?

(6) What effect will specific combinations of data have on system operation?

Black-box testing implies that the selection of test data as well as the interpretation of test results are performed on the basis of the functional properties of a piece of software. Black-box testing should not be performed by the author of the program who knows too much about the program internals. In new testing approaches, software systems are given a third external party for black-box testing after having successfully finished the internal glass box testing exercises.

Though centered around the knowledge of user requirements, black-box tests do not necessarily involve the participation of users. Among the most important black-box tests that do not involve users are functionality testing, volume tests, stress tests, recovery testing, and benchmarks. Additionally, there are two types of black-box test that involve users, i.e. field and laboratory tests (Karat, 90, 352). In the following the most important aspects of these black-box tests will be described briefly.

6.2 Functional Testing

Definition-based or specification-based testing is also known as functional testing or "black-box" testing. It identifies test cases based on the definition of what the software product (whether it be a unit (module) or a complete program) is intended to do. These test cases challenge the intended use or functionality of a program, and the program's internal and external interfaces. Functional testing can be applied at all levels of software testing, from unit to system level testing.

The so-called "functionality testing" is central to most testing exercises. Its primary objective is to assess whether the program does what it is supposed to do, i.e. what is specified in the requirements. There are different approaches to functionality testing. One is the testing of each program feature or function in sequence. The other is to test module by module, i.e. each function where it is called first.

Black-box testing is testing that occurs from the viewpoint of an end user. Black-box tests find bugs such as incorrect functions, interface problems, and database errors.

Black-box tests are also the only form of test the customer is likely to understand; mention "basis path testing" to a banker, and you'll have him frowning. Therefore, black-box testing is absolutely mandatory for acceptance testing. The customer must be able to understand these tests, so that he/she will know for sure whether or not you've met the contract requirements.

Required minimum: at least one black-box test per customer requirement.

White-box testing is performed early in the testing process, while black-box testing tends to be applied during later stages. Test cases should be derived which:

- reduce the number of additional test cases that must be designed to achieve reasonable testing, and
- tell us something about the presence or absence of classes of errors, rather than an error associated only with the specific test at hand.

The following types of functional software testing involve generally increasing levels of effort:

- **Normal Case:** Testing with usual inputs is necessary. However, testing a software product only with expected, valid inputs does not thoroughly test that software product. By itself, normal case testing cannot provide sufficient confidence in the dependability of the software product.
- **Output Forcing:** Choosing test inputs to ensure that selected (or all) software outputs are generated by testing.
- **Robustness:** Software testing should demonstrate that a software product behaves correctly when given unexpected, invalid inputs. Methods for identifying a sufficient set of such test cases include:
  - Test case generation by equivalence classes and Equivalence Class Partitioning,
  - Boundary Value Analysis,
  - Special Case Identification (Error Guessing), and
  - Random tests.

Equivalence classes minimize the number of tests necessary by representing the input space of the component by a few test cases that cover the entire set of possible inputs. Error guessing involves listing possible errors that could arise and generating test cases to ensure that these errors do not in practice happen.

Random testing involves randomly selecting input values from the entire input space of the component. It has been suggested that these random values should be chosen to reflect the expected operational input distribution. They also should reflect previous experience with similar components and systems and the bugs found in them.

These four techniques rely only on some notion of the input space and expected functionality of the component being tested. With software components, the user should know these facts and be able to create test cases around them.

While important and necessary, these techniques do not ensure that all of the most appropriate challenges to a software product have been identified for testing.

The functional testing methods identified above all emphasize individual or single test inputs. Most software products operate with multiple inputs under their conditions of use. Thorough software product testing should consider the combinations of inputs a software unit or system may encounter during operation. Error guessing can be extended to identify combinations of inputs, but it is an ad hoc technique. Cause-effect graphing is one functional software testing technique that systematically identifies combinations of inputs to a software product for inclusion in test cases.

Functional and structural software test case identification techniques provide specific inputs for testing, rather than random test inputs. One weakness of these techniques is the difficulty in linking structural and functional test completion criteria to a software product's reliability. Advanced software testing methods, such as statistical testing, can be employed to provide further assurance that a software product is dependable. Statistical testing uses randomly generated test data from defined distributions based on an operational profile (e.g., expected use, hazardous use, or malicious use of the software product).

Large amounts of test data are generated and can be targeted to cover particular areas or concerns, providing an increased possibility of identifying individual and multiple rare operating conditions that were not anticipated by either the software product's designers or its testers. Statistical testing also provides high structural coverage. It does require a stable software product. Thus, structural and functional testing are prerequisites for statistical testing of a software product.

6.2.1 Black Box or Functional Testing

All white-box tests have the disadvantage that the program's source code is needed to run the tests. Functional or black-box testing, however, aims to test a given program's behavior against its specification without making any reference to the internal structures of the program or the algorithms used. Therefore the source code is not needed, and so even purchased modules can be tested. The programs just get a certain input, and its functionality is examined by observing the output. This can be done in the following way:

- Input
- Interface
- Processing
- Output
- Interface

The tested program gets a certain input or the input is observed. Then the product does its job and generates a certain output which is collected by a second interface. This result is then compared to the expected output which has been determined before the test.

There are a lot of different ways to do black-box testing. Even to try to cover most of them would be far beyond the scope of this thesis, so again five representatives which should give a good impression have been chosen.

6.2.2 Functional Testing

Function testing is usually the first black box test. The main goal is to find divergences between the specification—a precise description of the program's behavior from the users point of view—or design, and the coded product. This is often done in the following way:

First, this specification is being analysed. For each of the program's input field, the allowed inputs are written down. It is useful to try to divide the possible inputs in so-called equivalence classes to reduce the number of possible inputs which should be tested.

Alternatively, a boundary value analysis can be done. The difference is that rather than choosing any element in an equivalence class as a representative, the focus is on the edges of the appropriate equivalence class. Once more, the triangle example helps to explain the usefulness of this test method. For all input values to represent a triangle, two conditions have to be fulfilled. First, all integers have to be greater than zero, and second, the sum of any two of them has to be greater than the third. A likely error for the program is that A + B = C is coded instead of A + B > C. Since the boundary value analysis explores situations on and around the edges of the equivalence classes, it helps to find bugs of this kind.

6.3 Black-box Testing Techniques

Black-box testing techniques are characterized by focusing tests on the expected behavior of a software component and ensuring that the resulting functionality is correct [Beizer, 1995]. In many cases this behavioral testing is done without the aid of source code or design documents. It is possible to provide input test cases and only test the outputs of the object for correctness. This type of black-box testing does not require knowledge of the source code and so is possible to do with software components.

Black-box testing is not strictly required to operate without access to the source code. Techniques such as control flow analysis and data flow analysis are black-box techniques that require the access to requirements documents and source code [Beizer, 1995]. They require that the internal behavior of the object be studied for correctness, making these techniques all but impossible to apply to software components.

To guide test case selection, the operational profile of the software component can be used. The operational profile identifies the criticality of components and their duration and frequency of use [Schneidewind, 1998]. Both the operational profile of the software component and the whole system must be taken into account.

Table 6.1: Black-box Testing Techniques

Technique	Description
Equivalence classes	Mark the input space into similar classes to allow on representative input to test for the entire class.
Error guessing	Based on experience, test possible or common errors that are possible.
Random tests	Pick randomly from the input space for the test cases.
Operational profile testing	Choose test cases based on the expected operational environment for the product.

6.4 Advantages of Black-box Testing

Advantages of Black-box Testing are listed:

- Black-box tests are reproducible.
- The environment the program is running is also tested.
- The invested effort can be used multiple times.
- Efficient when used on Larger systems.
- As the tester and developer are independent of each other, test is balanced and unprejudiced.
- Tester can be non-technical.
- There is no need of having detailed functional knowledge of system to the tester.
- Tests will be done from an end user's point of view. Because end user should accept the system. (This is reason, sometimes this testing technique is also called as Acceptance testing.)
- Testing helps to identify the vagueness and contradiction in functional specifications.
- Test cases can be designed as soon as the functional specifications are complete.

6.5 Disadvantages of Black-box Testing

- The results are often overestimated.
- Not all properties of a software product can be tested.
- The reason for a failure is not found.
- Test cases are tough and challenging to design, without having clear functional specifications.
- It is difficult to identify tricky inputs, if the test cases are not developed based on specifications.
- It is difficult to identify all possible inputs in limited testing time. So writing test cases is slow and difficult.
- Chances of having unidentified paths during this testing.
- Chances of having repetition of tests that are already done by programmer.

Black-box testing attempts to derive sets of inputs that will fully exercise all the functional requirements of a system. It is not an alternative to white-box testing. This type of testing attempts to find errors in the following categories:

(1) incorrect or missing functions,

(2) interface errors,

(3) errors in data structures or external database access,

(4) performance errors, and

(5) initialization and termination errors.

6.6 Testing Software Changes

Another aspect of software testing is the testing of software changes. Changes occur frequently during software development. These changes are the result of:

(1) debugging that finds an error and it is corrected,

(2) new or changed requirements ("requirements creep"), and

(3) modified designs as more effective or efficient implementations are found.

Once a software product has been baselined (approved), any change to that product should have its own "mini life cycle," including testing.

Testing of a changed software product requires additional effort. Not only should it demonstrate that the change was implemented correctly, testing should also demonstrate that the change did not adversely impact other parts of the software product. Regression analysis and testing are employed to provide assurance that a change has not created problems elsewhere in the software product. Regression analysis is the determination of the impact of a change based on review of the relevant documentation (e.g., software requirements specification, software design specification, source code, test plans, test cases, test scripts, etc.) in order to identify the necessary regression tests to be run. Regression testing is the rerunning of test cases that a program has previously executed correctly and comparing the current result to the previous result in order to detect unintended effects of a software change. Regression analysis and regression testing should also be employed when using integration methods to build a software product to ensure that newly integrated modules do not adversely impact the operation of previously integrated modules.

6.7 Equivalence Classes

This is a subset of black-box testing, but important in its own right. Most programs divide input into categories, or classes: a tax program may place a paycheck below \$500 in one tax bracket, a check from \$500 to \$1000 in another bracket, and a check for more than \$1000 in yet a third bracket. Each of these three brackets takes the program in a different direction, so you must test all three directions at least once.

Equivalence class is a portion of the component's input or output domains for which the component's behaviour is assumed to be the same from the component's specification.

An important metric connected to this testing is Equivalent Partition Coverage, Equivalence classes may be defined according to the following guidelines:

(1) If an input condition specifies a range, one valid and two invalid equivalence classes are defined.

(2) If an input condition requires a specific value, then one valid and two invalid equivalence classes are defined.

(3) If an input condition specifies a member of a set, then one valid and one invalid equivalence class are defined.

(4) If an input condition is boolean, then one valid and one invalid equivalence class are defined.

6.7.1 Equivalence Partitioning

An approach where classes of inputs are categorized for product or function validation. This usually does not include combinations of input, but rather a single state value based by class. For example, with a given function there may be several classes of input that may be used for positive testing. If function expects an integer and receives an integer as input, this would be considered as positive test assertion. On the other hand, if a character or any other input class other than integer is provided, this would be considered a negative test assertion or condition.

A technique in black-box testing is equivalence partitioning. Equivalence partitioning is designed to minimize the number of test cases by dividing tests in such a way that the system is expected to act the same way for all tests of each equivalence partition. Test inputs would be selected from each partition. Equivalence partitions are designed so that every possible input belongs to one and only one equivalence partition.

Equivalence partitioning is a method for deriving test cases. In this method, classes of input conditions called equivalence classes are identified such that each member of the class causes the same kind of processing and output to occur.

In this method, the tester identifies various equivalence classes for partitioning. A class is a set of input conditions that are is likely to be handled the same way by the system. If the system were to handle one case in the class erroneously, it would handle all cases erroneously.

Equivalence partitioning drastically cuts down the number of test cases required to test a system reasonably. It is an attempt to get a good 'hit rate', to find the most errors with the smallest number of test cases.

6.7.2 Designing Test Cases Using Equivalence Partitioning

To use equivalence partitioning, you will need to perform two steps:

- Identify the equivalence classes.
- Design test cases.

STEP 1: Identify Equivalence Classes

Take each input condition described in the specification and derive at least two equivalence classes for it. One class represents the set of cases which satisfy the condition (the valid class) and one represents cases which do not (the invalid class).

Following are some general guidelines for identifying equivalence classes:

(a) If the requirements state that a numeric value is input to the system and must be within a range of values, identify one valid class inputs which are within the valid range and two invalid equivalence classes inputs which are too low and inputs which are too high. For example, if an item in inventory can have a quantity of –9999 to + 9999, identify the following classes:

1. one valid class: (QTY is greater than or equal to -9999 and is less than or equal to 9999). This is written as (- 9999 < = QTY < = 9999)
2. the invalid class (QTY is less than –9999), also written as (QTY < –9999)
3. the invalid class (QTY is greater than 9999), also written as (QTY >9999)

(b) If the requirements state that the number of items input by the system at some point must lie within a certain range, specify one valid class where the number of inputs is within the valid range, one invalid class where there are too few inputs and one invalid class where there are, too many inputs.

For example, specifications state that a maximum of 4 purchase orders can be registered against any one product. The equivalence classes are: the valid equivalence class: (number of purchase orders is greater than or equal to 1 and less than or equal to 4, also written as (1 < = no. of purchase orders < = 4) the invalid class (no. of purchase orders> 4) the invalid class (no. of purchase orders < 1)

(c) If the requirements state that a particular input item match one of a set of values and each case will be dealt with the same way, identify a valid class for values in the set and one invalid class representing values outside of the set. For example, if the requirements state that a valid province code is ON, QU, and NB, then identify: the valid class code is one of ON, QU, NB the invalid class code is not one of ON, QU, NB

(d) If the requirements state that a particular input item match one of a set of values and each case will be dealt with differently, identify a valid equivalence class for each element and only one invalid class for values outside the set. For example, if a discount code must be input as P for preferred customer, R for standard reduced rate, or N for none, and if each case is treated differently, identify the valid class code = P the valid class code = R the valid class code = N the invalid class code is not one of P, R, N

(e) If you think any elements of an equivalence class will be handled differently than the others, divide the equivalence class to create an equivalence class with only these elements and an equivalence class with none of these elements. For example, a bank account balance may be from $0 up to $ 1,000,000 and balances $ 1,000 or over are not subject to service charges. Identify: the valid class: ($ 0 < = balance < $ 1,000) i.e. balance is between 0 and $ 1,000—not including $ 1,000 the valid class: ($ 1, 000 < = balance < = $ 1,000,000 i.e. balance is between $ 1,000 and $ 1,000,000 inclusive the invalid class: (balance < $ 0) the invalid class: (balance> $ 1,000,000)

6.8 Boundary Value Analysis (BVA)

6.8.1 Boundary Value

Boundary Value is an input value or output value which is on the boundary between equivalence classes, or an incremental distance either side of the boundary. The boundary value is that value separating equivalence classes. An equivalence class is a set of data for which the softwares behaviour is assumed to be the same.

For example the spec states that a field should accept from £0.01 up to and including £10. A message is generated indicating whether the entered field is too low or too high.

The boundary values in this case are £0.01, £0.02, £9.99 and £10.00 any amount in between is in the same equivalence class as they are all acceptable. Thus £2.48 and £9.98 should behave exactly the same.

6.8.2 Boundary Value Analysis (BVA)

Boundary value analysis is a methodology for designing test cases that concentrates software testing effort on cases near the limits of valid ranges. Boundary value analysis is a method which refines equivalence partitioning. Boundary value analysis generates test cases that highlight errors better than equivalence partitioning. The trick is to concentrate software testing efforts at the extreme ends of the equivalence classes. At those points when input values change from valid to invalid errors are most likely to occur. As well, boundary value analysis broadens the portions of the business requirement document used to generate tests.

Unlike equivalence partitioning, it takes into account the output specifications when deriving test cases.

BVA is different from equivalence partitioning in that it focuses on "corner cases" or values that are usually out of range as defined by the specification. This means that if function expects all values in range of negative 100 to positive 1000, test inputs would include negative 101 and positive 1001. BVA attempts to derive the value often used as a technique for stress, load or volume testing. This type of validation is usually performed after positive functional validation has completed (successfully) using requirements specifications and user documentation. Boundary Value Analysis is a test case design technique for a component in which test cases are designed which include representatives of boundary values.

The tester needs to understand what will happen at the boundaries of the behaviour for each component. For example, a field is required to accept amounts of money between £0 and £10. Does this mean up to and including £10 or £9.99? At the other end, can an amount of £0 be acceptable? Is the boundary set at the pound or penny level?

The analysts decides the boundary values are £0, £0.01, £9.99 and £10. Once this has been established, the tester can then set his test data.

The following tests are then to be executed:

A negative amount = rejected

0 = accepted this is on the boundary

null = rejected

£0.01 = accepted

£9.99 = accepted.

£10=rejected.

Items on the same side of the boundary value are said to be in the same equivalence class.

Thus, at the top of the range we only have to test three values. £9.99, £10 both of which should be accepted and £10.01 which is rejected.

An important metric connected to this testing is Boundary Value Coverage £10.98 and £20 are part of another equivalence class as they are too high. A negative amount of –£20 forms part of another class as it generates another message.

6.8.3 Boundary Testing

The boundaries between equivalence classes are favorite places for bugs to congregate. You should give special attention to the edge of each class and, if possible, try to go beyond the edge by entering illegal values (such as -$1). This method divides the input domain of a program into classes of data from which test cases can be derived. Equivalence partitioning strives to define a test case that uncovers classes of errors and thereby reduces the number of test cases needed. It is based on an evaluation of equivalence classes for an input condition. An equivalence class represents a set of valid or invalid states for input conditions.

This method leads to a selection of test cases that exercise boundary values. It complements equivalence partitioning since it selects test cases at the edges of a class. Rather than focusing on input conditions solely, BVA derives test cases from the output domain also. BVA guidelines include:

(1) For input ranges bounded by a and b, test cases should include values a and b and just above and just below a and b respectively.

(2) If an input condition specifies a number of values, test cases should be developed to exercise the minimum and maximum numbers and values just above and below these limits.

(3) Apply guidelines 1 and 2 to the output.

(4) If internal data structures have prescribed boundaries, a test case should be designed to exercise the data structure at its boundary.

6.8.4 Boundary Value Coverage

The percentage of boundary values of the component's equivalence classes which have been exercised by a test case suite. This is a metric indicating how much testing is required. It is important because a lot of defects are discovered at the boundary values. Thus if none or very few boundary value tests are left, then the risk of failure has been significantly reduced.

6.8.5 Performing Boundary Value Analysis

Once again, you'll need to perform two steps:

- Identify the equivalence classes.
- Design test cases.

But the details vary. Let's examine each step.

Step 1: Identify Equivalence Classes

Follow the same rules you used in equivalence partitioning. However, consider the output specifications as well. For example, if the output specifications for the inventory system stated that a report on inventory should indicate a total quantity for all products no greater than 999,999, then you will add the following classes to the ones you found previously:

- The valid class (0 < = total quantity on hand < = 999,999)
- The invalid class (total quantity on hand <0)
- The invalid class (total quantity on hand> 999,999)

Step 2: Design Test Cases

In this step, you derive test cases from the equivalence classes. The process is similar to that of equivalence partitioning but the rules for designing test cases differ. With equivalence partitioning, you may select any test case within a range and any on either side of it with boundary analysis, you focus your attention on cases close to the edges of the range. The detailed rules for generating test cases follow:

6.8.6 Rules for Test Cases

(1) If the condition is a range of values, create valid test cases for each end of the range and invalid test cases just beyond each end of the range. For example, if a valid range of quantity on hand is -9,999 through 9,999, write test cases that include:

- the valid test case quantity on hand is -9,999,
- the valid test case quantity on hand is 9,999,
- the invalid test case quantity on hand is -10,000 and
- the invalid test case quantity on hand is 10,000

You may combine valid classes, wherever possible, just as you did with equivalence partitioning, and, once again, you may not combine invalid classes. Do not forget to consider output conditions as well. In our inventory example, the output conditions generate the following test cases:

- the valid test case total quantity on hand is 0,
- the valid test case total quantity on hand is 999,999
- the invalid test case total quantity on hand is -1 and
- the invalid test case total quantity on hand is 1,000,000

(2) A similar rule applies where the condition states that the number of values must lie within a certain range—select two valid test cases, one for each boundary of the range, and two invalid test cases, one just below and one just above the acceptable range.

(3) Design tests that highlight the first and last records in an input or output file.

(4) Look for any other extreme input or output conditions, and generate a test for each of them.

6.9 Orthogonal Array Testing: Taguchi Method

Orthogonal Array Testing is a statistical testing technique implemented by Taguchi. This method is extremely valuable for testing complex applications and e-comm products. The e-comm world presents interesting challenges for test case design and testing coverage. The black box testing technique will not adequately provide sufficient testing coverage. The underlining infrastructure connections between servers and legacy systems will not be understood by the black-box testing team. A gray box testing team will have the necessary knowledge and combined with the power of statistical testing, an elaborate testing net can be set-up and implemented.

The theory Orthogonal Array Testing (OAT) can be used to reduce the number of combinations and provide maximum coverage with a minimum number of test cases. OAT is an array of values in which each column represents a variable-factor that can take a certain set of values called levels. Each row represents a test case. In OAT, the factors are combined pair-wise rather than representing all possible combinations of factors and levels.

A simple example: Three Factors and Three Levels Array is shown in table 6.2.

Table 6.2: Three Factors and Three Levels Array

	OS	Browser	Function
	Factor 1	Factor 2	Factor 3
Level 1	Win 98 SE	IE 4	Library
Level 2	Win Me	IE 5	Scheduling
Level 3	Win 2000	NS 6	Personal Inf.

Now given the example above, a tester would have to create 3^3 or 27 test combinations as shown in table 6.3.

Table 6.3: Total Number of Test cases

	Factor 1	**Factor 2**	**Factor 3**
1	1	1	3
?	1	2	2
3	1	3	1
4	2	1	2
5	2	2	1
6	2	3	3
7	3	1	1
S	3	2	2
9	3	3	2

Number of test cases table

By assigning values for each factor and then extrapolating for combined pairing, our total number of test cases drops to nine from 27. This simple but effective technique maximizes the required testing coverage.

6.10 Cause-Effect Graphing Techniques

Cause-effect graphing is a technique that provides a concise representation of logical conditions and corresponding actions. There are four steps:

(1) Causes (input conditions) and effects (actions) are listed for a module and an identifier is assigned to each.

(2) A cause-effect graph is developed.

(3) The graph is converted to a decision table.

(4) Decision table rules are converted to test cases.

6.11 Black-box Testing—With User Involvement

For tests involving users, methodological considerations are rare in SE literature. Rather, one may find practical test reports that distinguish roughly between field and laboratory tests. In the following only a rough description of field and laboratory tests will be given.

In field tests, users are observed while using the software system at their normal working place. Apart from general usability-related aspects, field tests are particularly useful for assessing the interoperability of the software system, i.e. how the technical integration of the system works. Moreover, field tests are the only real means to elucidate problems of the organisational integration of the software system into existing procedures. Particularly in the NLP environment this problem has frequently been underestimated. A typical example of the organisational problem of implementing a translation memory is the language service of a big automobile manufacturer, where the major implementation problem is not the technical environment, but the fact that many clients still submit their orders as print-out, that neither source texts nor target texts are properly organised and stored and, last but not least, individual translators are not too motivated to change their working habits.

Laboratory tests are mostly performed to assess the general usability of the system. Due to the high laboratory equipment costs laboratory tests are mostly only performed at big software houses such as IBM or Microsoft. Since laboratory tests provide testers with many technical possibilities, data collection and analysis are easier than for field tests.

To conclude, apart from the above described analytical methods of both glass and black-box testing, there are further constructive means to guarantee high quality software end products. Among the most important constructive means are the usage of object-oriented programming tools, the integration of CASE tools, rapid prototyping, and last but not least the involvement of users in both software development and testing procedures.

The above survey of glass and black-box testing methods has shown that although considerable work on development-oriented testing practices exists, there is much less work to date on user-oriented evaluation methods.

6.12 Random (Stochastic) Testing: Test Monkeys and Gorillas

While automation tools do your regression testing, you have more time to plan new tests and design new and interesting cases to try. Another type of automated testing, though, isn't designed to help run or automatically run test cases. Its goal is to simulate what your users might do. That type of automation tool is called a test monkey.

The term test monkey comes from the idea that if you had a million monkeys typing on a million keyboards for a million years, statistically, they might eventually write a Shakespearean play, Curious George, or some other great work. All that random pounding of keys could accidentally hit the right combination of letters and the monkeys would, for a moment.

The term 'monkey' that refers to a fully automated testing tool is common in the software testing arena. These test monkeys perform testing actions either randomly or stochastically—without any user bias. They assign test cases randomly and reportedly reveal about 10-20% of bugs.

Some of the features of test monkeys are:

(a) They can be used at any stage of the development cycle.

(b) They have the capability to use system resources to its extremes.

(c) They complement manual/automated testing.

Again these monkeys can be categorized into two divisions:

(1) **Dumb:** They have no idea about the legal inputs and the state of the system.

(2) **Smart:** They use the state tables and models and have the capability to choose the legal inputs.

"Smart monkeys" are valuable for load and stress testing; they will find a significant number of bugs, but are also very expensive to develop. "Dumb monkeys", on the other hand, are inexpensive to develop, are able to do some basic testing, but they will find few bugs. However, the bugs "dumb monkeys" do find will be hangs and crashes, i.e. the bugs you least want to have in your software product. "Monkey testing" can be valuable, but they should not be your only testing.

Test monkeys will test forever as long as they have electricity and the occasional but enough banana. When your software is released to the public, it will have thousands or possibly millions of people randomly pounding away on it. Despite your best efforts at designing test cases to find bugs, some bugs will slip by and be found by those users. What if you could supplement your test case approach with a simulation of what all those users would do, before you released your product? You could potentially find bugs that would have otherwise made it past your testing. That's what a test monkey can do!

Input are generated from probability distributions that reflect actual expected usage statistics e.g. from user profiles. The Random testing can be classified as:

- Dumb-monkey Testing
- Semi-Dumb Monkey Testing
- Brilliant Monkey Testing

6.12.1 Dumb-monkey Testing

The easiest and most straightforward type of test monkey is a dumb monkey. A dumb monkey doesn't know anything about the software being tested; it just clicks or types randomly. Listing 6.1 shows an example of Visual Test code that will randomly click and type 10,000 times. Inputs are generated from a uniform probability distribution without regard to the actual usage statistics. [Visual Test 6 Bible by Thomas R. Arnold, 1998]

Listing 6.1: Just a Few Lines of Code can Create a Dumb Monkey

```
1: RANDOMIZE TIMER
2: FOR i=1 TO 10000
3: PLAY "{CLICK "+STR$(INT(RND*640))+", "+STR$(INT(RND*480))+" }"
4: PLAY CHR$(RND*256)
5: NEXT iLine 1 initializes the random numbers. Line 2 starts
   looping from 1 to 10,000 times.
```

Line 3 selects a random point on screen between 0,0 and 640,480 (VGA resolution) and clicks it. Line 4 picks a random character between 0 and 255 and types it in.

The software running on the PC doesn't know the difference between this program and a real person except that it happens much more quickly. On a reasonably speedy PC it'll run in just a few seconds. Imagine how many random inputs you'd get if it ran all night!

Remember, this monkey is doing absolutely no verification. It just clicks and types until one of two things happens—either it finishes its loop or the software or the operating system crashes.

Note: If you don't believe that a dumb monkey can possibly find a serious bug, try running one on your favorite computer game or multimedia program. It's very likely that it won't last more than a few hours before crashing. It doesn't seem to make sense that simple random clicking and typing could find a bug, but it does for a couple of reasons:

Given enough time and attempts, just like the monkeys writing Shakespeare, the random inputs will eventually stumble onto a magic sequence that the programmers and testers didn't think of. Maybe the monkey enters some data and immediately deletes it or types in a huge string where a short one was expected. Who knows? It will find it, though.

A dumb monkey, with its continuous repetition and use, can expose bugs such as memory leaks that might not occur until many hours or days of normal use. If you've ever used software that seemed to become less and less stable the longer you used it, you've seen a problem that could have been found with a dumb monkey.

6.12.2 Semi-Smart Monkeys

Dumb monkeys can be extremely effective. They're easy to write and can find serious, crashing bugs. They lack a few important features, though, that would make them even more effective. Adding these features raises your monkey's IQ a bit, making him semi-smart.

Say that your monkey ran for several hours, logging thousands of random inputs before the software crashed. You'd know there was a problem but you couldn't show the programmer exactly how to re-create it. You could rerun your monkey with the same random seed but if it took several hours again to fail, you'd be wasting a lot of time. The solution is to add logging to your monkey so that everything it does is recorded to a file. When the monkey finds a bug, you need only to look at the log file to see what it was doing before the failure.

It's also a good idea to program your monkey to operate only on the software you're testing. If it's randomly clicking all over the screen, it could (and will eventually) click the exit command and stop the program. Since the monkey doesn't know that the program closed, it'll keep on going. Think about what would happen if the monkey was clicking all over your computer's screen—ouch! Most programmable automation tools provide a way to always target a specific application, or to stop working if the application is no longer present.

Another good feature to make your monkey semi-smart is crash recognition. If you started your monkey running for the night and it found a bug as soon as you walked out the door, you'd lose many hours of valuable test time. If you can add programming to your monkey to recognize that a crash has occurred, restart the computer, and start running again, you could potentially find several bugs each night.

6.12.3 Brilliant Monkey Testing

Moving up on the evolutionary scale is the smart monkey. Such a monkey takes the effectiveness of random testing from his less-intelligent brothers and adds to that an awareness of his surroundings. He doesn't just pound on the keyboard randomly he pounds on it with a purpose.

There are different levels of IQ in smart monkey testing. In the simplest, each input is considered independent of the other inputs. That is, a given test requires an input vector with five components.

In low IQ testing, these would be generated independently. In high IQ monkey testing, the correlation (e.g., the covariance) between these input distribution is taken into account. In all branches of smart monkey testing, the input is considered as a single event [Visual Test 6 Bible by Thomas R. Arnold, 1998]. The inputs are created from a stochastic regular expression or stochastic finite-state machine model of user behavior. That is, not only are the values determined by probability distributions, but the sequence of values and the sequence of states in which the input provider goes is driven by specified probabilities [Visual Test 6 Bible by Thomas R. Arnold, 1998].

A true smart monkey knows:

- Where he is
- What he can do there
- Where he can go
- Where he's been
- If what he's seeing is correct

Does this list sound familiar? It should. A smart monkey can read the software's state transition map, a formalized diagram that breaks the software into basic states, or conditions, and shows the means for moving from one state to the next. If the monkey can read all the state information that describes the software, it could bounce around the software just like a user would, only much more quickly, and be able to verify things as it went.

A smart monkey testing the Windows Calculator (see Figure 6.2) would know what buttons are available to press, what menu items are present, and where to type in the numbers. If it clicked the Help menu's About Calculator option, it would know that the only ways out were to click OK or the Close button. It wouldn't randomly click all over the screen, eventually stumbling onto one of them.

A smart monkey would know how to close the Calculator About dialog box. A smart monkey isn't limited to just looking for crashing bugs, either. It can examine data as it goes, checking the results of its actions and looking for differences from what it expects. If you programmed in your test cases, the smart monkey could randomly execute them, look for bugs, and log the results.

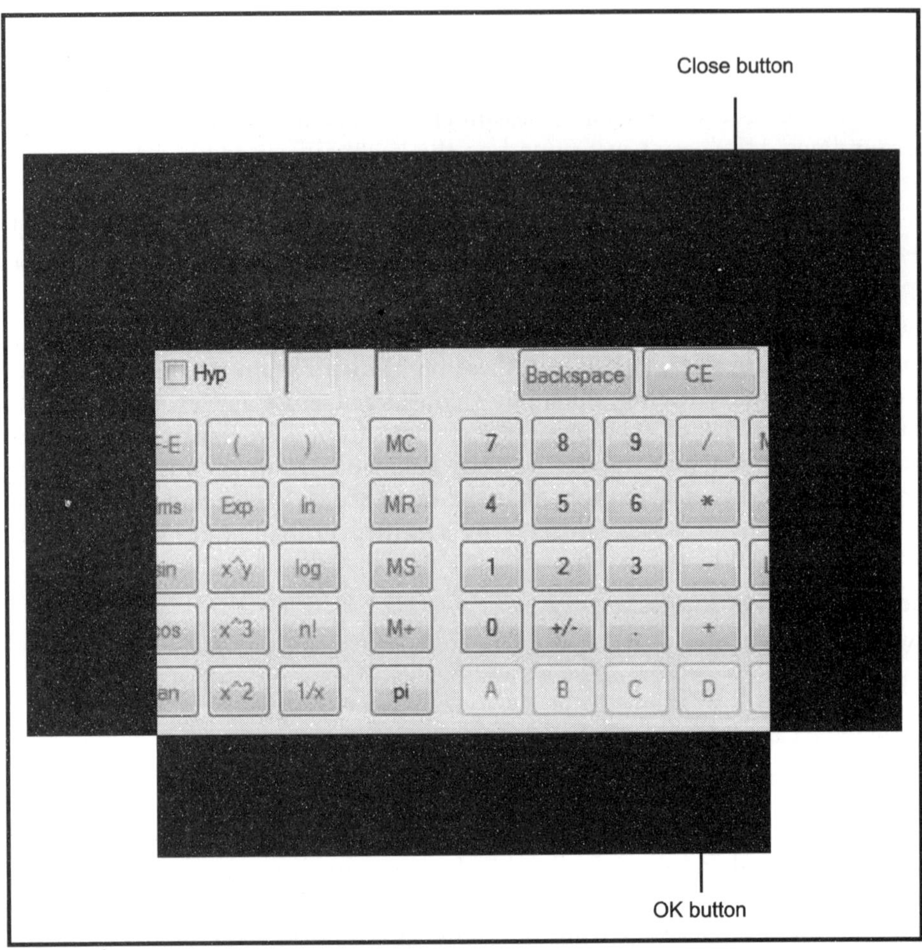

Fig. 6.2: Checking of Window's Calculator by Smart Monkey

6.12.4 KOKO: The Smart Monkey (Gorilla) Test

Figure 6.3 shows a smart monkey called Koko, named after the gorilla that could speak in sign language. To program Koko, you feed it the table that describes your software by defining each state, the actions that can be performed in that state, and claims that determine whether the result of executing an action is right or wrong.

The Koko smart monkey can be programmed to know where it is and what it can do.

When Koko runs, it drives the software to a known state, randomly selects an action based on a weighting that simulates real-world likelihood, performs that action, and then checks the result. If the action results in the software changing states, Koko knows that and uses a new set of actions that apply to that new state.

With such a system, you could simulate real-world usage of your software, compressing thousands of hours of use into just a few hours. Smart monkeys are truly bug-finding machines!

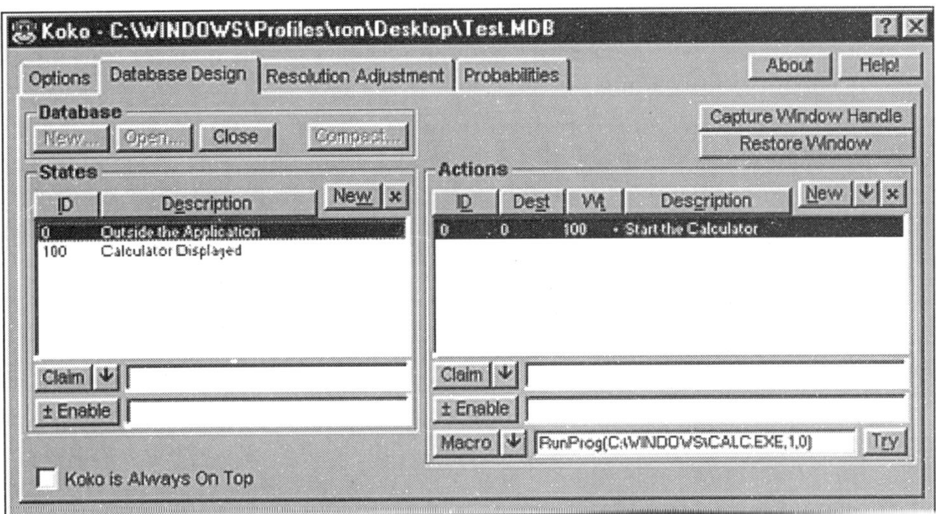

Figure 6.3: KoKo: The Smart Monkey

6.13 Monkey Test Tools

We get conflicting opinions about the efficacy of "monkey" test tools. Boris Beizer suggests in Black-box Testing that test monkeys aren't very useful for testing today's "professionally created software". His analysis concludes that the use of good testing practices will find more bugs than "keyboard-scrabbling or Rachmaninoff testing". But James Tierney, former Director of Testing at Microsoft has reported in internal presentations that some Microsoft applications groups have found 10-20% of the bugs in their projects using monkey test tools. However both the above assessments of monkey testing are correct.

There is no universal test tool that will find all the bugs in any software. Each tool has its uses, and some tools are more useful for certain projects, or at specific points in a project cycle, than others. Test monkeys are no exception. Wisely using them, tester can find new bugs cost-effectively. Use them carelessly, or exclusively, and you'll release a buggy product.

6.13.1 The Family of Test Monkeys

The term "monkey" is used to refer broadly to any form of automated testing done randomly and without any "typical user" bias.

While many of us find the "monkey" name appealing, others prefer the more technical sounding "stochastic" testing. Regardless, the essential elements are:

- The monkey is relatively ignorant of how humans use the product. It doesn't know how to build a Web page or create an amortization table, for example.
- The monkey can randomly choose from among a large range of inputs for testing, often all possible inputs.

Smart monkeys have some knowledge about how to access the user interface in the product they're testing. They know at a simple functional level what can be done, and more important, they understand what should happen when they do it. For example, they may know that choosing the New item on the File menu creates a new document, and they know that the new document will be displayed as a window with a particular class and text. If no new document window appears, or the window has the wrong caption or class, the monkey can identify the problem and report a bug.

Smart monkeys usually get their product knowledge from a state table or model of the software they test. Randomly traversing the state model, they choose from among all the legal options in the current state to move to another state, and then verify that they reached the next expected state. You can add illegal inputs to the monkey's repertoire if the model includes error handling states.

1. Dumb monkeys don't use a state table.
2. They have no idea what state the test application is in, or what inputs are legal or illegal.

Most important, they can't recognize a bug when they see one. The pure dumb monkey exemplifies Beizer's "keyboard scrabbling" test tool, and it isn't very useful for most projects. What can be useful is a not-quite-dumb monkey that's ignorant about your project, but understands its environment.

The early Apple Lisa and Macintosh groups developed a dumb monkey test tool with some limited knowledge of the Apple operating systems. Developers could test their application in monkey mode and the computer would act like an ignorant monkey, scrabbling with the keyboard and the mouse. Some developers required that their products survive a specified amount of monkey test time before they were released. Modern test monkeys know even more about their operating systems than the early Apple simian tools. For this discussion, dumb monkeys are application ignorant but environment savvy.

6.13.2 When to Use Smart Monkeys

In the ideal world, you could find all application bugs by reviewing the specifications and the code. You would never have to run any tests on the final product because it would be bug free. Most of us fall far short of this lofty goal. There are many reasons, but one of the most significant is the complexity of the application environment. To make thorough reviews, humans must be able to understand and mentally exercise the software in its operating environment. We can do that, with the proper training and skills, for embedded systems and even for some apparently complex software working in dedicated settings. Our grasp of the situation and the quality of our review efforts start to fail when our software must work in an event driven system, along with potentially thousands of other unrelated products. Add the possibilities of hundreds of thousands of users making simultaneous demands on our product, and our ability to find bugs by review alone dwindles.

Well crafted smart monkeys excel at finding bugs in such situations. If you accurately model the environment events in a state table, thousands of smart monkeys can read that table and present those events to your product. The monkeys will find combinations and sequences that human reviewers would never consider, although human users may create them after the product is released. Most of the commercially available load and stress testing tools depend on this smart monkey technology.

As per Brian Marick in his book *The Craft of Software Testing*, complex tests find more bugs than simple tests. But most of our automated tests are simple. We look for one major outcome after applying one input. Then we return the application to a known base state and execute another simple test. If the tests are well-thought out, they'll find good bugs. But they remain simple tests. When we return the application to a base state, we discard any "history" from previous tests. Real users seldom do that. Instead they chain many simple activities, one after another, to create complex situations.

Although testing team uses dumb monkeys to look for operating system bugs, they can be used to find quite a few application errors as well. There are four situations in every application product cycle where dumb monkeys can be cost effective:

- Dumb monkeys can find a lot of really good bugs, and save you testing time, early in the product cycle. The dumb monkey doesn't need to know anything about the user interface of the application. It doesn't matter whether the User Interface is totally changed from yesterday's build or half of it is missing. The monkey will test whatever it finds. So, you can start dumb monkey testing as soon as the new build arrives. The dumb monkey can explore the application and perhaps find nasty bugs while you're still adapting your formal automation suite to all the new UI changes.
- Dumb monkeys can give you very long runs of complex tests. Unless they find a crashing bug, they'll run for as many days as you let them, pushing memory and resources to their limits. If you have resource leaks or memory issues, dumb monkeys will help you find them.
- Near the end of the product cycle, when you think you've found all the nasty bugs, dumb monkey tests can help you increase your confidence. Running the dumb monkey for days at a time without failures gives you another measure of the stability of your application.
- The dumb monkey may be able to show you holes in your traditional test coverage. Run several hours of dumb monkey tests on a version of your application instrumented for coverage analysis and compare the results with a full pass of your non-monkey tests. If the monkey tests a function that's not touched by your traditional tests, you need to re-examine your test plan. If you have a state table for your application, teach the monkey to read it and check off each state as it tests your application. If it finds just one new state that's not defined on your state table, the monkey has exposed a whole new universe of untested bug possibilities in your application, something like a wormhole into the Delta Quadrant. At least one commercial tool uses the dumb monkey method to explore applications and create automation to maximize coverage while minimizing test time.

6.13.3 Making Useful Dumb Monkeys

Most team uses retail applications as test engines to look for operating systems bugs. Mostly good testers develop automated test suites for several hundred popular applications and run them often during the Windows product cycle. But there are thousands of additional applications one could use, if one had the time and testers to create the tests. Some of those applications might find us good Windows bugs and we'd like to have some inexpensive way to test them.

Some people experimented with dumb monkeys to test those applications. These dumb monkeys understand Windows basics. They know about menus and they can choose options on any menus they find. They can also recognize common Windows controls such as command buttons, check boxes, radio (option) buttons and edit boxes. They run a set of pre-defined tests on each control to make sure it's working properly. They can also recognize a few on the most common command buttons, such as OK and Cancel, and the most sophisticated monkeys automatically adjust to localized versions of Windows. They have created monkeys using several popular automation tools. Like Windows operating system, similar monkeys can be developed for other GUI operating systems using versions of automation tools specific to other operating systems.

6.13.4 Generic State Monkeys

Monkeys with GUI savvy can manipulate many Windows applications. But a few applications rely on custom controls to expose their functions to users. Most automation tools have trouble testing those applications because the tools can't find the controls the user must manipulate. If the automation tool can't find the controls, the monkey can't find them, either. That problem can be dealt with in several ways:

- Tell the monkey to click randomly a few times in every new window it sees. Occasionally the monkey clicks on one of those invisible elements and changes the application state.
- If the application has interesting areas such as toolbars that are invisible to the monkey, we tell it to focus its random clicks in those areas.
- Ask the monkey to randomly perform mouse actions, such as left-clicks, right-clicks and drags, or enter random text at the current insertion point, if the application relies on human users doing those things often.

A monkey with those skills can make some weird and futuristic drawings in Microsoft Paint or Corel Draw. These tools are sometimes called "generic state" monkeys, because, to be effective, they need to know five states:

- The test application is not running.
- The test application is running and is probably ready to accept test input.
- A new window appeared when a test was run.
- The new window has Windows controls on it that the monkey recognizes.
- The new window went away.

Given a state table with just these five generic states, this monkey can't log much useful information about an application's faults and failures. Most of the errors it sees are ambiguous and a human must examine the error log to decide what really happened. We call these "monkey noise" bugs and we try to avoid them. We do that by ignoring them entirely and using a different error oracle. The monkey starts the application in a debug session and we monitor the monkey's tests with a debugger. We want to find nasty crashing bugs that display the dreaded blue-screen-of-death. A debugger is very good at trapping those bugs. It automatically halts the monkey and allows a developer to examine the machine state when the bug occurs.

6.13.5 The Cost of Smart Monkey Testing

A good smart monkey tool is expensive to create. Like any test automation, building smart monkey test tools requires development and test resources. But the greatest single cost is generating the model or state table. It's not unusual to need a 50,000 node state table for a moderately complex product. Adding new features results in state explosion where the number of nodes increases geometrically. Maintenance becomes a major cost factor for large tables.

A good state table based on Petri nets or Markov chains may have value beyond the smart monkey that may help justify some of the expense. Even so, the cost of creating the table, and the monkey to run tests using it, often outweighs the value of the additional bugs found. The sad fact is that most smart monkeys are not easily adapted to other projects. Your monkey must pay back all its costs by finding bugs on the project it was designed to test.

Compared with smart monkeys, and most traditional automated and manual testing, dumb monkeys are dirt-cheap. A dumb monkey can test almost any application that can run on its operating system. So, you can leverage it to many unrelated projects.

You get the best results from a dumb monkey that knows a few things about your application. It will waste less time on useless mouse clicking if you can tell it about the interesting areas on the application's windows. But overeducating dumb monkeys isn't usually cost effective. Normally the target is to spend no more than thirty minutes teaching a dumb monkey about a new application.

Once you've given the dumb monkey the minimum information it needs to explore your application, set it up in a corner of your lab or office on an old, slow computer no one wants to use for regular testing. Have it start testing the application under a debugger and check its progress every day or so. If the monkey finds just one good bug, it will be the least expensive bug your team reports.

The hidden cost is creating the dumb monkey. Like any test tool, a good dumb monkey can be expensive to develop. But unlike many test tools, a mediocre or "beginner" dumb monkey has a good chance of finding some bugs, if you use it at the right time and for the right reasons. As the monkey proves its worth, you can add features and give it more skills. If you use Rational Visual Test on the Windows platform, you can start experimenting with dumb monkeys using a simplified monkey based on one of our Microsoft internal testing simians.

6.13.6 Choosing Wisely

Monkey testing should not be your only testing. Monkeys don't understand your application, and in their ignorance they miss many bugs. Monkeys won't add much value to embedded systems, or software running in simple environments, or projects that are difficult to automate.

Unless you already have an automation readable model or state table, smart monkeys will be very expensive to develop. They may be cost effective for critical parts of a project where the state table can be kept small. They're also valuable for load and stress testing. When used in the right places, smart monkeys will find a significant number of bugs.

Dumb monkeys that understand your operating system can be used on any application and get some basic testing done. A small amount of training on your specific application greatly improves their chances of finding bugs. Dumb monkeys will not find many bugs, but the bugs they do find will be crashes and hangs...the bugs you probably least want to have in your product.

6.14 Orthogonality

If you drop a rock in a pond, the still water will ripple as a reaction to the rock. This one action propogates ripples throughout the pond, maybe even reaching the farthest shores. This example illustrates something that is not orthogonal. One change in the pond, the presence of the rock, created changes throughout the whole pond.

In math orthogonal lines are defined as the following:

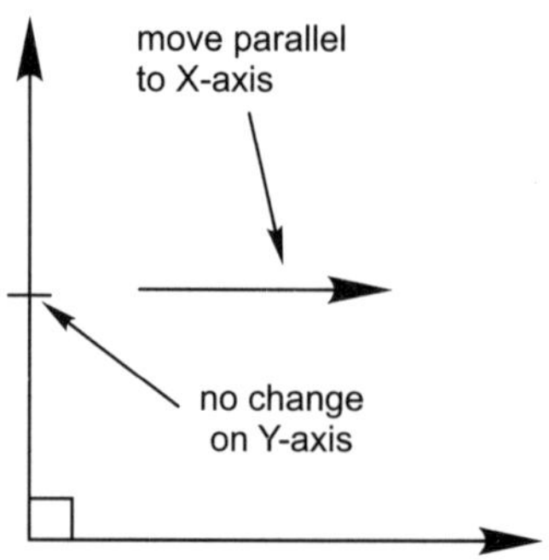

Fig. 6.4: Orthogonal Axis

These two lines are independent. When you move along the X-axis the Y value does not change and vice versa. This math example relates to orthogonality because a change in one part of your program (moving along the X-axis) should not affect a separate part (the Y value).

6.14.1 Event Planning

When you are planning an event such as a wedding reception or a business function, you want to make things run as smoothly as possible. Even though events are inherently time-coupled, you can try to decouple as much as possible. Here are some things that might be done:

- Separate the tasks to be done between helpers, i.e. Decorations, catering, invitations, etc.
- Keep the tasks separate so that each job is distinct, i.e. don't have the person handling the catering also pick up the decorative flowers.
- Run through a checklist to make sure every task was met sufficiently, i.e. make sure that the caterer got 200 servings of chicken.

Since responsibilities are clear-cut, if someone gets sick, it is easy to see where a replacement is needed. This idea will be used throughout this lesson to parallel planning an event with a software process.

Concepts of Orthogonality

- Design components that are self-contained.
- Components are independent with a well-defined purpose.

Benefits

- Orthogonal systems are easier to change and control.
- When components are independent, you can make truly local fixes. In interdependent systems, a "local" fix can ripple throughout other components.

Put plainly, orthogonality eliminates effects between unrelated things.

Productivity Gains and Risk Reduction

Two major attributes of orthogonality are increased productivity and reduced risk.

6.14.2 Gains in Productivity

(1) **Changes are localized.** This reduces development and testing time. It is easier to write small, self-contained components rather than a single large block of code.

(2) **Promotes reuse.** When responsibilities are specific and well-defined, components can combine more easily with new ones (in other programs).

Subtle gain in productivity when combining orthogonal components.

```
Component 1 => does M things
Component 2 => does N things
```

Combining these two components results in the ability to do M×N things.

Risk Reductions

- Diseased sections of code are isolated so it is easier to take out bad sections without affecting other components.
- Resulting system is more robust, i.e. A ripple of errors caused by a change in code is restricted to its component.
- Easier to test and thus better tested, i.e. Tests are easier to design and run on smaller components.
- System won't be as closely linked to a certain vendor, product, or platform.

6.14.3 Separation of Tasks

The tasks need to be well-defined responsibilities with minimal overlap.

The task separation depends on:

- The project.
- Any areas subject to change.
- The number of people available.

Here are the necessary steps:

- Separate infrastructure from application.
- Each major component will have its own subteam, i.e. database, communications, interface, and middleware.

Divide the application functionality between members of sub-groups.

With orthogonal groups, if a change needs to be made, the whole team does not need to discuss it. Only the sub-team making the change will need to meet since their responsibilities are separated from the other sub-teams. Even though tasks are distinct, it is still a good idea for sub-teams to communicate.

Task Separation in Event Planning for the event, a different group will be in charge of these areas:

- Decorations
- Catering
- Invitations
- Entertainment
- Location arrangements

Each has distinct responsibilities, so if the menu changes, only the catering group will have to meet to coordinate the change. Some groups might have to talk a bit. For example, the decoration group will need to know if their decorations will fit in the location provided.

6.14.4 Design

Synonyms: orthogonal systems, modular, component-based, layered.

Systems are made of cooperating modules, each independently implementing its functionality. Modules are sometimes layered:

- Each layer is an abstraction that uses the abstraction below it.
- The bottom layers are flexible to change without affecting code.
- Layering reduces large dependencies between modules.

(1) Design in event planning

The teams should work together. The invitation people can give the other groups an idea of how many people RSVP'd. The location group picks a location that will accomodate all the people. Then upon these things, the decorators and entertainment groups can know their space provided and the caterers can estimate how much food is needed. The decorators also can work upon what the location provides them with.

As for the good advice...Suppose the event is outside. The decorators should provide for a chance of rain. A canopy may be put up there just in case.

Coding

Ways to keep code orthogonal:

- Keep code decoupled => "shy code".
- Modules shouldn't share anything unnecessary or rely on each other.
- Avoid global data.
- Global data ties modules together that share data.
- Code is easier to understand and maintain if data is explicitly passed in.
- Avoid similar functions.
- Duplicate code reflects structural problems.

Making an Event Happen

The catering group does need to know how many RSVPs the invitation group received, but it doesn't need to know who RSVP'd.

The catering people shouldn't prepare tablecloths and centerpieces because this would duplicate the decorating committee's job and show a problem in the structure of group responsibility.

(2) Testing

With an orthogonal system, system testing can be performed at the individual module level. Unit testing is easier to specify and perform than integration testing.

Suggestion: Use built-in unit tests that run at each build process.

- There should be only one module to build and link a unit test.
- Only one module should be needed to fix a bug.
- When one fix is made, the problem should be fixed not create more problems.

(3) Testing the event

The different groups can perform unit testing on their part of the project to make sure they are on track. The decorations committee can check to see if their decorations will go up properly and if they fit the location. The catering committee can have their menu taste-tested. The invitations committee can retally their RSVP list. The location committee can make sure all the permits they need for the location are approved. The band can make sure that all their equipment works properly and fits in the space the location provides.

Class Exercise

You are writing a class called Parser that parses input lines into fields. Here are two examples. Which Java signature has a more orthogonal design?

Example 6.1

```
class Parser 1 {
public Parser1(InputStreamReader rdr) { ...
public void readNextLine ( ) throws IOException { ...
public int numFields ( ) { ...
public String getField(int fieldNo) { ...
}
```

Example 6.2

```
class Parser2 {
Parser2(String line) { ...
int numFields ( ) { ...
String getField(int fieldNo) { ...
}
```

Answer

`Class Parser2` is more orthogonal. It parses lines without focusing on details such as where the lines came from. Since it focuses on its own job, it makes the code easier to develop and increases flexibility. **`Parser2`** can parse lines coming from a file, created by another routine, or passed in through the environment.

REFERENCES

ANSI/IEEE standard 610.12-1990 -glossary of software engineering terminology.

Black Box Monkey Testing - Chapter 14 Visual Test 6 Bible by Thomas R. Arnold, 1998.

McGregor, John D. and Sykes, David A. *Practical Guide to Testing Object-Oriented Software.* Canada: Addison-Wesley, 2001.

Online Papers About Model-based Testing http://www.geocities.com/model_based_testing/online_papers.htm

Orthogonal Arrays and Linear Graphs by G. Taguchi, 1987.

Orthogonally Speaking, by Elfriede Dustin *STQE Magazine* volume 3, issue 5, September/October 2001 p. 46.

Software Testing Techniques by Boris Beizer, 1990.

Testing Object-Oriented Systems: Models, Patterns, and Tools (The Addison-Wesley Object Technology Series) by Robert V. Binder. October, 1999) Addison-Wesley Pub. Co.

The Art of Software Testing by Glenford J. Myers 1979.

STATIC WHITE-BOX TESTING

7

7.1 White-box or Structural Testing

For a long time, the majority of the programmers believed that programs are only written to be read by a computer. It was also their opinion that the only way to test a program is to execute it on the machine for which it was designed. This attitude often led towards badly structured, illegible, and nearly unchangeable programs.

But what if a programmer knows that he will have to present his product to other professionals? Additionally, such a presentation might disclose some bugs which are otherwise hard to find, resulting in a strong psychological influence on the programmer. He will automatically write programs which are simpler to read, better structured, and easier to maintain. During such a presentation the internal structure of a program is being disclosed with the main goal to detect faults. Therefore such a procedure is in general called a "White Box Test".

In addition to those tests done in teams, some other white-box tests have been derived from one of the oldest tests—the desk-test—a programmer checking his work at his desk. In the following some of the most common white-box tests out of both fields will be shown.

Code-inspections and walk-throughs—the two chosen representatives for white-box tests done in teams—have been two of the first methods of testing without the use of a computer (this is also called "human testing"). These test have a lot in common and share the same basic idea. They are static test methods which can already be used in very early phases of the development process. This makes it possible to detect faults in a stage in which they can still be removed without causing extremely high expenditures.

To give a better survey, the common order of events for these tests will be given now. They will be discussed in detail later in this chapter.

First, the team is assigned. Each member gets enough information so he can be well prepared when the team meets for the first time a couple of weeks later. During this meeting which lasts approximately two hours and should not be interrupted, an exact list of all faults found is produced. It is important that the group does not start to look for solutions, because this would require too much time and it would distract them from their work. They are only supposed to find the bugs—once more, testing is counter productive.

There is disunity in the literature about the ideal size of this team, but five persons are not a bad choice. Now, who should to be in such a team to have an optimal chance of success.

(1) The manager is the most important member of the team. S/H is the organizer, chairman, and responsible for the whole enterprise. It is absolutely required that he is acknowledged by all other members for his personality, and his specialized knowledge, and qualification. She/He has to control and lead the meeting, make sure that all bugs found are recorded correctly, and removed after the meeting. Last, but not least, he has to decide if it is necessary to meet again. Later she or he has to control if all faults found have been fixed.

(2) The design engineer who has to contribute his know-how about design to the group. She/He should not be one of those who made the design of program which is tested; he only has to have specialized knowledge about designing such a product.

(3) The programmer who has to contribute his knowledge about the programming language used. He also has to know a lot about coding in general. She/He must not be the one who coded the tested program.

(4) The tester who has to be an expert on procedures like this. It is her/his job to control the process in a way it is more likely to detect faults.

(5) The keeper of the minutes who should relieve the manager's administrative job and who should make sure that everything done gets recorded.

(6) The author who wrote the program the group is testing.

(7) And last, but not least, the user who should keep up the connection to the "outside world". He might spend hours without understanding anything the experts are talking about, but if he is able to find one single fault, he has already made up for his costs. He also increases the products quality if he manages that the final product is more similar to other user's expectations.

The Verification activities fall into the category of Static Testing. During static testing, you have a checklist to check whether the work you are doing is going as per the set standards of the organization. These standards can be for Coding, Integrating and Deployment. Reviews, Inspections and Walkthroughs are static testing methodologies.

(1) Dynamic

Testing involves working with the software, giving input values and checking if the output is as expected. These are the Validation activities. Unit Tests, Integration Tests, System Tests and Acceptance Tests are few of the Dynamic Testing methodologies. As we go further, let us understand the various Test Life Cycle's and get to know the Testing Terminologies.

(2) Static testing

Static testing is also called static analysis. By contrast with dynamic analysis, static testing does not require software to be executed with test data. Static analysis encompasses program proving, symbolic execution, anomaly analysis, inspections and code walkthroughs. Program proving requires specifying preconditions on inputs, and postconditions on outputs. Symbolic execution occurs when symbolic rather than numeric values of program variables are used. Anomaly analysis searches for anomalous program features (e.g., code that is never executed). The intent of the static style of testing is to analyze a software system and deduce its current operation as a logical consequence of the ensuing design decisions. Most importantly, the static mode of testing requires no execution of software (that stands in a sharp contrast with the previously discussed dynamic style of software testing). For instance, any modern compiler can help complete a part of static testing (static analysis of code). There are two main avenues pursued here. One hinges on highly formal methods of logic while the second approach relies on a number of heuristics and gets quite informal. With the growing complexity of software systems, the role of software testing becomes essential. A wealth of experience with software testing has resulted in the accumulation of sound testing practices and useful guidelines. One of these guidelines comes from Myers (1976).

As the name suggests, white box testing is opposed to its black box counterpart. White-box covers a wide range of techniques. They are all based on the internal structure, or code of the component.

This closeness to the code of an individual component makes it an essential element of Component Testing. White-box is often interchangeable with structural testing and glass-box testing.

The analysis and running of sometimes very complex code means that developers are most likely to use these techniques, as part of their develpment process.

7.2 White-Box Techniques

White-box is usually split into two groups. Static Analysis and Dynamic Analysis. The essential difference between them is that static techniques do not necessarily require the code to be executed.

7.2.1 White-Box Testing Methods

Testing the structure of the object is the foundation of white-box testing [Beizer 1995]. Reviewing code, requirements or design documents are all examples of testing, looking at a software process artifact to detect errors. Some strategies for white-box testing include source code statement coverage, branch coverage and condition coverage. These techniques are effective at ensuring that all the code has been exercised by the test cases, no malicious code is hiding in the component and that the structure of the code is well designed. Statement coverage ensures that every source statement is executed at least once. It does not, however, require that each statement be executed in each possible state the code can be in. Branch coverage requires that every possible outcome of a decision statement must be exercised. Condition coverage requires that every condition within a decision statement must achieve all possible values at least once [DeMillo et al., 1987].

These techniques, while effective at enumerating errors, are not feasible with COTS software since the user cannot expect to have any of the necessary artifacts. At best the user has a set of requirements that the system needs to be satisfied by the COTS software.

(1) Program slicing

Program slicing is a white box technique that uses data flow and control flow to produce a trace (slice) through the code that produces a specific behavior [Weiser 1984]. This slice can be used to reduce the amount of code that needs to be reviewed to track down a bug found with a particular behavior of the software. Since this is a white-box technique the source code is assumed to be available. The source code is necessary to do the control flow and data flow analysis. In practice, the slice is produced before program execution and during execution these statements are watched for bugs [Weiser, 1984].

Program slicing has also been applied as a software maintenance technique [Gallagher 1991]. Before a change is made it is applied to relevant slices to try to determine what effect the change will have on the behavior of the software. The authors claim this process can do away with regression testing as long as the changed slices produce the required behavior.

(2) Fault injection

Fault injection serves to determine how the software system will respond to faults arising during operation. These faults can include corrupted memory, failure of operating system subroutines or invalid input from a sensor, among others. The idea is to inject the faults that are possible and probable to encounter in the real world operation of the system. A fault tolerant system should be able to recover from some degree of these faults, with emphasis on some safety critical component not failing, i.e. medical devices, in a drastic way, i.e. harming the patient.

There are various ways to implement fault injection in software. Some common practices include wrapping the software in a container that muddles the output to other components, using debuggers to corrupt memory by overwriting portions of data or inserting extra instructions at compile time to corrupt the operation of the code.

With respect to COTS software, there is no chance to recompile the code, but certainly it can be wrapped and forced to produce bad outputs or given erroneous inputs. A good debugging tool could also be used to corrupt needed data, specifically argument lists after they have been passed to the software component. It would be difficult with COTS software and lacking the source code to corrupt specific data items.

7.3 Peer Reviews

Peer Reviews are considered a best industry practice for detecting software defects early and learning about software artifacts. Peer Reviews are composed of software walkthroughs and software inspections and are integral to software product engineering activities. A collection of coordinated knowledge, skills, and behaviors facilitates the best possible practice of Peer Reviews. The elements of Peer Reviews include the structured review process, standard of excellence product checklists, defined roles of participants, and the forms and reports. Software inspections are the most rigorous form of Peer Reviews and fully utilize these elements in detecting defects.

Software walkthroughs draw selectively upon the elements in assisting the producer to obtain the deepest understanding of an artifact and reaching a consensus among participants. Measured results reveal that Peer Reviews produce an attractive return on investment obtained through accelerated learning and early defect detection. For best results, Peer Reviews are rolled out within an organization through a defined program of preparing a policy and procedure, training practitioners and managers, defining measurements and populating a database structure, and sustaining the roll out infrastructure.

In software development, peer review refers to a type of software review in which a work product (normally some form of document) is examined by its author and/or one or more colleagues of its author, in order to evaluate its technical content and quality.

Management representatives should not be involved in the conduct of a peer review except when included because of specific technical expertise, or when the work product under review is a management-level document. Managers participating in a peer review should not be line managers of any other participants in the review.

Peer review (known as refereeing in some academic fields) is a scholarly process used in the publication of manuscripts and in the awarding of funding for research. Publishers and funding agencies use peer review to select and to screen submissions. The process also forces authors to meet the standards of their discipline and thus achieve scientific objectivity. Publications and awards that have not undergone peer review are likely to be regarded with suspicion by scholars and professionals in many fields.

7.3.1 Distinction from Other Types of Software Review

Peer reviews are distinct from management reviews, which are conducted by management representatives rather than by colleagues, and for management and control purposes rather than for technical evaluation. They are also distinct from software audits, which are conducted by personnel external to the project, to evaluate compliance with specifications, standards, contractual agreements, or other criteria.

Peer review processes exist across a spectrum of formality, with relatively unstructured activities such as "buddy checking" towards one end of the spectrum, and more formal approaches such as walkthroughs, technical reviews, and software inspections, at the other. IEEE Std. 1028-1997, "IEEE Standard for Software Reviews", defines formal structures, roles, and processes for each of the last three.

7.3.2 "Open Source" Reviews

In the open source movement, something like peer review has taken place in the engineering and evaluation of computer software. In this context, the rationale for peer review has its equivalent in Linus's law, often phrased: "Given enough eyeballs, all bugs are shallow", meaning "If there are enough reviewers, all problems are easy to solve".

7.3.3 How It Works

Peer review subjects an author's work or ideas to the scrutiny of one or more others who are experts in the field. These referees each return an evaluation of the work, including suggestions for improvement, to an editor or other intermediary (typically, most of the referees' comments are eventually seen by the author as well). Evaluations usually include an explicit recommendation of what to do with the manuscript or proposal, often chosen from a menu provided by the journal or funding agency. Most recommendations are along the lines of the following:

- to unconditionally accept the manuscript or proposal,
- to accept it in the event that its authors improve it in certain ways,
- to reject it, but encourage revision and invite resubmission, and
- to reject it outright.

During this process, the role of the referees is advisory, and the editor is under no formal obligation to accept the opinions of the referees. Furthermore, in scientific publication, the referees do not act as a group, do not communicate with each other, and typically are not aware of each other's identities. There is usually no requirement that the referees achieve consensus. Thus the group dynamics is substantially different from that of a jury. In situations where the referees disagree about the quality of a work, there are a number of strategies for reaching a decision.

Traditionally, reviewers would remain anonymous to the authors, but this is slowly changing. In some academic fields most journals now offer the reviewer the option of remaining anonymous or not; papers sometimes contain, in the acknowledgments section, thanks to (anonymous or named) referees who helped improve the paper.

At a journal or book publisher, the task of picking reviewers typically falls to an editor. When a manuscript arrives, an editor solicits reviews from scholars or other experts who may or may not have already expressed a willingness to referee for that journal or book division. Granting agencies typically recruit a panel or committee of reviewers in advance of the arrival of applications.

In some disciplines there exist refereed venues (such as conferences and workshops). To be admitted to speak, scholars and scientists must submit papers (generally short, often 15 pages or less) in advance. These papers are reviewed by a "program committee" (the equivalent of an editorial board), who generally requests inputs from referees. The hard deadlines set by the conferences tend to limit the options to either accept or reject the paper.

Typically referees are not selected from among the authors' close colleagues, relatives, or friends. Referees are supposed to inform the editor of any conflict of interests that might arise. Journals or individual editors often invite a manuscript's authors to name people whom they consider qualified to referee their work. Authors are sometimes also invited to name natural candidates who should be disqualified, in which case they may be asked to provide justification (typically expressed in terms of conflict of interest). In some disciplines, scholars listed in an "acknowledgments" section are not allowed to serve as referees (hence the occasional practice of using this section to disqualify potentially negative reviewers).

7.3.4 Criticisms of Peer Review

One of the most common complaints about the peer review process is that it is slow, and that it typically takes several months or even several years in some fields for a submitted paper to appear in print.

In addition, some sociologists of science argue that peer review makes the ability to publish susceptible to control by elites and to personal jealousy. The peer review process may suppress dissent against "mainstream" theories. Reviewers tend to be especially critical of conclusions that contradict their own views, and lenient towards those that accord with them. At the same time, elite scientists are more likely than less established ones to be sought out as referees, particularly by high-prestige journals or publishers. As a result, it has been argued, ideas that harmonize with the elite's are more likely to see print and to appear in premier journals than are iconoclastic or revolutionary ones, which accords with Thomas Kuhn's well-known observations regarding scientific revolutions.

However, others have pointed out that there is a very large number of scientific journals in which one can publish, making control of information difficult. In addition, the decision-making process of peer review, in which each referee gives his opinions separately and without consultation with the other members, is intended to mitigate some of these problems.

While some believe passing the peer review process is a certification of validity, those who study that process often hold a far more skeptical view.

7.3.5 Context of Use

Peer Reviews are considered a best industry practice for use on software projects. Senior managers consistently ranked Peer Reviews as the significant enabler of software product quality among all key process areas. These reviews are integral to the software product engineering life cycle activities associated with software requirements and specifications, designs and code, and test plans and procedures. The best practices for software management and engineering on the project and the context of use for Peer Reviews are shown in figure 7.1.

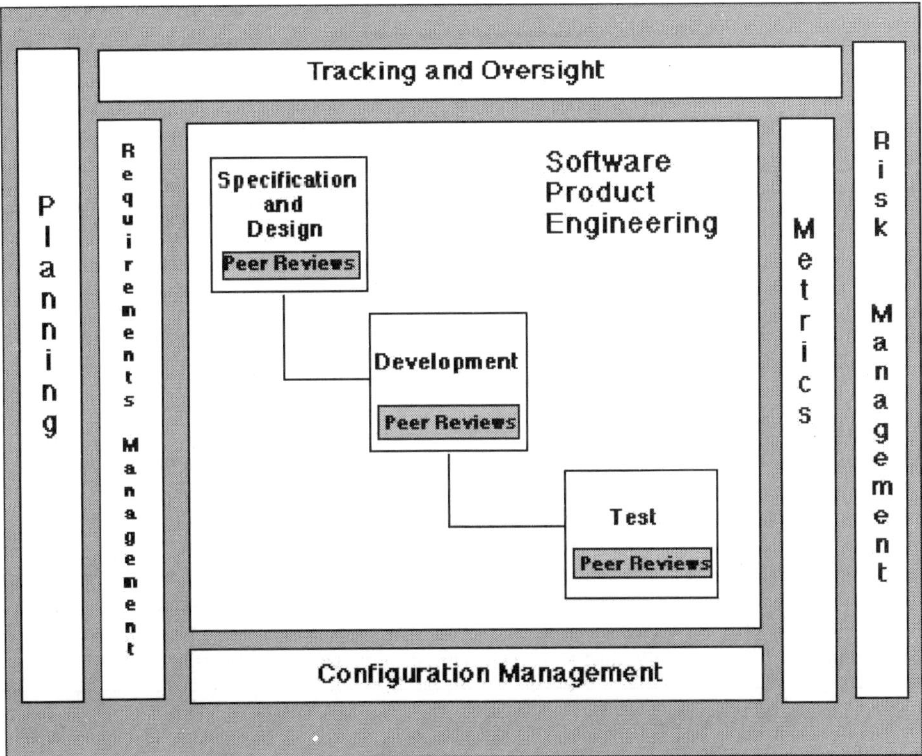

Fig. 7.1: Best Software Practice (Figure courtesy VBLAW)

Peer Reviews are composed of software walkthroughs and software inspections. Software inspections are the most rigorous form of Peer Reviews. Both software walkthroughs and software inspections are composed of a collection of coordinated knowledge, skills, and behaviors associated with process, standards, roles, and measurement. Peer Reviews are conducted as an integral part of each life cycle activity. See figure 7.2 Life Cycle Activity and Peer Reviews.

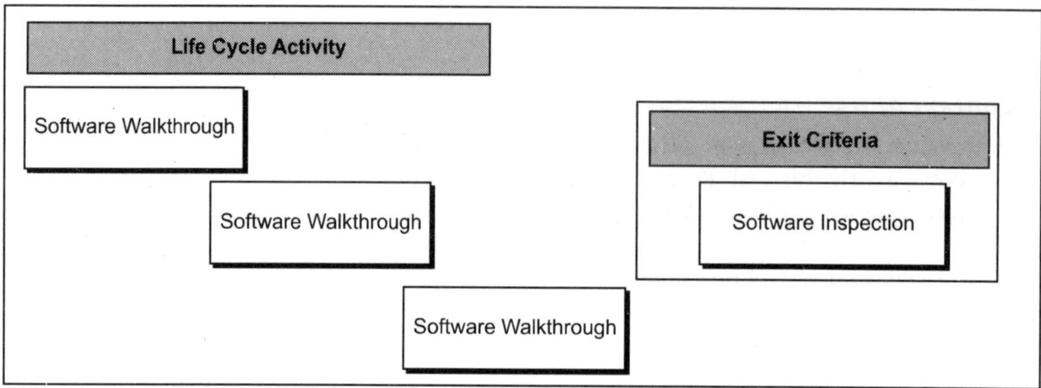

Fig. 7.2: Life Cycle Activities and Peer Reviews

7.3.6 Software Inspections and Walkthroughs Distinguished

Peer Reviews are a group activity organized to systematically reason about a software artifact. There are two types of Peer Reviews: software walkthroughs and software inspections. Each of these serves different purposes. Software walkthroughs are an informal review used to confirm the understanding of the producer and validate the approach being taken. Software inspections are a formal review used to verify that the artifact complies with the standard of excellence. In a life cycle activity, the software inspection is the exit criteria or gate that concludes the activity. See Table 7.1 Peer Reviews Scope.

Table 7.1: Peer Reviews Scope

Focus	**Software Inspection**	**Software Walkthrough**
Purpose	Do the job right Detect defects Conformance	Do the right job Learning Consensus
Initiation	Exit criteria for life cycle activity	Author request
Measurement	Product and process measurements	Instances

7.4 Elements of Peer Review

The Peer Reviews process is made up of several elements: the structured review process, defined roles of participants, system of checklists, and forms and reports. See Figure 7.3 Peer Reviews—Entry, Task, Verification, Exit and Figure 7.4 Elements of Peer Reviews.

(1) A structured review process is a systematic procedure integrated with the activities of the life cycle model. The process is composed of planning, preparation, entry criteria, conduct, exit criteria, reporting, and followup.

(2) A system of checklists governs each step in the structured review process and the review of the product itself, objective by objective. Process checklists are used as a guide for each activity of the structured review process. Product checklists house the strongly preferred indicators that set the standard of excellence for the organization's software products.

(3) The role of each participant in the structured review process is defined. The roles include the moderator, producer, reader, reviewer, recorder, manager, and consumer. Each role is characterized by particular skills and behaviors [Freedman/Weinberg 90].

(4) Forms and reports provide uniformity in recording issues at all software inspections, reporting the results to management, and building a data base useful in process management. Data collection utilizes three recording instruments: Inspection Record, Inspection Reporting Form, and Report Summary Form. The results of software walkthroughs are recorded as open issues and action items [Ebenau 94a].

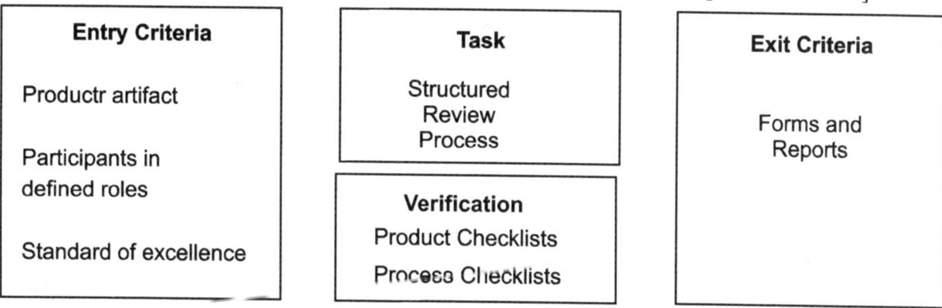

Fig. 7.3: Entry, Task, Verification and Exit Criteria in Peer Reviews

Elements	Software Inspection	Software Walkthrough
Structured Review Process	Planning, Preparation, Conduct, Report out, Followup	Planning, Optional Conduct, Followup
Standard of Excellence	Completeness, Correctness, Style, Rules of Construction, Multiple Views	Completeness, Correctness, Rules of Construction, Product and Engineering Practice
Defined Roles of Participants	Moderator, Recorder, Producer, Reviewer, Reader	Producer, Reviewer
Forms and Reports	Inspection Record, Inspection Reporting Form, Report Summary Form	Open Issues, Action Items

Fig. 7.4: Elements of Peer Reviews

7.4.1 Peer Reviews Roll Out

Peer Reviews has application throughout the software organization. Consequently, a systematic approach is needed to introduce it to all participants. The steps in the defined program for rolling out Peer Reviews within the organization include:

(1) Assess Peer Reviews practice

(2) Obtain management commitment

(3) Conduct Software Inspections training for practitioners, managers, and executives

(4) Prepare and disseminate Software Inspections Policy and Procedure documents

(5) Establish a coordination infrastructure, assign personnel, and formulate a program agenda

(6) Establish an inspection-based measurement program and database

(7) Set management objectives for planning, training, conducting, and using software inspections and measurements

(8) Continue to evolve the organization's process and product checklists

The initial step in the roll out is to conduct an assessment of the Peer Reviews practice. This will identify the strengths and weaknesses in planning, training, conduct, and reporting and use of results. Armed with this assessment, the change agent seeks management commitment and sponsorship for the improvements needed to offset the weaknesses. The following key practice indicators are assessed at regular intervals for each project in terms of approach, deployment, and results:

- The project follows a documented organization policy for performing software inspections.
- Adequate resources and funding are provided for performing software inspections on each software work product to be reviewed.
- Moderators and reviewers receive required training in how to lead software inspections, as well as in objectives, principles, and methods of software inspections.
- Software inspections are planned and documented.
- Software inspections are performed according to a documented procedure.
- Data on the conduct of the software inspections are recorded.
- Measurements are made and used to determine the status of the software inspections activities.
- The software quality assurance group reviews and/or audits the activities and work products for inspections and reports the results.

A clear management commitment is needed to approve and fund the training program including the cost of the instructor, training site, labor and burden for student attendance, and scheduling and administration of student enrollment and attendance.

With training underway and inspections being initiated by projects, Peer Reviews policy and procedure documents provide the guidelines for the well-defined process being deployed. The policy applies to all software development projects and states that each project involved in software development shall prepare, plan, conduct, and utilize software inspections. The purpose of the procedure is to provide the step by step instructions needed to carry out consistent examinations of work products on the project.

To fully stimulate the Peer Reviews roll out program among project personnel, an infrastructure of coordinators drawn from active projects is convened. These project coordinators meet periodically to share experiences, compare results, and discuss common problems.

As inspection results and measurements are accumulated, a measurement database and the operations for analyzing, reporting, and acting upon these measurements are established. The measurements are recorded in the Software Inspection Lab. These measurements include preparation effort, conduct time, and the artifact size in lines of code or pages inspected and for each defect detected the defect severity, defect category, defect type, and defect origin. Using the measurements, metrics are derived to continually assess the efficiency and effectiveness of the process and its operation. These metrics include:

- Minutes of preparation effort per defect
- Minutes of preparation effort per major defect
- Major defects per thousand lines
- Minor defects per thousand lines
- Lines per conduct hour
- Defects per session
- Preparation/conduct effort
- Lines per session
- Return on Investment

Software problem rates may be increasing. The results of the National Software Quality Experiment show no systematic improvement towards fulfilling the national goal of a ten times reduction in software problems. The quality goal is not being met by a wide margin. Instead problem rates are being pushed higher:

- With the emphasis on quicker, better, and cheaper
- With the trend towards code and upload practice as the life cycle model
- With the preoccupation on improving software process maturity and mastering the management track practices of the Software Engineering Institute's Capability Maturity Model for Software level 2, an obstacle to many
- With the downsizing of middle management and senior technical staff who often held the line on product quality.

While software inspections have been in use for over twenty-five years, defect prevention remains an immature practice. Defect prevention is a CMM level 5 key process area, and some organizations have achieved level 5. As more organizations seek to adopt the practice of defect prevention, its benefits and methods may become more well understood stimulating others to adopt the practice.

Similarly, defect prediction remains an underdeveloped practice. If software defects, faults, and failures can be predicted, perhaps they can be detected, controlled, and prevented. Model based techniques calibrated with defect detection early in the life cycle to predict defect rates in later life cycle activities have been demonstrated. More modest efforts utilizing software inspections data to estimate the number of defects remaining to be found in testing are being applied on the project [Harding, 98]. However, there is insufficient defect, fault, and failure data available from the nation's factory floor. In addition there is insufficient process, method, and tooling to combine defect data obtained through software inspections practice, software fault data obtained through software product test and use, and software failure data obtained through software system operation into predictions of trustworthy software system operation.

While the benefits and usage of software inspections on code artifacts is well known, there is increasing interest in extending software inspections to all phases of the life cycle including requirements, specifications, design, code, and test artifacts. The CMMI project with the inclusion of Peer Reviews in the Product Verification process area extends Peer Reviews to both systems engineering and software artifacts.

To achieve the best possible practice of software inspections, both managers and technical practitioners are encouraged to decriminalize defects. People make mistakes sometimes, yet software must be bit perfect. When managers and technical participants view with alarm the defects detected in software inspections, it produces a negative impact. On the other hand, when managers genuinely decriminalize defects and use their detection as a means to prevent their recurrence, it produces a positive result. During a software inspection session, the litmus test for decriminalization lies in the reaction of participants when a major defect is detected. Does the group say 'good catch' or 'bummer'?

With the growing recognition that fielding software involves a process of experimentation and with the increasing pressures of competition and demand for innovation, software walkthroughs may experience increasing in usage. Software walkthroughs encourage and support the learning essential to experimentation. In favoring the group interaction needed to achieve consensus, software walkthroughs may contribute to increased innovation in software products.

There is interest in automating software inspections. The value of programming languages with strong typing, robust compilers, static analyzers and traceability tools, and complexity metrics is recognized. However, software inspections is a reasoning activity and will remain essentially a human activity. The use of information technology innovations to support the logistics of preparation, scheduling, conduct, and results repository operations are sources for improved industry practice.

Software inspections are being conducted effectively using groupware tools. However, where global software development teams conducting geographically dispersed inspection sessions are using 'follow the sun' software development tactics, software inspection participants may be separated by both geography and time zones complicating the logistics of their application.

Software inspections usage is increasing in e-commerce applications where code and upload is the typical life cycle practice. In an environment of rapid change and frequent releases, there is an absence of robust testing and sometimes even regression testing.

7.5 Structured Review Process

The activities of the structured review process are organized for software inspections. Software walkthroughs may employ variations for planning, conduct, and followup.

(1) Planning

The structured review process begins early in the project when the manager plans for software inspections of requirements, specifications, designs, code, and test procedures. The schedule for each software inspection is recorded in the project's Software Development Plan [SDP] or project plan. A trained moderator is assigned to each software inspection, and moderator training is scheduled as necessary. The Software Quality Assurance (SQA) Plan also discusses the use of software walkthroughs and software inspections in terms of their contribution to product verification and validation.

(2) Preparation

Preparation is initiated by the moderator a week before the inspection session. The readiness of the product for inspection is assessed by the moderator and the producer. The moderator obtains the reviewers, recorder, and reader and briefs them on their roles along with the key principles of software inspections.

In assessing product volatility, the moderator ascertains the status of the baseline change activity and the completion of the preceding life cycle activity. The producer conducts a brief overview of the product to be inspected to assist the inspection team in their preparation for the inspection session.

The inspection materials are distributed to team members, the time and place for the inspection session are announced, and reviewers are encouraged to prepare individually for the inspection session. Individual preparation is the mother's milk of the software inspections process.

(3) Entry criteria

Entry criteria are checked by the moderator at the start of the inspection session. Before the conduct activity begins, the moderator determines that the software product is ready to be inspected and the inspection team is prepared to inspect it. The moderator again assesses the product volatility indicators. Inspection team members are asked for their preparation effort, and the recorder notes this information. Where the entry criteria are not satisfactorily met, the moderator may reschedule the inspection session.

The moderator script for directing the entry criteria includes:

1. Has the preceding life cycle activity been concluded?
2. Are there any changes to the baseline?
3. Are review participants in place and briefed?
4. Have all participants received all the review materials and checklists?
5. How many minutes of preparation did each participant perform?

(4) Conduct

The inspection session including entry, conduct, and exit is directed by the moderator and attended by the producer, reviewers, recorder, and reader. The manager does not attend. Some key principles govern the inspection session:

1. The inspection is limited to periods of peak concentration (1-2 hr.).
2. The product is reviewed, not the producer.
3. Issues are identified, not proposed solutions.

Each product component is inspected using the strongly preferred indicators found in the appropriate software product checklists. Each inspection team member in turn is asked if there is an issue to be raised for the product component and product checklist now before the group. If so, the issue is stated, discussed, and recorded. The producer may wish to obtain clarification of the issue at the time it is raised, but there is no need for the producer to defend or even explain the approach taken. The producer will have the opportunity to resolve the issue during the follow-up activity.

The moderator script for directing the conduct activity includes:

1. Are there any issues in completeness?
2. Are there any issues in correctness?
3. Are there any issues in style?
4. Are there any issues in rules of construction?
5. Are there any issues in multiple views?

(5) Exit criteria

Exit criteria are checked by the moderator at the close of the inspection session. The moderator verifies that all product components have been inspected and that the intended product checklists have been utilized. The recorder verifies that all the metrics have been recorded including preparation effort of each team member, the duration of the inspection session, and the size of the product being inspected as well as the defect type, defect category, defect severity, and defect origin for each issue raised. Finally, the moderator asks the producer for any closing comments, permitting the producer to have the last word.

The moderator script for directing the exit criteria includes:

(1) Have all product elements been inspected?
(2) Have all checklists been processed?
(3) Have the inspection results been recorded?
(4) Have metrics been collected?
(5) Would the recorder read back the issues?
(6) What should be the disposition of the inspection?
(7) Would the producer like an opportunity to comment?

(6) Reporting

The moderator with the help of the recorder reports the findings of the inspection session to the manager within a week. This report provides a review summary, the preparation effort and conduct time expended, the types of defects detected, and follow-up recommendations.

Follow-up

The follow-up rework on the product is performed by the producer. The followup actions are prepared jointly by the manager and the producer and entered in the project action log. As these follow-up actions are completed, the action log reflects the closure. Tracking issues to closure is an important indicator of software process maturity.

7.6 Software Walkthrough

The **walk-through** and the **code-inspection** technique are related to each other. The main difference is that the participants are supposed to think about good tests for the program during their preparation, when a walkthrough is planned. In the meeting they will execute those tests together manually on a sheet of paper or on a blackboard.

Once more, there is disagreement in the literature about the author's presence in the testing team. The main reason against his presence is that his work should be able to speak for itself. The documentation has to be clear, and ambiguous design or specification is taboo anyway.

The software walkthrough is organized to serve the needs of the producer or author of the software artifact in acquiring superior knowledge of all aspects of the software artifact. It is a learning experience. A desirable side-effect of the software walkthrough is the forging of a shared vision among the reviewers and consensus among participants on the approaches taken, product and engineering practices applied, completeness and correctness of capabilities and features, and rules of construction for the domain product. Since the software walkthrough caters to the needs of the author, it is the author who initiates the session. Consequently there may be several walkthroughs in each life cycle activity. Software walkthroughs yield open issues and action items. While these issues and action items may be tracked to closure, the only measurement taken is a count of the software walkthroughs held.

7.7 Code Inspection

After a small introduction by the manager, the author explains his source code in a presentation. The program is inspected in small steps. Any questions during the speech are discussed with the goal to detect faults. It is impressive how many bugs are found by the author himself while explaining the program to others. In other words, a lot of faults are found just by presenting a product to an audience.

Under all circumstances, the host has to prevent the team from trying to find fixes for the faults found. Those will be fixed by the author later, and he will get the chance to explain his fixes in a later meeting. This will also reduce the chance of new bugs created during the correcting—and those bugs are pretty likely.

Once again, the host is responsible for a productive atmosphere. This starts with the choice of the time for the meeting, continues with the prevention of external distractions, and includes things like the right moment to end the meeting. Since code-inspection is a extremely intellectual activity, it should not last longer than two hours. He should plan several meetings for longer programs, because it has turned out that in the average about 150 instructions are covered per hour. Another thing he has to take care of, is the members' attitude towards each other. For instance, as soon as the author regards the inspection as a personal attack, the lack of success is predeterminated. However, if the author keeps a egoless attitude, the meeting has a good chance to be very productive.

7.7.1 Static Code Analysis

Static analysis is the term applied to the analysis of computer software that is performed without actually executing programs built from that software (analysis performed on executing programs is known as dynamic analysis). In most cases the analysis is performed on some version of the source code and in the other cases some form of the object code. The term is usually applied to the analysis performed by an automated tool, with human analysis being called program understanding or program comprehension.

The sophistication of the analysis performed by tools varies from those that only consider the behavior of individual statements and declarations, to those that include the complete source code of a program in their analysis. Uses of the information obtained from the analysis vary from highlighting possible coding errors (e.g., the lint tool) to formal methods that mathematically prove properties about a given program (e.g., its behavior matches that of its specification).

Static analysis covers many different techniques. In terms of finding faults in the software, they are concerned with everything up to the early runs of the components functionality. This covers reviewing whether requirements and descriptions of the software are clear, unambigous and to standards. Once the code has been written it can be tested for standards compliance, syntax and complexity.

An example of a metric, derived from static analysis is McCabes Cyclomatic Complexity Metric. A figure is generated indicating the complexity of the component or components. The higher the complexity goes, the probability of a fault increases.

Static analysis can be undertaken manually or automatically depending on the type of test and the organisation. The most important technique is that of Reviews and Inspection. The more rigourous of the two is Inspection with a very clearly laid down framework for rigourously checking documentation and sometimes code. Proponents claim dramatic decreases in defects found in the final software. It is also known as Fagan Inspections after the man who introduced them at IBM.

Reviews are much less rigourous in their framework and range from simple walkthroughs from an analyst to formal technical reviews involving many stakeholders. Tools are available for static analysis. These include syntax parsers and data-flow analysers. Some people consider software metrics to be a form of static analysis. A growing commercial use of static analysis is in the verification of properties of software used in safety-critical computer systems.

7.7.2 Formal Methods

Formal methods is the term applied to the analysis of software (and hardware) whose results are obtained purely through the use of rigorous mathematical methods. The mathematical techniques used include:

- denotational semantics,
- axiomatic semantics,
- operational semantics, and
- abstract interpretation.

It has been proven that finding possible run-time errors—is undecidable: there is no mechanical method that can always answer truthfully whether programs may or may not exhibit runtime errors. This result dates from the works of Church, Gödel and Turing in the 1930s (see the halting problem and Rice's theorem). As with most undecidable questions, one can still attempt to give useful approximate solutions.

Some of the implementation techniques of formal static analysis include:

- model checking considers systems that have finite state or may be reduced to finite state by abstraction;
- abstract interpretation models the effect that every statement has on the state of an abstract machine (i.e., it 'executes' the software based on the mathematical properties of each statement and declaration).

7.7.3 Software Inspection

The software inspection is structured to serve the needs of quality management in verifying that the software artifact complies with the standard of excellence for software engineering artifacts. The focus is one of verification, on doing the job right. The software inspection is a formal review held at the conclusion of a life cycle activity and serves as a quality gate with an exit criteria for moving on to subsequent activities.

The software inspection utilizes a structured review process of planning, preparation, entry criteria, conduct, exit criteria, report out, and follow-up. It ensures that a close and strict examination of the product artifact is conducted according to the standard of excellence criteria spanning completeness, correctness, style, rules of construction, and multiple views. This close and strict examination results in the early detection of defects. The software inspection is led by a moderator and assisted by other role players including recorder, reviewer, reader, and producer. The software inspection is initiated as an exit criteria for each activity in the life cycle. Product and process measurements are recorded during the software inspection session and recorded on specially formatted forms and reports. These issues and defects are tracked to closure.

7.7.4 System of Software Inspection Checklists

Checklists are at the heart of software inspections. They fuel the structured review process and form the standard of excellence expected for the software product. Checklists provide the criteria for evaluating the quality of the product as well as progress within the process. Process and product checklists promote uniformity in the use of software inspections throughout a project and across an organization. Process checklists are used as a guide for each activity of the structured review process to ensure that the Software Inspections Process runs smoothly. Product checklists provide reviewers with the thorough technical focus needed to guide the review of each product component from all viewpoints. The system of checklists helps to overcome human limitations on information processing by focusing on just one consistent perspective at a time. See Table 7.2 for an example of a Design and Code Checklist and Table 7.3 for an example of a Specification Checklist.

Table 7.2: An Example of Design and Code Checklist

Completeness	Style
1. Has traceability been assessed? 2. Has available tool assistance been applied in assessing traceability? 3. Have all predecessor requirements been accounted for? 4. Where any product fragments revealed not to have traceability to the predecessor requirements? 5. What is the relationship of requirements to product component: 5.1 One to one 'simple analysis'? 5.2 Many to one 'straight toward'? 5.3 One to many 'complex'?	1. Are style conventions for block structuring defined and followed? 2. Are naming conventions defined and followed? 3. Are the semantics of the product component traceable to the requirements? 4. Are style convention or commentary defined and followed? 5. Are style conventions for alignment upper/lower case and lightning defined and followed? 6. Are templates used for repeating patterns? **Rules of Construction** 1. Are guidelines for program communication followed? 2. Is the interprocess communication protocol followed?

(*Contd...*)

Correctness 1. Are structured programming prime constructs used correctly: 1.1 Sequence: Is the function commentary satisfied or the sequence? 1.2 If the: If the test is true, is the function commentary satisfied? 1.3 If then else: If the test is true, the function commentary satisfied? 1.4 If the test is false, is the function commentary satisfied? 1.5 While-loop: If the condition is true, is the function commentary satisfied? Does the loop terminate? 1.6 Loop-until: If the condition is false, is the function commentary satisfied? Does the loop terminate? Is a one time loop acceptable? 1.7 For-do: Is the function commentary satisfied? Are there discrete steps through the loop? Is the loop in itialized and terminated property? 1.8 Case: For each leg, is the function commentary satisfied? Is the domain partitioned exclusively and exhaustively? 2. Are proper programs composed of multiple prime programs limited to single entry and single exit? 3. Are disciplined data structures used to manipulate and transform data? 4. Does the input domain span all legal values? 5. Does the input domain span all possible values? 6. Does the output range span all legal values? 7. For nodules, does the stated data span all legal values?	3. Are data representation conventions followed? 4. Is the system standard time defined and followed? 5. Are encapsulation, localization, and layering used to achieve object orientation? 6. Is logical independence achieved through event driven and process driven paradigms, late binding, and implicit binding? 7. Is scalability achieved through uniformity, parameterization, and portability? 8. Are fault tolerance, high availability, and security achieved? **Multiple views** 1. Has the logical view of user interface and object orientation consideration been assessed? 2. Has the static view of packaging consideration been assessed including program unit construction, program generation process, and target machine operations? 3. Has the dynamic view of operational considerations been assessed including communications, concurrency, synohronization, and failure recovery? 4. Has the physical view of execution considerations been assessed including timing, memory use, input and output, initialization, and finite word effects? 5. Has the product component been assessed for safety considerations? 6. Has the product component been assessed for year 2000 compliance? 7. Has the product component been assessed for security considerations? 8. Has the product component been assessed for open system considerations?

Table 7.3: An example of Specification Checklist

SPECIFICATION CHECKLIST COMPLETENESS	
1. Cope and Traceability 1.1 Is each operational capability fully descried in terms of its purpose and function? 1.2 Are all identified functions and data traceable to the higher level specification? **2. Completeness of Detail** 2.1 Is the decomposition of each identified function sufficiently fine-grained and uniquely allocated to a physical component? 2.2 Have all TBS and TBD indicators been replaced with the required information? 2.3 Are all logical operations specific completely? 2.4. Are all exception conditions explicitly identified and all necessary error processing defined?	**3. Data and Interface** 3.1 Has the necessary and sufficient set of input data been specified for each function? 3.2 For each function specified, are the required output data derived from the input data and accessible retained data? 3.3 Is the boundary of each identified function described in terms of all required input data and all required output data? 3.4 Is all the data identified that must be retained within the system for reference? 3.5 Is each inter-function data-flow or signal accounted for by both senders and receivers? 3.6 Are the semantics for each inter-function data flow or signal the same for all senders and all receivers?

3.7 Does each data item have specific initialization values and required range of permissible values? **4. Testability** 4.1 Does each requirement have a corresponding test requirement that identifies how it is to be verified and the required testing limits ? (Verification methods include: test and review of data, by inspection or observation, by data collection and analysis, or not required.) 4.2 Has the appropriate level of test been identified for verifying each requirement? (Level; of test include: unit, computer program element, or system test level.) 4.3 Has the appropriate level of test been identified for verifying each requirement? (Level of test include: unit, computer program element, or system test level.) 4.4 Have the stress test and regression test requirements for each test requirement been described? **CORRECTNESS** 1. Have the lighter level requirements been allocated correctly and appropriately to the specification? 2. Does each function specification and its inputs correctly produce the required outputs? 3. Is each equation correctly specified for performing the needed computations? 4. Is each logical operation correctly defined? 5. Is each interface signal identified in the interface design specification properly reflected in tie specification? 6. Is each external interface signal in the specification properly reflected in the respective interface design?	**STYLE** 1. Does the format ot the specification follow the documentation style guide? 2. For each mnemonic used, is it defined when first used and entered in the glossary with the page number of this definition? **RULES OF CONSTRUCTION** 1. Is interprocessor communication properly addressed? 2. Are inter function notifications properly addressed? 3. Are alternate modes considerations included? 4. Are data representation considerations properly accounted for? 5. Are design constraints properly accounted for? 6. Are control requirements properly accounted for? **MULTIPLE VIEWS** 1. Have initialization considerations been considered? 2. Has computer resource loading been assessed including memory, timing, and I/O? 3. Have alternate mode consideration been properly addressed? 4. Are the requirements sufficiently complete to support high level design? 5. Have user interface and display impacts been properly accounted for?

(1) Completeness

Completeness is based on traceability among software product artifacts of various types including requirements, specifications, designs, code, and test procedures. Completeness analysis may be assisted by tools that trace the components of a product artifact of one type to the components of another type. Completeness analysis of predecessor and successor artifacts reveals what sections are missing and what fragments may be extra. A by-product of the completeness analysis is a clear view of the relationship of requirements to the code product: straightforward (one to one), simple analysis (many to one), and complex (one to many).

The moderator script for inquiring about completeness includes:

1. Has traceability been assessed?
2. Have all predecessor requirements been accounted for?
3. Were any product fragments revealed not to have traceability to the predecessor requirements?
4. Was traceability found to be straightforward, simple, or complex?

(2) Correctness

Correctness is based on reasoning about programs through the use of informal verification and correctness questions derived from the prime constructs of structured programming and their composite use in proper programs [Linger 79], [McCabe 94]. Input domain and output range are analyzed for all legal values and all possible values. State data is similarly analyzed. Adherence to project specified disciplined data structures is analyzed. Asynchronous processes and their interaction and communication are analyzed [Prowell, 99].

The moderator script for inquiring about correctness includes:

1. Is the function commentary satisfied?
2. Are programs limited to single entry and single exit?
3. Is the loop initialized and terminated properly?
4. Does the input domain span all legal values?
5. Is there systematic exception handling for illegal values?
6. Are disciplined data structures used?

(3) Style

Style is based on project specified style guidance. This guidance is expected to call for block structured templates. Naming conventions and commentary are checked for consistency of use along with alignment, highlighting, and case. More advanced style guidance may call for templates for repeating patterns and semantic correspondence among software product artifacts of various types.

The moderator script for inquiring about style includes:

1. Are style conventions for block structuring followed?
2. Are naming conventions followed?
3. Are style conventions for commentary followed?
4. Are the semantics of the product component traceable to the requirements?
5. Are templates used for repeating patterns?

(4) Rules of construction

Rules of construction are based on the software application architecture and the specific protocols, templates, and conventions used to carry it out. For example, these include interprocess communication protocols, tasking and concurrent operations, program unit construction, and data representation.

The moderator script for inquiring about rules of construction includes:

1. Are guidelines for program unit construction followed?
2. Is the interprocess communication protocol followed?
3. Are data representation conventions followed?
4. Is the system standard time defined and followed?
5. Are encapsulation, localization, and layering used to achieve object orientation?
6. Is logical independence achieved through event driven and process driven paradigms, late binding, and implicit binding?
7. Is scalability achieved through uniformity, parameterization, and portability?
8. Are fault tolerance, high availability, and security achieved?

(5) Multiple views

Multiple views are based on the various perspectives and view points required to be reflected in the software product. During execution many factors must operate harmoniously as intended including initialization, timing of processes, memory management, input and output, and finite word effects. In building the software product, packaging considerations must be coordinated including program unit construction, program generation process, and target machine operations. Product construction disciplines of systematic design and structured programming must be followed as well as interactions with the user, operating system, and physical hardware.

The moderator script for inquiring about multiple views includes:

1. Has the logical view of user interface and object orientation considerations been assessed?
2. Has the static view of packaging considerations been assessed including program unit construction, program generation process, and target machine operations?
3. Has the dynamic view of operational considerations been assessed including communications, concurrency, synchronization, and failure recovery?
4. Has the physical view of execution considerations been assessed including timing, memory use, input and output, initialization, and finite word effects?

7.7.5 Defined Roles of Participants of Software during Software Inspections

Software Inspections are a reasoning activity performed by practitioners playing the defined roles of moderator, recorder, reviewer, reader, and producer. Some may name these roles facilitator, scribe, inspector, and author. Each role carries with it the specific behaviors, skills, and knowledge needed to achieve the expert practice of Software Inspections [Freedman/Weinberg 90].

Individuals attending the inspection session may take on more than one role. For example, the producer may also be a reviewer. The moderator and recorder roles are demanding ones, and the individual assigned is usually dedicated to the single role. The reader role is not always utilized in software inspections. When the reader is used, one of the reviewers, not the producer, is assigned this role. In software walkthroughs, the producer serves as reader.

(1) Manager

The manager is active in the planning, preparation, reporting, and follow-up activities. In planning, the manager identifies and schedules all software inspections in the project plan. The manager identifies personnel resource needs in terms of labor hours and allocates them to each inspection. The moderator is assigned by the manager who ensures that only trained moderators are appointed.

The manager generally does not attend the inspection session. Practitioners are wary that managers attending an inspection session might use the results in the personnel performance appraisal of the producer. In addition, reviewers are reluctant to identify defects in the artifacts of their peers in the presence of managers. However, if the manager is an expert in the application and must be present to make a technical contribution, the manager must first check management and organizational behaviors at the door convincingly and attend the inspection as a technical peer.

After the software inspection is conducted, the manager receives the moderator's report, meets with the producer to plan the followup, and administers the follow-up oversight.

(2) Moderator

The moderator is the keystone of the Software Inspections Process and is active in the preparation, entry criteria, conduct, exit criteria, and reporting activities. The moderator directs the activities of the software inspection. During the preparation activity, the moderator briefs the inspection team members on their roles in the structured review process, asks the producer to overview the software product to be inspected, distributes the inspection materials, and announces the time and place for the inspection session.

During the inspection session, the moderator directs the entry criteria, conduct, and exit criteria activities and facilitates the interaction among the inspection team members. The moderator intervenes as little as possible and as much as necessary to ensure that an effective and efficient software inspection session takes place.

A skillful moderator recognizes the role specific needs of inspection team members. For example, a producer with a "good catch" on his own product is called upon first. A talkative reviewer with little preparation effort is controlled. Where the moderator has issues to bring up, it is good form to insert these after the other team members have spoken. The moderator collaborates with the recorder in preparing the report for the manager on the findings of the inspection session.

(3) Producer

The producer is active during the preparation, entry criteria, conduct, exit criteria, and follow-up activities. The producer is responsible for creating the materials to be inspected. The producer attends the inspection as reviewer and is expected to raise issues. From time to time the producer may offer a technical explanation of the product as necessary.

The producer expects criticism of the product and need not offer any defense as issues are raised. It is understood that the producer may be in a protective state of mind with respect to the product being inspected. What is asked of the producer is that the protective state not be exhibited as defensive behavior. Where an issue is surfaced that is not understood by the producer, a dialogue may be needed to obtain clarification.

At the conclusion of the conduct activity, the producer is afforded the opportunity to comment on the inspection session and to acknowledge the value of the issues raised. The producer meets with the manager to plan the rework and performs the follow-up actions resulting from the inspection.

(4) Recorder

The recorder is active in the preparation, entry criteria, conduct, exit criteria, and reporting activities. The recorder completes the Inspection Record, the Inspection Reporting Form, and the Report Summary Form. The practice of the recorder is "to leave no bits on the floor". In other words, the recorder is expected to record every issue without exception.

During the entry criteria, the recorder notes the preparation effort of each inspection team member, the start and stop time of the meeting, the project and product name and size, and the life cycle activity for which the inspection is an exit criteria. As issues are raised, the recorder describes each issue and notes defect category, defect severity, defect type, and defect origin. The recorder uses the key word "investigate" in recording issues that may be defects but require additional research following the meeting. At the conclusion, the recorder tabulates the issues by defect type, severity, and category.

The role of the recorder is to be transparent to the inspection session and to record all issues completely and accurately. This requires a high degree of concentration, judgment, and technical knowledge.

(5) Reviewer

Reviewers are active in the preparation, entry criteria, conduct, and exit criteria activities. A reviewer is expected to spend sufficient time preparing and to raise issues and concerns about the software product. Reviewers are asked to refrain from proposing solutions and to direct their comments at the product not the producer. Reviewers accept the discipline imposed by the round robin, checklist structure of the inspection session. In return for accepting these responsibilities and disciplines, each reviewer is assured of an uninterrupted opportunity to raise issues.

(6) Reader

The reader is active in the preparation, entry criteria, conduct, and exit criteria activities. Where necessary, the moderator may ask the reader to read parts of the product aloud so as to focus attention on a particular trouble spot. The reader does this by paraphrasing not by reading line by line. Using the reader for this task helps promote the egoless behavior of the producer. The reader is responsible for bringing to the inspection session and being prepared to navigate any background materials, such as, baseline documentation and style guide.

(7) Forms and Reports

All data collected and reported during the Software Inspections Process is recorded by the recorder. This includes data about the product being inspected and about the inspection process itself. The requirements for data collection are defined and focus on three recording instruments: Inspection Record, Inspections Reporting Form, and Report Summary Form.

(8) Inspection Record

The Inspection Record is initiated during the entry criteria activity when the recorder gathers the preparation effort from each inspection team member. The name of the project and the product component are recorded along with the size of the product to be inspected. The life cycle activity for which this inspection serves as the exit criteria is recorded. The start time for the inspection session is entered at the beginning of the meeting, and the stop time is recorded at the close. Also at the close of the session, the disposition is recorded in terms of acceptance, reinspection, or conditional.

Table 7.4: Inspection Record

INSPECTION RECORD			
Project Name: Product Component: Start Time: ________ Stop Time: ________		Size: ________ lines ________ Elapsed Time: ________	Date: Pages ________
Role	**Name**	**Preparation Minutes**	**Additional Comments:**
Moderator			
Recorder			
Producer			
Reviewer			
Reviewer			
Reviewer			
Reader			
Total Prep Effort			
Checklists Used	**Disposition**		**Life Cycle Activity**
Completeness, Correctness, Style	—	Accept	Planning Requirements
Rules of Construction		Conditional	Specification
Multiple Views			Design
Technology		Reinspect	Code
Metrics			Test

7.7.6 Inspection Reporting Form

During the conduct activity as issues are raised, the recorder documents a description of each issue and assigns attributes that characterize the issue. Each issue is assigned a sequence number, and the page and line number are pinpointed. Similar issues that occur a few times are recorded as separate issues. An issue type that occurs an uncountably large number of times is recorded once.

A defect category is assigned as missing, wrong, or extra. A defect severity is assigned as major or minor. The defect origin is noted as the life cycle activity during which this defect was inserted. The defect type is entered. See Tables 7.4 and 7.5.

Table 7.5: Inspection Reporting Form

Inspection Reporting Form							
Issue Number	Page/ Line	Checklist	Defect Category	Defect Severity	Defect Type	Defect Origin	Defect Description
Defect Category: Missing., Wrong, Extra Defect Severity: Major, Minor Defect Type: Interface, Data, Logic, I/O, Performance, Functionality, Human Factors, Standards, Documentation, Symtax, Maintainability, Other.							

A major defect affects execution; a minor defect does not. In practice, some prefer to extend defect severity to include the extremes of critical and trivial. Other severity gradations used to classify defects, faults, and failures detected in testing and field operations are not used in software inspections. These test and operational execution-based severities often revolve around the criticality of the defect and its impact on sustaining testing or operations. Another dimension of defect severity is related to the effort needed to correct the defect.

The appropriate defect type is assigned as follows:

1. Interface: error in parameter list
2. Data: error in data definition, initial value setting, or use of disciplined data structures
3. Logic: error revealed through informal correctness questions spanning prime constructs of structured programming
4. I/O: error in formatting, commanding, or controlling I/O operations

5. Performance: error in managing or meeting constraints in computer resource allocations and capacities for CPU, memory, or I/O
6. Functionality: error in stating intended function or in satisfying intended function through refinement or elaboration
7. Human Factors: error in externally visible user or enterprise interface or interaction
8. Standards: error in compliance with product standards for construction or integration including programming style guidelines, open systems interfaces, or guidelines for the application domain architecture
9. Documentation: error in guidance documentation
10. Syntax: error in language defined syntax
11. Maintainability: error in uniformity and consistency
12. Other: any other error

7.7.7 Report Summary Form

During the exit criteria, the recorder completes the meeting stop time, verifies the completeness of all recorded results, and completes the Report Summary Form. This form is a frequency count of issues presented as a matrix of defect types by defect severity and defect category. This form serves several purposes. Since it cannot be constructed unless the recorder has completed the Inspection Reporting Form, it serves as an on-the-spot check of the recorded results. Once completed, weaknesses are highlighted and some opportunities for defect prevention suggest themselves. When the results of numerous inspection sessions are overlayed on the Report Summary Form, these frequency counts divided by the total defects serve as the probability of occurrence for each defect type, defect severity, and defect category. See Table 7.6 Report Summary Form.

Table 7.6: Report Summary Form

Report Summary Form						
Defect Types	Major Defects			Minor Defects		
	Missing	Wrong	Extra	Missing	Wrong	Extra
Interface						
Data						
Logic						
I/O						
Performance						
Functionality						
Human Factors						
Standards						
Documentation						
Syntax						
Maintainability						
Other						

7.7.8 Preparation for Expert Use

A collection of coordinated knowledge, skills, and behaviors facilitates the best possible practice of Peer Reviews. As Deming reminded us, there is no substitute for superior knowledge. In conducting Peer Reviews, superior knowledge is sought in the application domain, the computing platform both hardware and operating system, and programming language. In addition, participants must be knowledgeable in the Peer Review process and the standard of excellence expected in the product artifact.

For best results, participants filling certain defined roles must possess particular skills. The moderator needs facilitation, conflict identification, and conflict resolution skills. The recorder needs listening, synthesizing, and recording skills. The reviewer needs code reading skills.

Participants in Peer Reviews are expected to adopt certain behaviors known to contribute to effective and harmonious review sessions. First, the rules of civility apply. For example, one person speaks at a time, and personal attacks are not permitted. Second, since people make mistakes sometimes, it is necessary to decriminalize defects so that they do not remain hidden. Recognizing that, assigning blame for defects is discouraged. Third, participants are encouraged to direct their comments towards the product not the person who authored the artifact being reviewed. Finally, everyone is encouraged to give way to the individual who possesses superior knowledge.

7.7.9 Measurements

While many organizations have adopted software inspections, few have published their results. Those that have published results typically have done so following early successes in the new practice adoption cycle. Organizations with published results have included the Jet Propulsion Laboratory, Litton Data Systems, Bull HN Information Systems, Inc. AT&T Corp. and Lockheed Martin Corporation. While all used software inspections and have documented measured results, the particular adaptations are not well aligned, and the results do not lend themselves to systematic comparison.

7.8 Code Reviews

Using various reviews, inspections, and code walk-throughs in a software development project almost always has a positive affect on software quality, readability, and ease of understanding.

Important rules for conducting effective code reviews and walk-throughs are:

- The duration of a code review should be one hour. Occasionally, a two-hour meeting makes sense.
- A balance should be struck between the length of the review and the attention span of the reviewers.
- Participants must commit not only to attend the actual review, but also to read the material and attend a follow-up meeting to hear the presenter's response to comments made at the initial code review.
- Meeting coordinators must not let the meeting degenerate into a problem-solving session.

- Problems should be identified and assigned as action items to discuss in a follow-up meeting, after a solution has been devised.

The code review is designed to detect errors in the code or in the design, not to correct them.

7.9 Types of Structural Testing: White-Box Coding

Code-based testing is also known as structural testing or "white-box" testing. It identifies test cases based on knowledge obtained from the source code, detailed design specification, and other development documents. These test cases challenge the control decisions made by the program; and the program's data structures including configuration tables. Structural testing can identify "dead" code that is never executed when the program is run. Structural testing is accomplished primarily with unit (module) level testing, but can be extended to other levels of software testing.

The level of structural testing can be evaluated using metrics that are designed to show what percentage of the software structure has been evaluated during structural testing. These metrics are typically referred to as "coverage" and are a measure of completeness with respect to test selection criteria. The amount of structural coverage should be commensurate with the level of risk posed by the software. Use of the term "coverage" usually means 100% coverage. For example, if a testing program has achieved "statement coverage," it means that 100% of the statements in the software have been executed at least once. Common structural coverage metrics include:

- **Statement Coverage**—This criteria requires sufficient test cases for each program statement to be executed at least once; however, its achievement is insufficient to provide confidence in a software product's behavior.
- **Decision (Branch) Coverage**—This criteria requires sufficient test cases for each program decision or branch to be executed so that each possible outcome occurs at least once. It is considered to be a minimum level of coverage for most software products, but decision coverage alone is insufficient for high-integrity applications.
- **Condition Coverage**—This criteria requires sufficient test cases for each condition in a program decision to take on all possible outcomes at least once. It differs from branch coverage only when multiple conditions must be evaluated to reach a decision.
- **Multi-Condition Coverage**—This criteria requires sufficient test cases to exercise all possible combinations of conditions in a program decision.
- **Loop Coverage**—This criteria requires sufficient test cases for all program loops to be executed for zero, one, two, and many iterations covering initialization, typical running and termination (boundary) conditions.
- **Path Coverage**—This criteria requires sufficient test cases for each feasible path, basis path, etc. from start to exit of a defined program segment, to be executed at least once. Because of the very large number of possible paths through a software program, path coverage is generally not achievable. The amount of path coverage is normally established based on the risk or criticality of the software under test.

- **Data Flow Coverage**—This criteria requires sufficient test cases for each feasible data flow to be executed at least once. A number of data flow testing strategies are available.

7.9.1 White-Box Testing and Test Cases

White-box testing is a test case design method that uses the control structure of the procedural design to derive test cases. Test cases can be derived in a manner so that:

- Guarantee that all independent paths within a module have been exercised at least once,
- Exercise all logical decisions on their true and false sides,
- Execute all loops at their boundaries and within their operational bounds, and
- Exercise internal data structures to ensure their validity.

7.9.2 The Nature of Software Defects

Logic errors and incorrect assumptions are inversely proportional to the probability that a program path will be executed. General processing tends to be well understood while special case processing tends to be prone to errors.

We often believe that a logical path is not likely to be executed when it may be executed on a regular basis. Our unconscious assumptions about control flow and data lead to design errors that can only be detected by path testing. Typographical errors are random.

7.10 Loop Testing

This white-box technique focuses exclusively on the validity of loop constructs. Four different classes of loops can be defined:

1. Simple loops,
2. Nested loops,
3. Concatenated loops, and
4. Unstructured loops.

7.10.1 Simple Loops

The following tests should be applied to simple loops where n is the maximum number of allowable passes through the loop:

1. `skip the loop entirely,`
2. `only pass once through the loop,`
3. `m passes through the loop where m < n,`
4. `n - 1, n, n + 1 passes through the loop.`

7.10.2 Nested Loops

The testing of nested loops cannot simply extend the technique of simple loops since this would result in a geometrically increasing number of test cases.

One approach for nested loops:

1. Start at the innermost loop. Set all other loops to minimum values.
2. Conduct simple loop tests for the innermost loop while holding the outer loops at their minimums. Add tests for out-of-range or excluded values.

3. Work outward, conducting tests for the next loop while keeping all other outer loops at minimums and other nested loops to typical values.
4. Continue until all loops have been tested.

7.10.3 Concatenated Loops

Concatenated loops can be tested as simple loops if each loop is independent of the others. If they are not independent (e.g., the loop counter for one is the loop counter for the other), then the nested approach can be used.

7.10.4 Unstructured Loops

This type of loop should be redesigned.

7.11 Basic Path Testing

This method enables the designer to derive a logical complexity measure of a procedural design and use it as a guide for defining a basic set of execution paths. Test cases that exercise the basic set are guaranteed to execute every statement in the program at least once during testing.

Path testing has been one of the first test methods, and even though it is a typical white-box test, it is nowadays also used in black-box tests. The procedure itself is similar to the walk-through. First, a certain path through the program is chosen. Possible inputs and the correct result are written down. Then the program is executed by hand, and its result is compared to the predefined. Possible faults have to be written down at once.

There are different strategies about how to choose the path. The optimum would certainly be to follow each path through the module once, but this is not possible:

- Assume there is a little program which consists of a loop that is executed twenty times. Inside this loop are a case or some if instructions which allow ten different routes. The total number of paths through this little program would be 1020. Definitely nobody is able to trace this huge amount by hand provides a more detailed example.

Since the best solution is not possible, it is necessary to reduce the number of possibilities. There is no perfect solution to this problem, and those strategies should only be understood as hints for the "scout"—a human tester:

- In doubt prefer the shorter way out.
- Choose the path which involves less variables first.
- Use each instruction at least once.
- Do not ignore the important paths—even if they seem complex.
- Do not look over parts which seem to be difficult to understand.
- Last, but not least: trust your intuition.

It is also important to keep in mind that, due to the fact that conditions in a program are normally not completely independent of each other, not all paths are possible. For instance, there are only two different routes through the following program:

```
if (C) {
 instruction block A1
```

```
} else {
 instruction block A2
}
if (C) {
 instruction block B1
} else {
 instruction block B2
}
```

Assuming that the instruction blocks A1 and A2 do not influence the condition C then, regardless of whether the condition C is true or false, the paths A1-B2 and A2-B1 will never be used.

Example: A white-box test rationale for the Square Root function

The intention in white-box testing is to ensure that all possible feasible flow of control paths through a subprogram are traversed whilst the software is under test. This is not the same as saying that all statements in the subprogram will be executed as it is possible for all statements to be executed but for not all of the possible paths to be traversed. However, the converse is true; if all possible paths through a subprogram are traversed then all statements in the subprogram will necessarily be executed.

When considering the number of possible paths through a subprogram two other factors need to be remembered. The first is that some of the possible paths through a subprogram turn out upon investigation to be non-feasible paths. The second consideration is that the number of possible paths through a subprogram indicated by a flow graph analysis will indicate the minimum number of paths to ensure complete coverage. This may be less than the total number of paths which are possible when combinations of paths are allowed for. Examples of these two considerations will be given after the white-box testing of the Square Root function has been presented.

The number of possible paths through a subprogram is equal to the number of regions in the subprogram's flow graph. The final flow graph for the Square Root function, with the regions numbered, is as follows.

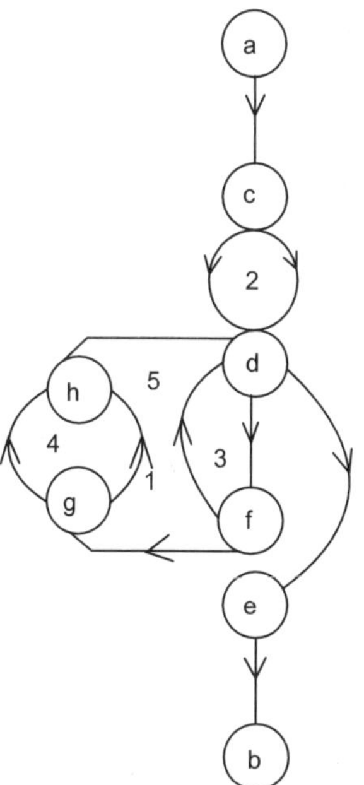

Fig. 7.5: Square root flowgraph with regions numbered

This indicates that there are five possible paths through the flow graph which can be described by listing the sequence in which the nodes must are visited. The five paths in the Square Root flow graph are as follows.

Path 1.	a c^1 d e b
Path 2.	a c^2 d e b
Path 3	a c^x d f g hdeb
Path 4	a c^x d f g^1 h d e b
Path 5	a c^x d f g^2 h d e b

The first two paths differ only in the arc which is followed between nodes *c* and *d*, to indicate which node is intended the nodes have been labelled 1 and 2 and the paths annotated to indicate which arc is intended. In the subsequent paths the arc traversed between *c* and *d* is shown as *x*, indicating that it does not matter which particular arc is followed.

The white box process continues by taking the black-box test plan and manually determining which of the paths will be traversed by each of the test runs. It is immediately obvious that with only three test runs in the black-box test plan there are not enough test runs to be certain that all five paths will be traversed.

A trace of the first test run from the black-box test plan will indicate that the second part of the *if* statement will be followed before the loop is entered and that the value of **CurrentError** when computed on line 0028 would be 0.0, causing the *if* condition on line 0036 to be true. Consequently the value of **CloseEnough** will be set to True and the loop will terminate after the first iteration. Relating this to the flowgraph this produces the path *a c d f d e b*, which is Path3 on the white-box test plan.

The second test run will also follow the second path of the selection before entering the loop. The *if* on line 0036 will evaluate false causing the *if* on line 0039 to be evaluated. This condition will evaluate false as the current guess will be 0.95 whose square (0.9025) is greater than Number (0.9). Following the end of both *if* statements the loop condition will evaluate true again and the loop will iterate for a second time. The path traversed so far would be `a c d f` g^1 `h d` and as the algorithm is known to terminate at some stage the path d e b would have to be traversed at some stage. Thus the complete path `a c d f` g^1 `h d e`, Path 4 from the white-box test plan, will have been known to be traversed during test run 2.

The third black-box test will differ from the second only in the arc which it traverses between nodes g and h. In this case the square will be larger than Number and the alternative path will be followed. The full path is `a c d f` g^2 `h d e`, which is Path 5 from the white-box test plan

Paths 1 and 2 will now have to be examined to determine if they are feasible. Both of these paths will be followed only if the body of the while loop is never entered. An examination of the source code will indicate that this can never happen. The loop is controlled by the value of the Boolean variable CloseEnough, for the loop body never to execute this variable will have to have the value true when the condition is evaluated for the first time. This is not possible as the value of the variable is set to false when the variable is declared. Paths 1 and 2 are thus examples of possible paths through a flowgraph which, upon investigation, turn out to be a non-feasible path.

Unfortunately the total number of feasible possible paths is not always the same as the number of possible paths which are produced from a flowgraph. The following two flow graphs and example implementations both have three regions, but differ in the number of paths.

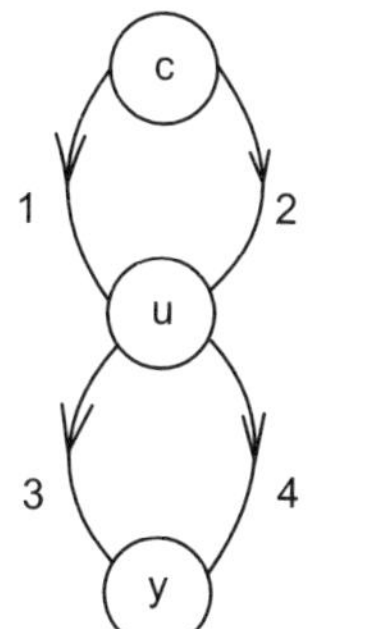

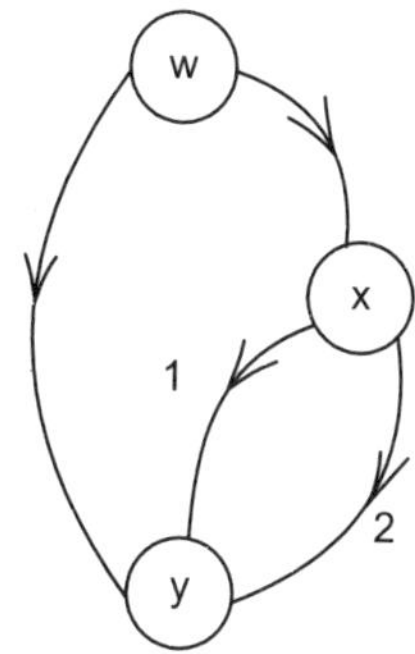

Fig.7.6: Path and Coverage

```
if Condition1 then
   -- First actions.
   else
   -- Second actions.
   end if;

   if Condition2 then
   -- Third actions.
   elsif
   -- Fourth actions.
   end if;
```

```
if Condition1 then
      -- First actions.
else

      if Condition2 then
      -- Third actions.
      else
      -- Fourth actions.
      end if;
     end if;
```

The reasons why the flowgraph on the left has a total of four feasible paths and the one on the right only three, despite the fact that both flowgraphs have the same degree of cylometric complexity are complex and are rooted in a branch of mathematics known as graph theory. Despite this problem the technique of flowgraph analysis and the subsequent counting of regions is still a valuable measure of cognitive complexity, and the number of bias paths which it indicates is the smallest number of distinct feasible paths which should be looked for. As this example indicates, there may also be more possible paths which be checked for when the flowgraph is used as the basis of white-box testing.

7.11.1 Domain Testing

In domain testing the goal is to check values taken by a variable, a condition, or an index, and to prove that they are outside the specified or valid range. It also contains checking that the program accepts only valid input, because it is unlikely to get reasonable results if idiocy has been entered. Colloquially, this part can be called “garbage in—garbage out” testing.

The following checks are suggested by Michael Krüger and Glenford J. Myers:

- Have all variables used been initialized correctly?
- Are all indices used to access an array inside the array’s dimensions?
- Are all those indices integers?
- Are all arguments in a comparison of the same type?

- Are all boolean expressions correct? Check logical operands like AND, and OR, and their priorities.
- Are there any "off by one" situations, like a loop which is executed too often, or a field index of an array which is increased by one?

Certainly, this list is by far not complete, but it gives a good impression of possible faults. It is known from experience that, if programs pass most of this tests, the number of bugs found by other tests is, according to expectations, lots lower.

Concluding this section is an example set of values which might be used to check a variable that contains a percentage. Keep in mind that the borders are of particular interest:

```
-4.00, -0.00, +0.00, 17.56, 100.00, 100.01, 102.25
```

7.12 Flowgraphs and White-Box Testing

The most expensive part of a software development process is the costs associated with its initial production, and most particularly its maintenance, during its life cycle. The attempted measurements in the previous chapter were concerned with the speed of execution which are most closely related to the costs of the machine on which the software will run. As a faster machine can be assumed to cost more than a slower one. The construction and maintenance costs are related more to the cognitive complexity of a software component, rather than its computational complexity, although in most cases it can be expected that these two concepts are closely related.

Flowgraph analysis is a static measurement technique which produces a measurement which seems intuitively related to the cognitive complexity of an algorithm. The technique of flowgraph analysis also lead to a second approach to testing software, a technique which is known as white-box testing. This chapter will commence with techniques of flow graph analysis before introducing white-box testing.

A flowgraph analysis is concerned with statically determining the number of different paths by which flow of control can pass through an algorithm. It can be argued that a developer or maintainer must be able to conceptualise the flow of control through an algorithm in order to fully understand its dynamic behaviour. Unless such an understanding is available the developer will not be able to fully predict the dynamic behaviour of the software and thus will not be able to ensure that all possible contingencies are allowed for in its design or implementation.

7.13 Flow Graphs

Flow graphs can be used to represent control flow in a program and can help in the derivation of the basis set. Each flow graph node represents one or more procedural statements. The edges between nodes represent flow of control. An edge must terminate at a node, even if the node does not represent any useful procedural statements. A region in a flow graph is an area bounded by edges and nodes. Each node that contains a condition is called a predicate node. Cyclomatic complexity is a metric that provides a quantitative measure of the logical complexity of a program. It defines the number of independent paths in the basis set and thus provides an upper bound for the number of tests that must be performed.

The Basis Set

An independent path is any path through a program that introduces at least one new set of processing statements (must move along at least one new edge in the path). The basis set is not unique. Any number of different basis sets can be derived for a given procedural design. Cyclomatic complexity, V(G), for a flow graph G is equal to

1. The number of regions in the flow graph.
2. V(G) = E - N + 2 where E is the number of edges and N is the number of nodes.
3. V(G) = P + 1 where P is the number of predicate nodes.

Deriving Test Cases

1. From the design or source code, derive a flow graph.
2. Determine the cyclomatic complexity of this flow graph. Even without a flow graph, V(G) can be determined by counting the number of conditional statements in the code.
3. Determine a basis set of linearly independent paths. Predicate nodes are useful for determining the necessary paths.
4. Prepare test cases that will force execution of each path in the basis set. Each test case is executed and compared to the expected results.

Automating Basis Set Derivation

The derivation of the flow graph and the set of basis paths is amenable to automation. A software tool to do this can be developed using a data structure called a graph matrix. A graph matrix is a square matrix whose size is equivalent to the number of nodes in the flow graph. Each row and column correspond to a particular node and the matrix corresponds to the connections (edges) between nodes. By adding a link weight to each matrix entry, more information about the control flow can be captured. In its simplest form, the link weight is 1 if an edge exists and 0 if it does not. But other types of link weights can be represented:

- The probability that an edge will be executed,
- The processing time expended during link traversal,
- The memory required during link traversal, or
- The resources required during link traversal.

Graph theory algorithms can be applied to these graph matrices to help in the analysis necessary to produce the basis set.

7.13.1 Producing a Simple Flowgraph

Although a flowgraph analysis can be made at the design stage this chapter will concentrate upon the production of flowgraphs from source code, as this is a prerequisite for the technique of white-box testing. To illustrate the techniques of flowgraph analysis, a flowgraph for the SquareRoot function introduced earlier in this section will be derived. The first implementation of the SquareRoot algorithm, is as follows.

```
function SquareRoot (Number: in FLOAT;
Accuracy: in FLOAT) re0urn FLOAT is
MaximumValue: FLOAT;
MinimumValue: FLOAT;
CurrentGuess: FLOAT;
CurrentGuessSquared: FLOAT;
CurrentError: FLOAT;
CloseEnough: BOOLEAN:= FALSE;
begin -- SquareRoot
if Number > 1.0 then
MaximumValue:= Number;
MinimumValue:= 0.0;
else
MaximumValue:= 1.0;
MinimumValue:= Number;
end if;
while not CloseEnough loop
CurrentGuess:= (MaximumValue + MinimumValue) / 2.0;
CurrentGuessSquared:= CurrentGuess * CurrentGuess;
CurrentError:= abs( Number - CurrentGuessSquared);
if CurrentError <= Accuracy then
CloseEnough:= TRUE;
else
if CurrentGuessSquared >= Number then
MaximumValue:= CurrentGuess;
else
MinimumValue:= CurrentGuess;
end if;
end if;
end loop;
return CurrentGuess;
end SquareRoot;
```

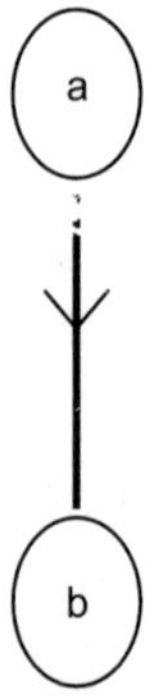

Fig. 7.7: Initial Square Root Flowgraph

The first stage in constructing a flowgraph is to note that at some stage flow of control will enter the subprogram and will at some stage leave the subprogram. This produces an initial flowgraph as follows:

A flowgraph consists of a number of nodes, shown as circles containing identifying letters, connected by arcs which have arrows indicating the direction in which flow of control will pass. The flowgraph above indicates that flow of control enters the subprogram at node a, flows through the arc and leaves at node b. The construction of the flow graph continues by refining the flow of control within the subprogram, between points a and b.

Refinement proceeds by dividing the implementation into parts where flow of control has a single entry and exit point. In the SquareRoot function there is a sequence of four parts. The first part comprises the declaration and initialisation of the local variables between lines 0017 and 0024, the second comprises the if structure between lines 0025 and 0031, the third is the while loop between lines 0032 and 0045 and the last is the single return statement on line 0046. The flow graph can be refined to reflect these three regions of code, producing the following flow graph.

The four parts where flow of control enters and leaves are shown between nodes a and c, c and d, d and e and between e and b. The first and last of these arcs require no further refinement as they represent regions where simple sequences of instructions, within which flow of control moves sequentially from instruction to instruction. The second arc requires further refinement which can proceed by substituting the standard two way flow graph for the arc between c and d. The standard two way flow graph is as follows:

Fig. 7.8: SquareRoot Flowgraph

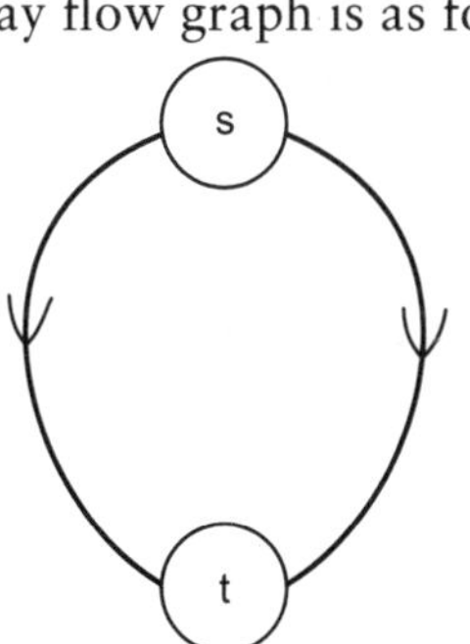

Fig. 7.9: Standard flowchart for a two-way selection

Flow of control enters the flow graph at node s and leaves at node t, following one of the two arcs connecting the nodes. This flowchart can be used to represent flow of control through if statements of the following forms:

```
One way if structure    Two way if structure
  if Condition then       if Condition then
  -- Actions.            -- First actions.
  end if;                     else
```

```
--Second actions.
end if;
```

For the one way *if* structure flow of control can cause the Actions to either be performed or omitted. For the two way *if* structure flow of control can cause either First actions or Second actions to be performed. The two possible flows of control are represented by the two arcs connecting the nodes. For more complex sequential selection structures, for example an elsif structure or a case structure of the following forms, a more complex flow graph would be required.

Three way elsif structure

```
if FirstCondition then
 -- First actions.
elsif SecondCondition then
-- Second actions.
   else
-- Third actions.
end if;
```

Three way case structure

```
case SelectionValue is
      when => FirstValueList
   -- First actions.
 when => SecondValueList
-- Second actions.
 when others =>
-- Third actions
 end case;
```

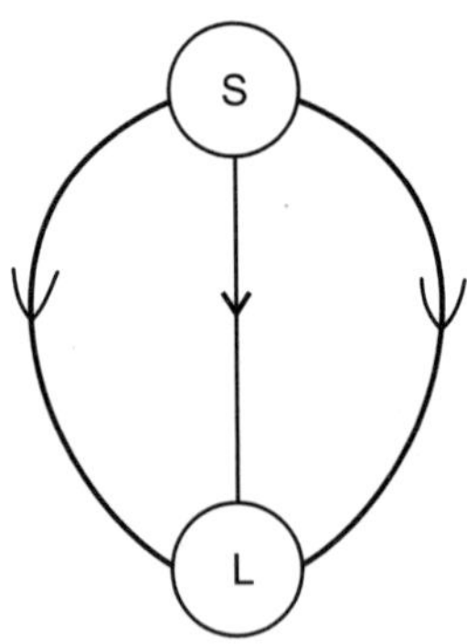

Fig. 7.10: Standard flowchart for a three-way selection

Additional `elsif` options or case options in the sequential selection structures will cause additional arcs connecting the two nodes to be added. Inserting a two-way selection flow graph into the SquareRoot flow chart to represent the two-way if structure between lines 0025 and 0031, will produce the flowgraph shown in Figure 7.11

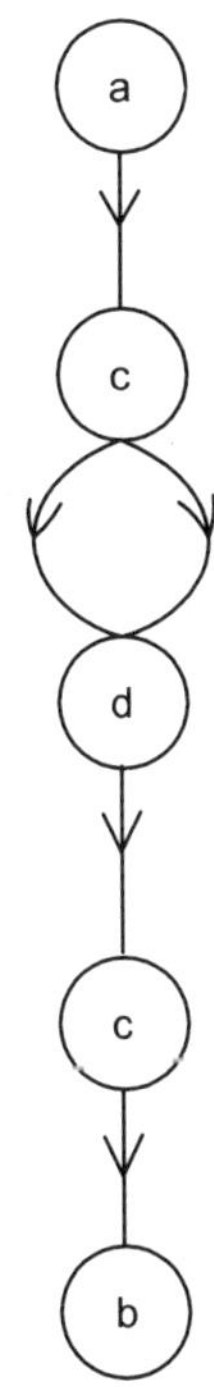

Fig. 7.11: SquareRoot function, second refinement

Refinement continues with the arc between nodes d and e which represent the while loop in the implementation. The standard loop flow graph is as shown in Figure 7.12.

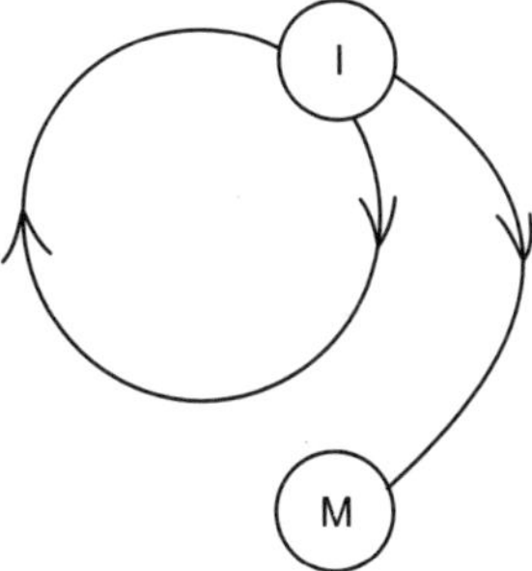

Fig. 7.12: Standard Loop flow graph

Flow of control can pass straight from node l to node m without following the circular arc back to the node. This would be the case for a while loop if the first time the condition controlling the loop was tested, it evaluated false. If a for loop was being represented then flow of control would avoid the circular route if the loop conditions were such that the body of the loop was not executed. The circular route represents the body of the loop and in circumstances where flow of control enters the loop body a representation of flow of control would indicate that node l was visited more than once indicating that the circular arc was followed. Inserting the standard loop flow graph into the **`SquareRoot`** flow chart produces the refinement as shown in Figure 7.13.

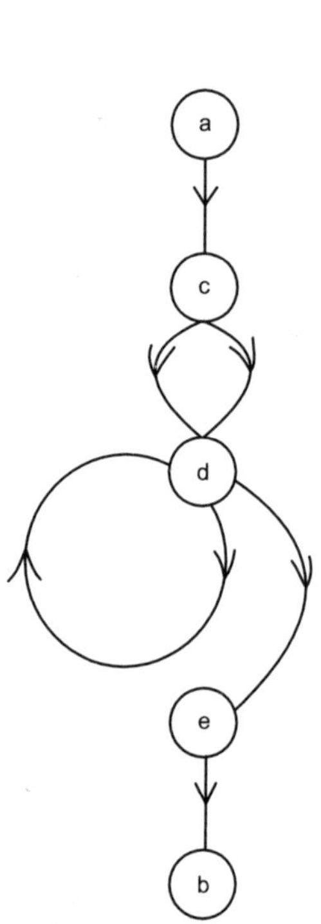

Fig. 7.13: SquareRoot function third refinement

Fig. 7.14: SquareRoot function fourth refinement

The construction of the flow graph continues by the refinement of the body of the loop. The first refinement would divide it into a sequence of two parts, the first is the sequence of statements between lines 0026 and 0028. The second part is the nested if statements between lines 0029 and 0037. Substituting a flow graph representing a sequence of two parts into the arc which represents the body of the loop produces the flow graph shown in Figure 7.14.

The arc between d and f represents a sequence of simple instructions and requires no further refinement, the arc between f and d represents the nested *if* statement which will have to be refined in two stages. The first stage of refinement will substitute a standard two way selection flowgraph to represent the outermost *if*, producing the flow graph shown in Figure 7.15.

The final refinement will replace one of the arcs between f and d with a two-way flow graph to represent the two-way *if* structure on lines 0039 to 0043. The final, completely refined, flowchart for the SquareRoot function is as shown in Figure 7.16.

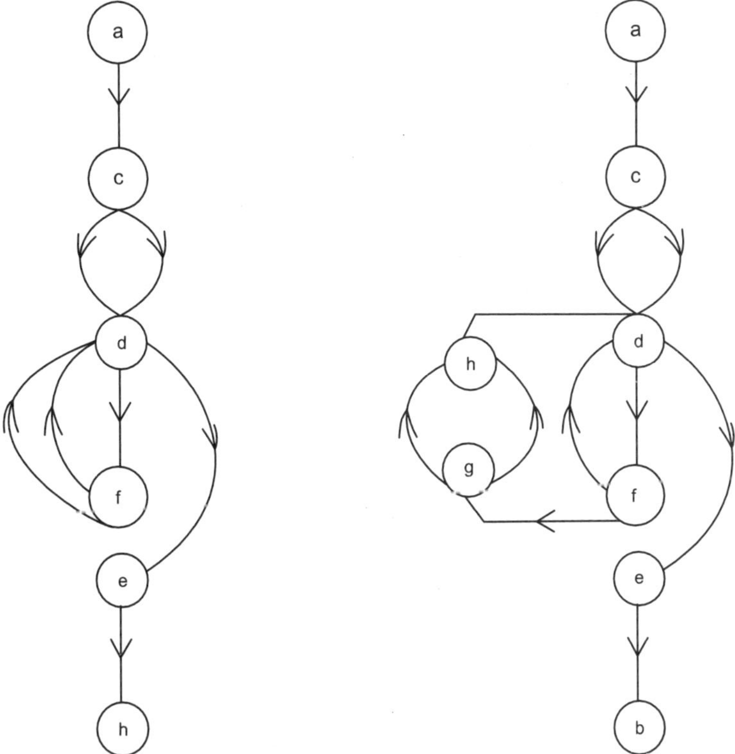

Fig. 7.15: SquareRoot function fifth Refinement

Fig. 7.16: SquareRoot function final Refinement

7.13.2 Flow Graphs and Testing

The technique of complexity measurement introduced above leads to a technique of testing known as white-box testing. Before introducing this technique in detail a black-box test rationale for the SquareRoot function will be developed in order that the two techniques can be subsequently compared.

A black-box test rationale for the `SquareRoot` function

Assuming that the `SquareRoot` function will always be called with legitimate parameters the black-box diagram, range diagrams, sub-range diagrams, list of test cases and test plan, produced using the techniques for black-box testing as follows:

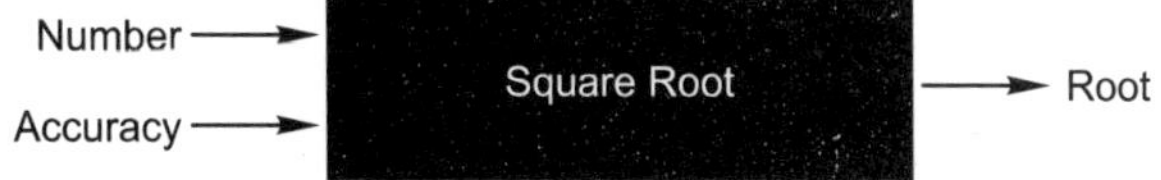

Fig. 7.17: Black Box Diagram of Square Root Function

The Number range diagram has been divided into two significant sub-ranges at the value 1.0, as values between 0.0 and 1.0 have square roots which are larger and numbers above 1.0 have square roots which are lower. This minimal black-box test plan will test the SquareRoot function using only three test runs. This might not seem a convincing test for this function and a realistic test regime might add some additional tests as the costs of testing are not very high compared with the increased confidence which they will yield. However as the intention in this part of the chapter is to compare black-box and white-box techniques only this minimal plan will be used in the comparison. In a more realistic testing environment where test plans were being produced for a large number of disparate subprograms then only a minimal plan would be used as the additional costs might not be justified.

7.13.3 Flowgraph Complexity Analysis

The complete flowgraph which has been produced by successive refinement from the source code now indicates all the possible paths by which flow of control can pass through the SquareRoot function. In its current state it provides a simple pictorial representation of the dynamic complexity of the subprogram, which can be compared visually with other flow graphs to compare the relative complexity of two or more subprograms.

A more satisfactory approach to deriving a measure of complexity from a flow graph would require some measurement of the graph. The most obvious measurement might be to count the number of nodes and the number of arcs. In the final SquareRoot flow graph above there are 8 nodes and 10 arcs. Each node represents a location within the software where a simple sequential flow of control joins with another simple sequential flow of control and each arc represents the flow of control through a simple sequence.

Although a count of the number of arcs and nodes gives some indication of the complexity of a flow graph, the real indication of the software's complexity is in the topological relationship of the nodes and arcs. The topology of a graph is the number of non-connected areas on the graph, each non-connected area is known as a region and number of regions is independent of the precise way in which the graph is laid out. The three flow charts shown in Figure 7.18 have a similar number of nodes and arcs, but the two right hand flow charts intuitively have a greater complexity than the left hand chart as they have a greater number of regions.

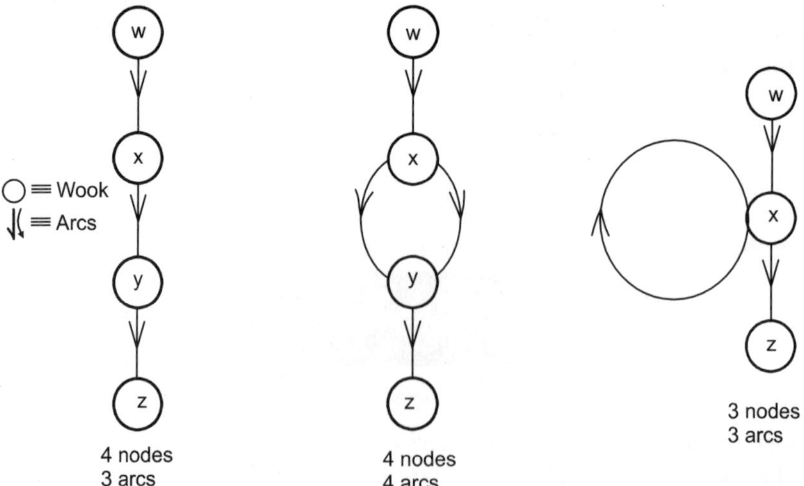

Fig. 7.18: Nodes and Arcs

The left hand flow graph has four nodes and three arcs, the middle four nodes and four arcs and the right hand flow graph three nodes and three arcs. The relationship between the number of arcs and the number of nodes is significant. Where a flowgraph has one fewer arcs than nodes it can be argued that every arc must connect one node with another node, without any two nodes being connected by more than one arc. This will produce a flow graph consisting of a single region, as shown on the left hand flow graph of Figure 7.19.

Continuing the argument it can be shown that there can never be less than this number of arcs as this would result in some nodes being unconnected with the rest of the flow graph. The situation where there are as many arcs as nodes produces flow graphs such as the two right hand graphs above where one arc must either duplicate an existing connection between two nodes or define a loop arc connecting a node to itself. In both cases the additional arc has changed the topology of the graph by defining a region within the graph. It can be shown that for every additional arc above the number of nodes another closed region is added to the graph. The sequence of flow graphs in Figure 7.19 illustrate that adding arcs increases the number of regions.

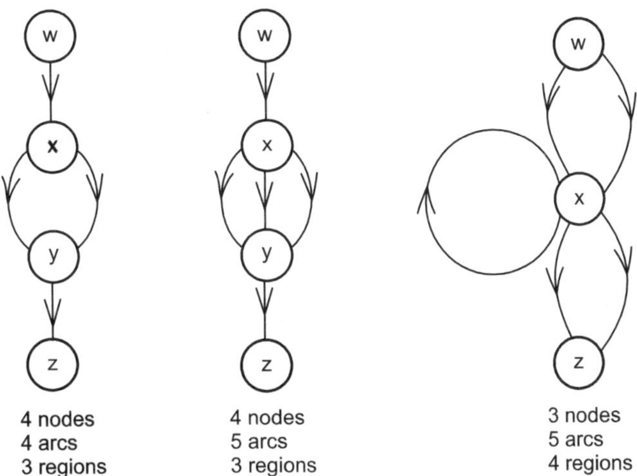

Fig.7.19: Nodes, Arcs and Complexity

Thus the number of regions in a flow graph is the most important indicator of complexity and can be derived either by counting the number of regions on the flow graph, including the external region in the count. Alternatively the number of nodes and arcs can be counted and the number of regions decided by using the formula:

```
regions = arcs - nodes + 2
```

This measure of the complexity of an algorithm, the number of regions in its flowgraph, is known as McCabes complexity metric. Although this technique established a metric for the complexity of an algorithm, it does not give any indication of the appropriate complexity which should be aimed for. Cognitive psychologists have determined that a human is only capable of maintaining and manipulating cognitive models which contain seven plus or minus two, i.e. between five and nine, cognitive chunks of information. Assuming that a region on a flow graph is equivalent to a cognitive chunk then it can be concluded that subprograms should not be constructed which contain more than a maximum of about nine regions and preferably should be limited to less than seven.

7.14 Cyclomatic Complexity

Cyclomatic complexity measures the amount of decision logic in a single software module. It is used for two related purposes in the structured testing methodology:

- First, it gives the number of recommended tests for software.
- Second, it is used during all phases of the software life cycle, beginning with design, to keep software reliable, testable, and manageable. Cyclomatic complexity is based entirely on the structure of software's control flow graph.

7.14.1 Control Flow Graphs

Control flow graphs describe the logic structure of software modules. A module corresponds to a single function or subroutine in typical languages, has a single entry and exit point, and is able to be used as a design component via a call/return mechanism. This document uses C as the language for examples, and in C a module is a function. Each flow graph consists of nodes and edges. The nodes represent computational statements or expressions, and the edges represent transfer of control between nodes.

Each possible execution path of a software module has a corresponding path from the entry to the exit node of the module's control flow graph. This correspondence is the foundation for the structured testing methodology.

As an example, consider the C function in Figure 7.20, which implements Euclid's algorithm for finding greatest common divisors. The nodes are numbered A0 through A13. The control flow graph is shown in Figure 7.21, in which each node is numbered 0 through 13 and edges are shown by lines connecting the nodes. Node 1 thus represents the decision of the "if" statement with the true outcome at node 2 and the false outcome at the collection node 5. The decision of the "while" loop is represented by node 7, and the upward flow of control to the next iteration is shown by the dashed line from node 10 to node 7. Figure 7.22 shows the path resulting when the module is executed with parameters 4 and 2, as in "euclid(4,2)." Execution begins at node 0, the beginning of the module, and proceeds to node 1, the decision node for the "if" statement. Since the test at node 1 is false, execution transfers directly to node 5, the collection node of the "if" statement, and proceeds to node 6. At node 6, the value of "r" is calculated to be 0, and execution proceeds to node 7, the decision node for the "while" statement. Since the test at node 7 is false, execution transfers out of the loop directly to node 11, then proceeds to node 12, returning the result of 2. The actual return is modeled by execution proceeding to node 13, the module exit node.

Annotated Source Listing for euclid

Print | Save | Convert | Close | Help

```
                         Annotated Source Listing

Program : Euclid                                                      01/15/96
File    : euclid.c
Language: instc
Module Module                                                    Start Num of
Letter Name                                 v(G) ev(G) iv(G)   Line  Lines
------ ----------------------------------------------------------- ----- ------
   A   euclid                                  3     1     1       2     19

        A0            euclid(int m, int n)
                      {/* Assuming m and n both greater than 0,
                         * return their greatest common divisor.
                         * Enforce m >= n for efficiency.
                         */
                          int r;
        A1                if (n > m) {
        A2                    r = m;
        A3                    m = n;
        A4                    n = r;
                          }
        A5 A6             r = m % n;        /* m modulo n */
        A7                while (r != 0) {
        A8                    m = n;
        A9                    n = r;
        A10                   r = m % n;    /* m modulo n */
        A11               }
        A12               return n;
        A13           }
```

Fig. 7.20: Annotated source listing for module "euclid."

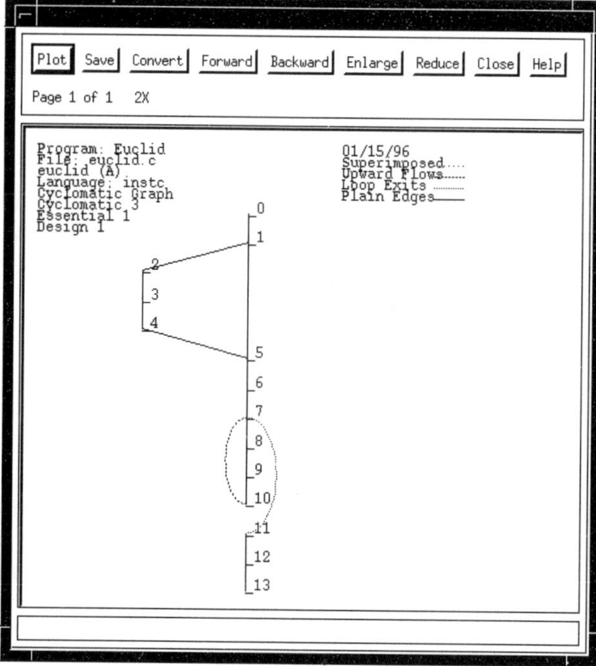

Fig. 7.21: Control flow graph for module "euclid."

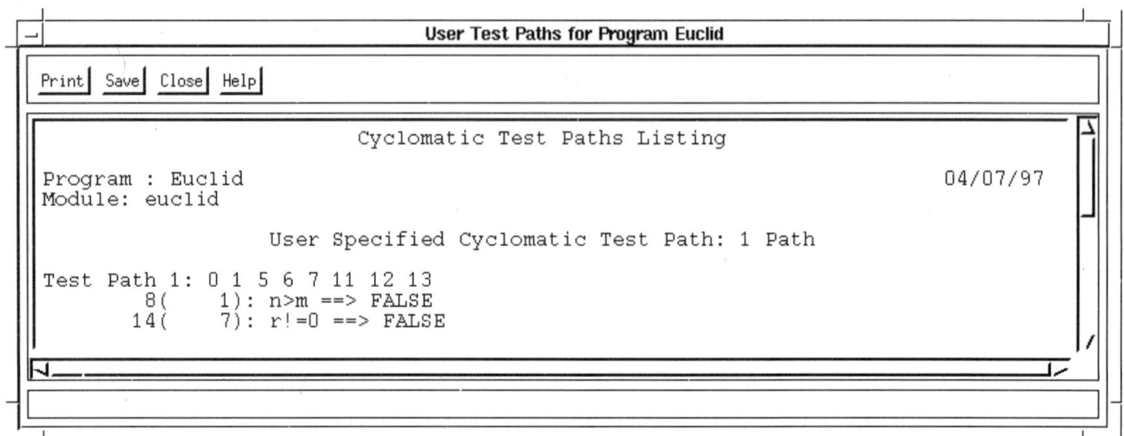
User Test Paths for Program Euclid

Print Save Close Help

Cyclomatic Test Paths Listing

Program : Euclid 04/07/97
Module: euclid

User Specified Cyclomatic Test Path: 1 Path

```
Test Path 1: 0 1 5 6 7 11 12 13
        8(    1): n>m ==> FALSE
       14(    7): r!=0 ==> FALSE
```

Fig. 7.22: A test path through module "euclid."

7.14.2 Definition of Cyclomatic Complexity, v(G)

Cyclomatic complexity is defined for each module to be e - n + 2, where e and n are the number of edges and nodes in the control flow graph, respectively. Thus, for the Euclid's algorithm example in section 7.14.1, the complexity is 3 (15 edges minus 14 nodes plus 2). Cyclomatic complexity is also known as v(G), where v refers to the cyclomatic number in graph theory and G indicates that the complexity is a function of the graph.

The word "cyclomatic" comes from the number of fundamental (or basic) cycles in connected, undirected graphs. More importantly, it also gives the number of independent paths through strongly connected directed graphs. A strongly connected graph is one in which each node can be reached from any other node by following directed edges in the graph. The cyclomatic number in graph theory is defined as e - n + 1. Program control flow graphs are not strongly connected, but they become strongly connected when a "virtual edge" is added connecting the exit node to the entry node. The cyclomatic complexity definition for program control flow graphs is derived from the cyclomatic number formula by simply adding one to represent the contribution of the virtual edge. This definition makes the cyclomatic complexity equal the number of independent paths through the standard control flow graph model, and avoids explicit mention of the virtual edge.

Figure 7.23 shows the control flow graph of Figure 7.21 with the virtual edge added as a dashed line. This virtual edge is not just a mathematical convenience. Intuitively, it represents the control flow through the rest of the program in which the module is used. It is possible to calculate the amount of (virtual) control flow through the virtual edge by using the conservation of flow equations at the entry and exit nodes, showing it to be the number of times that the module has been executed. For any individual path through the module, this amount of flow is exactly one. Although the virtual edge will not be mentioned again in this document, note that since its flow can be calculated as a linear combination of the flow through the real edges, its presence or absence makes no difference in determining the number of linearly independent paths through the module.

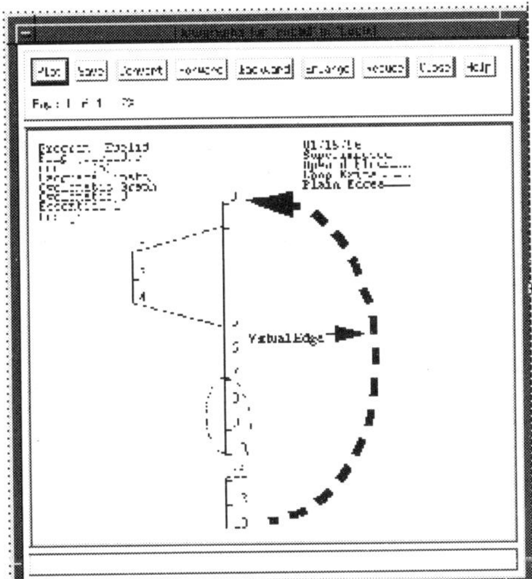

Fig. 7.23: Control flow graph with virtual edge.

7.15 Characterization of v(G) Using a Basis Set of Control Flow Paths

Cyclomatic complexity can be characterized as the number of elements of a basis set of control flow paths through the module. Some familiarity with linear algebra is required to follow the details, but the point is that cyclomatic complexity is precisely the minimum number of paths that can, in (linear) combination, generate all possible paths through the module. To see this, consider the following mathematical model, which gives a vector space corresponding to each flow graph.

Each path has an associated row vector, with the elements corresponding to edges in the flow graph. The value of each element is the number of times the edge is traversed by the path. Consider the path described in Figure 7.22 through the graph in Figure 7.21. Since there are 15 edges in the graph, the vector has 15 elements. Seven of the edges are traversed exactly once as part of the path, so those elements have value 1. The other eight edges were not traversed as part of the path, so they have value 0.

Considering a set of several paths gives a matrix in which the columns correspond to edges and the rows correspond to paths. From linear algebra, it is known that each matrix has a unique rank (number of linearly independent rows) that is less than or equal to the number of columns. This means that no matter how many of the (potentially infinite) number of possible paths are added to the matrix, the rank can never exceed the number of edges in the graph. In fact, the maximum value of this rank is exactly the cyclomatic complexity of the graph. A minimal set of vectors (paths) with maximum rank is known as a basis, and a basis can also be described as a linearly independent set of vectors that generate all vectors in the space by linear combination. This means that the cyclomatic complexity is the number of paths in any independent set of paths that generate all possible paths by linear combination.

Given any set of paths, it is possible to determine the rank by doing Gaussian Elimination on the associated matrix. The rank is the number of non-zero rows once elimination is complete. If no rows are driven to zero during elimination, the original paths are linearly independent. If the rank equals the cyclomatic complexity, the original set of paths generate all paths by linear combination. If both conditions hold, the original set of paths are a basis for the flow graph.

There are a few important points to note about the linear algebra of control flow paths. First, although every path has a corresponding vector, not every vector has a corresponding path. This is obvious, for example, for a vector that has a zero value for all elements corresponding to edges out of the module entry node but has a nonzero value for any other element cannot correspond to any path. Slightly less obvious, but also true, is that linear combinations of vectors that correspond to actual paths may be vectors that do not correspond to actual paths. This follows from the non-obvious fact that it is always possible to construct a basis consisting of vectors that correspond to actual paths, so any vector can be generated from vectors corresponding to actual paths. This means that one cannot just find a basis set of vectors by algebraic methods and expect them to correspond to paths—one must use a path-oriented technique such as that of section 6 to get a basis set of paths. Finally, there are a potentially infinite number of basis sets of paths for a given module. Each basis set has the same number of paths in it (the cyclomatic complexity), but there is no limit to the number of different sets of basis paths. For example, it is possible to start with any path and construct a basis that contains it.

The details of the theory behind cyclomatic complexity are too mathematically complicated to be used directly during software development. However, the good news is that this mathematical insight yields an effective operational testing method in which a concrete basis set of paths is tested i.e. structured testing.

7.15.1 Example of v(G) and Basis Paths

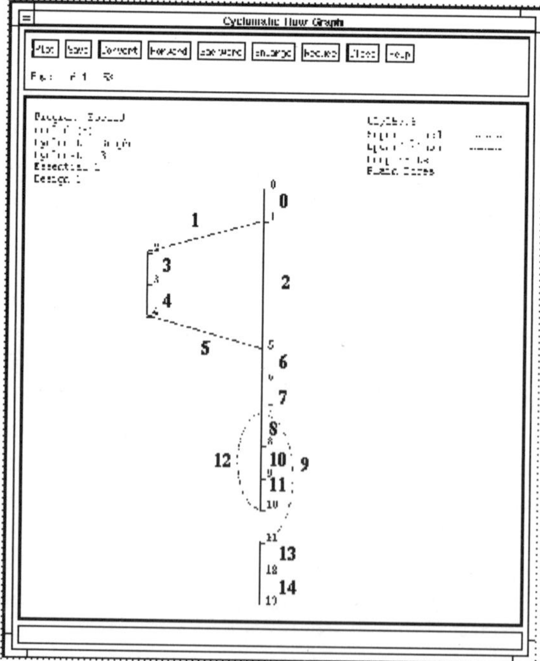

Fig. 7.24: Control flow graph with edges numbered

Figure 7.24 shows the control flow graph for module "euclid" with the fifteen edges numbered 0 to 14 along with the fourteen nodes numbered 0 to 13. Since the cyclomatic complexity is 3 (15 - 14 + 2), there is a basis set of three paths. One such basis set consists of paths B1 through B3, shown in Figure 7.25.

```
 Module: euclid
                 Basis Test Paths: 3 Paths
Test Path B1: 0 1 5 6 7 11 12 13
   8( 1): n>m ==> FALSE
   14( 7): r!=0 ==> FALSE
Test Path B2: 0 1 2 3 4 5 6 7 11 12 13
   8( 1): n>m ==> TRUE
   14( 7): r!=0 ==> FALSE
Test Path B3: 0 1 5 6 7 8 9 10 7 11 12 13
   8( 1): n>m ==> FALSE
   14( 7): r!=0 ==> TRUE
   14( 7): r!=0 ==> FALSE
```

Fig. 7.25: A basis set of paths, B1 through B3.

Any arbitrary path can be expressed as a linear combination of the basis paths B1 through B3. For example, the path P shown in Figure 7.26 is equal to B2 - 2 * B1 + 2 * B3.

```
Module: euclid
                 User Specified Path: 1 Path
Test Path P: 0 1 2 3 4 5 6 7 8 9 10 7 8 9 10 7 11 12 13
   8( 1): n>m ==> TRUE
   14( 7): r!=0 ==> TRUE
   14( 7): r!=0 ==> TRUE
   14( 7): r!=0 ==> FALSE
```

Fig. 7.26: Path P.

To see this, examine Figure 7.27, which shows the number of times each edge is executed along each path.

Path/Edge	0	1	2	3	4	5	6	7	8	9	10	11	12	13	14
BI	1	0	1	0	0	0	1	1	0	1	0	0	0	1	1
B2	1	1	0	1	1	1	1	1	0	1	0	0	0	1	1
B3	1	0	1	0	0	0	1	1	1	1	1	1	1	1	1
P	1	1	0	1	1	1	1	T	2	1	2	2	2	1	1

Fig. 7.27: Matrix of edge incidence for basis paths B1-B3 and other path P.

One interesting property of basis sets is that every edge of a flow graph is traversed by at least one path in every basis set. Put another way, executing a basis set of paths will always cover every control branch in the module. This means that to cover all edges never requires more than the cyclomatic complexity number of paths. However, executing a basis set just to cover all edges is overkill. Covering all edges can usually be accomplished with fewer paths. In this example, paths B2 and B3 cover all edges without path B1.

Note that apart from forming a basis together, there is nothing special about paths B1 through B3. Path P in combination with any two of the paths B1 through B3 would also form a basis. The fact that there are many sets of basis paths through most programs is important for testing, since it means it is possible to have considerable freedom in selecting a basis set of paths to test.

7.15.2 Limiting Cyclomatic Complexity to 10

There are many good reasons to limit cyclomatic complexity. Overly complex modules are more prone to error, are harder to understand, are harder to test, and are harder to modify. Deliberately limiting complexity at all stages of software development, for example as a departmental standard, helps avoid the pitfalls associated with high complexity software. Many organizations have successfully implemented complexity limits as part of their software programs. The precise number to use as a limit, however, remains somewhat controversial. The original limit of 10 as proposed by McCabe has significant supporting evidence, but limits as high as 15 have been used successfully as well. Limits over 10 should be reserved for projects that have several operational advantages over typical projects, for example experienced staff, formal design, a modern programming language, structured programming, code walkthroughs, and a comprehensive test plan. In other words, an organization can pick a complexity limit greater than 10, but only if it is sure it knows what it is doing and is willing to devote the additional testing effort required by more complex modules.

Somewhat more interesting than the exact complexity limit are the exceptions to that limit. For example, McCabe originally recommended exempting modules consisting of single multiway decision ("switch" or "case") statements from the complexity limit. The multiway decision issue has been interpreted in many ways over the years, sometimes with disastrous results. Some naive developers wondered whether, since multiway decisions qualify for exemption from the complexity limit, the complexity measure should just be altered to ignore them. The result would be that modules containing several multiway decisions would not be identified as overly complex. One developer started reporting a "modified" complexity in which cyclomatic complexity was divided by the number of multiway decision branches. The stated intent of this metric was that multiway decisions would be treated uniformly by having them contribute the average value of each case branch. The actual result was that the developer could take a module with complexity 90 and reduce it to "modified" complexity 10 simply by adding a ten-branch multiway decision statement to it that did nothing.

Consideration of the intent behind complexity limitation can keep standards policy on track. There are two main facets of complexity to consider: the number of tests and everything else (reliability, maintainability, understandability, etc.). Cyclomatic complexity gives the number of tests, which for a multiway decision statement is the number of decision branches. Any attempt to modify the complexity measure to have a smaller value for multiway decisions will result in a number of tests that cannot even exercise each branch, and will hence be inadequate for testing purposes. However, the pure number of tests, while important to measure and control, is not a major factor to consider when limiting complexity. Note that testing effort is much more than just the number of tests, since that is multiplied by the effort to construct each individual test, bringing in the other facet of complexity. It is this correlation of complexity with reliability, maintainability, and understandability that primarily drives the process to limit complexity.

Complexity limitation affects the allocation of code among individual software modules, limiting the amount of code in any one module, and thus tending to create more modules for the same application. Other than complexity limitation, the usual factors to consider when allocating code among modules are the cohesion and coupling principles of structured design: the ideal module performs a single conceptual function, and does so in a self-contained manner without interacting with other modules except to use them as subroutines. Complexity limitation attempts to quantify an "except where doing so would render a module too complex to understand, test, or maintain" clause to the structured design principles. This rationale provides an effective framework for considering exceptions to a given complexity limit.

Rewriting a single multiway decision to cross a module boundary is a clear violation of structured design. Additionally, although a module consisting of a single multiway decision may require many tests, each test should be easy to construct and execute. Each decision branch can be understood and maintained in isolation, so the module is likely to be reliable and maintainable. Therefore, it is reasonable to exempt modules consisting of a single multiway decision statement from a complexity limit. Note that if the branches of the decision statement contain complexity themselves, the rationale and thus the exemption does not automatically apply. However, if all branches have very low complexity code in them, it may well apply. Although constructing "modified" complexity measures is not recommended, considering the maximum complexity of each multiway decision branch is likely to be much more useful than the average. At this point it should be clear that the multiway decision statement exemption is not a bizarre anomaly in the complexity measure but rather the consequence of a reasoning process that seeks a balance between the complexity limit, the principles of structured design, and the fundamental properties of software that the complexity limit is intended to control. This process should serve as a model for assessing proposed violations of the standard complexity limit. For developers with a solid understanding of both the mechanics and the intent of complexity limitation, the most effective policy is: "For each module, either limit cyclomatic complexity to 10 (as discussed earlier, an organization can substitute a similar number), or provide a written explanation of why the limit was exceeded."

7.15.3 Examples of Cyclomatic Complexity

(1) Independence of complexity and size

There is a big difference between complexity and size. Consider the difference between the cyclomatic complexity measure and the number of lines of code, a common size measure. Just as 10 is a common limit for cyclomatic complexity, 60 is a common limit for the number of lines of code, the somewhat archaic rationale being that each software module should fit on one printed page to be manageable. Although the number of lines of code is often used as a crude complexity measure, there is no consistent relationship between the two. Many modules with no branching of control flow (and hence the minimum cyclomatic complexity of one) consist of far greater than 60 lines of code, and many modules with complexity greater than ten have far fewer than 60 lines of code. For example, Figure 7.28 has complexity 1 and 282 lines of code, while Figure 7.36 has complexity 28 and 30 lines of code. Thus, although the number of lines of code is an important size measure, it is independent of complexity and should not be used for the same purposes.

(2) Several flow graphs and their complexity

Several actual control flow graphs and their complexity measures are presented in Figures 7.28 through 7.36, to solidify understanding of the measure. The graphs are presented in order of increasing complexity, in order to emphasize the relationship between the complexity numbers and an intuitive notion of the complexity of the graphs.

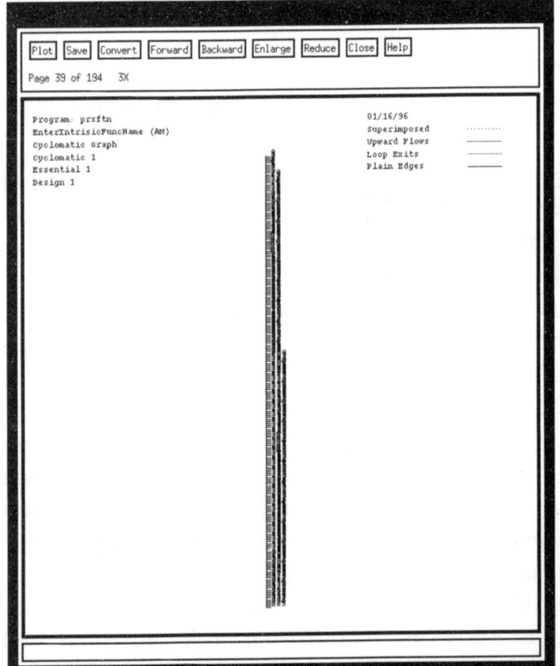

Fig. 7.28: Control flow graph with complexity 1

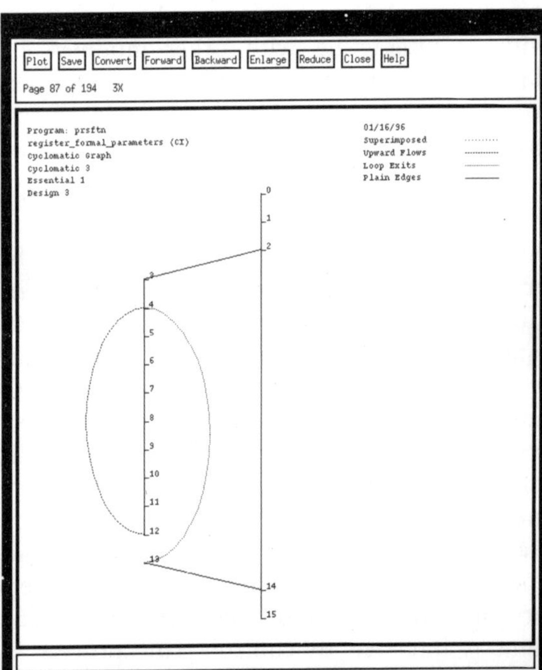

Fig. 7.29: Control flow graph with complexity 3

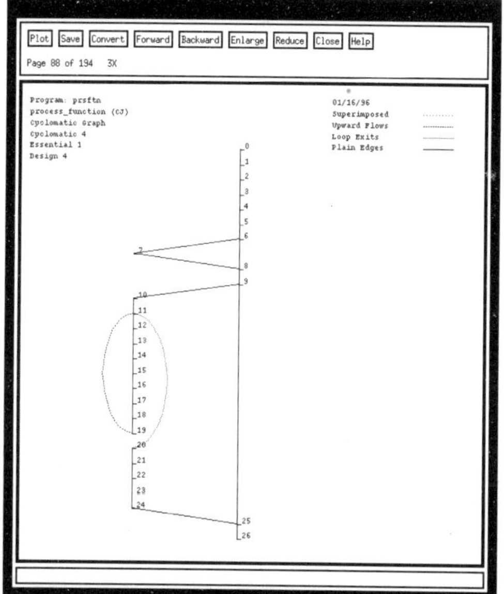

Fig.: 7.30: Control flow graph with complexity 4

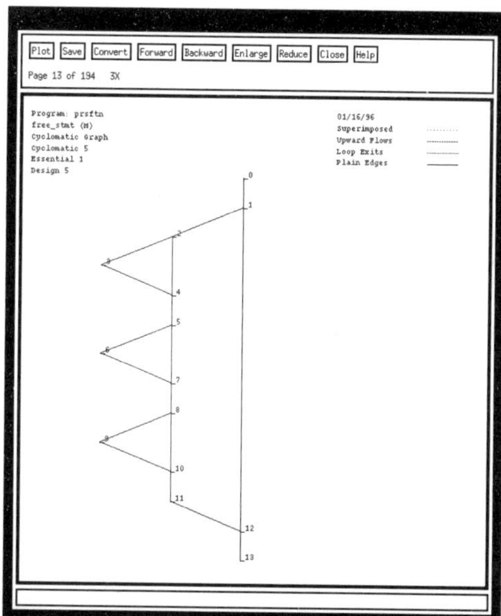

Fig. 7.31: Control flow graph with complexity 5

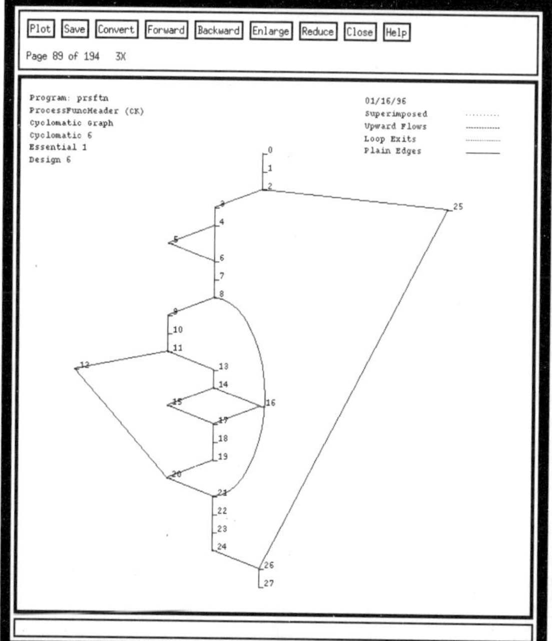

Fig. 7.32: Control flow graph with complexity 6.

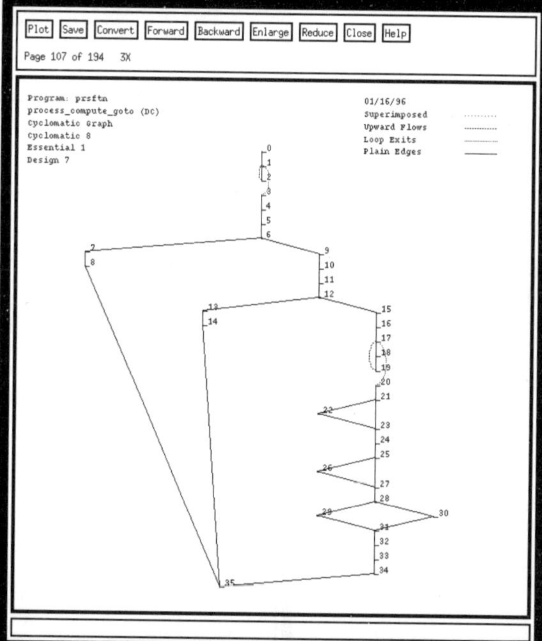

Fig. 7.33: Control flow graph with complexity 8.

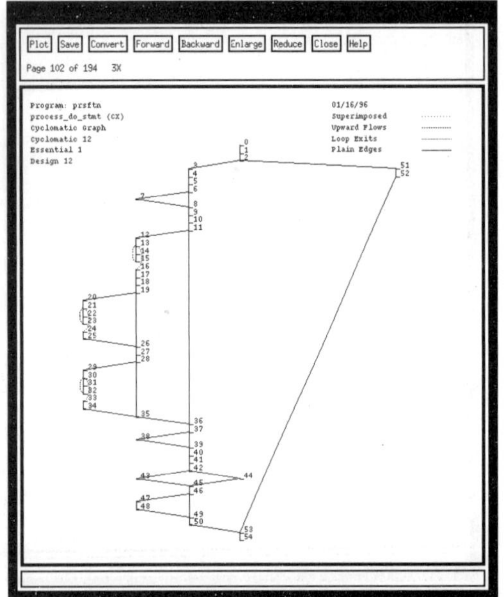

Fig. 7.34: Control flow graph with complexity 12.

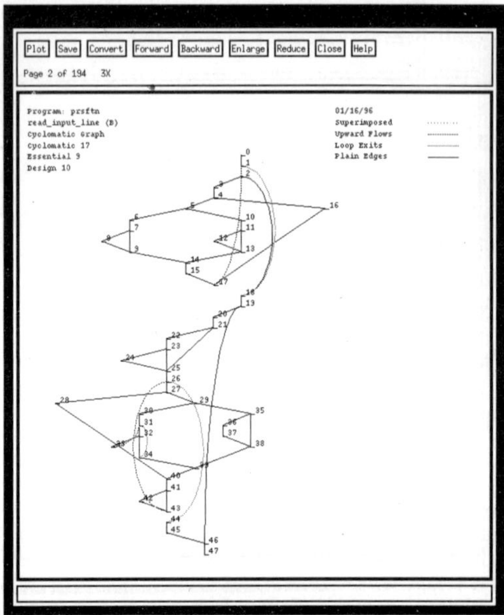

Fig. 7.35: Control flow graph with complexity 17.

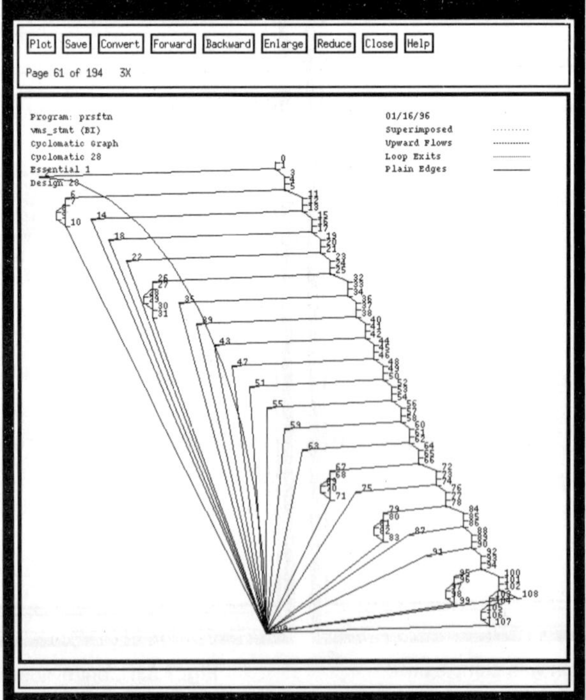

Fig. 7.36: Control flow graph with complexity 28.

One essential ingredient in any testing methodology is to limit the program logic during development so that the program can be understood, and the amount of testing required to verify the logic is not overwhelming. A developer who, ignorant of the implications of complexity, expects to verify a module such as that of Figure 7.35 with a handful of tests is heading for disaster. The size of the module in Figure 7.35 is only 30 lines of source code. The size of several of the previous graphs exceeded 60 lines, for example the 282-line module in Figure 7.28. In practice, large programs often have low complexity and small programs often have high complexity. Therefore, the common practice of attempting to limit complexity by controlling only how many lines a module will occupy is entirely inadequate. Limiting complexity directly is a better alternative.

7.15.4 Simplified Complexity Calculation

Applying the e - n + 2 formula by hand is tedious and error-prone. Fortunately, there are several easier ways to calculate complexity in practice, ranging from counting decision predicates to using an automated tool.

(1) Counting Predicates

If all decisions are binary and there are p binary decision predicates, v(G) = p + 1. A binary decision predicate appears on the control flow graph as a node with exactly two edges flowing out of it. Starting with one and adding the number of such nodes yields the complexity. This formula is a simple consequence of the complexity definition. A straight-line control flow graph, which has exactly one edge flowing out of each node except the module exit node, has complexity one. Each node with two edges out of it adds one to complexity, since the "e" in the e - n + 2 formula is increased by one while the "n" is unchanged. In Figure 7.37, there are three binary decision nodes (1, 2, and 6), so complexity is 4 by direct application of the p + 1 formula. The original e - n + 2 gives the same answer, albeit with a bit more counting, 12 edges – 10 nodes + 2 = 4. Figure 7.38 has two binary decision predicate nodes (1 and 3), so complexity is 3. Since the decisions in Figure 7.38 come from loops, they are represented differently on the control flow graph, but the same counting technique applies.

Multiway decisions can be handled by the same reasoning as binary decisions, although there is not such a neat formula. As in the p + 1 formula for binary predicates, start with a complexity value of one and add something to it for each decision node in the control flow graph. The number added is one less than the number of edges out of the decision node. Note that for binary decisions, this number is one, which is consistent with the p + 1 formula. For a three-way decision, add two, and so on. In Figure 7.39, there is a four-way decision, which adds three to complexity, as well as three binary decisions, each of which adds one. Since the module started with one unit of complexity, the calculated complexity becomes 1 + 3 + 3, for a total of 7.

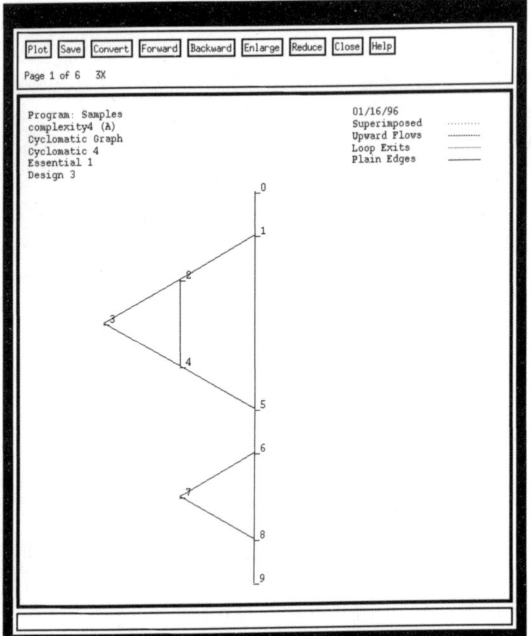

Fig. 7.37: Module with complexity four.

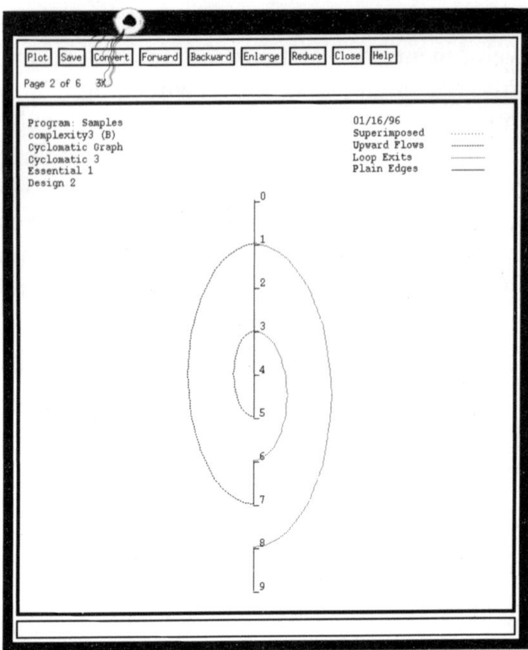

Fig. 7.38: Module with complexity three.

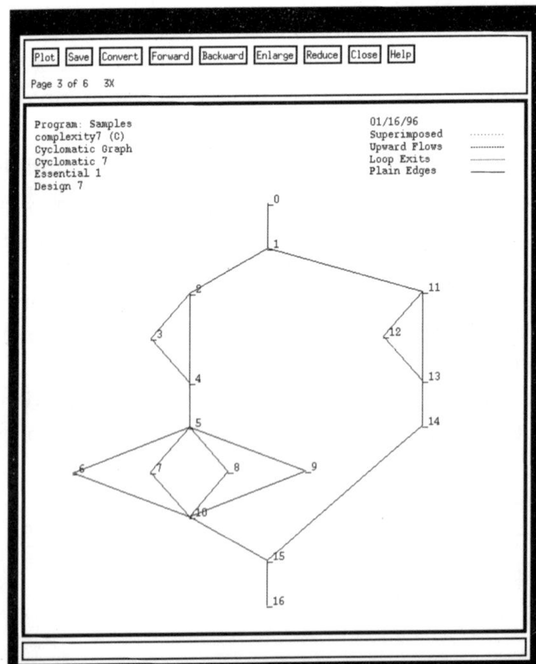

Fig. 7.39: Module with complexity 7.

In addition to counting predicates from the flow graph, it is possible to count them directly from the source code. This often provides the easiest way to measure and control complexity during development, since complexity can be measured even before the module is complete. For most programming language constructs, the construct has a direct mapping to the control flow graph, and hence contributes a fixed amount to complexity. However, constructs that appear similar in different languages may not have identical control flow semantics, so caution is advised. For most constructs, the impact is easy to assess. An "if" statement, "while" statement, and so on are binary decisions, and therefore add one to complexity. Boolean operators add either one or nothing to complexity, depending on whether they have short-circuit evaluation semantics that can lead to conditional execution of side-effects. For example, the C "&&" operator adds one to complexity, as does the Ada "and then" operator, because both are defined to use short-circuit evaluation. The Ada "and" operator, on the other hand, does not add to complexity, because it is defined to use the full-evaluation strategy, and therefore does not generate a decision node in the control flow graph.

Figure 7.40 shows a C code module with complexity 6. Starting with 1, each of the two "if" statements add 1, the "while" statement adds 1, and each of the two "&&" operators adds 1, for a total of 6. For reference, Figure 7.41 shows the control flow graph corresponding to Figure 7.40.

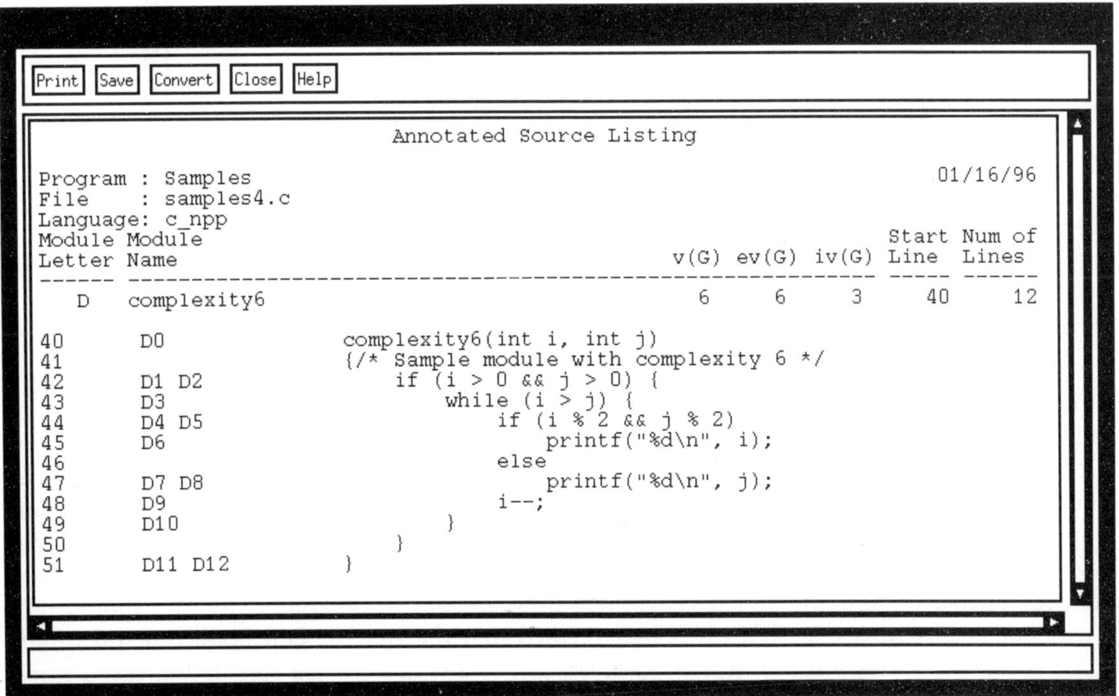

Fig. 7.40: Code for module with complexity 6.

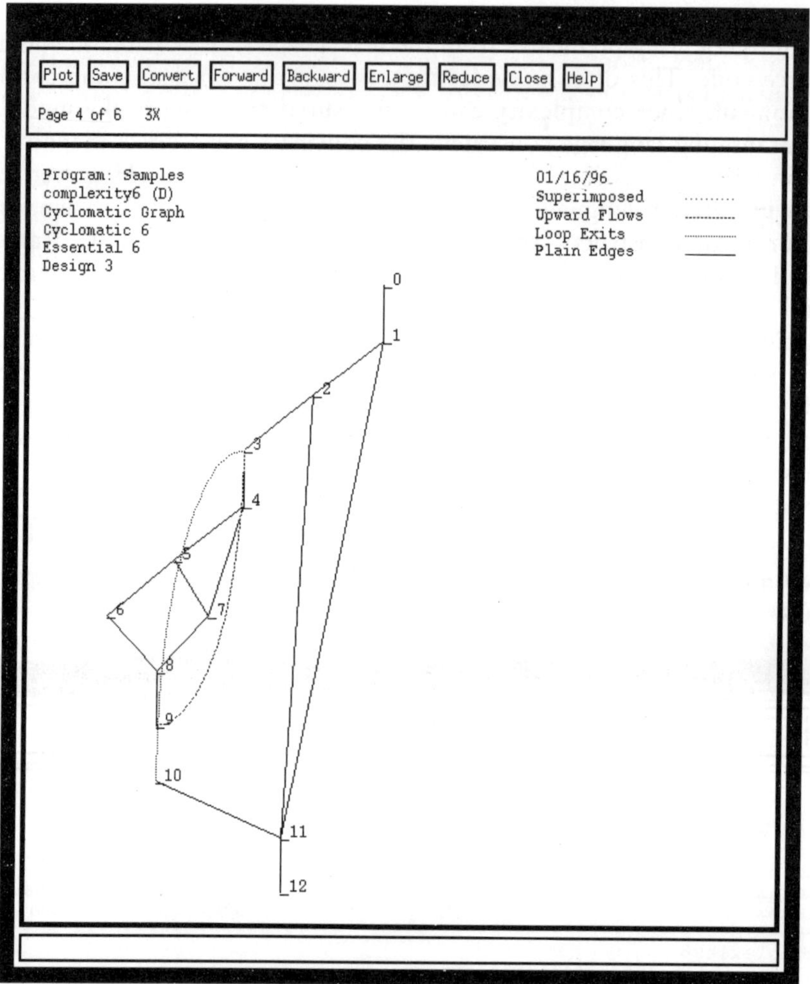

Fig. 7.41: Graph for module with complexity 6.

It is possible, under special circumstances, to generate control flow graphs that do not model the execution semantics of boolean operators in a language. This is known as "suppressing" short-circuit operators or "expanding" full-evaluating operators. When this is done, it is important to understand the implications on the meaning of the metric. For example, flow graphs based on suppressed boolean operators in C can give a good high-level view of control flow for reverse engineering purposes by hiding the details of the encapsulated and often unstructured expression-level control flow. However, this representation should not be used for testing (unless perhaps it is first verified that the short-circuit boolean expressions do not contain any side effects). In any case, the important thing when calculating complexity from source code is to be consistent with the interpretation of language constructs in the flow graph.

Multiway decision constructs present a couple of issues when calculating complexity from source code. As with boolean operators, consideration of the control flow graph representation of the relevant language constructs is the key to successful complexity measurement of source code. An implicit default or fall-through branch, if specified by the language, must be taken into account when calculating complexity. For example, in C there is an implicit default if no default outcome is specified. In that case, the complexity contribution of the "switch" statement is exactly the number of case-labeled statements, which is one less than the total number of edges out of the multiway decision node in the control flow graph. A less frequently occurring issue that has greater impact on complexity is the distinction between "case-labeled statements" and "case labels". When several case labels apply to the same program statement, this is modeled as a single decision outcome edge in the control flow graph, adding one to complexity. It is certainly possible to make a consistent flow graph model in which each individual case label contributes a different decision outcome edge and hence also adds one to complexity, but that is not the typical usage.

Figure 7.42 shows a C code module with complexity 5. Starting with one unit of complexity, the switch statement has three case-labeled statements (although having five total case labels), which, considering the implicit default fall-through, is a four-way decision that contributes three units of complexity. The "if" statement contributes one unit, for a total complexity of five. For reference, Figure 7.43 shows the control flow graph corresponding to Figure 7.42.

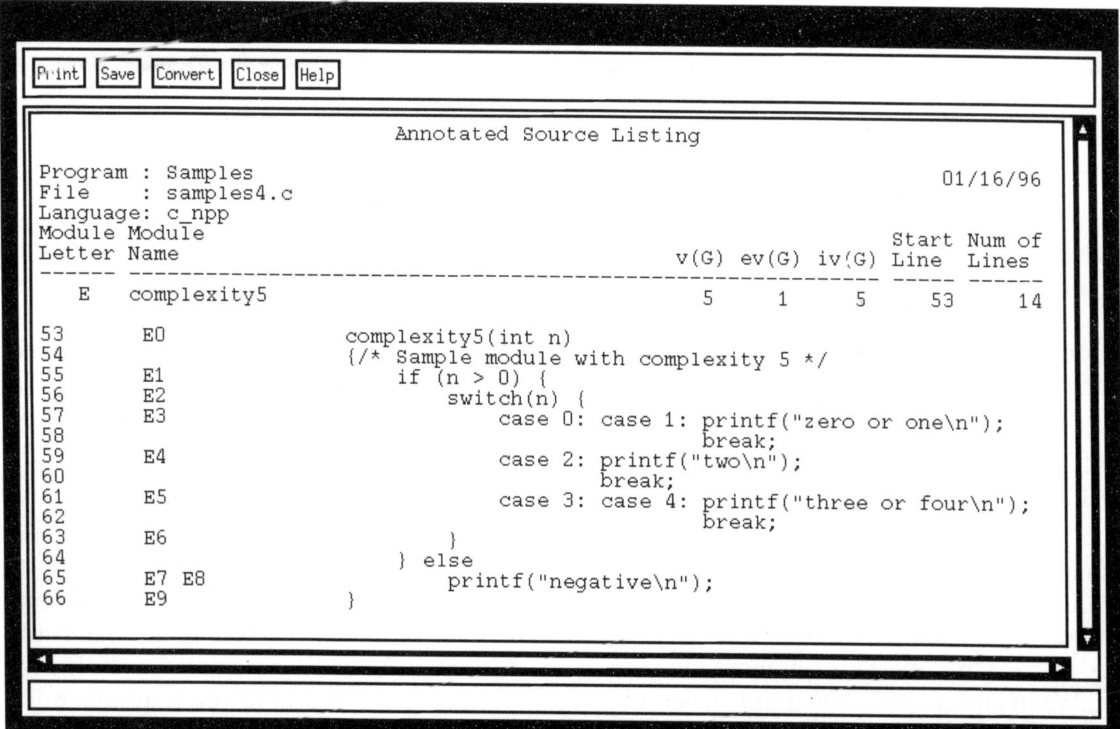

Fig. 7.42: Code for module with complexity 5.

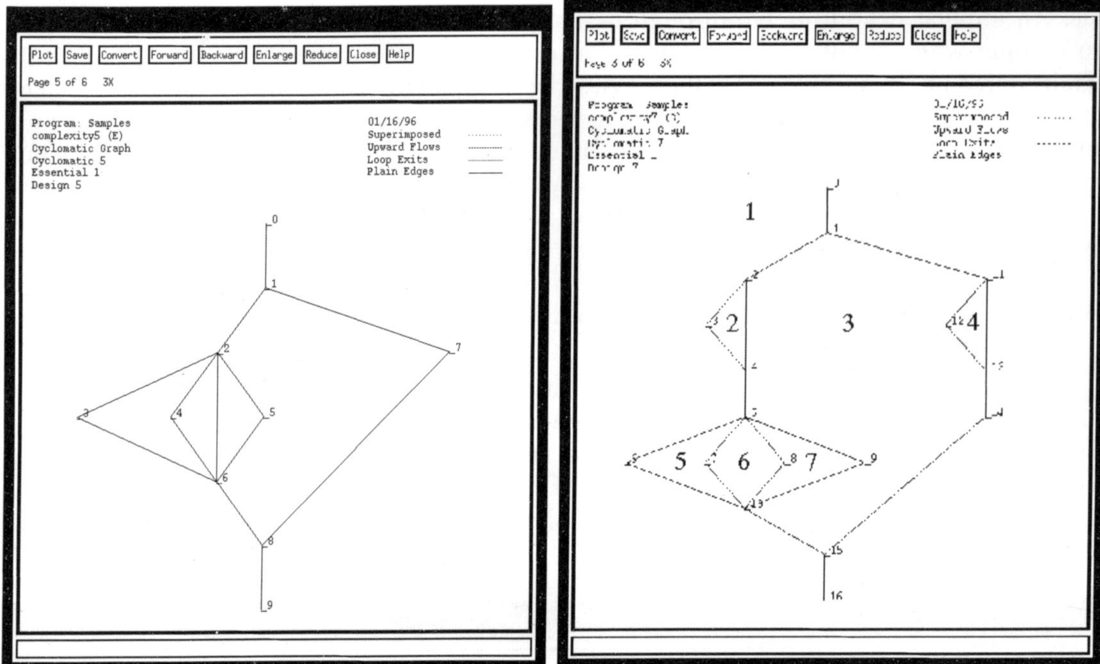

Fig. 7.43: Graph for module with complexity 5.

Fig. 7.44: Planar graph with complexity 7, regions numbered.

(2) Counting flow graph regions

When the flow graph is planar (no edges cross) and divides the plane into R regions (including the infinite region "outside" the graph), the simplified formula for cyclomatic complexity is just R. This follows from Euler's formula, which states that for planar graphs `n - e + R = 2`. Re-arranging the terms, `R = e - n + 2`, which is the definition of cyclomatic complexity. Thus, for a planar flow graph, counting the regions gives a quick visual method for determining complexity. Figure 7.44 shows a planar flow graph with complexity 7, with the regions numbered from 1 to 7 to illustrate this counting technique. Region number 1 is the infinite region, and otherwise the regions are labeled in no particular order.

7.15.5 Use of Automated Tools

The most efficient and reliable way to determine complexity is through use of an automated tool. Even calculating by hand the complexity of a single module such as that of Figure 7.46 is a daunting prospect, and such modules often come in large groups. With an automated tool, complexity can be determined for hundreds of modules spanning thousands of lines of code in a matter of minutes. When dealing with existing code, automated complexity calculation and control flow graph generation is an enabling technology. However, automation is not a panacea.

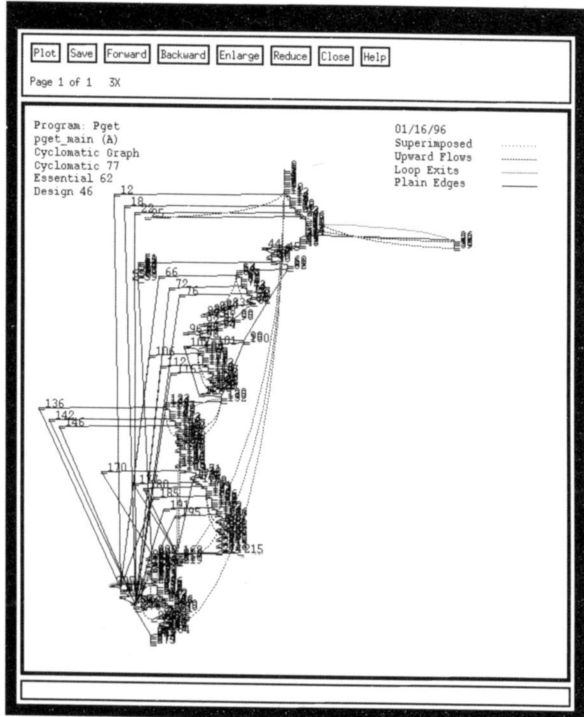

Fig. 7.45: Module with complexity 77.

The feedback from an automated tool may come too late for effective development of new software. Once the code for a software module (or file, or subsystem) is finished and processed by automated tools, reworking it to reduce complexity is more costly and error-prone than developing the module with complexity in mind from the outset. Awareness of manual techniques for complexity analysis helps design and build good software, rather than deferring complexity-related issues to a later phase of the life cycle. Automated tools are an effective way to confirm and control complexity, but they work best where at least rough estimates of complexity are used during development. In some cases, such as Ada development, designs can be represented and analyzed in the target programming language.

7.16 Structured Testing

Structured testing uses cyclomatic complexity and the mathematical analysis of control flow graphs to guide the testing process. Structured testing is more theoretically rigorous and more effective at detecting errors in practice than other common test coverage criteria such as statement and branch coverage. Structured testing is, therefore, suitable when reliability is an important consideration for software. It is not intended as a substitute for requirements-based "black-box" testing techniques, but as a supplement to them. Structured testing forms the "white-box," or code-based, part of a comprehensive testing program, which when quality is critical will also include requirements-based testing, testing in a simulated production environment, and possibly other techniques such as statistical random testing. Other "white-box" techniques may also be used, depending on specific requirements for the software being tested. Structured testing as presented in this section applies to individual software modules, where the most rigorous code-based "unit testing" is typically performed. The integration level Structured testing technique is described in section 7.20.

7.16.1 The Structured Testing Criterion

After the mathematical preliminaries of section 7.14 and especially 7.15 the structured testing criterion is simply stated: Test a basis set of paths through the control flow graph of each module. This means that any additional path through the module's control flow graph can be expressed as a linear combination of paths that have been tested.

Note that the structured testing criterion measures the quality of testing, providing a way to determine whether testing is complete. It is not a procedure to identify test cases or generate test data inputs. Section 6 gives a technique for generating test cases that satisfy the structured testing criterion.

Sometimes, it is not possible to test a complete basis set of paths through the control flow graph of a module. This happens when some paths through the module cannot be exercised by any input data. For example, if the module makes the same exact decision twice in sequence, no input data will cause it to vary the first decision outcome while leaving the second constant or vice versa.

A program with cyclomatic complexity 5 has the property that no set of 4 paths will suffice for testing, even if, for example, there are 39 distinct tests that concentrate on the 4 paths. As discussed earlier, the cyclomatic complexity gives the number of paths in any basis set. This means that if only 4 paths have been tested for the complexity 5 module, there must be, independent of the programming language or the computational statements of the program, at least one additional test path that can be executed. Also, once a fifth independent path is tested, any further paths are in a fundamental sense redundant, in that a combination of 5 basis paths will generate those further paths.

Notice that most programs with a loop have a potentially infinite number of paths, which are not subject to exhaustive testing even in theory. The structured testing criterion establishes a complexity number, v(G), of test paths that have two critical properties:

1. A test set of v(G) paths can be realized.
2. Testing beyond v(G) independent paths is redundantly exercising linear combinations of basis paths.

Several studies have shown that the distribution of run time over the statements in the program has a peculiar shape. Typically, 50% of the run time within a program is concentrated within only 4% of the code. When the test data is derived from only a requirements point of view and is not sensitive to the internal structure of the program, it likewise will spend most of the run time testing a few statements over and over again. The testing criterion in this document establishes a level of testing that is inherently related to the internal complexity of a program's logic. One of the effects of this is to distribute the test data over a larger number of independent paths, which can provide more effective testing with fewer tests. For very simple programs (complexity less than 5), other testing techniques seem likely to exercise a basis set of paths. However, for more realistic complexity levels, other techniques are not likely to exercise a basis set of paths. Explicitly satisfying the structured testing criterion will then yield a more rigorous set of test data.

7.16.2 Intuition Behind Structured Testing

The solid mathematical foundation of structured testing has many advantages. First of all, since any basis set of paths covers all edges and nodes of the control flow graph, satisfying the structured testing criterion automatically satisfies the weaker branch and statement testing criteria. Technically, structured testing subsumes branch and statement coverage testing. This means that any benefit in software reliability gained by statement and branch coverage testing is automatically shared by structured testing.

Next, with structured testing, testing is proportional to complexity. Specifically, the minimum number of tests required to satisfy the structured testing criterion is exactly the cyclomatic complexity. Given the correlation between complexity and errors, it makes sense to concentrate testing effort on the most complex and therefore error-prone software. Structured testing makes this notion mathematically precise. Statement and branch coverage testing do not even come close to sharing this property. All statements and branches of an arbitrarily complex module can be covered with just one test, even though another module with the same complexity may require thousands of tests using the same criterion. For example, a loop enclosing arbitrarily complex code can just be iterated as many times as necessary for coverage, whereas complex code with no loops may require separate tests for each decision outcome. With structured testing, any path, no matter how much of the module it covers, can contribute at most one element to the required basis set. Additionally, since the minimum required number of tests is known in advance, structured testing supports objective planning and monitoring of the testing process to a greater extent than other testing strategies.

Another strength of structured testing is that, for the precise mathematical interpretation of "independent" as "linearly independent", structured testing guarantees that all decision outcomes are tested independently. This means that unlike other common testing strategies, structured testing does not allow interactions between decision outcomes during testing to hide errors.

As a very simple example, consider the C function of Figure 7.46. Assume that this function is intended to leave the value of variable "a" unchanged under all circumstances, and is thus clearly incorrect. The branch testing criterion can be satisfied with two tests that fail to detect the error: first let both decision outcomes be FALSE, in which case the value of "a" is not affected, and then let both decision outcomes be TRUE, in which case the value of "a" is first incremented and then decremented, ending up with its original value. The statement testing criterion can be satisfied with just the second of those two tests. Structured testing, on the other hand, is guaranteed to detect this error. Since cyclomatic complexity is three, three independent test paths are required, so at least one will set one decision outcome to TRUE and the other to FALSE, leaving "a" either incremented or decremented and therefore detecting the error during testing.

```
void func()
   {
      if (condition1)
      a = a + 1;
      if (condition2)
      a = a - 1;
   }
```

Fig. 7.46: Example C function.

7.16.3 Complexity and Reliability

Reliability is a combination of testing and understanding. In theory, either perfect testing (verify program behavior for every possible sequence of input) or perfect understanding (build a completely accurate mental model of the program so that any errors would be obvious) are sufficient by themselves to ensure reliability. Given that a piece of software has no known errors, its perceived reliability depends both on how well it has been tested and how well it is understood. In effect, the subjective reliability of software is expressed in statements such as "I understand this program well enough to know that the tests I have executed are adequate to provide my desired level of confidence in the software." Since complexity makes software both harder to test and harder to understand, complexity is intimately tied to reliability. From one perspective, complexity measures the effort necessary to attain a given level of reliability. Given a fixed level of effort, a typical case in the real world of budgets and schedules, complexity measures reliability itself.

7.16.4 Structured Testing Example

As an example of structured testing, consider the C module "count" in Figure 7.47. Given a string, it is intended to return the total number of occurrences of the letter 'C' if the string begins with the letter 'A'. Otherwise, it is supposed to return -1.

The error in the "count" module is that the count is incorrect for strings that begin with the letter 'A' and in which the number of occurrences of 'B' is not equal to the number of occurrences of 'C'. This is because the module is really counting 'B's rather than 'C's. It could be fixed by exchanging the bodies of the "if" statements that recognize 'B' and 'C'. Figure 7.48 shows the control flow graph for module "count".

```
[Print] [Save] [Convert] [Close] [Help]

                        Annotated Source Listing

Program : Count                                                    01/18/96
File    : stex.c
Language: c_npp
Module Module                                                 Start Num of
Letter Name                             v(G) ev(G) iv(G)  Line  Lines
------ ------------------------------------------------ ----- ------
  A    count                               5     5     1     3     30

        A0             int count(string)
                       char *string;
                       { /* This module is incorrect.  Its specification is:
                          * If string begins with 'A' (eg "ABXCCZBZ") then
                          * return the number of  occurrences of 'C' (eg 2),
                          * otherwise return -1.
                          */
                          int index = 0, i = 0, j = 0, k = 0;
        A1                if (string[index] == 'A') {
        A2             L1:        index - index + 1;
        A3                        if (string[index] == 'B') {
        A4                            j = j + 1;
                                      k = 0;
        A5                            goto L1;
                                  }
        A6 A7                     if (string[index] == 'C') {
        A8                            i = i + j;
                                      k = k + 1;
                                      j = 0;
        A9                            goto L1;
                                  }
        A10                       i = i + j;
        A11                       if (string[index] != '\0') {
        A12                           j = 0;
        A13                           goto L1;
                                  }
        A14                   } else
        A15 A16                   i = -1;
                          return i;
        A17            }
```

Fig. 7.47: Code for module "count."

The "count" module illustrates the effectiveness of structured testing. The commonly used statement and branch coverage testing criteria can both be satisfied with the two tests in Figure 7.49, none of which detect the error. Since the complexity of "count" is five, it is immediately apparent that the tests of Figure 7.49 do not satisfy the structured testing criterion—three additional tests are needed to test each decision independently. Figure 7.50 shows a set of tests that satisfies the structured testing criterion, which consists of the three tests from Figure 7.49 plus two additional tests to form a complete basis=20

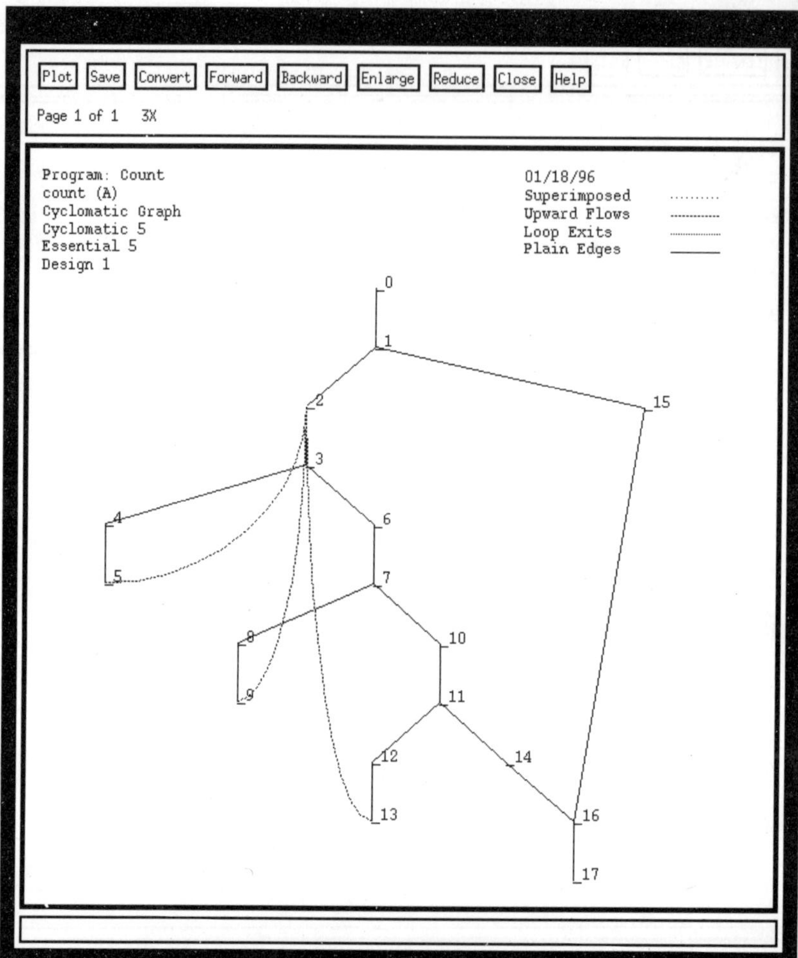

Fig. 7.48: Control flow graph for module "count".

Input	Output	Correctness
X	-1	Correct
ABCX	1	Correct

Fig.7.49: Tests for "count" that satisfy statement and branch coverage

Input	Output	Correctness
X	-1	Correct
ABCX	1	Correct
A	0	Correct
AB	1	Incorrect
AC	0	Incorrect

Fig. 7.50: Tests for "count" that satisfy the structured testing criterion.

The set of tests in Figure 7.50 detects the error (twice). Input "AB" should produce output "0" but instead produces output "1", and input "AC" should produce output "1" but instead produces output "0". In fact, any set of tests that satisfies the structured testing criterion is guaranteed to detect the error. To see this, note that to test the decisions at nodes 3 and 7 independently requires at least one input with a different number of `B's than 'C's.

7.17 Weak Structured Testing

Weak structured testing is, as it appears, a weak variant of structured testing. It can be satisfied by exercising at least v(G) different paths through the control flow graph while simultaneously covering all branches, however the requirement that the paths form a basis is dropped. Structured testing subsumes weak structured testing, but not the reverse. Weak structured testing is much easier to perform manually than structured testing, because there is no need to do linear algebra on path vectors. Thus, weak structured testing was a way to get some of the benefits of structured testing at a significantly lesser cost before automated support for structured testing was available, and is still worth considering for programming languages with no automated structured testing support. In some older literature, no distinction is made between the two criteria.

Of the three properties of structured testing discussed in section 7.16.2 two are shared by weak structured testing. It subsumes statement and branch coverage, which provides a base level of error detection effectiveness. It also requires testing proportional to complexity, which concentrates testing on the most error-prone software and supports precise test planning and monitoring. However, it does not require all decision outcomes to be tested independently, and thus may not detect errors based on interactions between decisions. Therefore, it should only be used when structured testing itself is impractical.

7.18 Integration Strategies

One of the most significant aspects of a software development project is the integration strategy. Integration may be performed all at once, top-down, bottom-up, critical piece first, or by first integrating functional subsystems and then integrating the subsystems in separate phases using any of the basic strategies. In general, the larger the project, the more important the integration strategy.

Very small systems are often assembled and tested in one phase. For most real systems, this is impractical for two major reasons. First, the system would fail in so many places at once that the debugging and retesting effort would be impractical. Second, satisfying any white-box testing criterion would be very difficult, because of the vast amount of detail separating the input data from the individual code modules. In fact, most integration testing has been traditionally limited to "black-box" techniques. Large systems may require many integration phases, beginning with assembling modules into low-level subsystems, then assembling subsystems into larger subsystems, and finally assembling the highest level subsystems into the complete system.

To be most effective, an integration testing technique should fit well with the overall integration strategy. In a multi-phase integration, testing at each phase helps detect errors early and keep the system under control. Performing only cursory testing at early integration phases and then applying a more rigorous criterion for the final stage is really just a variant of the high-risk "big bang" approach. However, performing rigorous testing of the entire software involved in each integration phase involves a lot of wasteful duplication of effort across phases. The key is to leverage the overall integration structure to allow rigorous testing at each phase while minimizing duplication of effort.

It is important to understand the relationship between module testing and integration testing. In one view, modules are rigorously tested in isolation using stubs and drivers before any integration is attempted. Then, integration testing concentrates entirely on module interactions, assuming that the details within each module are accurate. At the other extreme, module and integration testing can be combined, verifying the details of each module's implementation in an integration context. Many projects compromise, combining module testing with the lowest level of subsystem integration testing, and then performing pure integration testing at higher levels. Each of these views of integration testing may be appropriate for any given project, so an integration testing method should be flexible enough to accommodate them all. The rest of this section describes the integration-level structured testing techniques, first for some special cases and then in full generality.

7.19 Combining Module Testing and Integration Testing

The simplest application of structured testing to integration is to combine module testing with integration testing so that a basis set of paths through each module is executed in an integration context. This means that the techniques of sections 7.16 and 7.17 can be used without modification to measure the level of testing. However, this method is only suitable for a subset of integration strategies.

The most obvious combined strategy is pure "big bang" integration, in which the entire system is assembled and tested in one step without even prior module testing. As discussed earlier, this strategy is not practical for most real systems. However, at least in theory, it makes efficient use of testing resources. First, there is no overhead associated with constructing stubs and drivers to perform module testing or partial integration. Second, no additional integration-specific tests are required beyond the module tests as determined by structured testing. Thus, despite its impracticality, this strategy clarifies the benefits of combining module testing with integration testing to the greatest feasible extent.

It is also possible to combine module and integration testing with the bottom-up integration strategy. In this strategy, using test drivers but not stubs, begin by performing module-level structured testing on the lowest-level modules using test drivers. Then, perform module-level structured testing in a similar fashion at each successive level of the design hierarchy, using test drivers for each new module being tested in integration with all lower-level modules. Figure 7.51 illustrates the technique. First, the lowest-level modules "B" and "C" are tested with drivers. Next, the higher-level module "A" is tested with a driver in integration with modules "B" and "C". Finally, integration could continue until the top-level module of the program is tested (with real input data) in integration with the entire program. As shown in Figure 7.51, the total number of tests required by this technique is the sum of the cyclomatic complexities of all modules being integrated. As expected, this is the same number of tests that would be required to perform structured testing on each module in isolation using stubs and drivers.

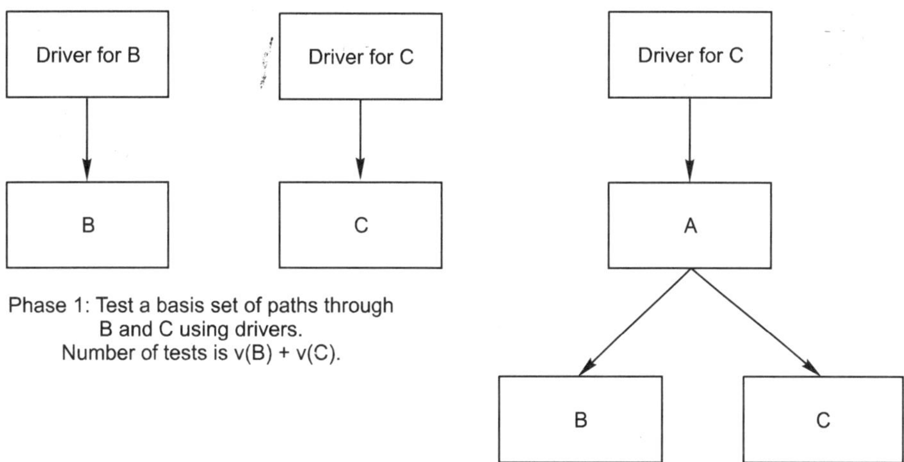

Fig. 7.51: Combining module testing with bottom-up integration.

7.20 Generalization of Module Testing Criteria

Module testing criteria can often be generalized in several possible ways to support integration testing. As discussed in the previous subsection, the most obvious generalization is to satisfy the module testing criterion in an integration context, in effect using the entire program as a test driver environment for each module. However, this trivial kind of generalization does not take advantage of the differences between module and integration testing. Applying it to each phase of a multi-phase integration strategy, for example, leads to an excessive amount of redundant testing.

More useful generalizations adapt the module testing criterion to focus on interactions between modules rather than attempting to test all of the details of each module's implementation in an integration context. The statement coverage module testing criterion, in which each statement is required to be exercised during module testing, can be generalized to require each module call statement to be exercised during integration testing. Although the specifics of the generalization of structured testing are more detailed, the approach is the same. Since structured testing at the module level requires that all the decision logic in a module's control flow graph be tested independently, the appropriate generalization to the integration level requires that just the decision logic involved with calls to other modules be tested independently.

7.21 Module Design Complexity

Rather than testing all decision outcomes within a module independently, structured testing at the integration level focuses on the decision outcomes that are involved with module calls. The design reduction technique helps identify those decision outcomes, so that it is possible to exercise them independently during integration testing. The idea behind design reduction is to start with a module control flow graph, remove all control structures that are not involved with module calls, and then use the resultant "reduced" flow graph to drive integration testing. Figure 7.52 shows a systematic set of rules for performing design reduction. Although not strictly a reduction rule, the call rule states that function call ("black dot") nodes cannot be reduced. The remaining rules work together to eliminate the parts of the flow graph that are not involved with module calls. The sequential rule eliminates sequences of non-call ("white dot") nodes.

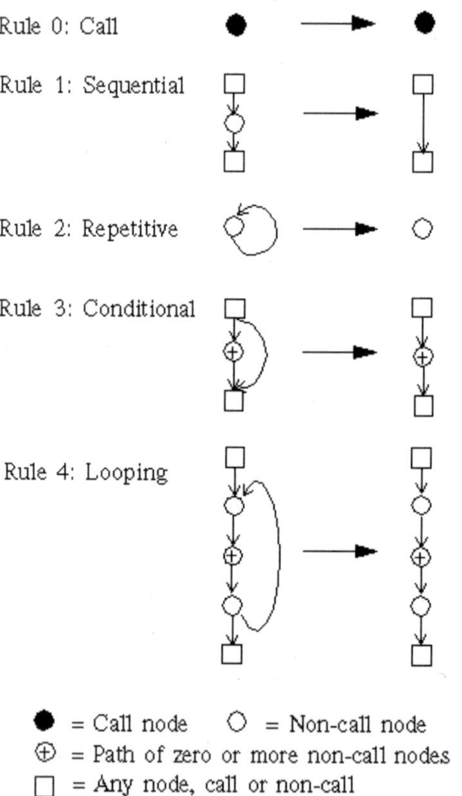

Fig. 7.52: Design reduction rules.

Since application of this rule removes one node and one edge from the flow graph, it leaves the cyclomatic complexity unchanged. However, it does simplify the graph so that the other rules can be applied. The repetitive rule eliminates top-test loops that are not involved with module calls. The conditional rule eliminates conditional statements that do not contain calls in their bodies. The looping rule eliminates bottom-test loops that are not involved with module calls. It is important to preserve the module's connectivity when using the looping rule, since for poorly-structured code it may be hard to distinguish the "top"of the loop from the "bottom". For the rule to apply, there must be a path from the module entry to the top of the loop and a path from the bottom of the loop to the module exit. Since the repetitive, conditional, and looping rules each remove one edge from the flow graph, they each reduce cyclomatic complexity by one.

Rules 1 through 4 are intended to be applied iteratively until none of them can be applied, at which point the design reduction is complete. By this process, even very complex logic can be eliminated as long as it does not involve any module calls.

Figure 7.53 shows a control flow graph before and after design reduction. Rules 3 and 4 can be applied immediately to the original graph, yielding the intermediate graph. Then rule 1 can be applied three-times to the left conditional branch, at which point rule 3 can be applied again, after which five more applications of rule 1 complete the reduction. The second application of rule 3 illustrates that a conditional structure may be eliminated even if its body contains a call node, as long as there is at least one path through its body that does not contain any call nodes.

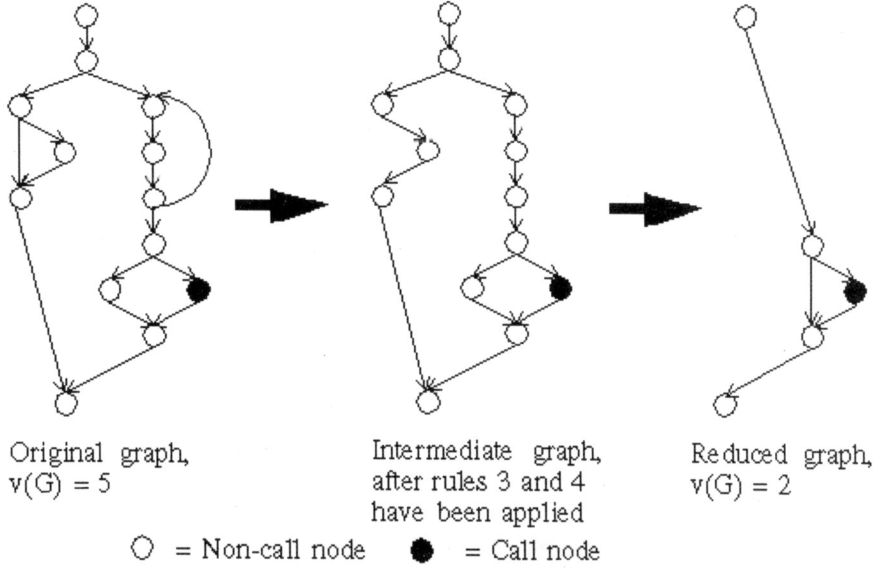

Fig. 7.53: Design reduction example.

The module design complexity, `IV(G)`, is defined as the cyclomatic complexity of the reduced graph after design reduction has been performed. In Figure 7.53, the module design complexity is 2. The design flow graph in Figure 7.54 displays the logic that contributes to module design complexity superimposed on the entire control flow graph for a module with cyclomatic complexity 6 and module design complexity 3.

When structured testing has already been performed at the module level, module design complexity can be used to drive integration testing, requiring a basis set of paths through each module's reduced graph to be tested in integration. For the bottom-up integration strategy discussed in section 7.16, the total number of integration tests becomes the sum of the module design complexities of all modules being integrated. Since module design complexity can be significantly less than cyclomatic complexity, this technique reduces the number of integration tests. It also simplifies the process of deriving data for each test path, since there are fewer constraints on paths through the reduced graph than on paths through the full graph.

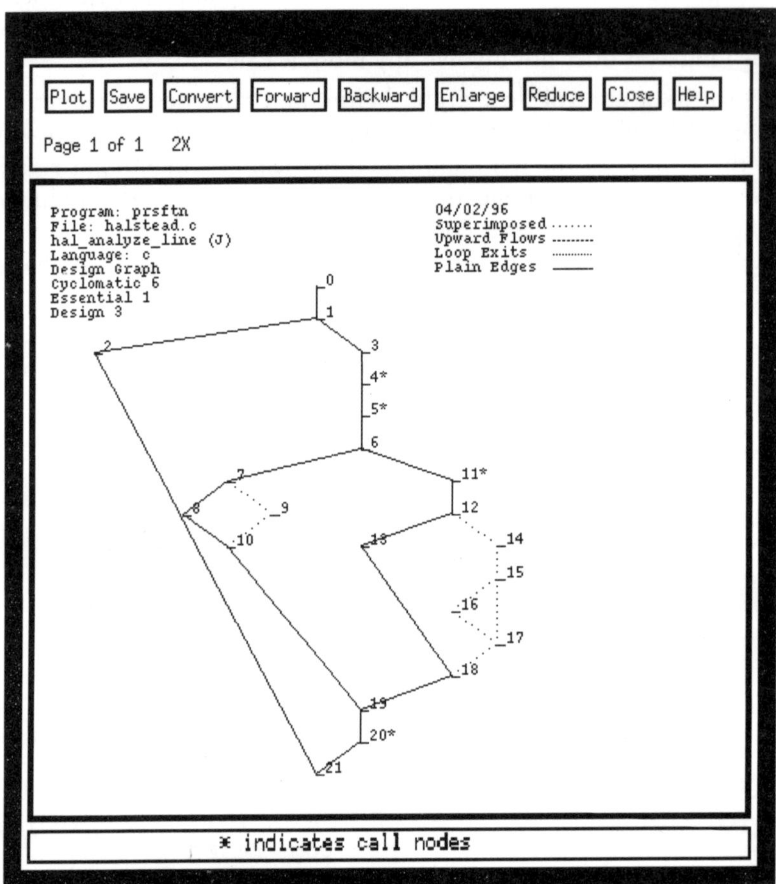

Fig. 7.54: Design graph with v(G) = 6, iv(G) = 3.

7.22 Integration Complexity

The integration complexity, S1, is defined for a program with n modules (G1 through Gn) by the formula: S1 = (SUM iv(Gi)) – n + 1. Integration complexity measures the number of independent integration tests through an entire program's design. To understand the formula, recall the baseline method of section 6 for generating a set of independent tests through an individual module. The analogous integration-level method generates a set of independent tests through the program's design. Begin with a baseline test, which contributes 1 to the S1 formula and exercises one path through the program's main module. Then, make each successive test exercise exactly one new decision outcome in exactly one module's design-reduced graph. Since the first "mini-baseline" path through each module comes as a result of exercising a path in a higher-level module (except for the main module, which gets its first path from the baseline test), each module contributes a number of new integration tests equal to one less than its module design complexity, for a total contribution of SUM (iv(Gi) - 1), which (since there are n modules) equals (SUM iv(Gi)) - n. Adding the 1 for the baseline test gives the full S1 formula.

A similar argument shows that substituting v(G) for iv(G) in the S1 formula gives the number of tests necessary to test every decision outcome in the entire program independently.

Figure 7.55 shows an example program with integration complexity 4, giving the control structure, cyclomatic complexity, and module design complexity for each module and a set of four independent integration tests.

Although a basis set of paths through each module's design-reduced control flow graph can typically be exercised with fewer than S1 integration tests, more tests are never required. For the most rigorous level of structured testing, a complete basis set of S1 integration tests should be performed.

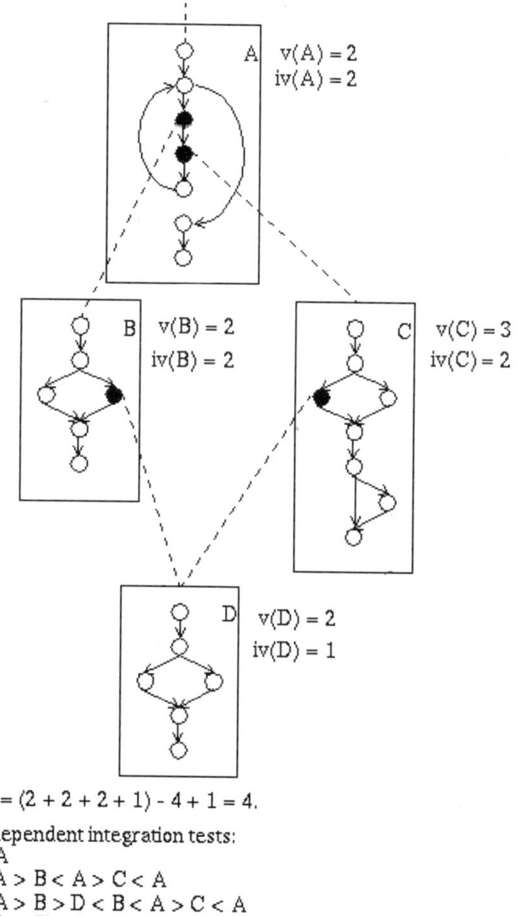

Fig. 7.55: Integration complexity example.

Integration complexity can be approximated from a structured design allowing integration test effort to be predicted before coding begins. The number of design predicates in a structure chart (conditional and iterative calls) can be used to approximate the eventual integration complexity. Recall the simplified formula for cyclomatic complexity from section 4.1, that for modules with only binary decisions and p decision predicates, v(G) = p + 1. The corresponding formula for integration complexity is that for programs with d design predicates, S1 will be approximately 7.14 and 7.15. The reason is that each design predicate (conditional or iterative call) tends to be implemented by a decision predicate in the design-reduced graph of a module in the eventual implemented program. Hence, recalling that iv(G) is the cyclomatic complexity of the design-reduced graph, combine the v(G) and S1 formulas to calculate the approximation that S1 = SUM iv(G) - n + 1 = SUM (iv(G) - 1) + 1 = SUM (v(GReduced) - 1) + 1 = d + 1, where d is the total number of decision predicates in the design-reduced graphs of the modules of the implemented program, and approximately equal to the number of design predicates in the original program design. Figure 7.56 shows a structured design representation with three design predicates and therefore an expected integration complexity of four.

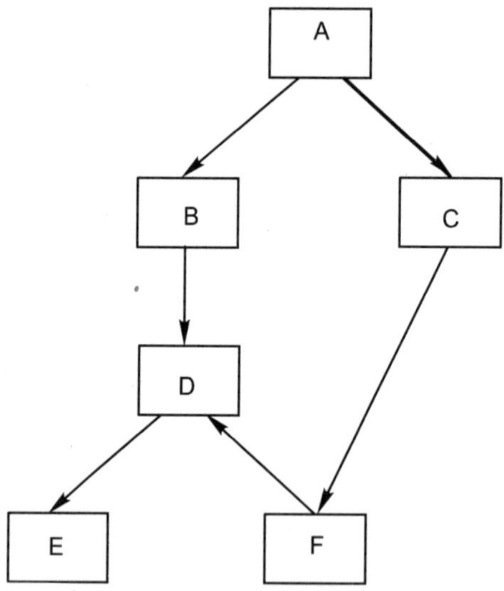

Fig. 7.56: Predicting integration complexity.

7.23 Incremental Integration

Hierarchical system design limits each stage of development to a manageable effort, and it is important to limit the corresponding stages of testing as well [WATSON5]. Hierarchical design is most effective when the coupling among sibling components decreases as the component size increases, which simplifies the derivation of data sets that test interactions among components. The remainder of this section extends the integration testing techniques of structured testing to handle the general case of incremental integration, including support for hierarchical design. The key principle is to test just the interaction among components at each integration stage, avoiding redundant testing of previously integrated sub-components.

As a simple example of the approach, recall the statement coverage module testing criterion and its integration-level variant from section 7.19 that all module call statements should be exercised during integration. Although this criterion is certainly not as rigorous as structured testing, its simplicity makes it easy to extend to support incremental integration. Although the generalization of structured testing is more detailed, the basic approach is the same. To extend statement coverage to support incremental integration, it is required that all module call statements from one component into a different component be exercised at each integration stage. To form a completely flexible "statement testing" criterion, it is required that each statement be executed during the first phase (which may be anything from single modules to the entire program), and that at each integration phase all call statements that cross the boundaries of previously integrated components are tested. Given hierarchical integration stages with good cohesive partitioning properties, this limits the testing effort to a small fraction of the effort to cover each statement of the system at each integration phase.

Structured testing can be extended to cover the fully general case of incremental integration in a similar manner. The key is to perform design reduction at each integration phase using just the module call nodes that cross component boundaries, yielding component-reduced graphs, and exclude from consideration all modules that do not contain any cross-component calls. Integration tests are derived from the reduced graphs using the techniques of sections 7.21 and 7.22. The complete testing method is to test a basis set of paths through each module at the first phase (which can be either single modules, subsystems, or the entire program, depending on the underlying integration strategy), and then test a basis set of paths through each component-reduced graph at each successive integration phase. As discussed in section 7.22, the most rigorous approach is to execute a complete basis set of component integration tests at each stage. However, for incremental integration, the integration complexity formula may not give the precise number of independent tests. The reason is that the modules with cross-component calls may not be connected in the design structure, so it is not necessarily the case that one path through each module is a result of exercising a path in its caller. However, at most one additional test per module is required, so using the S1 formula still gives a reasonable approximation to the testing effort at each phase.

Figure 7.57 illustrates the structured testing approach to incremental integration. Modules A and C have been previously integrated, as have modules B and D. It would take three tests to integrate this system in a single phase. However, since the design predicate decision to call module D from module B has been tested in a previous phase, only two additional tests are required to complete the integration testing. Modules B and D are removed from consideration because they do not contain cross-component calls, the component module design complexity of module A is 1, and the component module design complexity of module C is 2.

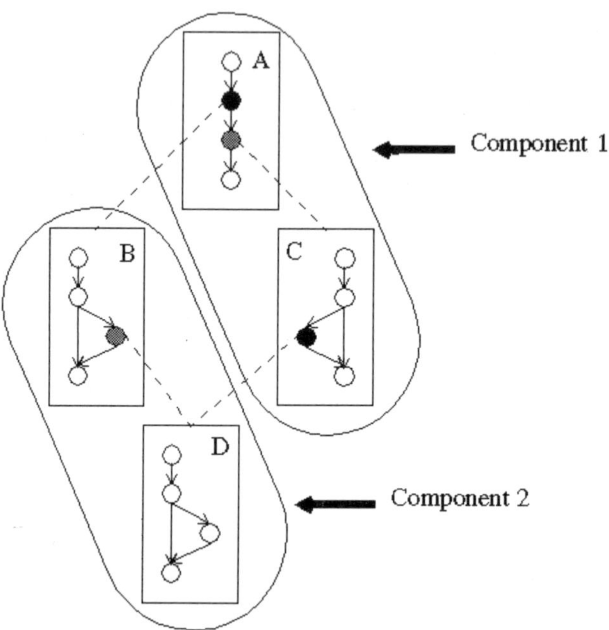

Independent component integration tests:
Test 1: A > B < A > C < A
Test 2: A > B < A > C > D < C < A
("X > Y < X" means "X calls Y which returns to X.")

○ = non-call node
● = cross-component call node
◉ = call node within a component

Fig. 7.57: Structured testing approach to incremental integration

7.24 Cyclomatic Complexity Metrics

Metrics are used in business model, CMMI, ISM3 and knowledge management. These measurements or metrics can be used to track trends, productivity, resources and much more. Typically, the metrics tracked are key performance indicators.

A software metric is a measure of some property of a piece of software or its specifications.

Since quantitative methods have proved so powerful in the other sciences, computer science practitioners and theoreticians have worked hard to bring similar approaches to software development

Cyclomatic complexity is a software metric (measurement) in computational complexity theory. It was developed by Thomas McCabe and is used to measure the complexity of a program. It directly measures the number of linearly independent paths through a program's source code.

The concept, although not the method, is somewhat similar to that of general text complexity measured by the Flesch-Kincaid Readability Test.

Cyclomatic complexity is computed using a graph that describes the control flow of the program. The nodes of the graph correspond to the commands of a program. A directed edge connects two nodes if the second command might be executed immediately after the first command.

Definition

$M = E - N + P$

where

M = cyclomatic complexity

E = the number of edges of the graph

N = the number of nodes of the graph

P = the number of connected components.

"M" is alternatively defined to be one larger than the number of decision points (IFs, UNTILs, ENDs...) in a module (function, procedure, chart node, etc.), or more generally a system.

Alternative definition

$v(G) = e - n + 2$

G is a program's flowgraph

e is the number of arcs in the flowgraph

n is the number of nodes in the flowgraph

Alternative way

There is another simple way to determine the cyclomatic number. This is done by counting the number of closed loops in the flow graph, and incrementing that number by one.

i.e.

M = Number of closed loops + 1

where

M = Cyclomatic number.

Note that there should be at least M test cases for testing the particular flow graph. This is the bare-minimum necessity to test the flow graph.

Key Concept

McCabe's rule of thumb is that "modules" with M of ten or more are error-prone. CASE structures are an exception. Due to their structure, they can have more than ten decisions without increasing the likelihood of errors.

The cyclomatic complexity of a section of source code is the count of the number of paths through the source code. For instance if the source code contained no decision points such as IF statements or FOR loops, the complexity would be 1 since there is only a single path through the code. If the code had a single IF statement there would be two paths through the code, one path where the IF statement is evaluated as TRUE and one path where the IF statement is evaluated as FALSE.

Cyclomatic complexity is normally calculated by creating a graph of the source code with each line of source code being a node on the graph and arrows between the nodes showing the execution pathways. As some programming languages can be quite terse and compact, a source code statement when developing the graph may actually create several nodes in the graph [for instance when using the C and C++ language "?" conditional operator (also known as the "ternary operator") within a function call interface].

In general, in order to fully test a module all execution paths through the module should be exercised. This implies a module with a high complexity number requires more testing effort than a module with a lower value since the higher complexity number indicates more pathways through the code. This also implies that a module with higher complexity is more difficult for a programmer to understand since the programmer must understand the different pathways and the results of those pathways.

One would also expect that a module with higher complexity would tend to have lower cohesion (less than functional cohesion) than a module with lower complexity. The possible correlation between higher complexity measure with a lower level of cohesion is predicated on a module with more decision points generally implementing more than a single well-defined function. However there are certain types of modules that one would expect to have a high complexity number, such as user interface (UI) modules containing source code for data validation and error recovery.

REFERENCES

Beizer, Boris. *Software Testing Techniques*, 2nd edition, New York: Van Nostrand Reinhold, 1990.

Howden. "Weak Mutation Testing and Completeness of Test Sets", *IEEE Trans. Software Eng.*, Vol. SE-8, No.4, July 1982, pp. 371-379.

John Joseph Chilenski and Steven P. Miller. "Applicability of Modified Condition/Decision Coverage to Software Testing", *Software Engineering Journal*, September 1994, Vol. 9, No. 5, pp. 193-200.

McCabe, Tom. "A Software Complexity Measure", *IEEE Trans. Software Eng.*, Vol. 2, No. 6, December 1976, pp. 308-320.

Morell, Larry. "A Theory of Fault-Based Testing", *IEEE Trans. Software Eng.*, Vol. 16, No. 8, August 1990, pp. 844-857.

Ntafos, Simeon. "A Comparison of Some Structural Testing Strategies", *IEEE Trans. Software Eng.*, Vol. 14, No. 6, June 1988, pp. 868-874.

Roper, Marc, *Software Testing*, London, McGraw-Hill Book Company, 1994.

RTCA/DO-178B, "Software Considerations in Airborne Systems and Equipment Certification", RCTA, December 1992, pp. 31, 74.

Woodward, M.R., Hedley, D. and Hennell, M.A. "Experience with Path Analysis and Testing of Programs", *IEEE Transactions on Software Engineering*, Vol. SE-6, No. 3, pp. 278-286, May 1980.

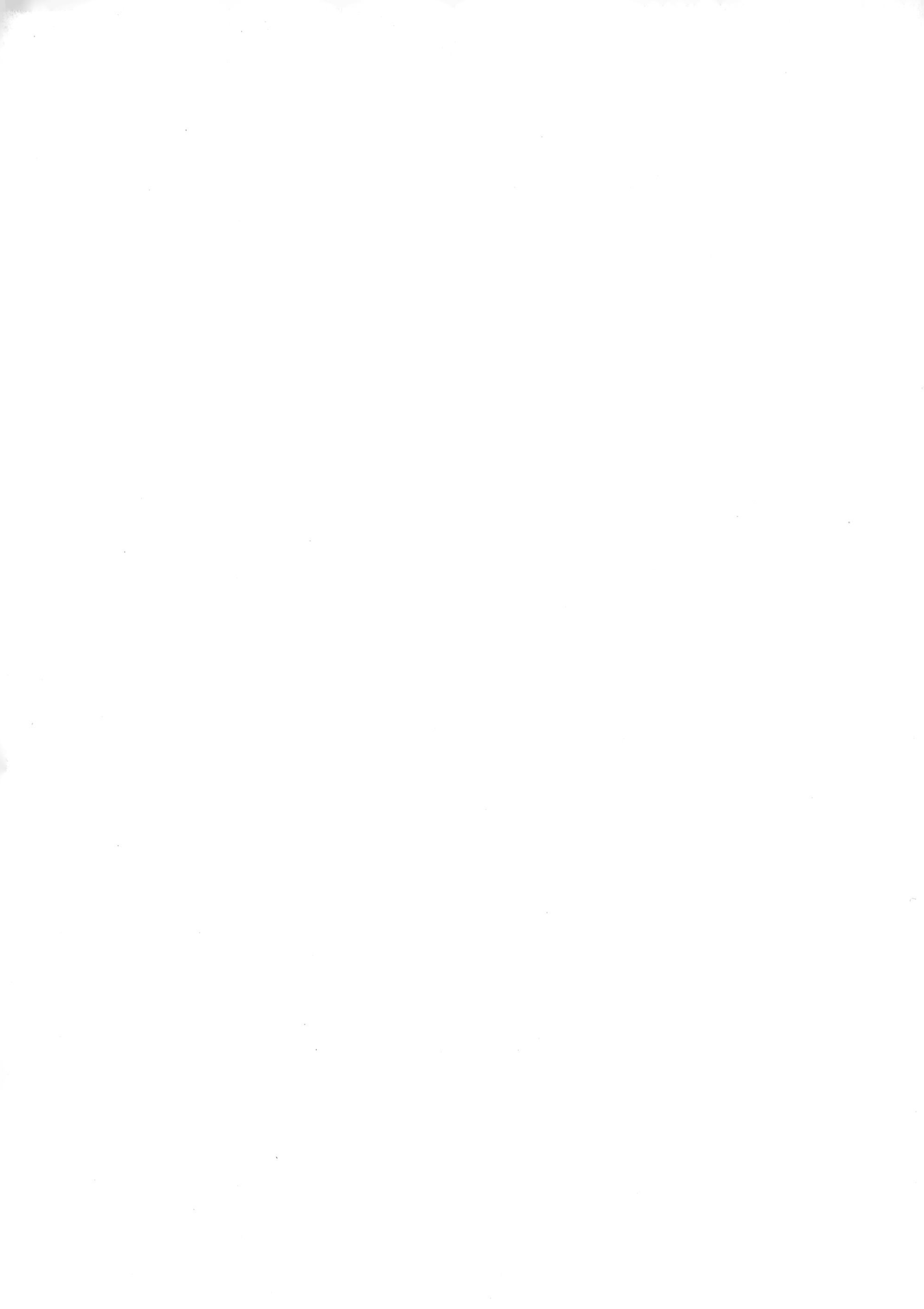